Rushton Dorman

The origin of primitive superstitions and their development into the worship of spirits and doctrine of spiritual agency

Rushton Dorman

The origin of primitive superstitions and their development into the worship of spirits and doctrine of spiritual agency

ISBN/EAN: 9783337282172

Printed in Europe, USA, Canada, Australia, Japan

Cover: Foto ©ninafisch / pixelio.de

More available books at **www.hansebooks.com**

OF

PRIMITIVE SUPERSTITIONS

AND THEIR DEVELOPMENT INTO THE WORSHIP OF
SPIRITS AND THE DOCTRINE OF SPIRITUAL
AGENCY AMONG THE ABORIGINES
OF AMERICA.

BY

RUSHTON M. DORMAN.

TWENTY-SIX ILLUSTRATIONS.

PHILADELPHIA:
J. B. LIPPINCOTT & CO.
LONDON: 16 SOUTHAMPTON STREET, COVENT GARDEN.
1881.

PREFACE.

THE study of archæological subjects is increasing in interest. Recent disclosures concerning the early condition and history of the human race have directed much attention to these subjects. Man's oral history crystallized in myths and superstitions reflects much light into a past which written history has not penetrated. Mythology is, therefore, a very important branch of anthropological science. Mythology in its broadest definition includes all pagan religious beliefs, commonly called superstitions, and cannot be confined to collections of fables and traditions, which are the folk-lore of peoples. It is the aim of this book to contribute facts to show the homogeneity of man's religious beliefs. Although the New World is the field of research in the present volume, the rudimentary forms of belief are shown to be the same there as elsewhere, and their systematic development is also the same. A striking illustration of this fact occurs to the writer, who, while among the negroes of the South, found among that uncultured people the same superstitions that prevailed in Africa, which were also the same as those found among equally uncultured peoples everywhere. The only way to account for their presence among the Southern negroes is to ascribe them to the natural outgrowth of the human mind, everywhere the same in the same stage of progress. Mythologists have studied myths without studying the superstitions which have found expression in the myths. They have exhausted resources in attempts to prove that the higher phases of belief and worship have been the most ancient and have become debased in the ruder forms. Voss endeavors to find in pagan myths a distortion of Hebrew revelations.

Dupuis, with his Sabaistic origin for cults, looks to astronomy for a solution. Abbé Banier finds in mythology "history in poetic dress." Creuzer sees nothing but symbols, and shows much erudition in his attempts to find their hidden meaning. Nearly all mythologists have fixed upon some locality where myths have originated, in the infancy of the human race, and whence they have spread, by transmission or migration, into the rest of the earth. Pococke and Sir William Jones locate their origin in the East; Rudbeck, in the North; Bryant, among the Hebrews. A new departure has been taken, however, in mythological science.

A work of the character of the present volume must necessarily be to a great extent a compilation. I have used great care to give credit to authors cited in this work, but, in order to escape quoting in full, in some cases have made abstracts of passages in such a way as to preserve their sense, without being able, however, to use quotation-marks, on account of such change. In such cases citations always occur, but it may not always be clear where the citation begins and ends. On this account I wish to acknowledge special obligations to the work of H. H. Bancroft on the Native Races of the Pacific Slope, Mr. Spencer's works on Sociology, and Mr. Tylor's Primitive Culture. I will also mention, as being specially full of information on subjects relating to the aboriginal tribes, the works of Mr. Schoolcraft, especially the large work, in six volumes, published at the expense of the United States government, but under his supervision; also the works of Messrs. Squier and Brinton; also Mr. Southey's History of Brazil.

A list of authorities cited in this work might be of some value as a bibliographical manual of the literature of the subject, but would add to the size and cost of this book, and only be superfluous when such exhaustive works as those of Messrs. Ludewig, Field, and Sabin have been published and can easily be obtained by those desiring such a work.

CHICAGO, February 9, 1881.

CONTENTS.

CHAPTER I.

INTRODUCTORY . . . 13

CHAPTER II.

DOCTRINE OF SPIRITS.

Spirits permeate all animate and inanimate nature—Fear of these spirits—Contests with spirits—Destruction and desertion of property—Spirits assume fairy forms—Demonology—Fear of evil spirits becomes worship—Doctrine of future rewards and punishments—Land of souls—Its localities and occupations—Difficulties of the journey thither—These difficulties dependent on the traditional difficulties of tribal migrations—Transmigration of spirits—Disease produced by them—The confessional as a cure—Sorcery—Couvade—Dreams a revelation from spirits—Prophecy . 19

CHAPTER III.

DOCTRINE OF SPIRITS (CONTINUED).

Worship of human spirits—Ancestral worship—Apotheosis—Culture-heroes—Fabulous forms assumed by mythical beings—Gods of Mexico, Central America, Bogota, and Peru—Idolatry—Its primitive forms—Grave-posts roughly hewn into the image of the dead and worshipped—Its later form an image of the deceased containing his ashes—Idolatry in aboriginal art—Supposed vitality of idols 69

CHAPTER IV.

FETICHISTIC SUPERSTITIONS.

Fetichism—Scalping fetichistic in conception—Inherence of spiritual force—Cannibalism fetichistic and a religious act—Eating images of gods a rite similar to the eucharistic—Superstitious fears about pronouncing the names of the dead—Tattooing fetichistic—Amulets—Primitive ornamentation fetichistic 141

CHAPTER V.

RITES AND CEREMONIES CONNECTED WITH THE DEAD.

Burial-customs—Care of the dead—Interment—Suspension—Cremation—Tombs the primitive altars—The mounds, their builders and uses—Burial-towers—Resurrection of the dead—Sacrifice—Food-offerings the primitive form—Human sacrifices—Tombs the primitive temples 163

CHAPTER VI.

ANIMAL-WORSHIP.

Its animistic origin—Immortality of the spirits of animals—Transmigration of human souls into animals—Omens—Manitology—Totemism—Animal names given to human beings—Traditionary descent of tribes from animals—Totemism in art—Heraldry—Totemic writing—Tattooing—Probable totemic origin of the animal mounds—Traditionary descent of animals from the human race—Metamorphosis—Animal dress—Worship of animals—Fabulous animals—Animals in the rôle of creators . 221

CHAPTER VII.

WORSHIP OF TREES AND PLANTS.

Worship of trees—Their supposed vitality explained by animism—Supposed descent of human beings from trees—Worship of plants—Personality ascribed to them—Origin of plants from human bodies—Those having medical properties supposed to be endowed with supernatural powers . 287

CHAPTER VIII.

WORSHIP OF REMARKABLE NATURAL OBJECTS.

Worship of mountains and dangerous places—Their supposed frequentation by spirits—Worship of volcanoes—Echoes and other noises supposed to be the voices of spirits—Traditionary descents of tribes from mountains—Metamorphosis—Worship of islands—Traditions of the origin of islands—Origin of the belief that the world was supported on the backs of animals—Worship of springs and fountains—Traditionary tribal descents from them—Their healing properties supernatural—Worship of rivers and lakes—Places of refuge 300

CHAPTER IX.

SABAISM.

PAGE

Worship of the heavenly bodies—Their personality—Their anthropomorphic nature—Animistic conceptions of them—Their romantic attachments to human beings—Their vitality—Their occupation by translated heroes—Crude notions concerning them—Eclipses—Astrology 325

CHAPTER X.

ANIMISTIC THEORY OF METEOROLOGY.

Tempests produced by hostile spirits—Coercive measures used to prevent them—Winds the manifestations of spiritual agency—Anthropomorphic representations of aërial deities 349

CHAPTER XI.

PRIESTCRAFT.

Priests—Sources of their influence—Medicine-men or doctors of rude tribes—Exorcism of evil spirits the method of curing diseases—Sorcerers—Miraculous powers ascribed to them—Rain-doctors—Witches—Rise of priestly hierarchies among the more civilized peoples—Priesthoods of Peru, Mexico, Yucatan, etc.—Monastic institutions of those countries—F a-tional institutions in the hands of the priests—Their influence in the State—Confessional—Priestly absolution saved criminals from legal penalties . 353

CHAPTER XII.

CONCLUSION 385

INDEX 393

ILLUSTRATIONS.

	PAGE
A FLYING HEAD (see page 281) .	*Frontispiece*
DACOTAH GOD OF THUNDER . . .	. . 83
HEYOKA	84
DACOTAH GOD OF WAR	. . 85
ATOTARHO, ANCIENT RULER OF THE IROQUOIS . .	. *faces* 86
GRAVE-POST HEWN TO THE LIKENESS OF THE DECEASED	. . . 118
TOMB OF AN ALASKAN CHIEF	. . 118
IMAGE OF AN INCA	. . 119
SEPULCHRAL URN OF THE MEXICANS . .	*faces* 120
SEPULCHRAL URN CONTAINING BRAZILIAN CHIEF .	. . 121
OJIBWAY IDOL	. 127
MOQUI IDOL	. . 127
STONES SLIGHTLY ALTERED TO A HUMAN RESEMBLANCE	. 130
BURIAL-TOWER OF PERU	. . 191
TOTEMIC WRITING	*faces* 239
THUNDER-BIRD OF THE HAIDAHS . .	. . 272
TCHIMOSE	. 278
FABULOUS ANIMAL OF THE WINNEBAGOES .	. 279
COMPOSITE FIGURE OF THE PERUVIANS .	. 284
GOD OF GRASS	. 299
ROCK-TEMPLE OF PERU	. 302
GOD OF THE SEA	. 323
SUN-HEAD	. 338
GOD OF THE AIR . . .	. . 352
PROPHET'S LODGE . . .	*faces* 363

PRIMITIVE SUPERSTITIONS.

CHAPTER I.

INTRODUCTORY.

THE object of this book is to reduce to a system of religious belief that multitude of superstitions that have germinated among uncultured peoples, and many of which remain as survivals in a higher culture, although they are inconsistent with the higher forms of religious belief among which they are found. We hope to trace all superstitions to a common origin. Success in tracing such superstitions to their source, connected with evidence that they have originated in error, or in ignorance of the truth, will certainly prove a benefit to man. The process of discovering these sources is, and always will be, an interesting labor to the anthropologist. The results of such research will certainly prove an interesting chapter in the history of man.

The doctrine of transmigration in the Orient, the animal worship of the Egyptians, the Sabaism of the Persians, are but stages of progress in a religious evolution. The pagoda of the Orient, the pyramid of Egypt, the temple of Greece, are but the representations in art of a superstition that finds its first expression in a more primitive form. The laws of evolution in the spiritual world can be traced with as great precision as in the material world. Much labor has been spent in the study of the laws of man's social progress, and much success has followed such effort. While a progressive movement must be recognized in all social institutions among peoples that have attained any degree of civilization, yet the tendency of all the evidence is to show that the highest development of religious culture among pagan nations has not attained to monotheism; on the contrary, the principles that control all religious thought among primitive peoples will work themselves out in polytheism among those peoples in lower stages of culture, or in pantheism among those of a higher culture.

That sublime definition, " God is a spirit, infinite, eternal, and unchangeable in his being, wisdom, power, holiness, justice, goodness, and truth," followed by that definition of the " chief end" of man, which is " to glorify God and enjoy him forever," is the high product of Christianity, which, if maintained in its purity, has nothing to fear from religious evolution.

All primitive religious belief is polytheistic. All savage tribes are full of the terror of invisible spirits which have been liberated by death. These spirits fill all nature, animate and inanimate. They are in the air, the wind, the storm, in the rock, the hill, the vale, in the river, the waterfall. They transmigrate into human beings, animals, plants, and even into inanimate stones, idols, and heavenly bodies, which are supposed to be animate thereafter. Hence originates the worship of ancestors, and also of animals, plants, stones, idols, and the heavenly bodies. Death, the liberator, and burial, have their religious ceremonies, and the tomb becomes the temple. These spirits liberated by death, or by sleep or a comatose condition, which are its equivalents in savage life, are abroad on the earth for a time, and can avenge themselves for past or present wrongs, in disease, which is a form of transmigration. They can appear in dreams, which is a form of prophecy.

Among primitive peoples the cure of diseases was given over to sorcerers, who were supposed to have some control over the evil-disposed spirits. This sorcery developed into the priestcraft of higher cultures, where exorcism of evil spirits still survives as one of the offices of the priests. In our own day those peculiar diseases which have defied medical skill, such as insanity, hysteria, and epilepsy, are relegated in many countries for cure to the priesthood. Even the primitive fetichism survives in the use of charms and amulets, and in the heraldic devices on many national flags and the armorial bearings of many families.

In tracing the origin of superstitions among savage or barbarous peoples, we will become convinced of the error of any writer who has affirmed that this or that people has no religion or religious feeling. Many such authors have contradicted themselves unwittingly by giving a long list of these superstitions; and I have often thought that they merely meant to convey the impression that the savages knew nothing of true religion. Let me say here that in all my studies upon this subject I have not found a people, no matter how savage, who have no religion, if the word is used in its broadest sense to embrace all superstition. I wish to speak of another error found in many books on the aboriginal tribes of America, where it is intimated that the belief in a Supreme Being has existed among them from an early time. No approach to monotheism had been made before the discovery of America by Europeans, and the Great Spirit mentioned in these books is an introduction by Christianity. Among the Northern tribes the Indian word *manitou* expresses their highest conception of deity. "Their gods were no whit better than themselves," says Mr. Parkman, "and when the Indian borrows from Christianity the idea of a supreme spirit, his tendency is to reduce him to a local habitation and a bodily shape. The idea that the primitive Indian had an Omnipotent Spirit to which he yielded his untutored homage is a dream of poets, rhetoricians, and sentimentalists." Mr. Keating says that the ideas that the Sauks had of the Great Spirit were that he had a human form, was white, and wore a hat. Mr. Dall says, "The Thlinkeets, like all American Indians, do not believe in a Supreme Being. Their feeble polytheism presents no feature worthy the name of such a belief." Mr. Schoolcraft says, "The Dacotahs do not understand the difference between a great Good Spirit and a great Evil Spirit. They think any spirit can do good when it chooses, or evil when it chooses." The Patagonians call God *Soychu*, but their word for the dead is *soychuhet*. The word *Con*, which has been used for the supreme deity of the Peruvians, originated in a blunder of the Spanish writers. It was a prefix to sacred names, and is the first syllable in *Conopa*, a stone idol. A close examination makes it evident that the Indians' idea of a Supreme Being was a conception no higher than might have been expected, and when they undertook to contemplate such a Being it became finite, and generally ridiculous. There is no Iroquois word that had such a primitive meaning as Great Spirit, or God. Perrot, after a life spent among the Northern Indians, ignores the idea that they had any conception of such a Being; and Allouez says the same of the tribes about Lake Superior. The tribes of California had no conception whatever of a Supreme Being. Mr. Powers says, "True, nearly all of them now speak of the Old Man Above, but they have the word and nothing more."

The American tribes afford a very favorable opportunity for such an investigation as the present. Without entering into the controversy as to the antiquity of the Red Race, I shall assume that it has occupied the territory of North and South America for a sufficient length of time to have developed its own culture in the varied stages of progress found at the time of the discovery by Columbus. Such an assumption is warranted by the best researches into their antiquity. I shall also assume that during the progress of their culture no interference from without has left any traces of itself. The best Americanists, after much study devoted to this subject, have so decided.

Without discussing the theory of the unity of the human race, I shall assume that the Red Race, if the unity of human races is true, was separated from the rest of the human family at such an early day that their mythology is indigenous, as was also their language.

All stages of progress are faithfully represented among them, from the most savage root-digger to the most civilized Peruvian. There were tribes of hunters, tribes of fishermen, and tribes of agriculturists. Art is also represented in all its forms. When we arise from a study of their mental characteristics, we cannot help being impressed with the fact that the human mind unfolds itself in all directions with as great regularity as does our physical nature. The growth of the mind is as certain in its order of development as is the growth of the body. It is due to these laws of development that the native of Patagonia has about the same superstitions as has the native of Alaska. The similarity is not due to contact between the several tribes of America. The differences in all the tribes are due to external influences, such as climate, soil, occupation, and also to their different degrees of progress in culture.

Progress in religious culture is coextensive with all other human progress among pagan nations. Pagan religion being the product of the human mind, and emanating from no higher source, will therefore have no great tendency to elevate humanity. Hence religious progress will always be in accord with progress in other directions.

The American savages agree in their religious views with the savages of other continents more than with the civilized peoples of their own. Says Mr. J. G. Müller, "The origin of their religions is found in their human nature. They have not received them from the peoples of the Old World, neither can they be understood if we try to derive them from thence."

Hence the study of comparative mythology can never have scientific value unless it is coextensive with the study of human progress in all directions. Too much effort has heretofore been directed to tracing a derivation of one system of mythological belief from another by contact or migration of myths. The growth of mythologies among all peoples has taken place according to the laws of man's spiritual being. There is therefore a great similarity of religious belief among all peoples in the same progressive stages. Even the similarity of the myths themselves is remarkable in cases where no transmission could possibly have taken place.

I shall not undertake to compare, to any extent, the superstitions of the New World with those of the Old World in this volume, as I intend to reserve that subject for another time; and I shall therefore confine my attention almost exclusively to a comparative study of the religious beliefs and traditions of the aborigines of the New World.

CHAPTER II.

DOCTRINE OF SPIRITS.

Spirits permeate all animate and inanimate nature—Fear of these spirits—Contests with spirits—Destruction and desertion of property—Spirits assume fairy forms—Demonology—Fear of evil spirits becomes worship—Doctrine of future rewards and punishments—Land of souls—Its localities and occupations—Difficulties of the journey thither—These difficulties dependent on the traditional difficulties of tribal migrations—Transmigration of spirits—Disease produced by them—The confessional as a cure—Sorcery—Couvade—Dreams a revelation from spirits—Prophecy.

THE primitive man fills his world with spirits, and his belief in this spirit life manifests and unfolds itself in all his varied superstitions. The places of the living are haunted with the spirits of the dead.

The Illinois, says Tonti, "fancy that the world is full of spirits, who preside over everything in nature, and that they are good or bad according to their caprice. It is upon this principle that all their foolish superstitions are grounded."[1]

The Hurons, says Charlevoix, believe in an infinite number of subaltern spirits, both good and bad. These are objects of their worship. Everything in nature has its spirit. Lest the spirits of the victims of their torture should remain around the huts of their murderers from a thirst of vengeance, they strike every place with a staff in order to oblige them to depart.

Mr. Greenhalgh relates the same custom among the Iroquois. He says, "Att night we heard a great noise as if ye houses had all fallen, butt itt was only ye inhabitants driving away ye ghosts of ye murthered."[2]

---

[1] Tonti's Account, 7.   [2] 1 Doc. Hist. N. Y., 16.

The Iroquois believe the space between the sky and earth is full of spirits.[1] In every tribe a death from time to time adds another ghost to the many that have gone before. Continually accumulating, they form a surrounding population, usually invisible, but occasionally seen.[2]

The Ottawas all believe in ghosts. "Once," said Mr. Barron, "on approaching in the night a village of Ottawas in confusion, they were all busily engaged in raising noises of the loudest and most inharmonious kind. Upon inquiring, I found that a battle had been lately fought between the Ottawas and Kickapoos, and the object of all this noise was to prevent the ghosts of the dead combatants from entering the village."[3]

The Choctaws also have their ghosts or wandering spirits, which can speak and are visible, but not tangible. Of the belief of the tribes about Hudson's Bay in spirits, Umfreville tells us they were so influenced by these superstitious ideas that they kept large fires burning all night, and slept only in the daytime. They often fired their guns at them. Among the tribes about Lake Superior you will frequently be awakened by the firing of guns. On inquiring for the cause, you will be told they are shooting the dead that trouble them. The Mohawks would never leave their dwellings at night, except in companies, for fear of evil spirits.[4]

In a war expedition, if any warrior fancies that he has seen the spirits of his forefathers, or heard their voices, he can oblige the warriors to retreat. The Ohio tribes were accustomed to bore holes in the coffin over the eyes and mouth to let the spirit pass in and out.[5]

Among the Eskimos, spirits trouble them by seating themselves near them and making faces at them. A meal is often spoiled in this way. They can generally drive them off by blowing their breath at them.[6]

---

[1] Hennepin's Contin., 55.
[2] 1 Spencer Soc., 234-35.
[3] 1 Keating's St. Peter's River, 109.
[4] Wood's N. E. Pros., 86.
[5] Dodge's Red Man O., 52.
[6] Lyon's Journal, 172.

"The natives of Brazil so much dread the manes of their dead, that some of them have been struck with sudden death because of an imaginary apparition of them. They try to appease them by fastening offerings on stakes fixed in the ground for that purpose."[1]

Among the natives of Costa Rica spirits are thought to infest everything. When anything has been lying around for some time, they beat it with sticks the day before they use it, to drive away the spirits. The spirits of the dead are supposed to remain near their bodies for a year.[2]

The natives of the Pacific slope suppose spirits to be present everywhere. On the northwest coast of America, at Stony Point, a burial-place of the Indians was considered to be haunted by them, and no Indian ever ventured there. Their usual superstitious reverence for and fear of anything belonging to the "memelose tillicums," or dead people, prevented their going near the spot.[3]

There was another locality near there, on the Shoal-Water Bay, the former site of an Indian village which had been deserted on account of dead people. The Indians were afraid to go back there on account of them, but if a white man went along they were willing to go, for the dead people were afraid of whites.[4]

The idea they have of their spirits is that they are hovering in the air; yet they are puzzled to know where the spirits of the whites got their wings from.[5] Association of ideas had not led them to this pleasing fancy of cultured minds.

Their superstition about names originates in their belief in spirits. The Indians of the Northwest Territory always change their own names when a relative dies, because they think the spirits of the dead will come if they hear the same name called that they were accustomed to hear before

---

[1] Nieuhoff's Brazil, 2; Churchill's Coll. Voy., 150.
[2] Gabb's Ind. Tribes, 503-4.   [3] Swan's Wash. Ter., 68.
[4] Ib., 77.   [5] Ib., 181.

death. For the same reason they avoid speaking the name of the dead person.[1]

They would not let Mr. Swan attend the burial of their dead, because, they said, the spirit of the dead person, and hosts of others hovering around, would see him and be displeased at his presence.[2]

Among many of the tribes their contests with spirits would often appear such realities that in their defence of themselves they would be covered with blood from the bruises received in their violent gesticulations. The spirits would often vanish by turning themselves into stone with a flesh-and-blood interior.[3]

This superstitious fear of places supposed to be haunted by spirits led to the destruction and desertion of dwelling-places, and thus served as a check to material prosperity and became an obstacle to progress.

The Ojibways pulled down the house in which any one had died, and chose another place to live in as far off as possible. Even with the death of an infant the same dread manifested itself. Mr. Kohl, while among them, visited a neighbor with a sick child in the morning. When he returned in the evening the lodge had disappeared, and all its inhabitants had departed. This revealed to him the child's death.[4]

It is quite remarkable to discover this same fear of the spirits of harmless children; but its cause is found in their superstitious ideas about disease. The Navajos would never occupy a lodge in which a person had died, but the lodge was burned.[5]

The Seminoles immediately removed from a house where death had occurred, and where the body was buried.[6]

A superstition is universally prevalent among the tribes of the Northwest, that when an abode has been deserted on account of a death, an evil spirit dwells there. The New England tribes would never live in a wigwam in which any person had died, but would immediately pull it down.[7]

---

[1] Swan's Wash. Ter., 189.   [2] Ib., 192.   [3] 1 Jes. Rel., 16.
[4] Kitchi-Gami, 106.   [5] 4 Schoolcraft, 214.   [6] 5 ib., 270.
[7] 10 Mass. Hist. Coll., 1st Series, 107.

The Arkansas burned the lodges in which any one had died.

Among the Abipones of Paraguay, when any one's life is despaired of, the house is immediately forsaken by his fellow-inmates. The custom of destroying and deserting the houses where death has occurred has undoubtedly arisen from a superstitious fear of the spirits of the dead. The same fear impels them to thrust the dead through some aperture other than the ordinary way of exit, and carry them away to a place of burial. By closing securely the hole which is made for the exit of the dead, the spirit, it was thought, would not be able to get back again into the lodge. A very curious custom sprang up in connection with this, by which they could investigate to their satisfaction whether the spirit had made any effort to return: they sprinkled ashes along the way to the place of burial.[1]

The Ojibways believe innumerable spirits are ever near; that the earth teems with these spirits, good and bad. Those of the forests clothe themselves with moss. During a shower of rain thousands of them find shelter in a flower. These spirits assume fairy forms, and also appear by means of transmigration in the varied forms of insect life. The Ojibway detects their tiny voices in the insect's hum. Thousands of them sport on a sunbeam.[2]

Thus the Ojibways have a fairy mythology. Burlington Bay is a great resort for these fairies. Whenever they are cornered they disappear under ground with a rumbling noise. They are thought to have great influence on the lives of the Indians. They attack their poultry and cattle, who soon thereafter die. They throw small stones through the windows of their houses. They dance over the ground like the down of a thistle. The Indians say the fairies are enraged at white people for destroying their forests.

The manifestation of spirits in fairy-like forms is not confined to the mythology of the Ojibways. The Dacotahs have

---

[1] 2 Dobrizhoffer, 265.   [2] Copway's Ojibways, 148–49.

land and water fairies of a mischievous character. They say they often see them.[1]

Among the Otoes, a mound near the mouth of White Stone River is called the mountain of Little People or Little Spirits, and they believe that it is the abode of little devils in human form, about eighteen inches high, and with remarkably large heads. They are armed with sharp arrows, with which they are very skilful, and are always on the watch to kill those who should have the hardihood to approach their residence. The tradition is that many have suffered from these little evil spirits. This has inspired all the neighboring nations with such terror that no consideration could tempt them to visit the hill.[2]

Mr. Kane tells a legend of the Nasquallies, who believed in a dwarf people, that were destroyed by birds, who stuck their quills into them. When the quills were extracted by one of their tribe, the fairies came to life again.[3]

Aisemid was a famous aërial spirit of the Western tribes, who carried a curious little shell, and could become visible or invisible as he chose.[4]

All the Indians imagine they see small spirits skip about over the plains and suddenly vanish; they dance in the moonlight on the tops of cliffs.[5]

The Shoshone legends people the mountains of Montana with little imps, called Ninumbees, two feet long, naked, and with a tail. These limbs of the evil one are accustomed to eat up any unguarded infant they find, leaving in its stead one of their own baneful race looking so much like the child that the mother will return and suckle it. If the little fiend seizes her breast she dies thereafter.[6]

The Tinneh also people their earth, sea, and air with spirits in the shape of fairies.[7]

---

[1] 3 School., Ind. Tribes, 232. [2] 1 Lewis and Clarke, 52-53, ed. 1814.
[3] Wanderings, 253. [4] 3 School., Ind. Tribes, 523.
[5] 3 ib., 408. [6] 3 Bancroft, Native Races, 157. [7] 3 ib., 142.

In Choctaw mythology, itallaboys are genii of very diminutive stature, but of great power. From them the conjurers receive their influence. They often ride by moonlight on deer, with wands in their hands, singing magic songs. They are invisible, intangible, and invulnerable. Thus we find a fairy mythology similar to that of Europe among the native races of America, embracing even the superstition of the Changelings.

"Sleep is thought by the Algic race to be produced by fairies, the prince of whom is Weeng. The power of this Indian Morpheus is exerted in a peculiar manner and by a novel agency. Weeng seldom acts directly in inducing sleep, but he exercises dominion over hosts of gnome-like beings, who are everywhere present. These beings are invisible. Each one is armed with a tiny club, and when he observes a person sitting or reclining under circumstances favorable to sleep, he nimbly climbs upon his forehead and inflicts a blow. The first blow only creates drowsiness; the second makes the person lethargic, so that he occasionally closes his eyelids; the third produces sound sleep. It is the constant duty of these little emissaries to put every one to sleep whom they encounter,—men, women, and children. They hide themselves everywhere, and are ready to fly out and exert their sleep-compelling power, although their peculiar season of action is in the night. They are also alert during the day. While the forms of these gnomes are believed to be those of little or fairy men, the figure of Weeng himself is unknown, and it is not certain that he has ever been seen. Iagoo is said to have seen him sitting upon a branch of a tree. He was in the shape of a giant insect with many wings upon his back, which made a low, deep, murmuring sound, like distant falling water. Weeng is not only the dispenser of sleep, but it seems he is also the author of dulness. If an orator fails, he is said to be struck by Weeng. If a warrior lingers, he has ventured too near the sleepy god. If children begin to nod or yawn, the Indian mother looks up smilingly and says they have been struck by Weeng, and puts them to bed."[1]

The Indian conception of the action of these invisible spiritual agents is aptly illustrated by an Ojibway legend of a warrior's spirit which returned from the field of battle and found his wife lamenting his death. He endeavored to talk to her, but she made no reply, except to remark to one near her that she felt a buzzing in her ears. The enraged husband, who did not realize the change from the material to the spiritual in his condition, struck her a blow on the forehead. She complained of feeling a shooting pain there. Thus the spirit was foiled in every attempt to make itself known.[2]

The Dacotahs believe that a mother, when her dead children think of her, will feel a pain in her breast, due to the action of the invisible spiritual agent.[3]

Thus the far-reaching effect of their doctrine of spiritual agency is evident.

Another form of spiritual manifestation is fire. Fire has always been regarded with more or less superstitious awe, because it is supposed to contain a mysterious spirit. Among the Hurons, a female spirit who was supposed to cause much of their sickness appeared like a flame of fire.[4]

Of the New England Indians, Josselyn says, "They have a remarkable observation of a flame that appears before the death of an Indian, upon their wigwams, in the dead of night. Whenever this appears, there will be a death."[5]

The Ojibways will never cut a stick that has once been on the fire. The reason of this superstition is that the fire has a spirit that has entered the wood and will get cut.

Among many of the tribes of America no cutting instrument could be used for some time after the death of a person, lest his spirit, the exact whereabouts of which they could not determine,

---

[1] Schoolcraft's Algic Res., 226, seq. [2] Jones's Traditions, 120.
[3] Neill's Minnesota, 70. [4] Jes. Rel., 16.
[5] Josselyn's Two Voyages, 133.

should get cut. Every object is supposed to be occupied by a spirit. The intelligence of these spirits is aptly illustrated by the following anecdote. A certain missionary to the Californians sent a native with some loaves of bread, and a letter, stating their number. The messenger ate a part of the bread, and his theft was consequently discovered. Another time, when he had to deliver four loaves he ate two of them, but hid the accompanying letter under a stone while he was thus engaged, believing that his conduct would not be revealed this time, as the letter had not seen him eating the loaves.[1]

This illustrates the natural tendency of the savage to believe that everything is inhabited by a spirit.

While upon the doctrine of spirits, let us trace the belief in evil spirits, and its gradual development into demonology. Although there was no moral dualism among the American nations, whereby all evil had become personified in a Satan, yet there were many tribes who had one or more evil spirits, to whose visits they ascribed personal and tribal calamities. I shall not, however, dwell long on this branch of their mythology, as the material for the subject has been employed to a great extent in tracing their belief in a future life, and their theory of disease. The Indians thought the inhabitants of the spirit-land act very much as they did when among the living. Hence each individual could do much harm as well as good. It was also thought that the next life was a time for retribution; and this idea is the key-note to demonology in primitive times.

The Comanches stood in great dread of evil spirits, which they attempted to conciliate. Their demons withheld rain or sunshine.[2]

All the appeals of the Mosquitoes are addressed to the evil spirits called Wulasha. These devils are the causes of all misfortunes and contrarieties that happen. The fear of these devils prevents them from going out alone after dark.[3]

---

[1] Baegert's, Smith, Rep., 1864, p. 379.
[2] 1 Bancroft, Native Races, 520.
[3] 3 ib., 479.

These Wulasha are supposed to strive for the possession of the dead. They have a religious ceremony in which we have a scene very similar to those represented upon Etruscan vases. Four naked men disguise themselves in performing their burial rite so that the Wulasha will not know them, and then rush into the hut, seize the dead body, drag it away, and bury it. Thus the dead are rescued from evil spirits.[1]

"They think that evil spirits destroy their crops and do them many grievous injuries."[2]

Thevet mentions an isle of demons near Newfoundland where the Indians were so tormented with them that they would fall into his arms for relief.

Among the Californians the most interesting feature of their religion was their belief in a body of demons. These malignant spirits have taken entire possession of the country about the Devil's Castle. In the face of divers assertions that no such thing as a devil proper has ever been found in savage mythology, Mr. Powers uses this language in reference to the belief of the Californian tribes: "Of course the thin and meagre imagination of the American savages was not equal to the creation of Milton's magnificent, imperial Satan, or of Goethe's Mephistopheles, with his subtle intellect and malignant mirth; but in so far as the Indian fiends or devils had the ability they are wholly as wicked as these. They are totally bad, but they are weak, undignified, absurd."[3]

Says Denis of the Brazilian tribes, "They complain without ceasing of the evil spirits that torment them. Houcha was the chief of the hierarchy of devils" among the Brazilians.

Ercono is the devil of the Moxos, and their foes were the Conos tribe. The devils of the Taos were called Tupas, and their enemies were the Tupis. Chelul is the devil of the Patagons, and a tribe called Cheloagas were their enemies.[4]

These linguistic evidences are very interesting in the study

---

[1] 1 Bancroft, 744.
[2] Roberts's Narrative, 267.
[3] 3 Bancroft, 158.
[4] 2 Rafinesque, 204.

of the mythologies, and are very consistent with their animistic theories. How natural that tribal enemies should become the devils of the tribe, and their spirits attempt to revenge the injuries of their lives!

Among the more civilized peoples demonology prevailed, and a tendency existed to exalt some one demon to a primacy.

The Nicaraguans had evil spirits, and a ceremony for expelling them from new dwellings.[1]

The Mayas of Yucatan had evil spirits who could be driven off by the sorcerers; they never came around when their fetiches were exposed.[2] They had a ceremony for expelling evil spirits from houses about to be occupied by newly-married persons.[3]

The Peruvians had devils who frequently put in an appearance. The Huancas have a legend that a great number of these devils once assembled and did much damage. One of their devils, called Huarivalca, is worshipped to this day, although he has disappeared and not been seen lately. There were spots which they said showed evidences of his presence. Supay was the prince of devils among them.[4]

The Toltecs have left a curious tradition of the destruction of many of their people by a demon, who would stalk into their midst, with long bony arms, and dash many of them lifeless. He kept up his persecution, appearing from time to time, and spreading disease, fear, and destruction, until they fled from their homes and lands.[5]

The Mexicans had an evil spirit, which often appeared in order to terrify and injure them.[6]

The assumption of pre-eminence by one or more demons is made easy by a belief in a local demon, who sometimes assumes the office of tribal demon or god. A local demon or malevolent spirit is usually ascribed to places where accidents re-

---

[1] 2 Bancroft, 785. [2] 2 ib., 697.
[3] Landa, xxxii. [4] Cieza, 179.
[5] 5 Bancroft, 281. [6] 1 Clavigero, Hist. of Mexico, 242.

sulting in death have occurred. An eddy in the river where floating sticks are whirled around and engulfed is not far from the place where one of the tribe was drowned and never seen again. What more manifest, then, than that the spirit of this drowned man dwells thereabout, and pulls these things under the surface, and even in revenge perhaps seizes and drags down persons who venture near? Soon there survives the belief in a water demon haunting the place. Some tribes had a curious way of finding drowned bodies. They would float a chip of wood, watch where it turned around, and drag there for the body.[1] The spirits of the drowned, with motives of revenge, dragged every object beneath the surface.

The primitive doctrine of souls obliges the savage to think of the spirit of the dead as close at hand. The tribes of Guiana suppose every place is haunted where any one has died. A superstitious fear soon instigates worship, and this worship, beginning at the tombs and burial-places of the dead, develops into the temple ritual of higher cultures.

"Most of the worship of the natives of Guiana," says Mr. Brett, "is directed to spirits, and generally to those of a malignant nature, which are unceasingly active in inflicting miseries on mankind. Pain in their language means 'the evil spirit's arrow.'"[2]

Among almost all of the American tribes the worship of spirits that are malicious, and not of those that are good, is a characteristic that has been noticed with much astonishment and commented upon by travellers and other writers. It is certainly natural that primitive worship, which is born of fear, should be directed to those malevolent objects that inspire fear. Another cause of this distinction in their worship is undoubtedly to be found in their belief that the wicked spirits remain upon the earth, and only the good ones pass over into a heavenly land, where they have naught to do with human affairs. The Ojibways thought good spirits inhabited the

---

[1] 1 Alexander's L'Acadie, 26.   [2] Brett's Ind. Tribes, 284.

upper empyrean and descended every few days to inquire after them. An invisible vine was supposed to form the connecting link, whose roots were in the earth and top in the sky. On this ladder the spirits passed up and down.[1] All ordinary and wicked spirits, however, remained on the earth, which was called the big plate where the spirits eat. Here we can trace the germ of the belief in a difference of locality for good and evil spirits. Among the Blackfeet, demons are worshipped with much ceremony and self-torture, in which they torment themselves without flinching or appearance of pain, in order to show the demons that it is useless to try to afflict them. There are evidences of demon-worship among the Cherokees, Chickasaws, Shawnees, and many other tribes, which I will not notice. To use the language of Mr. Shea, " pure unmixed devil-worship prevails through the length and breadth of the land."[2] The primitive conception of the spirit-land is not, except in a few cases, of a place in the sky, but of a place upon the earth and earthlike, where the ordinary avocations of life are carried on with less vicissitudes and hardship.[3]

Let us now notice the different opinions entertained as to the occupations of the spirit-life, and their doctrine of rewards and punishments. Mr. Tylor divides the subject of the future life into two theories, the continuance theory and the retribution theory. The first is that the future life is a reflection of this. Men are to retain their earthly form and earthly conditions, have around them their earthly friends, possess their earthly property, and carry on their earthly occupations. The other theory is that the future life is a compensation for this, where men's conditions are reallotted as the consequence, and especially as the reward or punishment, of their earthly life. The most primitive of these is the continuance theory. The shade of the Algonkin hunter hunts the spirits of the beaver and the elk with the spirits of bows and arrows, walking on the spirits of his snow-shoes over the spirit of the snow. The Brazilian

---

[1] Copway, 164.   [2] Catholic Missions, 25.   [3] 5 School., 403.

forest tribes will find a forest full of calabash-trees and game, where the souls of the dead will live.¹ Most of the tribes of North America thought that the spirits of the dead remained in form and feature as they had been in life. The belief respecting the land of souls varied greatly in different tribes. The prevalent idea was that the present life was continued with little change. The Ojibways think the soul after death enters a world where the souls injured in life haunt it. Even the phantoms of the wrecks of property destroyed during life obstruct its passage, and the animals to which cruelty has been shown in life torment it. After death enemies are also ready to avenge their injuries.² In this primitive form we can see the outline of the doctrine of future punishment.

Among the Ahts, a lofty birth or a glorious death gives the right of entering into a goodly land, where there are no storms or frost, but sunshine and warmth. The common people had to roam about the earth, in the form of some person or animal.³

The Brazilian tribes think the spirits of their chiefs and sorcerers enter a world of enjoyment while others wander about the graves.⁴

The Manacica chiefs were fed with a gum distilled from certain celestial trees in the spirit-land.

The Chibchas believed that men who died in war, and women in childbed, went directly into bliss, no matter how wicked they were.⁵

The Natchez and Tensas believed that after death the souls of their warriors went to reside in the land of the buffalo; but those who had not taken any scalps went to reside in a country inhabited by reptiles.⁶

We find everywhere the prevalence of the idea that the courageous would be specially favored in the spirit-world. This is

---

[1] 2 Tylor, Primitive Culture, 75–77. [2] 2 Keating, 255.
[3] 3 Bancroft, 521. [4] Bradford's American Antiquities, 345.
[5] 5 Herrera, 90.
[6] La Harpe's Historical Journal; French's Historical Coll., La., vol. iii. p. 18.

the primitive idea. The infliction of punishment for evil deeds soon appears, however. The Natches consigned the guilty guardian of their sacred fire, who let it go out, to one of those large mounds which are to be seen in the vicinity of the present city of Natchez. There he is doomed to languish forever, and to be eternally debarred from entering the world of spirits, unless he can make fire with two dry sticks, which he is ever rubbing together with desperate eagerness. Now and then a slight smoke issues from the sticks, the wretch rubs on with increased rapidity, and just as a bright spark begins to shoot up, the sluices of his eyes open against his will, and pour out a deluge of tears which drown the nascent fire. Thus he is condemned to a ceaseless work, and to periodical fits of hope and despair.[1]

The Sioux are of opinion that suicide is punished in the land of spirits by the ghosts being doomed forever to drag the tree on which they hang themselves; for this reason they always suspend themselves to as small a tree as can possibly sustain their weight.[2]

The Mayas of Yucatan believed in rewards and punishments in the future life. Living in a warm climate, their idea of happiness in the future life was to lie beneath the shade of the evergreen and umbrageous tree called yaxche. Herrera says, "The wicked were hungry and cold.[3] They think the souls of the deceased return to the earth if they choose, and, in order that they may not lose the way to the domestic hearth, they mark the path from the hut to the tomb with chalk."[4]

The Peruvians held the doctrine of future rewards and punishments. The greatest enjoyment of the good was rest of mind and body.[5] The souls can wander about the earth, although their heaven and hell are above and below the earth,

---

[1] Gayarre's La., 356.
[2] Bradbury's Travels, 89.
[3] Herrera, 176.
[4] Orozco y Berra, 157.
[5] 1 Garcilasso, 126–27.

and therefore they have anniversaries, at which food and supplies are furnished these souls.[1]

The Chippewyans think that bad souls stand up to their chin in water, in sight of the spirit-land, which they can never enter. Many believe, however, in transmigration for the wicked.

The New England tribes consigned their enemies to a place of misery, but they themselves had a very good time in the next world.[2]

Some tribes thought the wicked hunted and killed, in the next world, animals that were all skin and bone.

Thus we see the universal credence of all the tribes in the reality of a spiritual life and its rewards and punishments. Not only is that world inhabited by the spirits of their dead, but also all animate and inanimate substances, or shadows of substances. Its woods, streams, and lakes were more beautiful than the earthly. The soul's progress was not stopped by them, for they were but the shadows of material forms.

> "By midnight moons, o'er moistening dews,
> In vestments for the chase arrayed,
> The hunter still the deer pursues,
> The hunter and the deer a shade."

The region supposed to be haunted by the souls of the dead becomes wider as populations increase and scatter. Several counteracting influences have operated, however, to prevent the entire possession of the earth by these unseen powers. The most important of these influences has been the gradual separation of the spirit-world from the world of the living. Their entire separation is the last result of causes that for a time only removed it to localities proximate to the abodes of the living.

As nomadic tribes change their habitat, the spirit-land diverges from the abode of the living; and the difficulties of the road thither depend upon the nature of the hardships endured

---

[1] Jos. D'Acosta, bk. 5, chap. 7. [2] Wood's N. E. Pros., 104.

in migration. Most of the traditions agree that the spirits on their journey to the spirit-land were beset with difficulties and perils. There was generally a stream of water to cross, and only a narrow and slippery log to bridge the stream. Often they had to pass between moving rocks, which momentarily crashed together, grinding to atoms the less nimble of the pilgrims.[1]

As populations increase, burial-places are set apart, and the world of the dead becomes distinct from that of the living. In many cases the world of the dead, still near at hand, is an adjacent mountain. The genesis of this belief is clear. The Caribs buried their chiefs on mountains; the Comanches, on the highest hill in the neighborhood; the Patagonians, on the summits of the highest hills.[2] The Tupinambas located their heaven behind the great mountains which surrounded their country. The Mexicans also buried on their high places. Where caves are used for interments, they become the supposed places for the dead; hence develops the notion of a subterranean other world. The natives of Terra del Fuego believe that some of them after death are to return to those divine caverns where they were created and their deities reside.[3] Many of the savages of South America have a subterranean spirit-world where the pursuits are the same as in life.[4] The Zuñis had removed their spirit-world to a comfortable distance, where they would not be troubled with them daily; but they annually assembled on the top of a lofty mesa, and spent the entire day in communication with the spirits of the departed, who were supposed on that day to revisit that locality and hold converse with their friends and relatives, who carried them presents. This superstition is very similar to the custom of Roman Catholics on All Souls' Day.

The Dacotahs think each human body has four souls. After death one wanders about the earth, the second watches the

---

[1] Parkman's Jesuits, vol. lxxxii.   [2] 1 Spencer Soc., 218.
[3] 1 ib., 219.   [4] 2 Dobriz., 269.

body, the third hovers over the village, whilst the fourth goes to the land of spirits.[1]

Here we have a curious illustration of continuous survivals of more primitive beliefs. The soul which watches over the body represents the most primitive form of belief. The soul which hovers over the village represents one remove from the primitive belief. The soul which wanders about the earth represents another remove, and the fourth stage of progress assigns it to a distant land of spirits; but the three other beliefs are still surviving, and are the causes of their belief in this quadruplication of souls. The last forms of belief are undoubtedly due to the increasing tendency to migration as population increases.

A tribe that leaves its accustomed seat will have ever-recurring memories connected with that locality. They will desire when the spirit leaves the body to go back and visit the spirits of their ancestors and friends, whose souls are still living at their places of sepulture. An impulse is given to this belief by the superstitious fear of the dead by the living, who are very glad to get rid of them in this way.

Hence the tendency to locate the spirit-land elsewhere than in the midst of the living has been due to the migratory movements of tribes that are nomadic, or to the separation of the places of burial among populous settled peoples.

As migrations have proceeded in all directions, there must arise different beliefs about the direction of the world of spirits. In South America the Chonos and Araucanians go after death towards the west; whereas the Peruvians went east. The Central Americans went towards the east, while the Otomacks of Guiana went west. In North America the Chinooks have their paradise in the south, the Ojibways in the west, where the brave and good spend their time in pleasures, but cowards and the wicked wander about in darkness.[2]

The New England tribes thought the souls of the dead went

---

[1] Eastman's Legends, 129.   [2] Jones's Ojibways, 104.

to the southwest, where were their forefathers' souls.[1] The souls of murderers and thieves, however, wandered restlessly.[2]

Among many tribes the spirit-land is far distant from the place of the living. The soul is believed to take a long journey, only after the tribe has taken a long journey away from the place where their ancestors lived and died. It is generally to see its ancestors. If the tribe has formerly lived upon an island, their heaven is upon an island, as among the Caribs. If the tribe in its migrations has crossed a stream of water, as is generally the case, then the soul has a Stygian flood to encounter. If the tribe has crossed dangerous and difficult mountains, and has barely escaped their dangers, then a Scylla and Charybdis stand in the path of the soul.

The Potawatomies think the souls of the dead cross a large stream over a log which rolls so that many slip off into the water. One of their ancestors went to the edge of the stream, but, not liking to venture on the log, he came back two days after his death. He reported that he heard the sounds of the drum on the other side of the river, to the beat of which the souls of the dead were dancing.[3]

The Ojibways have traditions of the return of souls who have come to this stream, across which lies a serpent, according to their mythology, over whose body they must pass. A big strawberry lies by the side of the way to the spirit-land, which affords them refreshment on the journey.[4]

The soul of the Manacicas of Brazil is carried on the back of a sorcerer to the spirit-land. Over hills and valleys, across rivers, swamps, and lakes, to the Pass Perilous they fly. Here they have to get by a god Tatusio, who, if not satisfied with the conduct of the spirit, casts it into the flood.

These sorcerers who pretend to take charge of the soul, and when they have deposited it safely in the future home return to the earth, frequently come back, and say that Tatusio took

---

[1] Williams, Key to the Languages, 21. [2] Ib., 113.
[3] 1 Keating, 173. [4] Tanner's Narrative, 290.

it away from them and threw it into the water. They then ask for a canoe from the relatives, that they may go back with it and fish out the soul. This artifice is successful in getting them a good canoe, which they keep.[1]

The Chibchas had a great river that souls had to pass over on floats made of cobwebs. On this account they never killed spiders. In the future state, each family had its own location, as in this life.[2]

The Araucanian soul is borne across the Stygian flood by a whale, which does not succeed, however, in protecting it from a mythical hag, who tears out one eye if a toll is not paid her.[3]

The Mohaves believed that when their friends died they departed to a certain high hill in the western section of their territory; that they there pursued their avocation free from the ills and pains of their present life, if they had been good and brave. But they held that all cowardly Indians were tormented with hardships and failures, sickness and defeats. This hill, or hades, they never dared visit. It was thronged with thousands who were ready to wreak vengeance upon the mortal who dared to intrude upon this sacred ground.[4] The souls of those cremated were wafted thither on the curling smoke.

The Blackfeet believe that the spirits of the dead have to scramble up the projecting sides of a steep mountain before they can view the land of their ancestral spirits. Those who have imbrued their hands in the blood of their tribesmen fall down this mountain-side, and can never reach the top. Women who have been guilty of infanticide never even reach this mountain, but wander about the earth with branches of the mountain pine tied to their legs. The cries of wicked spirits are often heard above the country. Those that reach the happy land can have plenty of mushrooms, which are considered a great delicacy by Blackfeet spirits. He who has destroyed his neighbor's canoe stumbles over its wreck, which he cannot pass. The

---

[1] 3 Southey, 186–87.   [2] Bollaert, 12.   [3] 2 Molina, 91–92.
[4] Captivity of the Oatman Girls, 233.

spirits of animals and men injured in life haunt him. All the acts of life are deeply impressed on the green leaf of his memory.[1]

The Chippewyan, living in the regions of almost perpetual snow, wants to find a heaven in some more genial clime, and as his spirit moves onward the ice grows thinner, the air warmer, the trees taller. Birds of gay colors plume themselves in the warm sun. The swallow and the martin skim along the level of the green vales. The trees no longer crack beneath the weight of icicles and snow, and he sees no more the spirits of the departed dancing on the skirts of the northern clouds. His spirit craves a warmer heaven. A stone canoe is ready to take him over the dividing stream. No Charon demands a fare, but onward speeds the magic craft, with no visible impelling force, and lands him on the blessed shore, if he has not slaughtered more oxen than he could eat, or speared salmon to be devoured by the brown eagle, or gathered rock-moss to rot in the rain. These great crimes, in the moral code of the Blackfeet, will sink the canoe, and its occupant will flounder about in the water black with the heads of the unhappy.[2]

The Mosquito heaven was across a broad stream.

The future abode of Mexicans had three divisions. Their elysium was open to the souls of warriors, who were borne thither in the arms of Teoyaomique, Queen Consort of the God of War. Here awaited them the presents sent by loving friends below. These souls never tired, for they spent their days marching around the zenith as an escort to the sun. At evening they dispersed to the chase, or to the shady grove, after having delivered their precious solar charge to a new escort, composed of women who had died in childbed, who conducted it to its nightly couch of quetzal feathers, in which it reclined.

Although this is represented as the highest heaven, its joys would not appear as great to us as those of Tlalocan, where

---

[1] 1 Jones's Traditions, 245-50.   [2] 1 ib., 256-63.

happiness reigned supreme and sorrow was unknown. To this place were assigned those killed by lightning, and the drowned, and those dying of long and incurable skin diseases. Children sacrificed to Tlaloc played about its gardens.[1]

The Greeks assigned children to Erebus, as a penalty to prevent *infanticide;* but the Mexicans encouraged their *sacrifice* by assigning them to this place of happiness.

The third place, Mictlan, was a land of darkness and desolation, wherein were the souls of those who died of old age, or those who died in bed. There was no mercy in the Aztec Tartarus for those who died in bed among a race of warriors. The Mexican souls had to pass between two mountains that confronted each other. They were subjected to cutting winds. They had passes given them by the priest, who thrust little slips of paper in their hands. The journey ended with the passage of the "nine waters."[2]

In the Mexican heaven there were various degrees of happiness. The high-born warrior who fell gloriously in battle did not meet on equal terms the base-born rustic who died in his bed. The ordinary avocations of life were not dispensed with, but the man took up his bow again, the woman her spindle.

The road to paradise was represented to be full of dangers. Storms, monsters, deep waters, and whirlpools met the traveller on his way, who, however, almost always succeeded in reaching his destination, after having suffered more or less maltreatment on the way.[3]

The Northern Californians had a heaven where all met after death to enjoy a life free from want; but when the soul first escaped from the body, Omaha, an evil spirit, hovered near, ready to pounce upon it and carry it off.[4]

Among the natives about Clear Lake there is no contest, but a coyote waits for the soul and captures it: a good spirit may redeem it by paying a price. They kept up many demonstra-

---

[1] 3 Bancroft, 532-34.   [2] 2 ib., 604-5.   [3] 3 ib., 511-13.
[4] 3 ib., 523.

tions about the grave for three days, to scare away coyotes.[1] This superstition has arisen from the fact that the coyotes dig up the dead and devour them.

The Winnebagoes keep a fire on graves for four nights after burial, and keep the grass dug up, that bad spirits can have nothing to cling to.[2]

The Eurocs burn a light on the grave, and this beacon is kept burning a longer time in the case of the wicked, because they are thought to have a longer and more difficult passage to the spirit-land. Many are compelled to return, and transmigrate into birds, beasts, and insects.[3]

The Kailtas are carried to the spirit-land by a little bird, but if impeded by sins a hawk will certainly overtake them, and end their journey heavenward. The Cahroc path of the dead branches into two roads, one bright with flowers and leading to the great western land beyond the great waters, the other filled with thorns and briers, and the haunt of deadly serpents.

The Maricopa paradise is at their ancient home on the banks of the Colorado. There the spirits live on the sand-hills.

The Yumas located their paradise in a pleasant valley, hidden in one of the cañons of the Colorado, and they had gone so far as to separate the wheat from the chaff, for their wicked were shut up in a dark cavern, within view of their paradise, but its pleasures they could never enjoy, although within sight. The Navajo spirits had to travel far to reach their heaven. They had to cross an extensive marsh, in which many were bemired; but if they got through, they soon arrived at the home of two spirits,—one male and one female,—who sat combing their hair. After receiving a lecture on cleanliness, and obeying its injunctions, they passed on to the happy land. The Comanche spirits have not yet been confined to any locality, but want much more freedom than the circumscribed bounds of an Indian heaven can give them: so they hunt on the happy

---

[1] 3 Bancroft, 523.   [2] Eastman's Chicora, 21.   [3] 3 Bancroft, 524.

prairies of the setting sun, where the buffalo leads the hunter in the glorious chase, but at night they come back to their old homes and stay till break of day.[1]

The souls of the Sonora Indians dwell among the cliffs of their mountains, and the echoes there are their clamoring voices. Echoes throughout the Americas are the voices of spirits. In Nayarit the natives thought that most souls went to a common resort near their living habitat, but returned in the daytime in the shape of flies, in order to get something to eat.[2]

The Neeshenams had a heaven a long way off, and a stream to cross before getting to it. Their great ancestor, Eicut, presides over that happy land, whither he was led by his beloved wife, Yoatotowee. When she died, his grief knew no bounds; the light was gone from his eyes, the world was black and dreary. He fell into a trance; Yoatotowee came and stood beside him. He saw her; she turned, and started for heaven, the dance-house of ghosts. Eicut followed her into the spirit-land.[3]

The belief of the Mohicans regarding the separation of the soul is that it goes westward on leaving the body. There it is met with great rejoicing by the others who died previously. There they wear black otter- or bear-skins, which among them are signs of gladness.[4]

The Creeks believe the soul at death goes to the west and joins its friends.[5]

When a Kioway dies, his spirit travels toward sunset. A high mountain stands on the confines of the other world, upon which is a sentinel who informs the spirits when their friends are coming, and the spirits, with rejoicings, go forth to meet them.

The Dog-Ribs had located their heaven a great way off, for Chappewee, their ancestor, when his spirit took the long journey, carried three thousand roasted porpoises and thirty whales to supply him food on the way.[6]

---

[1] 3 Bancroft, 426-28.   [2] 3 ib., 528.   [3] 3 ib., 531-32.
[4] Wassenaer's Historie, Tr. Doc. Hist. N. Y., vol. iii. p. 29.
[5] Hawkins's Sketch, 80.   [6] 2 Jones, 2.

The heaven of the Tondanwandies is not far off, for they bury their dead in the morning, that the deceased persons may have time before night to reach their relations in another world.[1] The peaks of Costa Rica are the resort of their spirits, and their revellings can be heard at the distance of a mile or more.[2]

The Greenlanders assign two retreats for their departed souls; one the centre of the earth, the way to which appears difficult, because upon the path at a certain point they slide down a rocky defile, leaving blood all along the way.[3] It takes about five days to make this slide.[4]

Their spiritual body has evidently not been wholly dematerialized. The second abode for the dead is among the heavenly bodies, the path to which is along the Milky Way, called the path of the dead by this new school of Eskimo philosophers. It is curious to note here the prevalence of these two opinions upon the locality of their spirit-world. They have removed it from their living abode, and the first remove has evidently been to a subterranean abode, which is quite natural to a people living in underground houses a portion of the year. The new sect, becoming dissatisfied with this subterranean paradise, have turned it into a gloomy underground region. Mr. Crantz noticed that these two sects were quite hostile upon this subject.

Many mourning ceremonies had reference to the journey to the spirit-land. In the burial ceremonies of the natives of Alaska, if too many tears were shed, they said that the road of the dead would be muddy, but a few tears just laid the dust.[5]

Many traditions of a journey to the spirit-land and return are found. The following story is told of an old Indian chief of the Algonkins of Northern New Brunswick. His favorite son died; whereupon the father, with a party of friends, set out for the land of souls to recover him. They had to wade through a shallow lake several days' journey. This they did, sleeping at night on platforms of poles, which supported them above the

---

[1] Evans, Pedest. Tour, 57.   [2] Gabb, 506.   [3] Egede's Greenland, 205.
[4] 1 Crantz, 186.   [5] Dall, Alaska, 423.

water. At length they arrived in the realms of Papkootparout, the Indian Pluto, who rushed at them with his war-club upraised, but relented before striking. The bereaved father now begged hard for his son's soul, which was given him in the shape of a nut, which he was to insert in his son's body, and he would come to life. The adventurers returned to earth, and the father, who wished to take part in a dance of rejoicing which was begun, handed the bag containing the soul to a squaw to hold for him. She through curiosity opened the bag, and away went the soul to the realms of the Indian god of the dead.[1]

A Shawnee tradition tells of a brother who followed his sister into the land of spirits, seized her in the midst of a spirit-dance, placed her soul in a hollow reed, covered the orifice with the end of his finger, and brought her back to the earth, where gay festivities were indulged in on account of her return.[2]

Such stories of journeys to the spirit-land and a return are found in nearly every tribe.

Another destiny of the human spirits was transmigration. The transmigration of souls explains and renders intelligible all the various superstitions of pagan religions. A belief in this doctrine is found in every American tribe. The most primitive form of the belief was the most comprehensive. Before the separation of the abode of spirits from the abode of the living, disembodied spirits were everywhere present, seeking embodiment in some more material form. As the spiritual world became separated and became the abode of deserving souls, the undeserving souls were left to transmigrate until they were better fitted for the abode of the blest. The wicked generally entered noxious animals; those not so bad, the nobler animals and the bodies of infants.

Mr. Schoolcraft says, "The Indians of the United States believe in the transmigration of souls. The soul is thought to pass from one object to another, generally into the animal cre-

---

[1] Le Clerc, in Parkman's Jes., lxxxiii.
[2] 2 Gregg's Commerce of Prairies, 239.

ation. The individual can often determine the form of his future life for himself." [1]

The Northwestern tribes believe in transmigration; their departed souls can come back in human shape. The priests can transfer a soul released into a living body by blowing it through their hands.

The medicine-men of the Cocomes pretend to receive the spirit of the dead in their hands, and are able to transfer it to any one, who then takes the name of the dead person.[2]

When a body is burned among the Tacullies, the priest receives the spirit of the deceased into his hands, and, with a motion as though throwing it, he blows the spirit into some person selected, who takes the name of the deceased in addition to his own.[3]

Algonkin women who desired to become mothers flocked to the couch of those about to die, in hope that the vital principle as it passed from the body would enter theirs.[4]

A sorcerer among the Iroquois pretended he was once an oki (spirit) dwelling under the earth with a female spirit; that both of them ascended to the earth and hid beside a path until a woman passed, when they entered into her. After a time they were born, but not until he had quarrelled with and strangled his female companion, who came dead into this world.[5]

Permanent transition, new birth, or reincarnation of human souls is supposed to occur by the transmigration of the soul of a deceased person into the body of an infant. Many tribes buried dead children by the wayside, that their souls might enter into mothers passing by, and so be born again.

The Nootkans accounted for the fact that a distant tribe spoke the same language as themselves, by declaring them to be the spirits of their dead.

The Thlinkeets believe in the transmigration of the soul. It is not uncommon to hear a poor Thlinkeet say, when speaking

[1] 1 Schoolcraft, 33.   [2] 4 U. S. Ex. Exp., 453.
[3] Hazlitt, Br. Columbia, 32.   [4] Brinton, 270.
[5] Parkman's Jes., 92.

of a rich and prosperous family, "When I die, I should like to be born into that family."[1]

The Greenlanders think the soul may be taken out of the body and replaced; may be divided into parts and repaired when it loses a part. It can forsake the body during sleep, and be exchanged for that of some animal. They believe in the migration of souls. Widows make use of this doctrine to their great advantage; for if one of them can persuade any father that the soul of her deceased child has migrated into his son, or that the spirit of his deceased offspring animates the body of one of her children, the man will always do his best to befriend the child and widow.[2] As soon as a person dies, the soul is supposed to animate a new-born infant.[3] A young Eskimo woman, by the name of Avigiatsiak, had been a whale and a seal. When she was a seal she was caught, killed, and her head thrown beneath a bench. From thence she slipped into the body of the wife of the man who harpooned her, and was born a human being.[4]

Among the Kolushes the mother often dreams that she has seen the deceased relative who will transmit his soul to her child. In Vancouver's Island, in 1860, a lad was very much regarded by the Indians, because he had a mark similar to a chief who had died four generations before. They thought the dead chief had returned again.[5]

The celebrated Dacotah, Cloudy Sky, had lived three times on the earth. When his body was laid upon the scaffold at his first death, his spirit enlisted in the army of the enemies of the storm-god, and as they flew to battle with their shields before their breasts, the wind tore up the trees, and the waters cast their angry billows at the cloud; but the contest was brief, and they were conquerors, and the bow of bright colors rested between the heavens and earth. It was these cloud-battles that gave him his name of Cloudy Sky.[6]

A curious tradition among the Crows relates the incarnation

---

[1] Dall, 423.   [2] 1 Crantz, 185.   [3] 1 ib., 342.
[4] Rink, 450-51.   [5] 2 Tylor, 3-4.   [6] Eastman, 229.

of Storm Child. Black clouds gathered in midwinter; the thunder rolled and the lightning flashed, while strange noises alarmed the Crows. An inky cloud covered the peak of their mountain, and from its midst reached two long arms that deposited an infant on the earth. Soon the mysterious child which was given disappeared in the vapor. An old squaw who had not borne children for years stood looking on. No sooner did she see the child disappear in the vapor than she felt herself seized with violent labor-pains, and was delivered of a female child, perfectly green, like grass. The Indians all said it was the same child that had been in the cloud, and that the mysterious hands had no sooner deposited it than it was transferred to the woman. The squaw persisted that it was not the child of a man, though she was married. The Indians named it the Storm Child. Says Mr. Belden, "I often saw the Storm Child, and she is greatly feared and respected by her tribe."[1]

The Chibchas of Bogota believe in transmigration of souls into infants.[2]

Mr. Southey says "the Tucamas of Brazil hold the metempsychosis," or transmigration of human souls into human bodies.[3]

The Guaycurus[4] and the Guaranies believed in the same doctrine. "The Conchas held for certain that the dead again entered the bodies of those who were born."[5]

The Peruvians thought the souls of the dead returned after a time, and entered the bodies of infants at their birth.[6]

These few illustrations, selected from many more, will suffice to show the prevalence of the doctrine of transmigration, or reincarnation of human souls in human bodies. Let us now notice another form of the doctrine, the transmigration of human souls into animals. All peoples in early stages of culture draw little distinction between animal and man.

Primitive psychology, drawing no definite line of demarcation

---

[1] Belden, p. 215, seq.   [2] Bollaert, 5.   [3] 1 Southey, 590.
[4] 1 ib., 118.   [5] Cieza, 354.   [6] Bradford, 356.

between souls of men and of beasts, admits the transmigration of human souls into animals.

The nobler animals are generally, but not universally, selected as objects into which transmigration takes place. The architectural skill of the beaver, the wise aspect of the owl, the sweet plaint of the nightingale, the howls of beasts like the moans of children in pain, the sparkling orbs and tortuous stealthiness of the snake, supply hints at metempsychosis.[1]

The spirit freed

> "Fills with fresh energy another form,
> And towers an elephant, or glides a worm;
> Swims as an eagle in the eye of noon,
> Or wails a screech-owl to the deaf cold moon."

The Chinooks believe in the transmigration of souls into birds, beasts, fishes, and all animate objects.[2]

In Peru, as soon as a dying person draws his last breath, ashes are strewed on the floor of the room, and the door is securely fastened. Next morning the ashes are carefully examined to ascertain whether they show any impression of footsteps, and imagination readily traces marks, which are alleged to have been produced by the feet of birds, dogs, cats, oxen, or llamas. The destiny of the dead person is construed by the footmarks which are supposed to be discernible. The soul has transmigrated into that animal whose tracks are found.[3]

Mr. Hennepin says the Northern Indians related that they had seen a serpent come out of the mouth of a woman when she died.[4] Her soul had passed into its body.

The Powhatans refrained from doing any harm to small woodbirds, because they were animated by the souls of their dead chiefs.

A very popular bird for transmigration of the souls of the Hurons was the turtle-dove; and the Iroquois, as a part of the funeral rite, set free a bird to carry the soul away.[5]

---

[1] Alger's Doc. Fut. Life, 479. [2] Swan's Washington Territory, 174.
[3] Tschudi's Peru, 337. [4] Hennepin's Continuation, 122.
[5] Morgan's League, 174.

In Dacotah mythology a large fish which dammed up the waters of the St. Croix had in it the spirit of a Dacotah, and the only way of inducing his monstrous highness to take himself off and stop his obstruction of navigation was for an Indian woman, whom he had loved when a Dacotah, to entreat him to go to deeper water. She accompanied her request with a present of a little dish of bark, worked and ornamented very handsomely by herself.[1]

Among the South American tribes, the Abipones of Paraguay believe that the little ducks that fly about in flocks at night, uttering a mournful hiss, are inhabited by the souls of their dead.[2]

The Yurubas believed the souls of the dead entered into animals. The Mexicans also believed in such transmigration.[3]

The Caribs think human souls transmigrate into the bodies of beasts. A Guarany woman would start at seeing a fox, thinking the spirit of her dead daughter might be within it.

The totemic system is connected with transmigration. The Moquis think that after death they live in the form of their totemic animal. Those of the deer family become deer; the bear tribe become bears; and so on through the gentes.[4]

The doctrine of transmigration of human souls into animals is the source of their superstitious abstention from eating the flesh of some animals.

Darwin mentions a South American Indian who would not eat land-birds because they were dead men.[5]

The tribes akin to the Pomo will not eat grizzly bears, for the spirits of their dead enter into them. They will often beg to save the life of one of these animals.[6]

The California tribes abstain from large game, because they believe the souls of past generations have passed into their bodies.[7]

---

[1] Eastman, 163-64.
[2] 2 Dobrizhoffer, 74.
[3] Bradford, 357.
[4] Cozzens, 465.
[5] Naturalist's Voyage, 214.
[6] 3 Schoolcraft, 113.
[7] 5 ib., 215.

Hayes mentions an Eskimo woman who would not eat walrus, as her husband's soul had passed into it for temporary habitation. The Angekok always announces to the widow the animal into which her husband's soul has entered, and she never eats that animal.[1]

Nothing could be more natural to those who believe in the transmigration of human souls into animals, than to imagine that the best men would enter the nobler animals, while the common spirits entered the lower animals. The Tlascalans thought the souls of nobles animated the beautiful singing birds, while those of plebeians passed into weasels, beetles, and such creatures. The Icannis of Brazil thought the souls of brave warriors passed into beautiful birds that fed on pleasant fruits. Souls of cowards migrated into reptiles.[2]

The Tapuyas think the souls of the good and brave enter birds, while the cowardly become reptiles.[3]

The Arkansas thought their principal deities resided in some of the nobler animals, feeding in the forests, and perpetuity was kept up by transmigration.

The doctrine of transmigration of human souls into animals is found among all the tribes of the New World, but among the ruder tribes very little evidence of the limitation of this transmigration to evil spirits is found. Among a few of the Northern tribes it is found to a limited extent, but connected with a belief in a paradise for good spirits. The Ojibways thought the souls of the wicked passed into toads.[4]

We can recognize in the destiny of the departed souls, according to these rules of transmigration, the beginning of the doctrine of future rewards and punishments.

The Dog-Ribs think evil spirits assume the form of bears, wolves, and other animals, and in the woods and desert places they fancy they hear them howling and moaning.[5]

The Allequas supposed the soul must transmigrate until it

---

[1] Hayes's Arctic Researches, 199.   [2] 2 Tylor, 6-7; 3 Bancroft, 512.
[3] Orton's Andes, 170.   [4] Kohl's Kitchi-Gami, 219.
[5] Hartwig's Polar World, 329.

had become so good as to be able to pass into the ever-green prairies of the happy land. Some of the Western tribes thought that by eating those animals that did not contain the embodied spirits of their own tribe, whose flesh they abstained from eating, they would gather their souls and increase their own soul-power, and insure their getting into the spirit-land without further transmigration.[1]

It is among the South American nations that we find the doctrine most prevalent that wicked spirits transmigrate into animals. The Brazilian Indians thought evil spirits appeared in lizards, crocodiles, and other such reptiles.[2]

The Mbayas and Guaycurus of Brazil think the souls of the wicked pass into the bodies of wild beasts at death.[3]

Such is the doctrine of transmigration of wicked and inferior spirits into animals, and it certainly suggests a similarity to that of the races of the Old World, which Mr. Thoreau presents pleasantly in this strain: "All the shore rang with the trump of bullfrogs, the sturdy spirits of ancient wine-bibbers and wassailers still unrepentant, trying to sing a catch in their Stygian lake, who would fain keep up the hilarious rules of their old festal table, though their voices have waxed hoarse and solemnly grave, mocking at mirth."[4]

Another form of transmigration, according to the superstitious belief of barbarous peoples, appears in their theory of diseases and their cures; and a brief history of this remarkable superstition will now be given. As in normal conditions the man's soul inhabiting his body is thought to give it life and health and power to think, speak, and act through it, so an adaptation of the same principle explains abnormal conditions of body or mind, by considering the new symptoms as due to the operation of a second soul-like being, a strange spirit. "A man burning in fever, or pained and wrenched as though some live creature were tearing and twisting him within, rationally

---

[1] 3 Bancroft, 525.
[3] 1 Southey, 118; 3 ib., 392.
[2] Darwin, Nat. Voy., 243.
[4] Thoreau's Walden, 137.

finds a personal spiritual cause for his sufferings. When the mysterious unseen power throws him helpless on the ground, jerks and writhes him in convulsions, and impels him, with distorted face and frantic gesture not his, or seemingly even human, to pour forth wild, incoherent raving; or, with thought and eloquence beyond his sober faculties, to command, counsel, and foretell; such an one seems to those who watch him, and even to himself, to have become the mere instrument of a spirit which has seized him or entered into him. This is the savage theory of possession and obsession, which is their theory of disease and inspiration. There is this difference between possession and obsession. In possession the spirits enter into and inhabit the body; in obsession they hover about and affect it from outside."[1]

They are based on an animistic conception, most genuine and rational. This animism must assume the most prominent place in man's intellectual history. The doctrine underlying disease spirits and oracle spirits is the same, however strange it may appear. Many of those most diseased and abnormal and morbid have for the same reason become the great religious and prophetic teachers of humanity. Especially is this true among the uncultivated and primitive races, where all prophecy is a synonym of dream and all medical practice a synonym of sorcery. Disease being accounted for by an attack of spirits, it naturally follows that to get rid of these spirits is the proper means of cure. Nothing could display more vividly the conception of a disease or a mental affection, as caused by a spiritual being, than the proceedings of the sorcerer, who talks to it, coaxes or threatens it, makes offerings to it, and tries to entice or drive it out of the patient's body.

That the two great effects ascribed to such spiritual influence, namely, the infliction of ailments and the inspiration of oracles, are not only mixed up together, but often run into absolute coincidence, accords with the view that both results

---

[1] 2 Tylor, Prim. Cult., 123–26.

are referred to one common cause. The intruding spirit may be a human soul, or belong to some other class in the spiritual hierarchy. These spiritual beings are abroad upon the earth in large numbers, and their life is a continuation, and not a new life, in savage religion. They have revenge to satisfy, inspired by past and present wrongs. Again, those that have been wicked spirits when embodied are wicked when disembodied, and will seek to do all the injury to others in their power. The most primitive belief concerning the way in which these injuries are inflicted is that which attributes sickness and bodily harm to these disembodied spirits. Those that inflict sickness are really the demons of primitive times, although demonology in its modern form has not yet been fully developed. Thus we see that demonology, transmigration, disease, and dreams, although different branches of the same subject, are so interwoven in the study of the religion of the American nations that I have chosen to place them together in the same chapter, but study them separately, as far as it can be done, without a repetition of the facts that elucidate them all.

Disease is produced by the transmigration of one or more spirits, generally those of animals, into the sick person. Says Mrs. Eastman, "What the Dacotah most dreads is that some animal will enter his body and make him sick."[1] They thought that toothache was produced by the spirit of a woodpecker.[2] An old Dacotah, whose son had sore eyes, said that nearly thirty years before, when his son was a boy, he fastened a pin to a stick and speared a minnow with it, and it was strange that the fish after so long a time should come to seek revenge on his son's eyes.[3]

Among the Northern Californians, snakes and other reptiles appear to get most of the blame for their sickness. They discover the locality of the spirit in the body by barking at it for some time.[4]

---

[1] Eastman's Sioux. [2] Neill's Minnesota, 87.
[3] 2 Wiscon. Hist. Coll., 183. [4] 1 Bancroft, 354-55.

Among the wild tribes of Mexico the animals generally guilty are monstrous ants or worms.[1]

The natives of Brazil think disease is produced by the spirit of some animal entering the body of the patient, in revenge for some wrong, and the chief of the tribe, who acts as physician, asks the patient if he has offended a tortoise, deer, or other animal.[2]

Thus, among the Abipones of Paraguay, if they give the flesh of a tortoise, stag, or boar to dogs, it is an indignity to those animals, and punishment will overtake them. The soul of the animal will enter their bodies and afflict them.[3]

Paralysis was generally attributed to the agency of the spirit of a deceased person. The treatment consists in efforts to drive away the spirit by conjuring and uncouth noises.

According to the disease theory above given, the pathology of all diseases being nearly the same, their professed medicine-men treat all diseases nearly alike. Their efforts are expended in expelling the spirit, whatever it may be, which it is expected the medicine-man will soon discover, and, having informed the friends what it is, he usually requires them to be in readiness to drive it away as soon as he shall succeed in expelling it. This he attempts in the first place by incantations, intended to secure the aid of the spirits he worships, and then by all kinds of frightful noises and gestures, and by sucking the place where the pain is. As soon as he thinks he has succeeded in dislodging the spirit, he says the word, and two or more weapons are discharged at the door of the tent, to frighten the spirit as it passes out.[4] If they do not succeed in curing the patient, they excuse themselves by saying that they have not found the right animal.

Among the Six Nations the Indians had a singular way of discovering the right intruder in cases of extreme sickness. In the case of the illness of the wife of Ca-whic-do-ta, which oc-

---

[1] 1 Bancroft, 640.
[2] 1 Southey, 334.
[3] 2 ib., 263.
[4] 1 School., 250.

curred in 1793, fearing she was to die, the Indians gathered eight or ten bushels of ashes and placed them in a pile near the hut in which she lay. The ashes were then scattered around the cabin. By these manœuvres they hoped to discover what spirit visited the sick person by its tracks. The Western tribes had a still more singular way of discovering the intruding animal. Each medicine-man had diminutive wooden idols under some form of a quadruped, or bird, or fish. When any chief personage was sick, the priests were sent for, to bring their idols. They retired into a canoe to hold a consultation, and if they did not agree as to the malady or the mode of treatment, they settled the dispute by beating the idols against each other, and whichever lost a tooth or a claw was confuted.[1]

The departure of the animal was a cause of thanksgiving, even in the slightest affections. Thus, the Omahaws after an eructation say, " Thank you, animal."[2]

The way of curing sick patients among the Indians of Darien was to strip them stark naked and shoot small arrows at them. If an arrow opened a vein and blood rushed out, the people leaped with joy. The theory undoubtedly was that the intruding spirit had been pierced and compelled to come forth.

Among the Mapuches the sorcerer proceeds to frighten the evil spirit out of the patient. He makes himself as horrible-looking as he can, and begins beating a drum and working himself into a frenzy until he falls to the ground with his breast jerking convulsively. As soon as he falls, a number of young men outside the hut, who are there to assist him in driving off the evil one, begin yelling defiantly, and dashing at full speed, with lighted torches, around the hut. If this does not frighten the evil spirit off, but death takes place, it is attributed to witchcraft. A woman often acts as sorcerer.[3]

The Araucanians have the same ceremonies for cure of sickness.

The Mundrucus think sickness is caused by spirits, and the

---

[1] Dunn's Oregon, 91.   [2] 2 Long's Exp., 54.
[3] 2 Wood's Uncivilized Races, 562.

medicine-men fix upon the place where the evil spirit has located itself, and then suck the spot and blow smoke upon it.[1]

The Abipones think disease is produced by enemies, and murders are committed in many cases where disease results in death. An immense drum which makes a horrible bellowing is placed near a sick person's head to frighten away the evil spirit.[2]

The Central American tribes attribute sickness to evil spirits, and have medicine-men called sookias, who perform their incantations over the sick, whom they first surround with a little fence of charmed and painted sticks. If there is an epidemic in the town, they will surround the windward side with these sticks, with little grotesque images on them. If their success is not such as they expect in expelling the evil spirits, the inhabitants remove immediately and burn the village.[3]

The Patagonians thought sickness was caused by a spirit entering the patient's body. They believed every sick person to be possessed of an evil demon. The inhabitants of the West Indies also referred diseases to hostile demons, and the physician, after pulling and sucking the patient thoroughly, would go to the door of the house and pretend to blow something through his hands, saying, "Begone to the mountains, or where you will."[4]

The natives of Cumana thought the diseased were possessed with spirits. Their physicians sucked and licked the part affected, to draw out the distemper, spitting at short intervals. They said they drew out spirits. "If the disease increased, they tickled the throat with a stick till the patient vomited, which they carried into the field, saying, 'Go thy way, devil!'"[5]

The Koniagas in the Northwest, when a person falls sick, suppose some evil spirit has taken possession of him, and it is the business of the sorcerer to drive it out. He begins with a tambourine and incantations, and if this does not accomplish the purpose he falls upon the person of the sufferer, and, seizing

---

[1] 2 Wood's Uncivilized Races, 577.   [2] 2 Dobriz., 266.
[3] 1 Brown, 251.   [4] 1 Herrera, 163.   [5] 3 ib., 310.

the demon, struggles with it, overpowers it, and casts it out, while the assistants cry, "He is gone! he is gone!"[1]

The Nootkans ascribe disease to the influence of evil spirits. The patient is always starved, lest the food should be consumed by his internal enemy.[2] If the disease becomes serious, it is decided that evil spirits have fixed upon the patient's body for their dwelling-place, whereupon they begin a most violent pressure and kneading of the body,[3] evidently intending to make it very uncomfortable for the intruder.

Among the more advanced races of Mexico and Peru, an additional method of aiding in the cure of disease was found in the confession of sins.

The employment of the confessional in the cure of disease had a practical use. The disease was supposed to be produced by some avenging spirit, which might be appeased and turned aside from its revengeful purpose by the penitent admission of the wrong. Hence it was very common among semi-civilized peoples to have a confessional, and among the barbarous tribes it existed in a rude form, as the following illustration shows. In Honduras, if a native was met by a jaguar he would confess his sins aloud, imploring pardon. If the beast still threatened, he would say, "I have committed as many more sins: do not kill me."[4]

The Roman Catholics were quite astonished to find the confessional established before their arrival. The primitive belief that disease is produced by hostile spirits seeking revenge for some wrong would naturally result in confession, if the establishment of a priestly hierarchy outstripped the progress of medical science, conditions which we find fulfilled in the Mexican and Peruvian civilization. They both had an established priesthood, successors to the primitive sorcerers. But the wild and violent methods of these sorcerers would not be tolerated by a more cultivated people. They must yield to a more peaceful method of cure. The priest has assumed to himself

---

[1] 1 Bancroft, 85.
[2] 1 ib., 204-205.
[3] 1 ib., 246.
[4] 3 ib., 486.

the mediatorship between man and these revenging spirits, and a confession to him of all offences, followed by sacrifice and other penalties, served to propitiate the spiritual agents producing diseases. Coercion is supplanted by propitiation.

In Yucatan, difficulty in childbirth was supposed to be produced by some sin which had to be confessed. If the wife's confession did not answer, the husband was compelled to confess.[1] Sins committed twenty years before a sickness were thought to have come to give judgment at last, and were confessed and sacrifices offered to escape the penalty.[2] A married priesthood were the regular confessors, but in an emergency a husband confessed to a wife, and a wife to a husband.[3]

The natives of Salvador compelled confession of sins in case of sickness. The sins confessed were generally neglect of the worship of their gods. The Peruvians had the confessional, and it was a sin to conceal anything therein: all had to confess but the Inca, who confessed to the sun.[4]

The curious couvade, noticed by so many travellers, and which has been so difficult to explain, is a superstition that has arisen through fear of attacks of evil spirits. In the couvade the man takes to his bed when the wife gives birth to a child, and kills no animals. This fear of killing animals and carrying on their ordinary avocations arises from the supposition that the spirits of the animals will take advantage of the helplessness of the child, and avenge itself upon it in some disease.

Among the Caribs, in the West Indies, when a child is born, the father begins to complain and take to his hammock, and does not eat sometimes for five days together. After forty days the relatives and friends collect, and hack his flesh with agouti-teeth, and draw blood from all parts of his body. The wounds are then washed with pepper infusion. For six months he must not eat birds or fish, for whatever animals he eats will impress their likeness on the child, or produce disease by entering its body. The tribes on the east coast of South

---

[1] 2 Bancroft, 678.
[3] 3 ib., 472.
[2] 2 ib., 796.
[4] 4 Herrera, 348.

America practised the couvade, and thought if the father killed any animal it would harm the child. The idea seemed to be that the father must refrain from food the killing of which would bring harm to the child. Among the Arawaks the father can kill little birds and fish, but no large game.

Says Mr. Southey, speaking of the couvade among the Brazilians, "The father, according to a custom more widely diffused perhaps than any other observance which is entirely unaccountable, takes to his hammoc" during and after the birth of a child.[1] For fifteen days after the birth he ate no meat, did no hunting, and set no snares for birds.[2]

Among the Abipones the husband goes to bed, fasts a number of days, "and you would think," says Dobrizhoffer, "that it was he that had had the child."

The same custom prevails among the Coroados, the father abstaining from the flesh of animals. In Guiana the same custom prevails.

Among the Eskimos the husbands forbear hunting during the lying-in of their wives, and for some time thereafter.[3]

A curious custom of transferring disease-spirits to images, which are then carried away, is a method of cure that pertains to the subject of transmigration.

The Mexicans, to cure a raging fever, made a little dog of maize paste and put it on a leaf and left it on the roadside, saying the first passer-by would carry away the illness.[4] The spirit producing the disease entered the dog's image and was carried away. These curious methods of sending away the spirit of disease were common to the Old World as well as the New.

A favorite treatment among the Nahuas was to form a figure of corn dough. They introduced the disease into it and then carried it off and left it by the wayside. Of course it is the intruding spirit that is carried away in the image or figure, and the priest has succeeded in driving it out of the patient into the

---

[1] 3 Southey, 165.
[2] 2 ib., 368.
[3] Egede, 196.
[4] Motolinia, 130.

image, which is their equivalent of the scapegoat. It is quite remarkable to find this practice more common among the civilized American tribes than anywhere else, although it is found at certain stages of progress among all peoples.

The use of medical cures formed little or no part of the sorcerer's programme, and the few herbs that were discovered to have medical properties were themselves elevated into gods. Those that grew on burial-places had superstitious pre-eminence given them in these cures, showing the animistic nature of their cures and the tendency of the primitive mind.

Sometimes diseases of the consumptive or non-acute kind are produced by the prolonged absence of a person's soul from his body. Such a case came under Mr. Jones's observation, where the sorcerer told a sick man that his soul had gone away from him, and was in the bank of a river with the manitous who reside there.[1]

The Aht sorcerer undertakes to bring back truant souls into bodies that have been bereft of them; also effects interchanges of souls.[2]

This theory of the absence of the spirit from the body during life and the incoming of another spirit, explains a large class of phenomena which are accounted for by the presence of the strange spirit. The body perhaps struggles violently in the throes of a nightmare. The inference is that this usurping spirit uses the body in this violent way. Sometimes the new spirit is not willing to go out when the other returns, and then we would have a case of possession, and the struggle might become so fierce and sharp that the person would behave like a maniac, and the intruding spirit would be dubbed a demon. Again, upon the same theory these cases of possession by an unclean, or, in other words, an intruding spirit, would not be confined to the sleep superstition, but some audaciously wicked spirit would occasionally attempt to force an entrance when the spirit is not away; and then we have epilepsy, and the falling

---

[1] Jones's Ojibways, 271. [2] Sproat's Scenes of Savage Life, 169.

sickness. Again, sometimes the body does things involuntarily. What has caused this? Evidently an intruding spirit has produced contortions, and makes the body do things its owner does not wish. Hysteria is produced by an intruder, and its uncontrollable and meaningless laughs and sobs are those of the newcomer. Its movements are felt in the globus hystericus. Again, sneezing and yawning are involuntary, and these are the work of the intruder; and hence quite a body of superstitions have grown up around these, many of which have survived to the present day.

The next branch of the subject of the employment of spirits, and their invisible agency, will be that of dreams. Dreams are produced by the temporary transmigration of an outside spirit into the troubled person, or they are the real experiences of the wandering soul of the sleeper. Among the Ahts, when a person starts in a dream with a scream, a relative will cut his arms and legs, and sprinkle the blood around the house as a sacrifice to the spirit which is troubling him. If the vision continues, they throw articles on the fire.[1] This sacrifice appeases the intruding spirit.

The influence of dreams is so great upon the life of the American Indians that every act and thought is predicated upon this superstition. Many instances are found where Indians have dreamed of seeing a bear, or some other animal, at a certain place, whose flesh they need to keep them from starving; and such credence do they give to this dream that they will start after the game. Such a case is mentioned in Tanner's narrative. The mother of a young hunter dreamed that she saw a bear at a certain place which she described. A young son following the description found a bear in the place indicated, and killed it.[2]

A few such coincidences have strengthened their faith in dreams. The Nootkans find out where fish and berries are most abundant by means of dreams. Obedience was yielded to dreams.

---

[1] Sproat, 173.   [2] Tanner, 52-53.

Charlevoix mentions an Iroquois who dreamed of having a finger cut off, and forthwith proceeded to cut it off when he awoke.[1]

An Iowa chief, having dreamed that he would die after the happening of a certain event, prepared himself for death after the event happened, and expired without any previous indisposition.[2]

Says Hind of those savages about Hudson's Bay, "If one of them dreams he will die, he cannot be saved." An Indian dream is an inspiration. The inspiring agent is a spirit. Its communication in the dream becomes an oracle to them, more implicitly believed than ever was oracle of Dodona or Pythian Apollo. Their doctrine of dreams is closely connected with their belief in the transmigration of souls, for their doctrine of the transmigration is much broader than the Pythagorean. Death did not have to loose the bands of the spirit to give it freedom to migrate, in the Indian philosophy. In sleep it wandered away from the body, and while gone another from the spirit-land could usurp its vacant throne. Each man was, however, his own channel of inspiration, and his own interpreter. The spirit was not connected with the body by a luminous band exceedingly ethereal, yet so sensitive as to warn the wanderer of danger or encroachment, as is imagined by some modern spiritualists, but its connection was severed, and it sometimes took a long journey to converse with the sun or moon, or this or that star.

Their crude anthropomorphic conceptions of the heavenly bodies did not make it presumptuous to think of conversing with the sun; many of them in their dreams have taken a pleasant walk with that luminary. Little Raven, an Ojibway, walked over mountains and high up into the vault of heaven with "the big sea-water" far beneath. He at last beheld the sun sitting with a lamp behind him. The sun told him his future life, and then sent him back to earth to live till it was

---

[1] 2 Voyage, 156. [2] Stoddard's Louisiana, 425.

fulfilled.[1] Little Raven, on account of this dream, was confident of living until his mission was accomplished.

Indians of the Algonkin stock believe that communications from superior beings take place in dreams. Not only the future in this life, but their life after death, is revealed to them in this way. Many of their ideas of the future life are the result of these dreams.[2]

The savage considers the events in his dreams to be as real as those of his waking hours. The dream is the first important act of their lives, and takes place soon after they become adults. They have discovered that fasting is a very sure method of inducing these dreams, and each one goes to some secluded place as soon as he arrives at maturity, to dream, and in this way to select a guardian spirit. After fasting the necessary time in his solitary retreat, whether it be a cave, a forest tree, or the lofty summit of some neighboring mountain, the dream comes, and home the famished recluse hastens, happy in the inspiration of the hour. Sometimes he is so reduced by starvation he cannot return without help; but anxious friends who have sought out the lost one are ready when the sacred act is over to lend their aid.

In these first dreams, which are religious acts, the first or the most prominent thing they dream about becomes their manitou (fetich), and on awaking all their efforts are directed toward obtaining this object. To dream of anything that is proof against the arrow or tomahawk makes them proof against the enemy, and brave warriors. To dream of an animal of any kind makes them imagine they will have the qualities of that animal. Birds were favorite manitous, for he who had a bird for his manitou could escape from impending danger as easily as that animal.

We can see what a great influence these dreams would have upon almost every act of their life. To illustrate more particularly; chiefs when organizing an expedition for war would call

---

[1] Kohl, 206–7. [2] Tanner's Narrative, 290.

their men together and inquire of them, one by one, what they had dreamt of during their fast-days, and what manitous they could rely on for assistance. All who had dreamed of war, or things proof against the arrow or tomahawk, were always selected for these war expeditions. The Ojibways have a tradition of a body of warriors who once went out to victories more astonishing than that of Marathon. The secret of their success was that every man selected for the expedition had had a dream that nerved him for the field of battle.

Dreams all through life have a great significance, though not so great as these first dreams. For instance, if a band of warriors is on its way to the enemy's country, it will turn back if a chief has one or more unfavorable dreams. All dreams before and during the expedition are carefully observed and considered, and all the individual manitous of their first dreams are carried along as fetiches to the war, and the most implicit faith is shown in these, although they have so much evidence all the time before their eyes of their uselessness.

A large part of the religious belief of the Dacotahs is made up of dreams.

The Indians of New England had superstitious regard for their dreams. One who dreamed that the sun had darted a beam into his breast was so frightened thereby he lay awake and fasted ten days and nights.[1]

An Ojibway damsel, whom Copway knew, had fasted ten days and nights in a lonely cave near Grand Island. Here she waited for inspiration of the spirits. She fled from her home to the rocky cave, and, though sought in woodland and in glade for two days, she was not found by her anxious friends. At last, one evening, as the sun was sinking below the horizon, they beheld, standing on a lofty peak, the lost maiden gazing at the departing sun. She was soon found sitting in the cave, and, although a rivulet of pure water coursed along at her feet, she touched it not, for she was fasting that she might have dreams,

---

[1] Williams, Key, 39-40.

and they came. The clouds rolled beneath her. She looked back on the path she had followed, and around it she beheld the lightning's flash. Up she went, and on one side rolled the deep broad ocean, on the other the lofty mountains of the west stretched their heads into the clouds. She dreamed she had a companion who touched her head, when one-half of her hair was changed to snowy whiteness. She awoke; her soul was satisfied. She was to be blessed with old age, and with the most perfect confidence she believed she would not die till her hair turned white.[1]

The Brazilians had the same superstitious confidence in the inspiration of dreams as the Northern tribes. Before an expedition into an enemy's country, if many of the tribe dreamt of eating their enemies it was a sure sign of success; but if more dreamt that they themselves were eaten, the expedition was given up. The dreams of their prophetesses when in a trance produced by being fumigated with petun were received as oracles.[2]

Among the Chiquitos a dream will make a whole horde forsake their place of sojourn, and induce an individual to abandon his wife and family.[3]

The Guaranies noted their dreams with apprehensive credulity.[4] Among the natives of Paraguay dreams were prophecies: an Abipone juggler would sit upon an aged willow overhanging some lake, and abstain from food for several days until he began to see into futurity through the medium of dreams.[5]

The conjurers of Hispaniola fasted three or four months to obtain communication with the evil spirits, and when reduced to extreme weakness had a hellish apparition, to use the language of Herrera, in which they were informed whether the seasons of the year would be favorable or not, and how many children would be born, and how many live, and other such inspirations. These were their oracles.[6]

---

[1] Copway, Ojibways, 150–58. [2] 1 Southey, 204. [3] 1 ib., 335.
[4] 2 ib., 371. [5] 2 Dobriz., 67–68. [6] 2 Herrera, 15.

The native of Honduras repaired to a river, wood, or hill, where, in an obscure place, he might fall asleep and dream. In these dreams the first animal he saw would be his nagual, their equivalent of the Northern manitou.[1]

The civilized tribes watched their dreams after the birth of a child, and interpreted them as a revelation of the future of the child.[2] The Mayas believed implicitly in the fulfilment of these dreams.[3] The same was true among the Nahuas, who had a certain order of priests who made the interpretation of dreams their special province.[4]

Many of the folk-tales among the tribes of North America describe the dreamy experiences of youthful Rip Van Winkles who have, with so much vivid reality, lived out twenty years of incident in twenty-four hours. Many imaginative persons have passed into the dream-land, loved some spirit form that has presented itself to their disordered minds, have had children grow up around them, and in the midst of these delightful associations awoke. Their dreams are remembered as realities, and their awaking is called a return from the spirit-land.

A curious tradition to illustrate this point is told of a Winnebago who died with love for a phantom woman who appeared in a spiritual body and, beckoning to him, called,—

> "Mishikiwakwa, come,
> And thou shalt be prest
> To a faithful breast,
> And thou shalt be led
> To a bridal bed."

The romantic Winnebago, after pining away in his attachment to the dreamy shadow that had called him in some ecstatic vision of the night hour, died, and went to drink with her of the crystal streams in the land of souls, and bring her berries from the hills and flowers from the vales.[5]

---

[1] 4 Herrera, 138.   [2] 4 ib., 141.
[3] 2 Bancroft, 796.   [4] 2 ib., 212.
[5] 2 Jones, Traditions, 278–80.

DOCTRINE OF SPIRITS. 67

Among many of the tribes we find a mythical tree or vine, which has a sacredness connected with it of peculiar significance. It always forms a connecting link and medium of communication between the world of the living and the dead. It is generally used by the spirits as a ladder to pass downward and upward upon, when their religious conceptions have located the land of spirits in an upper empyrean. The Ojibways had one of these vines, the upper end of which was twined around a star. Many traditions are told of attempts to climb these heavenly ladders. These myths have undoubtedly found place in the Indian folk-lore on account of some dream many times told and well adapted to fill a want in the human mind. The wish has become father to the thought, and a way to the spirit-land over the vine or the tree has been found just as satisfactory as was the ladder of Jacob to the ancient Hebrew world. If a young man has been much favored with dreams, and the people believe he has the art of looking into futurity, the path is open to the highest honors. The future prophet puts down his dreams in pictographs, and when he has a collection of these, if they prove true in any respect, then this record of his revelations is appealed to as proof of his prophetic power. The old people meet together and consult them, for the whole nation believe in these revelations. If convinced, they give their approval, and he is declared a national prophet.[1]

Among the Iroquois, Hiawatha gave his revelations to his nation through the medium of dreams.[2]

Many of the mystic ceremonies of the Iroquois, as well as those of all the other tribes, designed for the cure of the sick and the welfare of the community, have been dictated by dreams and transmitted as a sacred heritage from generation to generation.

To aid in bringing on dreams and visions, drugs were used, especially among the natives of the Mexican countries and those of South America. The Omaguas, on the Amazon, use

---

[1] 1 Schoolcraft, 113-14.   [2] Parkman's Jesuits, lxxxii.

narcotic plants, under the influence of which they are subject to extraordinary visions. The inhabitants of the West Indian islands snuffed cahoba, and by its intoxicating influence put themselves in communication with the spirits, as they thought. The Mundrucus of North Brazil would administer intoxicating drinks to seers, who would discover murderers by their dreams. The Peruvian priests threw themselves into an ecstatic condition by a narcotic drink, called tonca, made from the *Datura sanguinea*, or fetich herb. The Mexican priests made themselves ecstatic and saw spirits by the use of intoxicating drinks.

Mr. Heckewelder describes the same custom among the Delaware medicine-men, who were made to drink decoctions of an intoxicating nature until their minds became bewildered, so that they saw extraordinary visions. The North American Indians held intoxication by tobacco to be supernatural ecstasy.[1] This accounts for their use of tobacco in so many of their religious ceremonies.

Tobacco was called the holy herb among many Brazilian tribes, because it induced visions in which they saw spirits.

---

[1] 2 Tylor, 416-17.

CHAPTER III.

DOCTRINE OF SPIRITS (CONTINUED).

Worship of human spirits — Ancestral worship—Apotheosis—Culture-heroes—Fabulous forms assumed by mythical beings—Gods of Mexico, Central America, Bogota, and Peru—Idolatry—Its primitive forms—Grave-posts roughly hewn into the image of the dead and worshipped—Its later form, an image of the deceased containing his ashes—Idolatry in aboriginal art—Supposed vitality of idols.

IN his earliest state of culture man is an ignorant, consistent, natural spiritualist. The broader spiritualism of savage life is more full and thoroughly consistent than that of modern times.

Mr. Spencer says, "It is unquestionably true that the first traceable conception of a supernatural being is the conception of a ghost." "Whatever is common to men's minds in all stages must be deeper down in thought than whatever is peculiar to men's minds in higher stages, and if the later product admits of being reached by modification and expansion of the earlier product, the implication is that it has been so reached." "When, instead of wandering groups, who continually leave far behind the places where their members lie buried, we come to settled groups whose burial-places are in their midst, and among whom development of funeral rites is thus made possible, we find that ghost-propitiation becomes an established practice."[1]

The fear of spirits inspired acts of worship. The superstition that spiritual agency produced personal calamities would naturally develop an appeal to spirits, together with rites and ceremonies intended to appease their malevolent designs.

Says Schoolcraft, "The Dacotahs stand in fear of the spirits

[1] 1 Spencer, 305-6.

of the departed, because they thought it was in their power to injure them in any way they pleased."[1] They tried to keep these spirits pleased, by making feasts to the dead.[2] They prayed to the spirits of the dead for intervention in their behalf in the ordinary pursuits of life. Mr. Prescott gives the following prayer as a specimen: "Spirits! have mercy on me, and show me where I can find a deer."[3] The principal dance of the Dacotahs was a sacred rite in honor of the souls of their dead.[4]

The Mandan religious ceremonies consisted in acts which they supposed appeased the spirits of their dead. They crawled on their hands and knees around a row of skulls which they kept near the village. They cut their flesh with knives, and prayed to and conversed with the spirits of their dead, which were supposed to be present in the skulls. The women would often bring their work and sit and keep company with, and talk to, the skull of a husband for hours together.[5]

The Koniagas worshipped dead whalers just before they started on a whaling-expedition, and the Kadiaks seemed more attracted to the dead than to the living. Their mourning ceremonies were very elaborate and of a religious nature. Sacrifices were often made to their dead.

The Thlinkeets, Kenai, and Tinneh celebrated annual festivals in commemoration of the dead. One of the most important religious ceremonies of the Ojibways was the feast of the dead, when they kindled a fire at their graves, and burned meat in sacrifice. They prayed to the dead.[6] They always offered a portion of their daily food to the spirits of the dead by putting it on the fire, where it burned while they were eating.[7] The Virginians worshipped the manes of those buried in their tumuli. The Abipones of Paraguay had annual religious ceremonies to the spirits of their dead. The Guaranies also worshipped their dead, and carried round with them little boxes containing their relics.

---

[1] 2 Schoolcraft, 195.   [2] 2 ib., 199.   [3] 2 ib., 226.
[4] Eastman's Legends, 33.   [5] 1 Catlin's Illustrations, 90.
[6] Jones, Ojibways, 98.   [7] Beach, Ind. Mis., 376.

The Mexicans worshipped the spirits of all women that died in childbed. There were oratories raised to their honor in every ward that had two streets crossing. In these were kept images of them. The famous superstitions the world over about cross-roads are familiar, probably, to the reader. These haunted places where two roads cross are appropriate localities for the spirits of mother and child who die together. The Mexican cross-roads were their favorite haunts, and on certain days of the year the people made offerings at the cross-roads of bread kneaded into figures of butterflies, also toasted maize.

Cihuacoatl appears to have been the patroness of such women. They prayed to her in their trouble. If they died before childbirth the body was sacred, and every effort was made to steal it, to be divided into amulets. Hence it was guarded for four days and nights by the family of the deceased. What a remarkable proof that spiritism was the secret of their religious life! The value of these bodies consisted in their being surcharged with a double portion of spiritual power. The superstition can find no other rational explanation than this. The grave of the unfortunate woman was turned into a bivouac of armed forces. The body they guarded was a holy relic, which many were eager to win, who prowled around the nightly camp-fires of the little band that guarded her grave. Wizards watched for a chance to obtain a left arm of the dead wife, which had a special power in their profession.[1]

Among the praises sung to her by the mourners of her fate were many clothed in all the beauty of a matchless verbiage: "O woman strong and toil-enduring! O child beloved, beautiful and tender dove! Thou hast conquered! Up with thee! Break from sleep! Already the morning shoots through the clouds. Thither, to the house of thy father, let thy sisters, the celestial women, carry thee."[2]

The savages that inhabited the banks of the Orinoco worshipped the dead, and their skeletons were hung up in rude

---

[1] 3 Bancroft, 364.   [2] 3 ib., 366.

huts or temples. All the bones of their dead were kept like so many relics.

"The rudimentary form of all religion," says Mr. Spencer, "is the propitiation of dead ancestors." The worship of human spirits is more universal than pure ancestral worship. It is doubtful whether ancestral worship is comprehensive enough to explain all the facts connected with the worship of spirits. It is limited in its definition, and the worship of spirits is inclusive of it as well as all other worship of pagan peoples.

Ancestral worship is found in America connected with the worship of human spirits. It was most prevalent among the more civilized peoples, but nowhere had it assumed that elaborate form found among the Chinese. Ancestral worship might properly be called the state religion of Peru. The living Incas worshipped their royal ancestors. The Peruvian village Indians worshipped the founder of the village from whom they claimed descent; the village patrons were the mummies of these ancestral aboriginal inhabitants.[1] In addition, each family worshipped the bodies of its ancestors, which were often adorned with costly garments, and had priests attached to them who made the offerings.[2] These dead bodies were worshipped every day.[3] Some of the Peruvians would carry the dried corpses of their parents around the fields, that they might see the state of the crops.

Among the natives of Trinidad Island, feasts are held in honor of their ancestors, at which they worship them. The natives of the Ladrone Islands worshipped the bones of their ancestors, which they kept oiled in their houses.

The Haytians called their ancestors zemis, and worshipped them. Some zemis were bad, and sent diseases, hurricanes, and other catastrophes; others were good. Some were male, some female.

At the annual feast to the dead among the Central American tribes, the relatives prostrated themselves and called loudly

---

[1] Arriaga, 89.   [2] Ib., 14.   [3] Ib., 63.

upon the dead. The Woolwas placed a gruel of maize on the grave for some time after burial.¹

The Tlascaltecs had an annual festival of the dead, when the lords and priests spent several days in the temple weeping for their ancestors, and singing their heroic deeds. The families of lately deceased persons assembled upon the terraces of their houses, and prayed to their dead heroes who had fallen in battle, who were rewarded with canonization, and their statues placed among the images of the gods.²

The Aztecs had two festivals of the dead each year, at which they burned incense and made offerings to the dead in the temples, and the people blackened their bodies and prayed to their dead relatives. The Miztecs had an annual festival to the dead, which was kept in all its primitive significance. On the eve of that day the house was prepared as if for a feast. A quantity of food was spread upon the table, and the inmates went out with torches in their hands, bidding the spirits enter to the feast. They then returned and squatted around the table with crossed hands and eyes lowered to the ground, for it was thought the spirits would be offended if looked upon. In this position they remained till morning, praying to their unseen visitors. The food was supposed to have had all its virtue extracted by these spirits.³

Speaking of ancestral worship among the Northern tribes, Mr. Henry says, in his captivity among those about Lake Superior, that at their feasts the master of ceremonies calls upon the manes of deceased relatives to be present and partake of the food which has been prepared for them, and to assist them in the chase. They offer at every feast, and almost all their meals, a portion of their food to their dead ancestors.

Among the New England Indians ancestral worship is seen in their reverence for the souls of their forefathers, which had gone to the southwest, to the court of their great god Cantan-

---
¹ 1 Bancroft, 745.   ² 2 ib., 331.   ³ 2 ib., 622-23.

towit, whose anthropomorphic and ancestral character is seen in the traditionary accounts of him.[1]

Among the Mandans there was a tradition of a first man who promised to be their helper in time of need, and went away. It came to pass that the Mandans were attacked by foes. One Mandan proposed to send a bird to the great ancestor to ask for help; but it was decided no bird could fly so far. Another thought a look would reach him; but the hills walled him in. Then said the third, thought must be the surest way to reach the first man. He wrapped himself in his buffalo robe, fell down, and thought a prayer.[2]

The Mingo tribes revere and make offerings to the first man. Many Mississippi tribes say the first man ascended into heaven and thunders there.[3]

The principal god of the Maypuris, of Brazil, was Eno, from whom they claimed descent as an ancestor. This word Eno forms the root of the word for man in the dialects of the Panos, Guaranies, Omaguas, and other tribes who have probably descended from the same ancestor.

The Moquis worshipped a great father and mother from whom they sprang. Traditionary first parents in many tribes were deified, and often figured in the rôle of creators. Among the Dog-Ribs, Chapewee, the first man, was creator of sun and moon.

The Nicaraguans said Tamagostad, a man, and Cipattonal, a woman, from whom they descended, made heaven and earth, and they were their gods whom they served. They formerly walked on the earth, and were just like them. The remotest ancestors that are remembered have become divinities, remaining human in physical and mental attributes, and differing only in power.[4] The mythical creator of the natives of the Antilles was their ancestor.

The cosmogony of the tribes of interior California shows

---

[1] Williams's Key, 21.
[3] 2 ib., 312.
[2] 2 Tylor, 311.
[4] 1 Spencer, 313.

the anthropomorphic character of their creator, for the world was produced by union of brother and sister, she protesting against the incest ineffectually. From this union sprang all animate creation, and even inanimate, according to some authors.[1] They claimed that these creators were not of the human family, but this assumption on behalf of an apotheosized ancestor is generally found among all the tribes. The traditions reveal their nature, for their progeny was Ouiot, an ancestral chief, who was plainly a historical character.[2] Some time after the death of Ouiot, whose tyranny led to his destruction by poisoning, arose the great Chinigchinich, a leader and founder of the order of sorcerers. His life was one of beneficence, and his memory was revered among the Indians of California. He was deified and much worship paid to him. He looks down upon them from the stars.[3]

The worship of living persons who, on account of some physical peculiarity or mental superiority, are supposed to have within them an incarnated spirit, is found in America, and is not inconsistent with their worship of the dead. Diaz mentions a curious case: " In the centre of the Chiapanese army was a woman, aged and immoderately fat, who was esteemed by them a goddess and had promised them the victory."[4]

D'Acugna also mentions the case of an Indian of a Brazilian tribe, who presumptously set himself up to be a god and received the homage of a great many.

Mr. Dobrizhoffer mentions the case of an Indian sorcerer at the town of St. Joaquin, in Paraguay, who was adored as a divine person by a lot of foolish women.[5]

The Indians of Tolteque worshipped an old Indian whom they had dressed up in a particular way and installed in a hut, where they offered sacrifices to him. His godship, who had no manner of work to do, was regaled with all the good things the village afforded, and willingly sustained the character he

---

[1] Boscana's Chinigchinich, Tr. in Life in Cal., 243. [2] Ib., 246.
[3] Ib., 254–56.   [4] Diaz, 61.   [5] 2 Dobriz., 81.

had been made to assume. A great many instances of such worship of the living are found.

"It was the custom of the natives of New England, at the apprehension of any excellency in men or women, to cry out, 'Manitou!' which means, 'he is a god!' This they do if they see one man excel others in wisdom, valor, and strength. They called the English 'gods.'"[1]

Anything which transcends the ordinary, the savage thinks of as supernatural. The remarkable man or hero shares this superstitious reverence. This remarkable man may be simply the remotest ancestor, remembered as the founder of the tribe. He may be a chief famed for strength and courage. He may be a sorcerer of great repute. He may be an inventor of something new that is useful. He may be a stranger of superior race, who brings to them arts and knowledge. Whoever he is, if he is regarded with awe during life he will be regarded with increased awe after death. The propitiation of his ghost being sought more than the propitiation of ghosts less feared, he will become a culture-hero, with an established worship.

The apotheosis after death of those who have become distinguished in life as benefactors or rulers renders them the objects of a general worship, which is not ancestral because participated in by all.

Montezuma appears to have been worshipped by the New Mexican tribes. They extol his miraculous powers. He planted maize at night which in the morning was grown and ripened. He was immaculately conceived by a drop of dew falling on the exposed breast of his mother as she lay asleep in a beautiful grove.[2] The estufas are Montezuma's churches, where they worship him.

The Arawaks had a culture-hero, named Arawanili, who appears in their traditions to have been the discoverer and founder of their system of sorcery. Before his time the spirits inflicted continual misery on mankind, but by this mystery

---

[1] Williams's Key, 111.   [2] Cozzens's Marvellous Country, 434-35.

they could be restrained in their practices. Arawanili was translated without death. He appears to be the principal deity of the Arawaks.[1]

A famous god among the Caribs was Bohito I., who was evidently an early priest and legislator. He is said to have established sorcery. Bohito II. introduced medical knowledge and the burning of the dead, and was apotheosized. Bonito III. brought music to them.[2] This trimurti appeared to stand at the head of the Haytian pantheon.[3] Another prominent figure was Oubekeyeri (man from above), who introduced agriculture and house-building.[4]

The worship of dead chiefs prevailed among the more civilized peoples. Balboa says the Peruvians worshipped all their dead chiefs, and offered them sacrifices at certain seasons of the year. An ancient Curaca, mentioned by Cieza, was worshipped with great reverence by many villages. His body was in a grotto under a tent, with a diadem on its head, and magnificently clothed. The Indians did not even dare to look upon him. He had been a just and wise counsellor of one of the Incas.

The Mexicans in their great feast of the tenth month gave divine names to their dead chiefs and other famous persons who had died in war. Idols were made in the image of these persons and put with the other deities. Says Camargo, "They then called them Teotl so-and-so, meaning god or Saint so-and-so." The Mayas worshipped their dead chiefs. Among the Isthmians a dead chief was dried and hung up in his own palace, and on the anniversary of his death food was brought to him. The arms which he formerly used, and models of the canoes he used, were placed in the presence of the body. They then celebrated a festival in his honor.

There was a tendency among all the tribes to deify heroes. Thus originates the worship of particular gods. Among primi-

---

[1] Brett, 292–93. [2] 1 Rafinesque, American Nations, 189–92.
[3] 1 ib., 189–92. [4] 1 ib., 196.

tive peoples the ghosts and manes of the dead are feared. Superstitious fear of these ghostly spirits pervades the savage communities. There is not, however, among such a people, as yet, a pantheon, nor has such pre-eminence been attained by any member of a savage tribe as to entitle him to deification. Equality in the social status of peoples seldom produces apotheosis. Giants are the first mythical heroes that emerge from the chaos of their past. Nameless generally, they are only identified with a locality. Gradually, however, as nations emerge from a condition of barbarism, leaders of these progressive movements become culture-heroes; and if, perchance, in these progressive movements a despotic form of government should arise, under the leadership of a man of despotic nature, and be isolated amid a surrounding barbarism, the religious condition of such a people will and must be deplorable. All the paraphernalia of apotheosis will lend its glitter to the exaltation of the despot, but at the expense of the spiritual degradation of the people. Costly funeral ceremonies and magnificent tombs at the monarch's death will be followed by as abject a spiritual worship as was the homage given him in life. Human sacrifices will soon be added to the offerings with which his tomb-temple has been filled. Human sacrifice is a very convenient way of disposing of the multitudes of barbarous captives taken in the wars. Besides this, the apotheosized warrior king will delight in the blood of his enemies, who are now sent to be his slaves in the spirit-world. Very soon a myth of immaculate conception will account for the birth of so elevated a personage, and if, perchance, another monarch of similar courage or virtue appears, then an incarnation, according to the doctrine of transmigration, is accorded him. The last great act in the drama of apotheosis will be translation. Death must be robbed of this one victim, that the triumph of the hero may not be limited. Then comes a myth of translation, and we have a full-fledged heathen god, with a personality, and a name, and a throne, and a court, and a moral nature no different from that of the living king. This is the thread that runs through the mythological story of every civilized people, and especially is it true of the civilized American nations. Before taking up the pantheons of the more civilized races, let us notice some of the culture-heroes and mythical characters that can be found among the more uncivilized tribes.

Torngarsuk is the principal god of the Greenlanders. The most popular representation of him is as a giant with one arm. He is the one consulted by the Angekoks in disease. But Torngarsuk's wife or mother, the stories do not agree which, is the most feared of any of their deities. She is reputed by many to be the daughter of the famous Angekok who tore Disko Island from the continent, near Baals River, and towed it a hundred miles farther north. She lives under the ocean in a large house. Sea-fowls swim about in the tub of train-oil under her lamp. Seals, exceedingly vicious, guard the portals of her palace.[1] Her human character is unquestionable.

Another god is Innertirrirsok, who is spirit of the air. Erloersortok is a ghastly character in their pantheon, who feeds upon the intestines of the dead.[2]

The Ingnersuit are fabulous beings that live beneath the surface of the earth, in cliffs along the sea-shore. They are often seen entering through mounds of turf. They have the shape of men, and their life is like the Greenlander's. They act as the guardian spirits of the Kayakers. But they are not all good. Some without noses persecute the Kayakers.[3]

The Kayarissat are giant Kayakers. They raise storms and bring bad weather. The Mermen are fabulous creatures who inhabit the sea. They are fond of fox-flesh, which is sacrificed to them. The Toruit are inland giants, living under the earth. They enter through places hidden by vegetation. They, however, go to sea in foggy weather, without kayaks, sitting on the surface of the water. The Erkigdlit have the shape of man in the upper part of their body, but are dogs in their lower

---

[1] 1 Crantz, 190–91. [2] Egede, 185–86. [3] Rink, 46.

limbs.[1] These deities of the Greenlanders are evidently anthropomorphic.

Manabozho undoubtedly occupies the Olympic throne in the Ojibway pantheon. He was no more nor less than a great brave and chief, about whom many folk-tales are told. Manabozho lives in a wigwam, with two squaws to make up his family circle. The Ojibways did not ascribe omnipotence to him. Their crude ideas of the helplessness of their gods when involved in difficulties is illustrated by a story they tell of Manabozho. They say he went up into a tree-top to stop a noise produced by two branches rubbing against each other. When he had pulled the branches apart they sprang together again and caught Manabozho and held him suspended for three whole days. His appeals to the animals resulted in jibes and ridicule, and the wolves ate up his breakfast which he left under the tree. A bear at last helped him out of his difficulty. When he returned home he gave both of his wives a severe beating,[2]—a touch of human depravity surviving in a god.

Manabozho had three brothers, named Chibiabos, Wabasso, and Chokanipok. This last he accused of killing his mother, because he was the last born of quadruplets, whose birth resulted in her death. He destroyed him, after many contests. Wabasso went north, and was changed into a white rabbit, and is considered a great spirit. Chibiabos and Manabozho lived together in great happiness, until Chibiabos, venturing out on the ice too far one day, was drowned. Manabozho made the shores resound with his wails of sorrow on account of the death of his brother. Such was the mythological family from whom the Algonkin tribes trace descent. In a war between the turtles and Manabozho he barely escaped destruction in a flood produced by the turtles. He reached a place of safety, however, carrying his grandmother under his arm. She is a prominent character in their traditions, and is called the great-grandmother of all. She remains at home in her lodge all the time,

---

[1] Rink's Traditions, 47.   [2] Kohl's Kitchi-Gami, 388-89.

in order that no one may call on her in vain. They thus deny her omnipresence.[1]

Manabozho discovered that the maple-tree could produce sugar. He killed the ancient monsters of their traditions, whose bones are frequently found. He cleared the streams of obstructions. He has now gone to live on an immense flake of ice in the Arctic Ocean.[2]

Manabozho was the reputed ancestor of the Algonkin race. He was the inventor of picture-writing, the founder of Meda worship, the maker of the earth, the sun, and moon. From a grain of sand he fashioned the habitable land, and set it floating on the waters, till it grew to such a size that a young wolf, running constantly, died of old age ere he reached its limits. Manabozho was a mighty hunter of old. The Great Lakes were the beaver-dams he built, and when the cataracts impeded his progress he tore them away with his hands. After watching the spiders spread their webs to trap flies, he devised the art of making nets to catch fish. In the autumn, ere he composes himself to sleep, he fills his pipe and takes a godlike smoke, and the clouds float over the hills and woodlands, filling the air with the haze of an Indian summer.[3]

He was reputed to have been born at Mackinaw. According to ancient tradition, there is a chain of mountains and an immense lake to the northwest of Lake Superior—probably meaning the Rocky Mountains and the Pacific Ocean—where he was particularly fond of living.[4]

This god, says Father Allouez, according to the traditions of the natives, crossed at a single step a bay eight leagues in width. Manabozho once went angling for the king of fishes, but was swallowed, canoe and all. He smote the monster's heart with his war-club till the fish would fain have cast him up into the lake again, but the hero set his canoe fast across the fish's throat inside and finished slaying him. When the dead

---

[1] Tanner's Narrative, 192. [2] 1 Schoolcraft, 317–19.
[3] Brinton's Myths, 176–77. [4] Chateaubriand's Travels, 41–42.

monster drifted ashore, the gulls pecked an opening, through which Manabozho came out.[1]

With entire unanimity all branches of the Algonkins, including the Powhatans of Virginia, the Delawares, the warlike hordes of New England, the Ottawas of the far North, and the Western tribes, spoke of this "chimerical beast," as one of the old missionaries calls him, as their common ancestor. The totem of the great hare, whose name he bore, was looked upon with respect.[2]

He has not always borne the ludicrous character that has been given him latterly. Mr. Brinton thinks it passing strange that such an insignificant creature as a hare should receive this apotheosis, and says, "No explanation of it in the least satisfactory has ever been offered." The totemic system of the Indians is a solution of it. Manabozho, a hero of the gens of the hare, has distinguished himself in their early history, and the process of deification has gradually gone on, with an accretion of folk-tales and traditions, in which his acts have become more and more superhuman, until nothing was too great for Manabozho.

Wabun, Kabun, Kabibonocca, and Shawana are four Algonkin gods, who preside over the winds from the cardinal points. These gods of the winds were ancestral spirits. Shingebiss was a mythical character of the Ojibways. He had probably been an early sorcerer in that tribe, for they have many stories to tell of his metamorphoses. His great triumph over the god of the weather is curiously told in one of their folk-tales. How he managed to live nobody knew: it was a mystery to the wild foresters around him. Yet on the coldest day he would catch fish. His success enraged Kabibonocca, god of the northwest, who sends the cold and storms, and he determined to freeze him out. He poured the cold blasts of the north upon him and piled up the snow-drifts. Failing in this, he decided to visit Shingebiss in person, and entered his lodge one night, while he sat by the burning logs; Kabibonocca began to melt, and he was glad to leave the imperturbable Shingebiss to enjoy

---

[1] 1 Tylor, 337.   [2] Brinton, 175.

his warm fire. Shingebiss had thereafter the reputation of being a great spirit who was too much for the god of the wind.[1]

> "Windy god! I know your plan:
> You are but my fellow-man;
> Blow you may your coldest breeze,
> Shingebiss you cannot freeze."

The Waindegoos were giants as tall as pine-trees. They were invulnerable and cannibals, and passed through the forests as a man does through grass.[2] They had the human form, as had also the famous giant god called Aggodagoda, who was uniped. He hopped over rivers and valleys at a bound.[3] Among the Ojibways there was a god called Pabookowaih, the god that crushed diseases; also a goddess Wahneetis, goddess of health,[4] who was his spouse. The worship of these gods was undoubtedly confined to a family or gens, as they had no tribal reputation. Their images were of human form.

The name of one of the Dacotah divinities is Wahkeenyan. His teepee is supposed to be on a mound on the top of a high mountain in the far west. The teepee, or tent, has four openings, with sentinels clothed in red down. A butterfly is stationed at the east, a bear at the west, a fawn at the south, and a reindeer at the north entrance. He is supposed to produce the thunder. He has a bitter enmity against Unktayhee, and attempts to kill his offspring. The high water and floods were supposed to be caused by his shooting through the earth and allowing the water to flow out. When the lightning strikes their teepees or the ground, they think that Unktayhee was near the surface of the earth, and that Wahkeenyan, in great rage, fired a hot thunderbolt at him.[5] Fig. 1 is a representation of this god hurling these thunderbolts, and shows his human form.

FIG. 1.

---

[1] 3 Schoolcraft, 324–25.   [2] Jones's Ojibways, 156–60.
[3] 3 Schoolcraft, 521.   [4] Jones's Ojibways, 87.
[5] 1 Minn. Hist. Coll., 267, seq.

The Jupiter Maximus of the Dacotahs is named Unktayhee. He fills the rôle of creator. He made man in this manner. The earth being finished, he took a deity, one of his own offspring, and, grinding him to powder, sprinkled it upon the earth, and this produced many worms. These matured into infants, which became full-grown Dacotahs. They think the bones of the mastodon are the bones of this god, and preserve them with great care.[1] Morgan's Bluff, near Fort Snelling, is the residence of Unktayhee. Under the hill, they say, is a subterranean passage for the use of the god. They often pretend to see this god passing through the air and over the hill,[2] and represent him with human form.

Heyoka is the antinatural god of the Dacotahs. He appears in four forms; sometimes as a tall and slender man with two faces, like the Janus of ancient mythology. He holds a bow in his hand streaked with red lightning; also a rattle of deer-claws. The second form is a little old man with a cocked hat and enormous ears, holding a yellow bow. The third, a man with a flute suspended from his neck. The fourth is invisible and mysterious, and is the gentle zephyr which moves the grass and causes the ripple of the water. Heyoka is a perfect paradox. He calls bitter sweet, and sweet bitter; he groans when he is full of joy, he laughs when he is in distress; in winter he goes naked, and in summer wraps up in buffalo robes. Those whom he inspires can make the winds blow and the rains fall.[3] He uses a frog for an arrow-point. He keeps a zoo-

FIG. 2.

---

[1] 1 Minn. Hist. Coll., 267, seq.   [2] Eastman, 210.
[3] 1 Minn. Hist. Coll., 268, seq.

logical garden within his court-yard. Among the animals are a deer, elk, and buffalo. He hurls meteors at his enemies in self-defence, and uses the lightning which surrounds his house to kill his game with.[1] Fig. 2 is a representation of this god.

Takinshkanshkan is a deity of the Dacotahs, and is supposed to be invisible, yet, everywhere present. He is full of revenge, exceedingly wrathful, very deceitful, and a searcher of hearts. His favorite haunts are the four winds and the granite boulders strewn on the plains of Minnesota. He is never so happy as when he beholds scalps warm and recking with blood.[2] The East, West, North, and South each had a deity presiding over them, but of an undoubtedly anthropomorphic character. The translation of the names indicates Man of the East, Man of the West, Man of the North, and Man of the South. Witkokaga is another god, who deceives animals into being taken.[3] Canotedan is the Dacotah god of the forest, and lives in a tree. When he wants anything, he can be found sitting on a branch. He has powers of attraction, and draws around him all the birds of the forest. He wages constant war with the gods of the elements, and kills one occasionally,—which does not exterminate them, however. The Dacotahs have a god of the grass, who can make them crazy, and a god of war. All of these spiritual beings were anthropomorphic.

FIG. 3.

Fig. 3 is a rough representation of the god of war.[4]

The Great Spirit is borrowed from the whites, to complete their pantheon. The Dacotahs have giants who stride over the largest rivers and the tallest trees with ease.

Among the Iroquois the stonish giants figure in their folk-

---

[1] 2 Schoolcraft, 225.
[2] 1 Minn. Hist. Coll., 268.
[3] Eastman, xxxi.
[4] 3 Schoolcraft, 485–87.

lore, and undoubtedly represent an invading tribe whose valor tested the Iroquois to the utmost. Plate II. is a representation of one of their culture-heroes, whose name was Atotarho. He was an early ruler, whose hair was represented in snake forms, as was that of Medusa. Many of the characters in the Iroquois pantheon have assumed the human form, or, in other words, are ancestral. Hiawatha is one of the most prominent. He taught the Six Nations arts and knowledge. He taught them to raise corn and beans. His wisdom was great, and the people listened to him with admiration. There was nothing in which he did not excel. He was a good hunter, brave warrior, and eloquent orator. He selected a beautiful spot on the southern shore of Cross Lake. He erected his lodge, planted his field of corn, and selected a wife. Here he was resorted to for advice and instruction. Soon there arose a great alarm at the invasion of a ferocious band of warriors from the north. The public fear was extreme. A great council of all the tribes was appointed to meet on an eminence overlooking Onondaga Lake. Three days had elapsed, and there was a general anxiety lest Hiawatha should not arrive. Messengers were despatched for him. They found him in a pensive mood, and he communicated to them his strong presentiments that evil betided his attendants at the council. The messengers urged him to come, and he put his magic canoe in the water, and it moved without paddles. His only daughter took her seat in the stern. Soon they entered on the bright bosom of the Onondaga. The great council saw the well-known canoe approaching, and sent up shouts of welcome as the venerated man landed in front of the assemblage. As he and his daughter ascended the banks, a loud sound was heard in the air, and a dark spot was discovered descending rapidly. Terror seized the Indians, and they scattered in confusion to escape the impending calamity. Hiawatha's daughter was the doomed object. A white bird with a mighty swoop crushed the girl to the earth, and not a human trace of her could be discovered. Not a muscle moved in the face of Hiawatha. He passed on to the head of the council. His

ATOTARHO.

(ANCIENT IROQUOIS CHIEF.)

advice was given and adopted, and Hiawatha's mission was accomplished. He went down to the shore, and assumed his seat in his mystical vessel. Sweet music was heard in the air, and, as its cadence floated on the ears of the wondering multitude, an apotheosis was taking place. Hiawatha in his magic canoe rose in the air higher and higher, and vanished from sight.[1]

Thus was this great and good man translated, according to the traditions of his people. The sun-worship of the Iroquois is ancestral in its character, as they believe the sun to be a man, but their legend has not come down to us relating the earthly career of this solar man, as in many other tribes. Iosco, another mythical hero, confirmed their ideas of this luminary by visiting him and taking a day's journey with him around the world.[2]

Jouskeha was the Iroquois mythical character who figured as the creator of the world and the father of the human race.[3]

Areskoui was another of their deities to whom sacrifices were offered. Father Jogues saw a female prisoner burned as a sacrifice to Areskoui.[4] The god of thunder was supposed to be a giant in human form.[5] Two gods of the Iroquois appeared among the Natches; for their goddess Athaensic was the female chief of evil spirits, and Jouskeha of good spirits, in both tribes.[6] They were the reputed ancestors.

Among the New England tribes a god called Squanto, to whom they ascribed all good, and another god, Tanto, to whom they ascribed all evil, were worshipped. Tanto produced death and carried the dead to his wigwam.[7] They were ancestral. Pampagussit was the name of the sea-god of the New England Indians.[8] He was represented with human form. Yotaawit was god of fire, Nanepaushat was god of the moon, and Keesuckquand god of the sun. "They had their he and she saints, even as the papists," says Roger Williams.[9] Another of their

---

[1] 3 Schoolcraft, 315–17. [2] 5 ib., 402. [3] Parkman's Jesuits, lxxvii.
[4] Ib., lxxvii. [5] Ib., lxix.
[6] 2 Chateaubriand, 40. [7] 2 Maine Hist. Coll., 94.
[8] Williams's Key, 98. [9] Ib., 110.

gods was named Moshup, who lived at Martha's Vineyard with his wife and five children. He used to catch whales, and pluck up large trees to roast them with. He once sent his children to play ball on the beach that joined Noman's Land to Gay Head. He then cut with his toe a line in which the water followed and cut them off. His wife mourned them so much that he threw her away in a fit of rage. She fell upon Seconet, near the rocks, where she lived some time, exacting contribution of all who passed there by water. After a while she was changed into a stone: the shape of this stone remained until the English broke it up for relics.[1]

Wakon is the principal god and ancestor of the Osages.[2]

The Indians on the Columbia River believe that men were created by a deity named Etalapass, but when made they were imperfect, having a mouth that was not opened, eyes that were fast closed, hands and feet that were not movable. A second divinity, whom they call Ecanumu, having seen men in this state of imperfection, took a sharp stone and laid open their mouths and eyes; he gave agility also to their feet, and motion to their hands.[3]

Kareya, the ancestor of the Karoks of California, was the creator of their world. They have the stool upon which he sat when upon the earth. Since the advent of Christianity he has been elevated to the divine primacy of Supreme Being.

Gard is the name of the culture-hero of the Yuroks. He gave them their language, and now lives in their mountains. He has recently been elevated to the dignity of Supreme Being, as no other is so well adapted to represent the Christian God to their minds.[4]

He was also ancestral god of the Hupas. Many of the incidents of his life are remembered by them. "Clean was his heart," say they. He was translated, according to their myths, in a thick cloud of smoke, which floated to the land of

---

[1] 1 Mass. Hist. Coll., 1st Series, 139. [2] 1 Rafinesque, 160.
[3] Franchere's Voy., 258. [4] 3 Ethnol. of Powell's Exp., 64.

spirits.[1] This is undoubtedly a myth connected with his cremation.

The creator of the Maidus was a man from whom they descended.[2]

Quahootze is the principal god of the Nootkans. He stills the tempests and controls the storm. They chant and pray to him. A human victim was formerly offered at his annual festival, but now a boy with knives stuck through his flesh appears as a substitute. Matlose is a famous hobgoblin of the Nootkans. He is a very Caliban of spirits: his head is like the head of something that might have been a man, but is not. His monstrous teeth and nails are like the fangs and claws of a bear. Whoever hears his terrible voice falls like one smitten, and his curved claws rend prey into morsels with a single stroke.[3] Huge images, carved in wood, stand in their houses, intended to represent the form and hold in remembrance the visit of a god in the guise of an old man who came up the sound long ago in a copper canoe and instructed them in many things.[4] The Nawloks are fabulous beings, part human, with whom their sorcerers are supposed to commune and obtain their prophecies.[5]

Yehl stands at the head of the Thlinkeet pantheon. He is kind, and loves men; not so with Khanuk, who could raise a magic darkness that would frighten Yehl into helplessness. Yehl cannot die or become older. Chett is a great Northern rukh, that snatches up and swallows a whale without difficulty. The flash of his eyes produces the lightning.[6]

The anthropomorphic nature of these gods is beyond question. Yehl and Khanuk lived formerly on the earth, and were born of a woman whose race has passed away. Khanuk was god of war and the patron of every fearless brave. He sends epidemics and bloodshed to all who displease him, while Yehl crosses the purposes of his dark-minded brother. Yehl had

---

[1] 3 Ethnol. of Powell's Exp., 81. [2] 3 ib., 287. [3] 3 Bancroft, 151.
[4] 3 ib., 151. [5] 3 ib., 150. [6] 3 ib., 146.

great skill in the use of the bow and arrow. They have a traditionary incarnation of Yehl in one of their mighty hunters. A disconsolate mother went to the sea-shore to weep for her lost children, and while there a dolphin pitied her and told her to swallow a small pebble and drink some sea-water, which she did, and in proper time Yehl was born. His first famous exploit was to shoot a crane, called, when translated, "crane that can soar to heaven." In the skin of this bird he clothed himself whenever he wished to fly. Yehl's contests with his uncle for revenge made much of their folk-lore. Yehl had other incarnations, in one of the most romantic of which he was transformed into a blade of grass and got into a girl's drinking-cup and was swallowed by her and born again. The balance of his life was spent in stealing benefits for mankind, and in his adventures, metamorphosing himself at pleasure. His black plumage was obtained in an adventure where he attempted to escape through the chimney of a hut.[1] He had the fogs and clouds at his command, and would draw them around him to escape his enemies.[2]

The Okanagans have a god Skyappe, and also one called Chacha, who appear to be endowed with omniscience; but their principal divinity is their great mythical ruler and heroine Scomalt. Long ago, when the sun was no bigger than a star, this strong medicine-woman ruled over what appears to have now become a lost island. At last the peace of the island was destroyed by war, and the noise of battle was heard, with which Scomalt was exceeding wroth; whereupon she rose up in her might, and drove her rebellious subjects to one end of the island, and broke off the piece of land on which they were huddled, and pushed it out to sea, to drift whither it would. This floating island was tossed to and fro and buffeted by the winds till all but two died. A man and woman escaped in a canoe and arrived on the mainland, and from these the Okanagans are descended.[3]

---

[1] 3 Bancroft, 100-3.   [2] 3 ib., 149.   [3] 3 ib., 154.

The Acagchemen races of California appear to reverence an ancestor by the name of Ouiot, who was a great warrior and ruler of the early day. He grew old, however, and useless, and, as was their custom, they poisoned him, and he died, and was succeeded by a greater, named Ouiamot, who came dancing among them when assembled for some purpose, and entered into league with their medicine-men and confirmed their power. He then returned to the stars whence he came.[1]

The Pericues of Lower California were divided into two sects, worshipping two hostile divinities who waged a war of extermination on each other, and who were historical characters.

Niparaya was the name of one, whose wife, though possessing no body, bore him, in a divinely mysterious manner, three children. This young god made men by drawing them up out of the earth. He died, and an owl appears to represent him. Another god was Tuparan, whom Niparaya appears to have defeated in battle and confined under the earth. This was another way, undoubtedly, of expressing his death and burial. His followers continue to be his sectaries.[2]

The tribes in the neighborhood of Trinity River had their great ancestor Wappequemow, who was a giant who quarrelled with a great god at the mouth of the Klamath and was banished thence. Next in their pantheon comes the great Omaha, who is invisible and brings misfortune on mankind. Next is Makelay, a veritable fiend, as swift as the wind, moving in great leaps as the kangaroo moves. The sight of him is death to mortals.[3] They were represented in human forms.

The most curious mythological characters among the natives of Northern California are those mysterious people called the Hohgates, who have left an immense bed of mussel-shells near the Crescent City. These Hohgates, seven in number, were famous hunters of seals. One day, being out at sea in their boat, they struck a huge sea-lion with their harpoon, and, standing by their line, were dragged with fearful speed toward a great

---

[1] 3 Bancroft, 166.   [2] 3 ib., 169.   [3] 3 ib., 176.

whirlpool that lay to the northwest, where spirits shiver in its dark cold, and even the living suffer from its winds. Just as the boat reached the dreadful current, the rope broke, and the sea-monster was swept alone in the whirl, while the Hohgates were caught up into the air, their boat floating steadily toward the empyrean until the translated heroes landed where the Seven Stars now shine.[1]

The inhabitants on the Rio Grande adored three ancestral gods, called Cocopo, Cacina, and Homace, to the first of whom a temple was raised some ten feet wide and twice as deep. At the end sat the idol of stone or clay, representing the god bearing some eggs in one hand and some ears of maize in the other. In this temple an old woman presided as priestess, and directed the ceremonies by which the natives implored rain,—a blessing the more necessary as the streams frequently ran dry.[2]

The Araucanian pantheon is composed of Pillan, Epunamun, Mulen, and Guecubu. Pillan signifies the spirit, and it appears that he had acquired a great pre-eminence over all others. His anthropomorphic character is written plainly in his polity, which is a prototype of the Araucanian. Undoubtedly he was an early ruler and the founder of their government, and when he disappeared his administration of affairs in the spirit-world would not vary from the earthly. Epunamun was their god of war. Mulen was their beneficent deity, and always the friend of the human race. He is the antagonist of Guecubu, who is their malevolent deity and the author of all evil. If a horse tires, it is because Guecubu has ridden him. Death is brought about by this demon, who suffocates them. These gods have a hierarchy of genii or active spirits,[3] and were historical characters.

At the head of the pantheon of the Tupinambas was Tupa, which is their word for father, and was used for the Supreme

---

[1] 3 Bancroft, 177. [2] Shea's Cath. Missions, 79.
[3] 2 Molina, 84–86.

Being after the introduction of Christianity. Although he was the god of thunder, still his character was that of a beneficent being.[1] Next stood Zome, who taught them the use of the mandioc. The woods made a path for Zome in his progress, and the rivers opened to give him passage. He could also walk upon the waters. He commanded the tempests. The most ferocious animals crouched submissive at his feet.[2] They pointed out his footsteps imprinted on the shore.

The Manacicas had a triplet of deities, called Urapo, Urasana, and Uragozoriso, two of them good and one bad, and a host of spiritual attendants, including the souls of their enemies. They would come with a noise through the air and enter the hut prepared for them, which shook at their presence. This rude temple had a holy of holies, into which none but priests were allowed to enter. When the oracles were pronounced, these spirits returned to the air whence they came. They had a goddess Quipoci, who appears to have been a sweet singer of early times.[3]

The Yuracares of Brazil had a divine hero, Tiri, who was suckled by a jaguar.[4]

Among the Tamanacas of Guiana a hero-god, Amalavaca, piled rocks upon each other until a famous cavern, which was called his house, was formed. He was no other than their primitive ancestor. He, with his brother Pochi, another mythical hero of this people, gave the surface of the earth its present form. The pictographs on the rocks are his handwriting.[5]

Among all of the culture-heroes of the civilized races of America, Quetzalcoatl is the pre-eminent one. There can be no doubt that he was a historic character. Descriptions of his personal appearance are found in the historic fragments of those peoples among whom he lived. Quetzalcoatl came to Tulla. He had a broad forehead, large eyes, and flowing

---

[1] 1 Southey, 227. [2] Warden's Researches, 189.
[3] 3 Southey, 184. [4] 1 Tylor, 282.
[5] 2 Humboldt's Personal Narrative, 471, seq.

beard, and was clad in a white robe. He held a sickle in his hand. His habits were ascetic. He was never married, yet was chaste and pure in his life. He condemned sacrifices, except of fruits and flowers. When addressed on the subject of war, he stopped his ears with his fingers. He loved peace. He instructed people in agriculture, metallurgy, and the arts of government. He was one of those benefactors of their species who have been deified by the gratitude of posterity. His age was the golden age of Anahuac; a veritable mythical age, too, for under him the earth teemed with fruits and flowers without the labor of culture. An ear of Indian corn was as much as a single man could carry. The cotton as it grew took the rich dyes of human art. Stalks of the amaranth were so large people climbed them like trees. Such a man as this in the semi-civilized state of Tulla is a marvel. His character was more exemplary than any other human being of whom we have any account in America. He was like a meteor that flashes across a dark sky and is gone. Tezcatlipoca, whose worship was quite opposite in its character to that of Quetzalcoatl, triumphed, however, with his sanguinary ritual, which was celebrated with human sacrifices. A struggle ensued in Tulla between the opposing systems, which resulted favorably to the bloody deity, and the faction who sought to establish his worship in preference to the peaceful and ascetic service of Quetzalcoatl triumphed. But Quetzalcoatl was allowed to depart in peace. Myriads of rich-plumed songsters made the air melodious as they accompanied him on his journey. The flowers by the wayside gave forth unusual volumes of perfume at his approach. A few devoted followers clung to him in his travels. He next appeared at Cholula. War was not known during his sojourn there. The enemies of the Cholulans came with perfect safety to his temple, which is one of the most interesting relics of antiquity, and the sculptor and architect flourished under the patronage of the great god king. After twenty years he passed down to the sea, and, entering his wizard skiff, made of serpent-skins, embarked, after bestowing his blessing upon four young men who had followed him thither in their devotion.[1]

Most prominent among the peculiar reforms of Quetzalcoatl, and the one that is reported to have contributed most to his downfall, was his unvarying opposition to human sacrifice. This sacrifice had prevailed from pre-Toltec times at Teotihuacan, and had been adopted more or less extensively in Culhuacan and Tulla. By Quetzalcoatl it was absolutely prohibited in the temples of the latter capital, and thus the powerful priesthood of Otompan and Culhuacan was arrayed against him. Again, it is thought that under Quetzalcoatl the spiritual power became so dominant as to excite the jealousy and fears of the nobility in Tulla, who were restless under priestly restraint.[2]

Tezcatlipoca, the persecutor of the great priest of Tulla, became the greatest god adored in these countries. Creator of heaven and earth, recompenser of the just and the unjust, his name means shining mirror. According to tradition, he descended from heaven by a rope made of spiders' webs. Stone seats were placed in the corner of the streets for him to rest upon, which no other person was ever allowed to use. Of course this adulatory worship is due to his success in attaining the primacy. His true character is shown as the sorcerer. His triumph is that of sorcery and semi-barbarous religion over an attempted reformation. The tradition of the visit of Tezcatlipoca to the sick Quetzalcoatl gives us a vivid insight into the nature of the struggle of the contending forces. The account is as follows. There came at last a time in which the fortunes of Quetzalcoatl and his people the Toltecs began to fail, for there came against them three sorcerers who were gods in disguise,—Tezcatlipoca, Huitzilopochtli, and Tlacapevan. Tezcatlipoca turned himself into a hoary-headed old man and went to the house of Quetzalcoatl when sick, and demanded to see the sick man. He gave him a draught, which worked its spell to induce Quetzalcoatl to leave his pontifical throne

---

[1] Short, 269-71; 1 Prescott, 58-60.   [2] 5 Bancroft, 261.

and palace and become a wanderer. In Cholula he found a resting-place for twenty years, and yet after that lapse of time the magic spell was still upon him, and again he left his work of civilizing to flee from the dread sorcerer's charm.

Tezcatlipoca, though a magician and of the religious order, allied himself to the civil power in the following manner. He disguised himself, and, while selling green peppers in the market-place of Tulla, the only daughter of the temporal lord of the Toltecs saw him by chance from the palace-windows, and was smitten with love for the disguised god. She sickened and languished with love for the handsome pepper-vender. He was brought into the palace, went in to the princess and remained with her, and she became well. Innumerable acts of sorcery did he now perform, many of them in punishment of the Toltecs for their hostility to him. He at last won his way to the control of the civil and religious affairs, and the Mexicans were subdued into submission to the most bloody religious worship ever established on the face of the earth. In the midst of their progress in the arts of civilized life, a cessation of progress in religious life took place. The retreating figure of Quetzalcoatl would have shuddered to look back and see the dark pall that the great sorcerer was hanging around his redeemed land. Although so many supernatural acts are ascribed to Tezcatlipoca, yet he was undoubtedly a culture-hero and the founder of Tezcuco. His father was king of Tulla probably about 752 A.D., and it was undoubtedly after his death that Tezcatlipoca strove for the supremacy at Tulla, appearing there with many metamorphoses. Quetzalcoatl, according to that eminent anthropologist, Mr. Waitz, was originally a man, a priest in Tulla, who arose as a religious reformer among the Toltecs, but was expelled by the adherents of Tezcatlipoca, who had been, according to Francis of Bologna, a great prince. They made an image of him and worshipped it.

Apotheosis of monarchs among the Mexicans was a natural consequence of their earthly autocracy. From the moment of his coronation the Aztec sovereign lived in an atmosphere of adulation unknown to the mightiest potentate of the Old World. Reverenced as a god, the haughtiest nobles—sovereigns in their own provinces—humbled themselves before him. Absolute in power, the fate of thousands depended upon a gesture.[1]

In his coronation oath he promised to make the sun shine, the clouds give rain, the rivers flow, and the earth bring forth fruit in abundance.[2]

We will next notice the goddess Citlalicue, to whom women prayed. She had many children in the upper world, but finally brought forth a flint knife which was thrown to the earth, and from it sprang sixteen hundred heroes. Xolotl, who was one of these heroes, went to the regions of Mictlanteuctli, the Mexican Pluto, and got a bone of a dead man, that he might create a new race of men in place of those destroyed in one of their traditionary destructions. The god of the dead pursued him when he discovered the theft. Xolotl stumbled in his flight and broke the bone, but escaped with it. When sprinkled with the blood of the heroes, the bone became a male and female.[3]

This Promethean legend of the Mexicans is repeated with different incidents throughout American mythology.

Centeotl, goddess of corn, had five temples in Mexico. Next to Quetzalcoatl, this goddess was the most beneficent in the Mexican pantheon. She elicited the love of her worshippers. There were no human sacrifices to her, but she was contented with the sacrifice of doves, quails, and leverets, which they offered in great numbers. They looked to her for deliverance from the cruel slavery they were under to the other gods. Mictlanteuctli, god of the under-world, was supposed to dwell in a place of great darkness, in the bowels of the earth. Sacrifices were always made to him at night, and his priests were painted a black color. Both Centeotl and Mictlanteuctli were represented in human form.

---

[1] 2 Bancroft, 143-44.   [2] 2 ib., 146.   [3] 1 Clavigero, 245-46.

Mixcoatl, goddess of hunting, was the principal deity of the Otomies, who were a tribe of hunters. She had two temples, however, in Mexico, where wild animals were sacrificed to her. She was the Diana of the Mexican pantheon, and represented a hunter condition. There appears to have been another deity bearing this name,—and a male. He seems to have been god of thunder. He was represented with a bundle of arrows in his hand. He was the principal deity of the ancient Chichemecs, but held in high honor by the Nahuas, Nicaraguans, and Otomies. He rode upon the tropical tornado, and was lord of the lightning. He is probably identical with Camaxtli. It is not uncommon, where adoption of tribal gods takes place, to change their profession without changing their name. Thus, the god of hunting, of a tribe of hunters, if established in the pantheon of a tribe whose pursuits are not the chase, will be assigned to other duties, and the whole form of worship gradually changed. One of the ceremonies of this god, however, observed by the Mexicans, was a great hunt in the fourteenth month, when the celebrants wended their way to a mountain-slope, and drove deer, rabbits, hares, coyotes, and other game together and began their slaughter in honor of this hunting god. A portion of the game was sacrificed to the god. Later in the month, human sacrifices were made by the Mexicans; but I think this was a late introduction by the advocates of a bloody ritual, and after sacrifice had reached its greatest height of enormity. Another fact has some bearing upon this subject. The sacrifices of this hunting god appear to have been synchronous with those of the gods Tlamatzincatl and Yzquitecatl, and their ceremonies conducted together; and, since human sacrifices were offered to these two deities, they would eventually be introduced into the worship of the hunting god.

Opochtli was god of fishing. He was believed to be the inventor of nets and other instruments of fishing. His image was like a man. The sacrifices to him were pulque, smoking-canes, and other vegetable substances. No human sacrifices are mentioned, and therefore no departure from the primitive worship.[1]

Texcatzoncatl was god of wine. This Aztec Dionysus had companion deities, who as a class bore the remarkable name of "the four hundred rabbits." This, taken in connection with the fact that four hundred priests officiated in the temple of this god, would point to a time when a family bearing the totemic name of the rabbit had consecrated themselves to the worship of an ancestor, and had gradually grown into a priestly caste, maintaining the worship of their god among many other rival deities. Upon the head of the image of this god was a vessel for the reception of wine, which was ceremoniously poured into it.[2]

Ixtlilton was a god of physic, who cured sick children. He was represented by a living man decorated with certain vestments. His temple was a temporary structure of painted boards, in which were kept many jars containing a fluid like black water, which was given the sick child to drink. This is a remarkable piece of imposture, which was only possible among a people all of whose religious conceptions of a deity were colored by anthropomorphism. Here we see a man assume the functions of a deity, with a priesthood attached to his service, whose blessing was supposed to impart curative power to a useless decoction. The same god appears to have been used for the detection of crime; for when a feast was given to him by a private person, he would come to the house of the feast-giver with music, and preceded by the smoke of copal incense, and after feasting he would examine a jar containing the black water above mentioned, and if a piece of straw, or a hair, or any dirt was found therein, it was a sign that the giver of the feast was a thief, or adulterer, or doer of some kind of evil, and he was confronted with the charge accordingly.[3] This god appears to be a personification of primitive sorcery surviving in a higher civilization.

---

[1] 1 Clavigero, 256; 3 Bancroft, 410.   [2] 3 Bancroft, 418.
[3] 1 Clavigero, 257; 3 Bancroft, 409–10.

Tlazolteotl was the goddess of sensual pleasure. The Mexicans invoked her to free them from the disgrace following the exposure of illicit love. Her principal devotees were lustful men and courtesans. She does not, however, bear the wholly depraved character of her votaries, for the Mexicans never attributed to their gods those shameful irregularities which the Greeks and Romans imputed to theirs.[1] She had no very prominent place in the minds of the people. Her mythical home was in a pleasant plain, watered by innumerable fountains, where she passed her time in the midst of delights and ministered to by a host of inferior deities. No man was able to approach her, but she had in her service a crowd of dwarfs, buffoons, and hunchbacks, who diverted her with their songs and dances and acted as messengers to such gods as she fancied. So beautiful was she, no woman in the world could equal her. The garden of her palace was filled with flowers, the touch of any one of which would make one love to the end and love faithfully. She would not allow that any man could resist her temptations. Yappan, the Simeon Stylites of the New World, retired to a great stone in the desert, and there dedicated his life to penitential acts. No spot could be found in the austere, continent life of the anchorite, and the many women sent by the gods to tempt him to pleasure were repulsed and baffled. The chaste victories of the lonely saint were applauded in the upper world, and he was about to be transformed into the higher life. Then it was that Tlazolteotl felt herself slighted, and, wrathful, contemptuous, rose in her evil beauty and descended to earth. That day her singing dwarfs were silent, her messengers undisturbed by her behests, and away into the desert she sped, fairer than eye can conceive, and advancing toward the lean, penance-withered man on his sacred height, her sweet voice sent a thrill through his mortified flesh. "She had come to comfort him," she said, and down from the rock he came, and helped the goddess

---

[1] 1 Clavigero, 257.

ascend, and, alas! in a cloud of shame the chaste light of Yappan went out forever. Tlazolteotl, flushed with victory, left the poor recluse humbled on his deserted rock, all his nights and days of fasting gone for naught. He was transformed into a scorpion, and crawls in and out from under the stone on which he had his abode.[1]

Xipe was the god of the goldsmiths. Those who neglected his worship would be afflicted with sores and itch. He appears to have had his origin in Jalisco, and was especially honored on the sea-shore. His image was of the human form. Human sacrifices disgraced his altars. Those who stole gold or jewels were always offered, and often prisoners of war were sacrificed to him. The hearts of the victims were placed in the mouth of the idol with a golden spoon. Napatuctli was god of the mat-makers and workers in water-flags and rushes. His idol wore a black and white skirt adorned with little sea-shells. He was a beneficent deity, and was known as "he that was large and liberal." His image was that of a man. He had two temples in Mexico.[2]

Omacate was the god of mirth. His image, which was that of a man, was brought to, and presided at, the banquets. If this was neglected, this god would mix hairs with the food of the guests, and this was a great disgrace.[3]

Mexitli, often called Huitzilopochtli, was god of war and the principal deity of the city of Mexico. He was immaculately conceived by a woman called Coatlicue, and born with a shield in his hand and a crest of feathers on his head. Coatlicue was a very pious woman, and spent much of her time in the temple. One day when walking in the temple she beheld descending in the air a ball made of feathers, which she seized and kept in her bosom. The ball disappeared, and Mexitli was the result. Mexitli's first act was to kill his brothers and sister, who had conspired to destroy their mother on account of her supposed

---

[1] 3 Bancroft, 377–79. [2] 1 Clavigero, 257; 3 Bancroft, 417.
[3] 1 Clavigero, 258; 3 Bancroft, 408.

fall from virtue. His early life inspired mankind with terror. He became the leader of his people, conducted them for many years in their great migration, and settled them finally where the great city of Mexico was built. He was the founder of that city, in which was built for his worship the superb temple so admired by the Spaniards.[1] Like all primitive heroes, he was supposed to be gifted with miraculous power, and his birth and death were surrounded with mystery. An incarnation accounted for his birth, and an apotheosis rewarded his life. Pinailton, who was Mexitli's war-lieutenant, came in for a share of worship, and was appealed to on all sudden occasions when the delay of formality kept them from the presence of Mexitli. Coatlicue, his mother, was goddess of flowers and patron saint of the flower-dealers, who were numerous in Mexico. She had a festival in the spring, when the flower-dealers presented her with beautiful braids of flowers.[2]

Toci was goddess of medicinal herbs. She was called "our ancestor," or "grandmother." At her religious ceremonies she was represented by a woman, who was then sacrificed to her. This representative was treated with all the reverence due a goddess.[3]

The goddess Xilonen seems to be connected with agriculture and the vegetable world, as well as Centeotl and Toci. She is represented by a woman who was to be offered to her in sacrifice during her religious ceremonies. A peculiarity connected with the human sacrifice in the case of these agricultural gods appears to be the flaying of the victim, whose skin is torn off and worn by the priests for a time. It would appear to represent the tearing off of the husk or outside covering of the corn and other vegetable substances used by the people.

The goddess Chalchihuitlicue had power over the waters of the sea and rivers, to drown those who went down to them. She raised tempests and caused boats to founder. In her left

---

[1] 1 Clavigero, 254-55.   [2] 1 ib., 257.   [3] 3 Bancroft, 356-58.

hand she held the leaf of the white water-lily; in her right a boat in the shape of a cross. In her honor were celebrated the ceremonies of the lustration of children. Two of these baptisms were practised on every infant,—one immediately after birth, when prayer was offered to this goddess of waters to purge the infant of the vices inherited from its father and mother. "All spot and defilement let the water carry away," said the celebrant of this ceremony, who then immersed the child. The second baptism took place about five days thereafter, at some time considered propitious by the diviner. The ceremony in its formal part was nearly similar to the first, but it had more of a spiritual significance. The first was a practical act, where washing the body of the newly-born babe was an essential feature. The second was more of a typical cleansing of the spirit and a dedication to the goddess of water. The last baptism was not an immersion. It was accompanied with the ceremony of naming the child.

Tlaloc was the god of rain and the fertilizer of the earth. He resided where the clouds gather on the highest mountain-tops. He had many attendant deities passing under the same name. He had only one eye. They prayed and sacrificed to him for rain. He received a very large share of the ceremonial worship of the Mexicans. Xinhtecutli was the god of fire. Upon the back of the image of this god was a dragon's head. This form of representation of the gods is familiar to us in the art of Nicaragua and other neighboring regions. Human sacrifices and an elaborate ceremonial worship were given this god. Teoyaomique was a goddess who collected the souls of those who died in war. She was represented in an image as holding her head in her hands, while two snakes issued from the neck where the head should have been.[1] Jacateuctli was god of merchants. He was represented as a man walking with a staff. The Mexicans also had a god of the tennis-court, as Herrera calls it, or a patron deity of the ball-play. His priest

---

[1] 3 Bancroft, 400.

blessed the ball-ground before the game began. The winner of the game sacrificed to this god.[1]

In Michoacan the goddess Xaratanga occupied the first place in the affections of the Terascos, although she transformed their princes into snakes because they appeared drunk at her festivals. Her name is associated with the downfall of the native dynasty. She was evidently a historic character. She assumed at last a secondary place, because Curicancri was exalted over her by the Chichemec rulers of the country. Manovapa, the son of Xaratanga, was worshipped, as was also Teras, from whom the Terascos took their name and were descended. Surites, a high-priest who preached morality and was considered an inspired prophet, also had a share of their worship.[2]

The Chiapenec pantheon had twenty gods, all of whom were heroes, ancestors, or first rulers of the people inhabiting Chiapas. Imox appears to have been the first settler of this country, and was worshipped. Costahuntox was another of their gods, who is represented with ram's horns on his head. Chimax was a great military leader, and, although captured and burned by enemies, he was apotheosized. Been appears to have been god of travellers. Among the other gods, Igh, Chanan, Yabalan, Tox, Moxic, Lambat, Molo, Elab, Evob, Hix, Chabin, Chic, Cahoh, and Aghul appear to have had little related of them, but were human beings elevated to the position of deities.

Votan is a mythical character who appears to have been one of the earliest culture-heroes of the Mayas of Yucatan; but some authorities make him the descendant of Imox. He describes himself in his book on the origin of the race as being a snake. Votan founded the great city of Palenque, the metropolis of a mighty kingdom, and one of the cradles of American civilization. It is a curious fact that a tribe of natives called the Snakes was found near Palenque and in the neighborhood where Votan's life was spent. The name of

---

[1] 2 Herrera, 341. [2] 3 Bancroft, 445-46.

Snake, which he has given himself, was undoubtedly his totemic or family name. Votan was apotheosized. Ah-Hulneb, named the chief archer on account of his exploits before death, received after death divine honors in the island of Cozumel, whither he had probably carried the Maya civilization. After his death his tomb became an object of veneration, and a temple was built on his royal sepulchre. The island was named after his successor, who also had a sumptuous temple there, in which he was represented in the form of a swallow. Within the temple of Ah-Hulneb a gigantic terra-cotta statue of him was placed, where he appeared dressed as a warrior and holding an arrow in his hand. This statue was hollow, and placed close to the wall, so that a priest could speak through it. So famous did this oracle become, and so great was the multitude of pilgrims flocking thither, that it was found necessary to construct roads to it from all the chief cities of Yucatan, Tabasco, and Guatemala. Zacal-Bacab, Caual-Bacab, Chacal-Bacab, and Ekel-Bacab were gods of the air, and were anthropomorphic.[1] The deities of the Mayas of Yucatan, says Lizana, were their good kings, whom gratitude or fear had made them place among the gods. Hunabku, who was the father of Zamna, their great culture-hero, appears to stand at the head of the Maya pantheon in point of time, and his spouse, Ixazalvoh, who was the inventor of weaving, was also apotheosized. The principal god or culture-hero of the Mayas of Yucatan was Zamna, who was an early lawgiver and civilizer. He invented the Maya hieroglyphic art. He was founder of the royal house. He died at an advanced age, and was buried at Izamal, where a sacred temple was erected in his honor. It was a favorite shrine for Yucatec pilgrims, especially those who were diseased. Prayer and presents offered to Zamna were supposed to bring cures. He was said to have raised the dead.[2]

Of all the apotheosized heroes of Yucatan, Kinich Kakmo was the most remarkable. Son of the sun, he dedicated to

---

[1] 3 Bancroft, 466.   [2] 5 ib., 618; 3 ib., 464.

that luminary a magnificent temple in the village of Izamal. He became personified in the sun.[1]

Pizlimtec, an ancient priest, was deified under the name of Ahkin-Xooc. Ahkin means magician. He undoubtedly attained his distinction through the practice of sorcery. He was also god of poetry and music.[2]

Izona, who appears to have been called the father of men, and was probably an early historical character, was an object of their worship. He had a son Bacab, who attained divine honors. He was divinely begotten; for, according to the traditions, he was born of a virgin Chibirias, who was the daughter of Ixchel, the Yucatec medicine-goddess.[3] Echua was the patron god of merchants and travellers. To him travellers erected every night an altar and burned incense thereon.[4] Cuculcan, the founder of Mayapan, has been considered identical with Quetzalcoatl. Although this identity has not been established, yet there is some probability of it. Many of the followers of Cuculcan were deified, two of whom became gods of fishes, two of farms, and one of thunder. They wore full beards, says the account of them, showing their anthropomorphic character.[5] Chilam Cambal was their god of strength, says Ayeta; Citboluntum was god of health, and Xuchitun of song. There can be no doubt that all of these gods of the Mayas were deified men. All their kings and heroes, for whom they had gratitude or fear, were apotheosized.[6]

Another Maya divinity, by the name of Hunpictoc, had a temple toward the southwest from Izamal. This name was the title of one of the chiefs of the nobility, to whom were confided the safety of the king and the security of the temples. This was the most respectable position under the prince, and his eminent services were probably rewarded with an apotheosis.[7]

---

[1] 2 Brasseur, Hist. Mex., 5.   [2] 2 ib., 11.   [3] 3 Bancroft, 462.
[4] Cogolludo, bk. 10, ch. 8.   [5] 3 Bancroft, 465.
[6] Cogolludo, 198.   [7] 2 Brasseur, 47.

His name signifies "commander of eight thousand lances." Yucemil was god of death. Food was sacrificed to him. If he became hungry, human beings were his victims. Baklun Cham was the Maya Priapus, and was worshipped in a magnificent temple at Merida. Chac was god of agriculture. Abchuy-Kak was another apotheosized warrior. He became god of war, and his statue was borne in the van of the army by four of the most illustrious captains, and received an ovation all along the route. Yxchebelyax was god of painting and writing.[1] Xibalba was the god of evil, or the devil of their religion. Ayeta gives the name of Multimtizec to this god, and the change of this name to Xibalba was probably brought about by their hostile connection with the rising Xibalban empire, hereafter noticed. Most of the Maya gods have evidently gained their celebrity as historical characters. Very little is told of most of them, but their anthropomorphic character is unquestionable.

The Mijes, a Maya nation, surrounded the birth and death of their hero Condoy with the mystery preceding an apotheosis. A prince of indomitable courage, undertaking great conquests, he was defeated, and, with his followers, driven into the mountain-range of Cempoaltipec. He and his followers were hunted down like the beasts of the forests, and would fain have hidden themselves in the dens of animals. Condoy, in their traditions, had no father or mother, and disappeared as mysteriously as he came.[2] They cherished his memory, and thought he had been translated among the gods.

The deities of the Quiches of Guatemala were apotheosized men. Hun Hun Ahpu and Vukab Hunahpu are historical characters who figure extensively in Quiche traditions. These two culture-heroes appear to have gotten into difficulty with the princes of Xibalba, and were beheaded. This tradition shows their anthropomorphic character. The head of Hun Hun Ahpu was placed between the withered branches of a calabash-tree, whereupon the tree became immediately laden

---

[1] 3 Bancroft, 466-67.   [2] 3 Brasseur, 48-49.

with fruit, and the head turned into a calabash. The tree was thenceforth held sacred, and it was sacrilege to touch it. A princess, however, disobeys the injunction, becomes pregnant, and brings forth two sons, named Xbalanque and Hun Ahpu,[1] who after many adventures overthrow the Xibalban princes, and apotheosize Hun Hun Ahpu, whom they recognize as their father by the mystery of an incarnation. Zipacna and Cabraken were Herculean princes of the royal house of Xibalba at the time of the struggle that ensued, and for their heroism had godlike honors in their mythology. The primitive condition of this early Xibalban monarchy is shown in the traditions. Vucub Cakix, the monarch, was shot by Hun Ahpu and Xbalanque while eating fruit in a tree-top. Zipacna, his son, who carried mountains on his shoulders, had to be destroyed by craft. He lived on crabs. Hun Ahpu and Xbalanque made an artificial crab, which he followed into the cave of a mountain which had been previously mined by them. The mountain fell on him and crushed him. Thus ended the Hercules of their mythology. Cabraken was poisoned, and, when the strength had gone out of him, tied and buried alive.[2] Thus ended the dynasty of Vucub Cakix. Monarchs that climbed trees, and princes that crawled on the earth after crabs, were supplanted by Hun Ahpu and Xbalanque, the young agriculturists, whose enchanted tools worked of themselves while they were away on the mountain-side hunting deer. The dawn of agriculture had begun before the hunting life had closed. While the Quiche-Cakchichel empire was in process of formation, a great rivalry arose, as should be expected, between the gods of the respective branches. The great ancestors of the Quiche branch appear to have been rejected by a portion of the nation, who favored the introduction of the new gods Tohil Avilix and Hacavitz. Tohil appears to have been the creator of fire, and probably represented an era of progress. As a condition of granting the privilege of this great discovery to others, he in-

---

[1] 3 Bancroft, 479-80. [2] 5 ib., 172-73.

sists upon an agreement to worship him. Tohil appears in their early history as the leader of a great migration. His followers on their way are much annoyed, according to tradition, by the attacks of wild animals, meaning undoubtedly wild tribes inhabiting the regions through which they passed. Balam Quitze, who appears to have been high-priest of the migrating tribe, and his companions, brought these wild beasts and offered them before Tohil, Avilix, and Hacavitz. This introduction of human sacrifice enraged the tribes of the invaded country. At last great hostility to Balam Quitze and his companions was aroused in the mountain-tribes, who found it hard, however, to track the invaders on the fog-enveloped summits of the Guatemalan heights. The followers of Balam Quitze found it equally difficult to overcome the tribes that were arrayed in hostility against them. It was at last agreed to submit the new gods, Tohil, Avilix, and Hacavitz, to an ordeal, and if they proved to be the great and worthy gods they were represented, then there would be a submission to them. A strange plot was entered into to test their virtue, for two beautiful virgins were sent to wash linen in the stream where Tohil, Avilix, and Hacavitz were bathing in the form of young men. They were subjected to the great temptation, but they maintained their godlike dignity and virtue. They were the representatives of a higher morality and a progressive civilization. At last the great priest Balam Quitze prepared to die, after all the tribes were subjected and the Quiche empire established. He had been a faithful priest and leader. The traditions say that he disappeared suddenly and mysteriously.[1]

Tohil, the principal god of the Quiches of Guatemala, appears to have been the discoverer of fire. This fire he produced by stamping with his sandal. Tohil was a great leader of the people at a period in their history when under him they went forth from their native land. They endured much hardship. A sea, however, parted for their passage, and water miraculously

---

[1] 5 Bancroft, 548-52.

favored them in their migrations, as it has done in the traditions of almost all other peoples. It does not require much investigation to detect apotheosized men in the Quiche gods Tohil, Avilix, and Hacavitz. They were ancestral gods who were once men, and from whom the Quiches claim to have sprung. Other gods of Guatemala are Xchmel, Xtmana, and Gucumatz, who is identical probably with Quetzalcoatl, who, it will be remembered, when exiled sought refuge among other peoples.

The *Chahalka* were Guatemalan household gods, who presided over houses. When they built a house they dedicated the central part to these gods, and kept a place of sacrifice to them. They prayed to them that good fortune should favor the house.[1] They are identical with the spirits of their dead relatives,[2] and a survival of house-burial. Incense was burned and sacrifices made to these ancestral deities.

Pezelao appears to have been the principal god of the Zapotecs. He was their god of the dead and lord of the sacred places of Yopaa.[3]

The spiritual pontiff of Yopaa was looked upon as a god by the Zapotecs, whom the earth was unworthy to hold, or the sun to shine upon. No one dared look upon him, but all fell with their faces to the ground. The most powerful lords never entered his presence without bare feet.[4] Pitao Peeci, another of their gods, presided over auguries and divination,[5] and was undoubtedly an ancient high-priest. Pitao Pecala inspired their dreams. Cociyo was the rain god, and gave or withheld the showers as he pleased.[6] Wichaana was god of fish, and was thought to be their creator. The earliest ancestor remembered by a people is usually elevated to this position. Piltzinteolli, the child-god, a representation of whose youthful form was reared in several places in Jalisco, had offerings of the choicest fruit and flowers.[7] In Oajaca, as might be expected of a people

---

[1] Ximenez, 188. [2] 3 Bancroft, 481.
[3] 3 Brasseur, 26. [4] 2 Bancroft, 142-43.
[5] 2 ib., 27. [6] 2 ib., 27.
[7] 3 ib., 444-47.

who regarded living kings and priests with adoration, apotheosis was common. Petela, an ancient Zapotec cacique, was worshipped in the cavern of Coatlan. At one end of this subterranean temple a yawning abyss received the foaming waters of a mountain-torrent, and into this were thrown human sacrifices, gayly dressed and adorned with flowers. Pinopia, a saintly princess of Zapotecapan, was worshipped in another place. Her corpse had been miraculously conveyed to heaven.[1] Wixepecocha, a reformer and prophet of the Zapotecs, was worshipped. A statue of this god was found near Tehuantepec.[2]

The principal goddess of the natives of the province of Cerquin, in Honduras, was Comizagual, a woman who came among them from other parts, according to tradition. She was skilled in the art of magic, and came into their province flying through the air. She had three sons without being married, and, according to the usual traditions in such cases, without knowing man. After ruling with equity, she was translated in the following manner: she ordered her bed brought out of the house, when there came a great flash of lightning with thunder, and Comizagual was never seen more.[3]

Oviedo says the Nicaraguans knew nothing of the "One Creator." The anthropomorphic character of their creators is evident from what Oviedo tells us of Tamagostad and Zipaltonal. These Nicaraguan creators were a man and woman, from whom the Indians claimed descent. They asserted, with the greatest assurance, that their ancestors were the greatest gods. In their description of them they gave them the same color as the Indians, and said they ate the same things.[4] Since they were themselves anthropophagi, they said their gods delighted in human flesh.[5]

Nezahualcoyotl, king of Acolhuacan, in popular belief was

---

[1] 3 Bancroft, 457. [2] 4 ib., 372.
[3] 4 Herrera, 137. [4] Oviedo, 19-26.
[5] Ib., 61.

placed among the gods, even though he died after the Spanish inroad; but the age of apotheosis was about closing.

The most prominent personage in the Isthmian pantheon was Dabaiba. She is described as a native princess whose reign was marked by great wisdom and many miracles, and who was apotheosized after her death. She was said to control the thunder and lightning, and to bring showers or produce drought as she pleased.[1]

Xolotl was the leader of the first Chichemec invasion.[2] He was deified. Wanacace was another of their gods, and ancestor of the branch of the Chichemecs called Wanacaces. Hereti was also one of their primitive heroes, who became a patron saint.[3]

The worship of great national gods did not supplant the worship of family gods, but supplemented it, as in the case of the classical nations of antiquity. Thus often we find the husband worshipping his family god and the wife hers. Thus, Iri Ticatame, in departing from his capital, took his god Curicaneri with him, while his wife took her god Nasoricuare wrapped up in a rich cloth.[4] She was no more willing to desert her family god than was Rachel to leave behind her the idols of her father Laban.

Bochica was the leading mythical character in Bogota. He had the fabulous age of two thousand years ascribed to him, and this time was all employed in elevating his subjects. The Chibchas apotheosized Bochica as the founder of their laws and institutions. Bochica lives in the sun, and has the privilege of standing at the head of their pantheon. His wife Chia was deified with him, and occupies the moon. The powerful Tomagata, one of their oldest caciques, was deified.[5] Another of their deities was Bachue, a beautiful female, from whom they descended. She after a period of time disappeared by metamorphosis; but statues of gold and wood are still to be seen

---

[1] 3 Bancroft, 498. [2] Ixtlilxochitl, 1re partie, 29.
[3] 3 Brasseur, 80. [4] 5 Bancroft, 512.
[5] Bollaert, 48.

representing her. Their patron deity was Chibchacum, although his power was not so great as that of Bochica. Chibchacum in an angry mood brought a deluge on the people of the tableland. Bochica punished him severely for this act, and obliged him thenceforth to bear the burden of the earth. He was the Atlas of the New World. He had not arisen above subjection to fatigue, for he occasionally shifted the earth from one shoulder to another, and he sometimes did this so carelessly that severe earthquakes were produced. Neucatocoa was the god of revelry and drunkenness, and was the Bacchus of the Chibchas. He appears to be the only one not bearing a strictly anthropomorphic character. He is represented as a bear covered with a mantle. Sorro was the god who had charge of the boundaries of their fields.[1]

Gacheta is a famous virgin who conceived and brought forth Garanchaca, a famous chief who ruled over them. She declared the sun to be the father of her boy. This is another case of immaculate conception.

Xue, a great benefactor of his people, has received a place in their pantheon. He appears to have been a great preacher to whom large concourses of people repaired for instruction. He also taught them to spin and weave.[2]

The Muyscas of Bogota had a god named Queteba, who fashioned the surface of the earth as it now is. With a single blow he opened a cliff in the Andes, through which flows the river Funha.[3]

The historical deities were those which initiated men into social life and were founders of civil or religious institutions. Although the worship of spirits which was so prevalent among all the uncivilized tribes still survived among the more civilized nations, yet the worship of culture-heroes was peculiarly distinctive of the latter. The chief of these deified men in the Peruvian history was Viracocha, who more than once appeared in human form to the Inca of the same name, saying he was the

---

[1] Bollaert, 12-13.   [2] Ib., 21-22.   [3] Brinton's Relig. Sent., 240.

brother of Manco Capac. The Inca ordered a magnificent temple to be constructed to this apparition. In the temple stood a statue of the deity as he appeared to the Inca, in which he was represented as a man with a beard. Viracocha was of large stature, and his power so great that he brought down the mountains, raised the valleys, and made water spring from the rocks. He taught the people to love one another. They formed idols in his likeness and reared temples to his glory. He passed toward the north, but their legends appear to confirm his reappearance some time after on a different mission. He now healed the sick and gave sight to the blind, but after having been subjected to persecution he went to the sea-shore and spread his mantle upon its waves, went away, and has never been seen since.[1]

Another culture-hero is Ayarache, who founded Pacaritambo. He was so strong he could throw down the hills. He appears to have used a sling. Ayarache was at last enticed into a cave by his two brothers, who immediately stopped up the mouth of it with stones. In his efforts to get out, many mountains and high hills fell down upon him, and thus ended Ayarache.[2] His two brothers, Aranca and Ayarmango, erected the town of Tamboquiro, and appear to have been sorcerers. Although they had dealt so treacherously with their brother, they pretended to commune with him and obey his directions, given from time to time. Aranca was at last turned into a stone, but Ayarmango founded the city of Cuzco, and was known thereafter as Manco Capac.[3] He deified his two brothers.[4]

All the Incas after death enjoyed deification, and their apotheosis began in life. The Peruvians also adored heroes in some of the provinces, which worship prevailed before the conquest of the Incas. In the ancient town of Huahualla they sacrificed to the mummies of Caxaparca and his son Huaratanga, both dressed in the garb of warriors.[5] In Quichumarca they worshipped Huari and his two brothers. Apuyurac was wor-

---

[1] 4 Herrera, 285.   [2] 4 ib., 286.   [3] 4 ib., 287-89.   [4] 4 ib., 290.
[5] Rivero and Tschudi, Ant., 163-66.

shipped in the town of Hupa, and also his son in the town of Tamor. The race of Sopac worshipped Apri-Xillin and his son Huayna. In the valley of Janja, Huarivilca was worshipped, and a sumptuous temple constructed to him. The family deities were generally the entire bodies of their ancestors, so arranged in the tombs that they could see them and offer them sacrifices.[1] The natives of Quito adored Pacha and Eacha, who were gods, but had formerly been heroes.[2]

This cursory examination of the pantheons of the more civilized nations has been made for the purpose of showing that their gods were historical characters and their worship was the worship of human spirits.

I will now notice the worship of idols, as it is closely connected with the subject of the worship of human spirits. Idolatry in its lowest form, and its development under higher conditions of civilization, can be advantageously studied among the native races of America. Conspicuous by its absence among many of the lower tribes, image-worship comes plainly into view among those in the upper levels of savagery. The Mandans howled and whined and made their prayers before puppets of grass and skins. The Virginians had idols with temples set apart for them, and a priesthood. To supply the demand of the natives of the West India Islands for idols, one island near Hayti had a population of idol-makers. In Mexico, idolatry attained its full development. In the higher culture of Peru, the idols of conquered provinces were carried, half trophies, half hostages, to Cuzco, to rank among the inferior deities of the Peruvian pantheon, while the nobility of the empire were advancing one step higher to the worship of the heavenly bodies.[3]

Mr. Spencer thinks the savage may have been prepared to suspect animation in inanimate things by discovering plants and animals embedded in rock. I am persuaded that idolatry owes its origin to the belief that disembodied spirits are everywhere present, ready to transmigrate into inanimate objects,

---

[1] Rivero and Tschudi, Ant., 169–70.   [2] Bollaert, 84.   [3] 2 Tylor, 172–73.

and that they will enter readily any image that bears any resemblance to the body formerly inhabited by that spirit, or any image containing any fragment of that former body. The more civilized races made images of persons while living, or soon after death, and into these were put their ashes or some part of their body after death. This they thought insured the presence of the spirit in that idol, and the priests strengthened the credulity of the people by speaking through these images in such a way as to deceive them into the belief that the images spoke.

Among the more primitive peoples a rude idolatry appears. When a child dies among the Ojibways they cut some of its hair and make a little doll, which they call the doll of sorrow. This lifeless object takes the place of the deceased child. This the mother carries for a year. She places it near her at the fire, and sighs often when gazing on it. She carries it wherever she goes. They think that the child's spirit has entered this bundle and can be helped by its mother. Presents and sacrificial gifts are made to it. Toys and useful implements are tied to the doll for its use.[1]

La Poterie mentions the same custom among the savages of the Canadas. This is the most primitive form of idolatry.

Among the Northwestern tribes, says McKenny, "I have noticed several women here carrying with them rolls of clothing. On inquiring what these imported, I learn that they are widows, who carry these bundles when their husbands die. This bundle is called her husband, and she must never be seen without it. If she walks out, she takes it with her. If she sits down, she places it by her side. This badge of widowhood she is compelled to carry until some of her husband's family takes it away."[2] When presents are given round, this bundle, or "husband," comes in for an equal share, as if living.[3] A mother, on losing her child, prepares an image of it and fixes it in a cradle, and goes through the ceremony of nursing

---

[1] Kohl's Kitchi-Gami, 108.   [2] McKenny's Tour, 292.   [3] Ib., 293.

it for a year.[1] The Knistenaux, who killed their parents when old, always made a bunch of feathers tied with a string into a doll-shaped image of them, and treated it with superstitious reverence.[2]

The next step is to make images out of wood or roughly-hewn stones which require but little alteration to make them into the representation desired. A good many of the tribes of British America and the Northern United States made these rough idols and worshipped them.

Among many tribes whose art is still in a rude state, a gravepost is roughly hewn into the image of the person over whose body it is placed. Mr. McCoy says, "Among the Ottawas we often discovered at the heads of their graves a post somewhat proportioned to the size of the deceased. When any one visited the grave, they rapped on the post with a stick to announce their arrival to the spirit. On the upper end of this post was cut a slight resemblance of the human face." The Indians not far from Quebec, while the Jesuit priests were among them, whenever any one died, cut his portrait and put it on the grave, "anointing and greasing that man of wood as if living," says Father Lalamant. Among the Algonkins a post was generally placed on the graves of the dead and their portraits carved thereon.[3] The Alaskans ornamented all their graves with carved and painted faces.[4] This rude form of preserving images of the dead represents a primitive form of idolatry, and connects it with the worship of the dead.

"Outside of the Indian graves of the Northwest are frequently found the images of those buried," says Mr. Brown, who found three figures carved out of wood placed outside a grave. One of the figures represented a man who had a rifle over his knee ready to guard the bodies from desecration. The figure of a woman was postured as if knitting a mat.[5]

---

[1] McKenny's Tour, 293-94.   [2] Brinton, 275.
[3] 2 Charlevoix, Journal, 185.   [4] Whymper, 101.
[5] 1 Brown's Races, 109.

The natives of Chile decorate the graves of their chiefs with figures representing the chief and his wives placed around the grave. Each figure is cut from a huge log of wood ten or twelve feet high. These rude figures are carved by professionals, who get enormous prices for their work. Sometimes as high a price as an ox is given for one of these rude figures. No grandee is considered buried unless his grave is decorated with these figures.[1]

Fig. 4.

In the West Indies the tombs had planks over them, some of which bore the likeness of the entombed person.[2]

Fig. 4 illustrates the configuration of the grave-post into the likeness of the deceased. It is the headstone of a Nicaraguan grave.[3]

Fig. 5 is an image of the son of an Alaskan chief placed over the tomb.

Fig. 5.

Images of men and women were made and placed near the bodies of those deposited in the bone-houses or primitive temples of the tribes of the Southern United States. "Their temples had rows of statues round about them on the four sides, and a row of women opposite a row of men. These statues were placed opposite the dead bodies" which they were made to represent in life.[4]

Among the Isthmians the image of a great warrior was made at death and carried in procession to the place of burial.[5]

The same custom prevailed in Peru. The images of the dead were made and set up in their tombs and worshipped.

---

[1] 2 Wood's Uncivilized Races, 567; Smith's Araucanians, 309.
[2] 1 Herrera, 266.
[3] Pim and German's Dottings, Plate.
[4] 3 Picart, 113.
[5] 3 ib., 176.

All the Incas had this honor conferred on them, and their images were carried in the funeral processions, and sacrifices made to them.¹ Fig. 6 is an image of one of the Incas, and was an object of worship.

Fig. 6.

They also made statues of their chiefs during their lives, and these statues, made in the likeness of the chief, were served as if they had been alive, and villages were set apart to provide them with necessaries.

Among the Mayas, merchants who died away from home, or warriors who were killed in battle whose bodies could not be found, were represented by images which were made of them, and these images received all the funeral ceremonies which their bodies would have received. If any one was drowned and the body lost, they made an image of it, which they treated in the same manner. To these images they made offerings.

Among the Mayas of Yucatan images of all those who died were made and worshipped.² They cut off the heads of their lords and chief men when they died and kept them along with their statues. They made wooden statues of their dead parents, and left a hollow in the neck where they put in their ashes and kept them among their idols.³

Among those tribes where cremation has supplanted interment, a statue of the deceased is made, to contain his ashes or to be placed beside the vessel containing them.

The Mexicans preserved the ashes, hair, and teeth of the dead and put them in little boxes, above which was placed a wooden figure shaped and adorned like the deceased.

The Aztec monarchs were cremated, and their ashes, charred bones, and hair gathered together in an urn, near which was placed a statue of the monarch attired in his royal habiliments.⁴

---

¹ Jos. d'Acosta, book 5, chap. 6.
³ 5 Herrera, 175.
² 2 Bancroft, 800.
⁴ 2 Bancroft, 611.

The Tarascan kings were cremated and their ashes and valuables made into a figure which was dressed in royal habiliments, with a mask for its face.[1]

The Scyris had in their tombs a hollow figure of the deceased, within which were placed stones of divers colors and shapes, denoting the age and other biographical data of the deceased.[2] These images were objects of worship.

The Mayas made hollow clay images, or hollow statues of wood, in which they placed the ashes of the burned bodies of their monarchs. They offered food to these images at their festivals. Thus cremation led those peoples practising it to a different form of idolatry than that of making and worshipping grave-posts that were carved into the image of the deceased. Cremation among the more civilized peoples led them to the manufacture of hollow images of the dead, capable of holding their ashes, or of urns to contain the ashes, near which stood the image of the deceased.

Many of these sepulchral vases, made to hold the ashes of the dead, had upon the outside of them a representation of the deceased, and then they became the apparent objects of worship. On Plate III. we find such a burial-vase of the Mexicans. Among all the Nahua nations, offerings of choice viands, wine, and flowers were placed before these caskets containing the dead.[3] The Mayas erected temples over the urns containing the ashes of the dead.[4] The Peruvians placed the ashes of Viracocha in a small jar of gold, and offered sacrifices to it.[5] The Peruvian cavaliers of royal blood, Curacas, and other magnates, were deposited in large vases of gold and silver in the form of urns, which were found in the meadows and woods.[6] They worshipped these specimens of pottery.

One of the most famous Huacas worshipped by several provinces in Peru was in the form of a large jar surrounded by eight other jars. Near it were many small rabbits which had

---

[1] 2 Bancroft, 621. [2] Bollaert, 88. [3] 2 Bancroft, 618. [4] 5 Herrera, 175.
[5] Rivero and Tschudi, Per. Ant., Tr. Hawks, 166. [6] Ib., 200–1.

PLATE III.

SEPULCHRAL URN.

DOCTRINE OF SPIRITS.   121

been offered in sacrifice.[1] Many of their conopas, or family gods, were such clay jars, hollow within. Twin children dying at an early age were placed in earthen pots and worshipped as sacred beings. Thus it will be seen that the worship of these hollow clay images or jars is due, not to any special reverence for the image itself, but because they were used as burial-urns and contained the ashes or some portion of the body of the deceased. This subject is well illustrated by Fig. 7, representing the burial-urn of a Brazilian chief.[2]

FIG. 7.

It is very difficult to determine just how far we might go in making the art of the American nations tributary to the elucidation of their religious history. It is probable that all primitive art reflects the religious life of the people, even if religion did not originate their art. The first form of art among the American aborigines, exclusive of the manufacture of their rude implements, is undoubtedly seen in their ornamentation, which was fetichistic, which will be treated under the head of feti-

---

[1] Rivero and Tschudi, 168–69.   [2] Denis, Brésil, 404.

chism. The next progressive step was toward idolatry, which was followed by elaboration of sepulchral structures culminating in temples. "By a superstition indigenous to all lands, people without records have left their annals in their graves. In the belief that their wants and occupations would be the same in the spirit-land as they were here, they had their household and personal effects interred with them. We can scarcely regret the prevalence of a delusion which has been the means of making us acquainted with the arts and habits of peoples of whom otherwise we could have known little."[1]

The pottery found in the tombs is a very large part of it fashioned after some object of veneration. Very little of it is perfectly plain and free from a quasi-idolatrous shape or picture representing some man, animal, or mythological character. A Peruvian vase is of special interest on account of the light it reflects upon one of the modes by which Peruvians perpetuated the features and characters of prominent men. It is a vase bust, representing the head of the famous cacique Ruminhauy. The features are strongly developed, and with indisputable traits of an individual's portrait. These baked clay busts preceded marble statuary in the Old World. Thus it will be seen what a prominent feature of their religious history their art history becomes. The worship of urns used in urn-burial has of course resulted from the association of the urn with the person deposited in it. The same is true of the idols which were made to hold the ashes of the dead. The worship is not at first directed toward the material part of the urn or idol, or even the representation it may have upon it of the deceased, but it is directed toward the spirit supposed to reside there. In the case of the conopas and other images, the theory of the entry of a spirit into anything representing natural objects explains the apparently unreasonable worship of material things. Many mythical characters appear on their vases.

Gateways to towns were often of idolatrous forms. The

---

[1] Ewbank's Brazil, Appendix.

monolithic gateway of Tiahuanaco gives us a mythological group of representations of condor, tiger, serpent, and sun, surrounding a central human figure, toward which winged human-headed figures are kneeling. It was the custom of pagan nations to adorn the gateways of cities and entrances to temples and palaces with one or more figures of deities who were the protecting genii of the place. A former monarch was often selected for this responsible position. Frequently, however, one or more persons were buried alive beneath the walls of the gateway, that their spirits might be ever present to guard the place.

The belief in the vitality of idols can be illustrated by many curious facts. The inhabitants of Lambayeque, Peru, said they came from the north, bringing with them an idol of green stone called Llanpallec, which represented their ancient chief. They built a temple for this idol at a place called Chot. When they attempted to remove this idol from its temple after many generations, it became very much enraged and brought on them drought and famine. It was somewhat appeased by their throwing the chief who had committed this sacrilege into the sea.[1]

The belief of idolatrous nations in that vitality of images which makes them capable of feelings of pain and pleasure, and which endows them frequently with a capacity for speech and motion, is due to the imposture of priests. The idols of pagan nations which have temples and priests attached to them are generally hollow and so placed that they can be spoken through by priests or others attached to their temples. Thus originated the belief in oracles. This imposture of priestcraft was very prevalent among many of the American peoples. The Haytian idols were hollow, and so large that the priests could speak through them and delude the people, who thought the idol spoke.[2] The priests would often get inside of these idols in order to practise this imposition. This rendered it necessary to make those large idols which were used in the temples of

---

[1] Squier's Peru, 169.   [2] McCulloh's Ant. Res., 108.

the more civilized American races. Many of these were found in Mexico and Yucatan and the West India islands. In the island of Barbadoes an enormous clay idol was found, whose head alone weighed sixty pounds.[1]

The Virginia Indians had an idol in one of their temples which the priest moved about before the people and made it answer questions. They thought it was alive.[2]

An idol mentioned by Martyr, which was found in the West Indies and was made of wood, was thought by the natives to go about by itself. It would hide itself in the woods, and they would search a great while to find it, and bring it back.[3]

Says Roman Pane, the natives of Hispaniola had many idols which they thought spoke to them, and when food was placed before them and left there, and the priests devoured it, the idols were thought to have eaten it. He mentions many such cases of imposture. "Guamorete, a man of note, had a cemi (idol) in his house, which, when his house was burned by his enemies, got up and went a bowshot from the place, near to a water. He would come down from on top of the house where he was put. He had two crowns grow on his head. Another cemi had four feet like a dog's, and was made of wood. He would often at night go out of the house into the woods, and when brought home again and bound with cords, yet he would get away into the woods again; and when the Christians came he broke away and went into a morass, where they tracked him, but never saw him again. There was another one which they found in a ditch. It was a log which appeared to have life in it. Taking it out, they built a house to it. It went out of that house several times and returned to the place whence they brought it. At another time they bound and put it in a sack, and yet it went away as before." The same author says the Indians will often see a log of wood, and through some hallucination will think it directs them to make it into an idol, which they immediately do. In the valley of Rimac, Peru, there was an idol in the

---
[1] 1 Edwards's West Indies, 51.   [2] 3 Picart, 113.   [3] Decades, 47.

figure of a man, which answered questions and became famous as an oracle. Thus idols were supposed to have all the sagacity and passions of human beings.

The Tarascos in their migrations appear to have been led by an idol, and their city Izintzuntzan was founded upon a spot pointed out by a supposed auspicious omen, for a multitude of gorgeous birds congregated in the air above their idol, and formed a brilliant canopy for the sacred image.[1]

Uxmal is said to have been destroyed through the anger of their idols, who were outraged because a new clay god was made by a usurper and worshipped by the people.[2]

This supposed vitality of idols was taught by the priesthood, who by this means increased their influence and power.

In Hispaniola, the Spaniards found a conspiracy between the cacique and priesthood to deceive the people. Hearing that a certain idol spoke to the people, the Spaniards were present at one of these performances, and they found that the statue was hollow, with a hollow tube connecting with it, through which the priest spoke to the people. The cacique begged the Spaniards not to disclose this to the Indians, because by that artifice he kept them in subjection.[3]

Among the tribes formerly inhabiting the territory of the United States idolatry did not prevail to the same extent as it did among the more civilized races. Many rude idols have been found, however, which were objects of worship. On the Saskatchewan were found four painted posts about five feet high. The features of a man were roughly carved on each post and smeared with patches of vermilion and green-colored paint over the cheeks, nose, and eyebrows. These were the images of the dead. "When decorated with fresh paint, feathers, strips of leather, and a painted robe of elk, moose, or buffalo-skin, these idols inspire the most superstitious awe among the savages, who carve and ornament them; but the awe of many becomes terror when these images are illumined by fire at night."[4]

---

[1] 5 Bancroft, 516. [2] 5 ib., 633. [3] 1 Herrera, 160. [4] 1 Hind's Nar., 402.

In the town of Franklin, Illinois, was found a very rough figure of an idol. It was a stout stick of timber, hewn out so as to resemble an Indian with four faces.[1]

Among the Senecas an image was discovered in 1802, which was made of wood and was nearly decayed to the ground. It had the form of a man, and was whimsically painted and decorated with skins. The rotten condition of this god occasioned much agitation among the Indians. Some were for taking it into the woods and leaving it there with plenty of provisions. They reluctantly consented that it should be destroyed if he who destroyed it should take upon himself the responsibility of any harm that might threaten the nation in consequence. This fearful idol was tumbled into the river by the Christians, while the Indians gazed upon it with reverential awe as it floated away. A curious illustration of the idolatrous superstition of the natives of North Carolina is related by Mr. Haywood. To encourage the young men to be industrious in planting their maize and pulse, they annually placed a kind of idol in the field dressed up exactly like an Indian. This image none of the young men dared approach, because the old men would not allow it. They told them that it was a former warrior who had died many years ago, but had now come back to see if they worked well. The old men sat around the image, paying it the most profound respect and maintaining silence.[2]

The Northwestern tribes had idols, before which their religious ceremonies were performed. An idea prevailed that while these rites were going on a spirit entered into the wooden idol.[3]

Rude idols have been found among most of the tribes of the Algonkin race. Fig. 8 is a rough idol of the Ojibways. Among the nations of Oregon every house had its idols.[4]

The New Mexican tribes made images of all of their dead and worshipped them.

---

[1] Boies' De Kalb County, 463.   [2] Haywood's Nat. and Ab. Hist. Ten., 229.
[3] Dall's Alaska, 389.   [4] Dunn, 182.

DOCTRINE OF SPIRITS. 127

The Moquis had little images made of wood or clay, gaudily painted and gorgeously decorated with feathers. These images are suspended from the rafters of their houses by a string, and are objects of worship. Fig. 9 is one of their idols.[1]

Fig. 8.   Fig. 9.

Idols were found in many parts of Georgia, although Bolzius, Bartram, Adair, and others deny, either positively or inferentially, the existence of either idols or images within the limits then occupied by the Georgia Indians. Subsequent investigations prove, by the discovered presence of the images themselves, that idol-worship was here practised. The Creeks had at one of their war towns a carved statue of wood, which they worshipped.[2] The ornamented posts, the wooden images, and figures of men and animals sketched upon the Creek houses have long since perished. Next in the order of durability are small images of burnt clay, which occur in various parts of the

---

[1] Cozzens's Marvellous Country, 487; and Plate LXII. in Hayden's Geological Survey of Colorado.   [2] McCulloh's Ant. Res., 107.

State. Three stone idols were found in the Etowah valley of Georgia. Two of these represented the male human figure in a sitting posture; the third represented a female figure. Many terra-cotta images were found.[1] A small shrine was found in Chatooga County hewn out of the solid rock, and within which was seated on a pedestal an image.[2]

This removes the doubt we might have of the worship of idols by some population formerly inhabiting this region of country. Mr. Jones appears to think these are not the remains of Cherokee art, but of some people who preceded them. Mr. Jones mentions the existence of a few idol pipes, in which a human figure was represented in a sitting posture. In their countenances the devotional idea was forcibly expressed.[3]

Among the inhabitants of that region of country now called Tennessee, idolatry in a rude form has left many remains of itself among their antiquities. The relics, which are somewhat unique and more interesting than all others in this region, are stone and clay images varying in height from six inches to two feet, and found in great numbers by all diligent explorers. Images are frequently found in the mounds of Tennessee. These images were without doubt placed upon the mounds and received worship.[4] Evidences of sacrificial offerings to these images are found in the graves.

The vast system of idolatry prevalent at the time of the discovery among the South American and Central American tribes is testified to by all the early writers. The greater number of historical gods of the Peruvians had figures made of them in stone and wood. Some of these were of enormous size. Near Hilavi such a statue was found near the sculptured sepulchres three times a man's height, with two monstrous figures beside it. In front of each of these idols was an altar. It took thirty persons three days to destroy these images. The idol Rimac was a human figure found in a magnificent temple. Deputations from different countries came to worship this idol

---

[1] Jones, Antiq. of Southern Indians, 432–33.   [2] Ib., 431.   [3] Ib., 402–3.
[4] Haywood's Nat. Ab. Hist. Tenn., 151.

and bring it offerings. The idol Huaca Catequella, which foretold the death of Inca Yupanqui, was famous throughout Peru. The son of the Inca, out of revenge, destroyed the temple of this idol, but the idol was rescued by the priests. The idol Umina, with a face half human, made of an emerald, was deeply venerated.[1]

The Purahas, near Quito, worshipped idols of clay with a human head, but with the mouth at the top of the head, for convenience of pouring in the blood of the sacrificed victims.[2]

Among the Mayas of Yucatan the family idols were so reverenced that they were considered the most valued part of the inheritance left by those who died.[3] The Brazilian tribes made gigantic idols of plaited palms, and also had their family idols, which often lay neglected in the corners of their houses until a time of need or war came.[4] The Tupinambas had idols in the image of men set up in the woods, where the sorcerers offered sacrifices to them and consulted the spirits supposed to reside in them.[5] They were their oracles. The missionary Cardenas is said to have overthrown more than twelve thousand idols among the Brazilian tribes.[6]

Among the Patagonians every family had its own household wooden image.[7]

Mexico was divided into wards, and each ward had an idol-god of its own, with temple and temple service.[8]

Every house in Mexico had its idols, one near the place where they slept, and another near the door.

Idols were so numerous on the chief island in Lake Peten that it took one hundred men a whole day to destroy them.[9]

In Granada there was a multitude of idols to which temples were dedicated. Their houses also contained idols. They were so devoted to idolatry that wheresoever they went they

---

[1] Rivero and Tschudi, 172-74.
[2] Bollaert, 86.
[3] Landa, 27.
[4] 1 Southey, 621.
[5] Denis, Brésil, 20.
[6] 2 Southey, 382.
[7] Nar. Adventure and Beagle, ed. 1839, p. 90.
[8] 3 Herrera, 194.
[9] 3 Bancroft, 483.

carried an idol. In battle they would hold an idol with one arm and fight with the other.[1]

Closely connected with the subject of idolatry is that of the worship of stones. These stones are sometimes reverenced on account of their similarity to the human figure, or the figure of some animal. Such stones are called shingabawassins by the Ojibways. They have all the essential character of idols, and are supposed to be the locality of some god.[2] Figs. 10 and 11 represent two of these stones. Their similarities to the

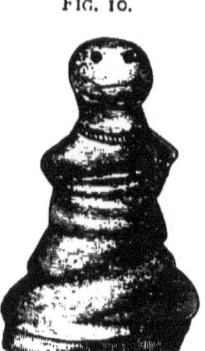
FIG. 10.

FIG. 11.

human or animal form are frequently noticed, and are generally accounted for by a metamorphosis; they almost always have some tradition connected with them, which makes them the objects of superstitious fear. The Aricaras have a legend that three stones in their country that resemble a man, woman, and dog are a young Indian girl and her lover and the dog that followed them when they left their homes because the girl's parents refused their consent to their marriage.[3] They were worshipped.

A curious case of metamorphosis occurred near Scarborough's Hill, at Chinook Point. Two rocks are shown there which are two metamorphosed men who belonged to the fabu-

---

[1] 4 Herrera, 90.   [2] 1 Schoolcraft, 94.
[3] 1 Lewis and Clarke, 107; Tylor's Researches, 113.

lous age of giants. This tale is told of them. One of them was wading in the water of Shoalwater Bay for crabs, when an aquatic monster swallowed him. His brother called the giants to his aid, and collected great fir-trees, dried spruce, and other trees wherewith to build a fire, and brought huge stones to be heated. The fire was made, the water in the bay evaporated. The great sea-monster was killed, ripped open, and the man released.[1] The giants were metamorphosed into these stones soon after. At the mouth of the Walla Walla two stones, human-shaped, were thought to be two Kiuse girls metamorphosed by a jealous husband, and were objects of worship.

The Standing Rock is a famous stone in the Indian country on the Upper Missouri. It is a little boulder twenty-eight inches high. The Indians look on it as sacred, and have painted and adorned it with colored ribbons and tails of animals. The following myth gives it its sacred character. A young Aricara woman, wife of a celebrated brave, was spirit-broken because her husband took a second wife. She went out on the prairie and sat broken-hearted and refusing food until she died and was turned into that rock. All of the women of the tribes located thereabout repair to this rock and make their offerings whenever they are afflicted with domestic difficulties.[2]

In a cavern on the banks of the Kickapoo there is a gigantic mass of stone presenting the appearance of a human figure. The Indians say that it is a metamorphosed Indian woman, who, having received several wounds in battle, was left, and nearly perished of hunger. She was converted into this monument, which they hold in great fear, and never pass without offering sacrifices to it. They say it formerly had the power of killing those that approached it.[3]

Schoolcraft tells the following tradition of metamorphosis: "An Indian, while passing across Winnebago Lake on a beautiful summer day, espied at a distance in the lake before him a

---

[1] Swan's Washington Territory, 69. [2] Beach, 388. [3] 1 Keating, 251.

beautiful female form standing in the water. Her eyes shone with a brilliancy that could not be endured, and she held in her hand a lump of glittering gold. He immediately paddled toward the attractive object, but as he came near he could perceive that it was gradually altering as to its shape and complexion; her eyes no longer shone with brilliancy, her face lost the hectic glow of life, her arms imperceptibly disappeared, and when he came to the spot where she stood, it was a monument of stone having a human face, with the fins and tail of a fish. He sat a long while in amazement, fearful either to touch the superhuman object or go away and leave it. At length, having made an offering of the incense of tobacco, and addressed it as the guardian angel of his country, he ventured to lay his hand upon the statue to lift it into his canoe, when it disappeared." [1]

The Laches worshipped every stone as a god, and said they had all been men, and all men were converted into stones after death, and the day was coming when all stones would be raised as men. The shadows of stones were the manifestation of the gods in them.[2] The inhabitants of Istlavacan had a rock three feet high and one foot thick, supposed to be a distorted human face, which they reverenced.[3]

Many stones of the shape of men and women, found in Peru, are, according to tradition, beings metamorphosed. Arriaga mentions metamorphoses of men to stones, and the worship of these stones.

How vividly this recalls to our minds the myth of Deucalion and the derivation of the Greek word λαοι (people), the primitive meaning of which was "stones"! The famous Oneida stone from which the Oneidas claim descent, is an illustration of mythical descent from stones. Mr. Schoolcraft thinks they were prompted to this absurdity by the use of metaphorical language; but I am convinced that cases of this kind have arisen from a mythical metamorphosis. Much of the stone-

---

[1] Schoolcraft's Nar. Journal, 406. [2] Piedrahita, bk. 1, ch. ii.
[3] 3 Bancroft, 482.

worship has arisen in this way, as we have seen by the myths I have cited in reference to these stones. If we remember that a mythical character is often the subject of such a metamorphosis, and such mythical character may have been one from whom a tribe claims descent, then we have all the premises for such a conclusion as the Oneidas arrived at. This stone became a place for national sacrifice.[1] The Dacotahs claimed descent from a stone, and offered sacrifices to it, calling it grandfather. They thought the spirit of their ancestor was present in this stone, which is their altar for national sacrifices. The Ojibways had such stones, which they called grandfather.

Animation was ascribed to all stones that were objects of worship. In cases of supposed metamorphosis, the spirit remained in the stone notwithstanding the change.

Many of the rocks which presented any similarity to man or animal were supposed to be inhabited by spirits, and were held in great awe by the Indians, whether a metamorphosis was ascribed to them or not. Spirits transmigrated into stones, and this made them objects of worship.

A curious illustration of such transmigration is found among the Peruvians. A certain stone supposed to be animated by a spirit, which had commanded resistance to the Inca Rocca, was ordered thrown from the top of a mountain by this Inca, when a parrot flew out of it and entered another stone, which the Indians still point out and worship.[2]

In Central America, when a lord died, a stone was put into his mouth to receive his soul.[3]

The Mexicans buried a small green stone with the dead, and this was called the principle of his life, and into it the soul was thought to pass.

The natives of Mizteca worshipped an emerald which was inhabited by a spirit which had transmigrated thither. In Esmeraldas there was a great emerald which belonged to the lord of Manta. It contained a powerful spirit, and was an object of

---

[1] Schoolcraft's Iroquois, 46–47.   [2] Montesinos, 147.   [3] Ximenez, 211.

great veneration. On certain occasions it was displayed and worshipped. It cured diseases, and pilgrimages were made from all parts, of those afflicted, to sacrifice and pray to the stone.[1]

It would not be inconsistent for peoples holding such ideas to ascribe vitality and power of activity to stones; and such is the fact. There were many traditions among the Mexicans about their famous stone, which was selected for a sacrificial stone. On its way to Mexico, notwithstanding all the honors paid it, it broke through the causeway, and carried the high-priest and many others to the bottom of the lake. According to tradition, it spoke frequently on the journey to that city.[2]

Among the Brazilians, the most popular charms worn by the Indians are stones called muira-kitans, which appear to be stones cut from rocks at the bottom of lakes. There is a tradition that they were alive in the lake, and the women, by giving them a drop of their blood, could catch them.[3]

Among the natives of the West Indies food was regularly offered to certain stones that were objects of worship, and they supposed the food was eaten when it disappeared.

The Ojibways thought some of the stones that were worshipped by them moved about from place to place.[4]

The following story of a Northern Indian illustrates the supposed vitality of stones and the worship paid them on this account. Opposite La Pointe was an isolated boulder, which was a huge erratic rock. Otamigan, an Indian well known among the whites, sacrificed to this stone, and never passed it without laying an offering of tobacco on it. He often went to pay worship to it. His attention was attracted to it in the following way. He sat down to rest himself at one time opposite this rock, and as he was looking at it the rock oscillated, made a bow, and advanced toward him. This transient giddiness of Otamigan produced the greatest veneration in his mind

---

[1] Cieza, 183-84.
[3] Smith's Brazil, 581-82.
[2] 5 Bancroft, 471.
[4] McKenny's Tour, 402.

for this rock, and he considered it thereafter as his protecting god.[1]

Among the Ojibways, in the copper region, the erratic blocks of that ore were considered highly mysterious, and were raised to the dignity of idols. Mr. Kohl tells a story of an Ojibway chief who was willing to give him his daughter, or anything else he had, but a mass of copper in a forest, which had been his and his ancestors' protective genius. Through it he said he had won victories in battle, preserved his health, and been successful in the hunt. At last he consented to part with it, but he sacrificed the price given to his guardian spirit, after having made as sharp a bargain as he could, and laid five pounds of tobacco in its place in the forest.[2] It was the spirit that inhabited this lump of copper that gave it its significance, and when the metal was removed from its locality it lost its sacred character, and the tobacco was supposed to satisfy the spirit lurking about the place.

Says Allouez, "The Ottawas often find at the bottom of Lake Superior pieces of pure copper weighing from ten to twenty pounds. I have often seen them in the hands of the savages, and, as they are superstitious, they look upon them as so many divinities. For this reason they preserve these pieces of copper wrapped up among their most precious movables. There are some who have preserved them for more than fifty years. Others have had them in their families from time immemorial, and cherish them as household gods. For some time there was visible a great rock entirely of copper, the top of which projected above the surface of the water. This gave occasion to by-passers to go and cut off pieces from it. Nevertheless, when I passed by that place, nothing could be seen of it. I believe that the storms, which here are very frequent and similar to those on the sea, have covered this rock with sand. Our savages wanted to persuade me that it was a divinity, and had disappeared for some reason which they did not state."

---

[1] Kohl's Kitchi-Gami, 59.   [2] Ib., 62–64.

We find among the inhabitants of both hemispheres at the first dawn of civilization a peculiar predilection for stones which, on account of some peculiarity of color or natural form, are looked upon with superstition. West of Rock River a stone was found which the Indians venerated, and had adorned with paint and a feather. It was a piece of syenite that differed from all the rocks in this vicinity. They made offerings to it.[1] Mr. Keating mentions many other such places, all objects of worship. The White Dog gens of the Ojibways resided near a rock, which on account of its form was an object of great superstition to them.[2]

The Dacotahs propitiated those spirits which were supposed to be embodied in oval-shaped stones by sacrifices of tobacco and other trifling articles.[3] When a Dacotah is troubled in spirit and desires to be delivered from real or imaginary danger, he will select a stone that is round and portable, and, placing it in a spot free from grass and underbrush, he will streak it with red paint, and, offering to it some feathers, he will pray to it for help.[4] The Ojibways regard round stones with awe. They will pick them up, paint them, clear away the grass, make an offering, and then pray the stone to deliver them from danger.[5] The Red Pipe-Stone quarry is a famous place to inspire the Indians with religious feelings. There are five large erratic boulders near here, where not a blade of grass is broken or bent by the feet of man. The Indians venerate these so reverently that they stand at a distance and offer tobacco by throwing it toward these boulders, and then they solicit permission of the spirits supposed to reside here to carry away some of the stone:[6] they would not dare carry away any of it without these propitiatory offerings. The Northwestern Indians had stones from which they asked rain or wind, or a cessation of it.[7] About fifty-five miles above Fort Gratiot was the White Rock, an enormous detached mass of transition limestone

---

[1] 1 Keating, 298.   [2] ib., 149.   [3] 1 Minn. Hist. Coll., 461.
[4] Neill's Minnesota, 60.   [5] 3 Schoolcraft, 229.   [6] 2 Catlin, 203.
[7] 1 Brown's Races, 59.

standing in the lake at a distance of half a mile from the shore. The White Rock is an object which had attracted the early notice of the Indians, who are the first to observe the nonconformities in the appearances of a country. And it continues to be one of the places at which offerings are made. These tributary acknowledgments are generally useless articles. There does not appear to be any obligation upon individuals to make them, or to renew them at any regular periods.[1]

At the entrance to Lake Superior there is a high rock in the shape of a man, which the Indians call the master of life. Here they make their offerings by throwing tobacco into the water. By this they intend to make an acknowledgment to the rock for the blessings they enjoy.[2]

Near Peoria there is a sacred stone resembling the figure of a man. The Indians who pass by pay their adorations to it, and believe it has an influence over their fortunes.[3] One on Little Manitou Creek is supposed to resemble the bust of a man whose head is decorated with the horns of a stag. On Stone Idol Creek, some few miles from the Missouri, there are two other stones resembling the human form, and a third like that of a dog, all of which are objects of veneration. Another, near Big Manitou Creek, is inlaid with flints of various colors and covered with figures of animals. Stones were also oracles. Any rock or stone of extraordinary appearance becomes the object of general veneration.[4]

In the country of the Mandans there is a smooth, porous mineral body twenty feet in circumference, called the Great Medicine Stone. To this stone a deputation is sent every spring, who, after smoking and presenting the pipe before it, retire to an adjacent wood and return in the morning to read the destinies of the nation, which they imagine they see written thereon in certain marks.[5]

---

[1] Schoolcraft's Nar. Journal, 87, seq.   [2] Long's Voyages, 43.
[3] Pittman's European Settlements, 42.
[4] 1 Hind, 364; 2 Beltrami, 175; Kercheval's Valley of Va., 48.
[5] 3 Warden's U. S., 581.

In Guatemala a stone was the oracle through which a god gave his decision to the people after having been consulted by the judges. To the westward of Patinamit there was a mound that commanded the city. On it stood a round small building six feet high, in the middle of which was a pedestal formed of a shining substance resembling glass. Seated around this building, the judges heard and decided upon the causes brought before them; before executing a sentence, however, it was necessary to have it confirmed by an oracle, for which purpose three of the judges quitted their seats, and proceeded to a deep ravine, where there was a place of worship, wherein was placed a black, transparent stone. On the surface of this tablet the deity was supposed to give a representation of the fate that awaited the criminal. If the decision of the judges was approved, the sentence was immediately inflicted. If nothing appeared on the stone, the accused was set at liberty. This oracle was also consulted in the affairs of war.[1]

Thus it will be seen that stones were worshipped because they were supposed to be animated by spirits, and the worship was idolatrous in its nature. Before leaving the subject of idolatry, let us notice its use in sorcery. All of the tribes of both continents use idolatry in their sorcery. When they wish to injure any one, they make an image of the person. They then injure this image, expecting the person to suffer as acutely as though the injury was inflicted on his body. They sometimes burn these images, and then they expect the death of the person. They pretend to cure disease by means of the same superstition; for, having made an effigy of the supposed evil spirit producing the disease, generally thought to be an animal, they will destroy this image, and thereby expect to destroy the disease.[2]

When they want to overcome any one who resists their love, they make an image of the person, and into this image they introduce love-powders. If the image has a lock of hair or

---

[1] Juaro's Guatemala, 384. [2] Kohl, 282.

any part of the person desired to be affected attached to it, these powders will work their charm on the person as effectually as if really taken by such person.[1]

The sorcerers are often told to transfer from the sick person to some other, who is the patient's enemy, the disease they are called to cure. This they can always do when they can get an image of that person.[2]

The same superstition is resorted to in times of famine, to bring animals within the power of the hunter. A little image is made to represent the animal which they wish to obtain in the hunt; then the part representing the heart is punctured with a sharp instrument. After this ceremony they will start out with full confidence of success.[3] Sometimes simply a grass or cloth image of the animal is made and hung up in his wigwam. After repeating an incantation he shoots at the image, and if the arrow enters it he will succeed in killing the animal.[4]

To prove the universality of this curious superstition among all the tribes, I will select a few authorities. Says Charlevoix, "Amongst the Illinois and almost all the other nations, they make small figures to represent those whose days they have a mind to shorten, and which they stab to the heart. At other times they take a stone, and by means of certain invocations they pretend to form such another in the heart of their enemy."[5]

The Ojibways believe that by drawing the figure of any person in sand or ashes, or on clay, or by considering any object as the figure of a person, and then pricking it with a sharp stick, or other substance, or doing in any other manner that which done to a living body would cause pain or injury, the individual represented, or supposed to be represented, will suffer accordingly.[6]

The Malemutes of the Northwest made images to represent children which they wished to have, and fondled the idol as if

---

[1] Kohl, 396–97.
[2] 2 Keating, 159.
[3] Tanner's Narrative, 174.
[4] 1 Schoolcraft, 372.
[5] 2 Charlevoix, 166.
[6] Henry's Captivity.

it was a real child.[1] They expected to obtain children by this means.

Another form of this superstition about the representation of any person or thing was shown in their fear of having their photographs taken. They refused to risk their lives before a photographic apparatus. They said those who had their photograph had their spirit, and they did not wish this to pass into the keeping of others who could torment it at pleasure.[2] The Yanktons accused Catlin of producing a great scarcity of buffalo by putting a great many of them in his book.[3] They refused at first to be painted by him, on account of the same superstition. These paintings were supposed to have their life in them. He had great difficulty in overcoming this superstition. The Araucanians would not allow their portraits to be taken, lest the possessor might obtain some magical influence over them. I will not dwell longer on these fetichistic conceptions in this chapter, but will treat of the subject more fully in the next.

---

[1] 1 Bancroft, 82. [2] 1 ib., 245.
[3] 2 Catlin's Illustrations, 194.

CHAPTER IV.

FETICHISTIC SUPERSTITIONS.

Fetichism—Scalping fetichistic in conception—Inherence of spiritual force—Cannibalism fetichistic and a religious act—Eating images of gods a rite similar to the eucharistic—Superstitious fears about pronouncing the names of the dead—Tattooing fetichistic—Amulets—Primitive ornamentation fetichistic.

THE fetichism of primitive peoples is not a meaningless superstition, as generally represented, but has grown from the roots of their religious belief. A fetich is not the inanimate, powerless, material thing to them that it is to us, but is redolent with life. The idol is filled with a spirit; it speaks in the oracle. So the fetich, whether a medicine-bag, or image, or claw of beast or bird, is filled with a spirit. This imaginary animation gives fetichism its power over the savage mind. The fetichistic superstition has prolonged its life to our day. It survives in amulets, charms, talismans, seal-rings, heraldry. Among early peoples it originated their ornamentation with feathers, teeth, shells, animal skins, and similar articles of personal adornment, including tattooing. Idolatry and fetichism are closely akin, but an idol is not, strictly speaking, a fetich; it is always an object of worship, whereas fetiches are not always objects of worship, but are often connected with sorcery. They are generally amuletic in their character. Their supposed supernatural power is used to ward off evil from their owners or bring them good fortune; they are also used to bring evil upon others. They are generally regarded as subject to the will and control of their owners, and are, therefore, generally not objects of such reverence as inspires worship. The doctrine of fetiches has led to many superstitions that may properly be called fetichistic, and a few of these will explain the origin of the fetichistic sentiment. Among these were scalping and the taking and preservation of the heads of enemies by so many primitive peoples. It was thought that the possession of any part of an enemy placed that enemy in the power of the possessor. This superstition seems to be based upon the belief that each portion of any animate body, or inanimate body supposed to be animate, had also a portion of the spirit that appertained to the whole. Hence, whoever possessed a part of the material substance possessed also a portion of the spiritual, and although it was only a portion, generally a very small part, yet it gave the possessor a control over the whole, which he would never have succeeded in getting in an ordinary way. This explains the whole system of sorcery as practised among ancient peoples, and all its kindred superstitions. Hence arose a desire to prevent any part of the body from getting into the possession and under the control of others. For this reason sorcerers and witches were anxious to get some part of the person upon whom they wished to work their spells, and enemies were very anxious to get some part of their enemy into their possession. Friends were just as anxious to preserve them, and would risk their lives to prevent the scalp of a tribesman from falling into the enemy's hands. Individuals would conceal their nail-parings and hair, and even their saliva, with superstitious fear of its falling into the hands of the unfriendly. Even the clothes of a person were supposed to be permeated by his spiritual life. This belief in the inherence of spiritual life is shown in the fact that, in washing their soiled clothes, many of the tribes were very careful to dispose of the water so that no one could obtain any of it. This superstition was akin to the fetichistic, where a part of the soul is thought to inhere in every part of the body and in everything the body touched.

Quite a curious illustration of their belief on this subject is found in the marriage of the fishing-nets. The Hurons married their nets every year to young girls of the tribe, with much more formality than that observed in human wedlock. The Algonkins of the Ottawa had the same ceremony yearly, in the middle of March, and, as it was difficult to find virgins, mere children were chosen. The net was held between them, and its spirit was harangued. They said the spirit of the net appeared to them when it had any complaint to make. The animation ascribed to these nets was due beyond doubt to the spiritual substance of the fish which was thought to inhere in them. This whole ceremony is meaningless, except by this inherence or transmigration of spiritual life, which explains it.

Preserving parts of dead enemies was fetichistic in conception. The Omaguas cut off the heads of their enemies and preserved them in their houses. The teeth they strung and wore as necklaces.[1] The Mundrucus of Brazil kept the heads of slain enemies. They had a preparatory process for preserving them. The custom of wearing the skulls of slain enemies as fetiches was the origin of trepanning. Those trepanned skulls were found in Peru, and also among the Northern tribes. This custom is very prevalent among the barbarous tribes on the other continent, but among the Americans scalping appears to have generally superseded it; yet upon the monuments of the Mexican nations the entire skull is seen strung to the belts of many of the heroes whose achievements are pictured thereon.

Scalping was universal among the Northern tribes, and was fetichistic in origin. The Osages planted on their graves a pole with an enemy's scalp hanging to the top. Their notion was that by doing this the spirit of the victim became subjected to the spirit of the buried warrior.[2] Mr. Brown thinks that scalping has superseded the taking of the whole head, on account of the difficulty of carrying the entire head.[3] This view is confirmed by the fact that many tribes scalped the heads of those taken in war only when they travelled a great distance. Sorcerers pretended to hold converse with the departed spirit through the scalp of the deceased.[4]

The Indians of the Algonkin stock living around the Great

---

[1] 3 Southey, 703. [2] 1 Tylor, 460.
[3] 1 Brown's Races, 67. [4] 1 Bancroft, 569.

Lakes, in addition to the practice of scalping, cut fingers, arms, and other limbs from their enemies, which they keep as long as they can, and toward which they show as strong a spirit of revenge as though the whole person was present and in life.[1] The Californians do not appear to scalp enemies, but the head, hands, or feet are preserved as trophies.[2] The savages of New Granada wore the teeth of slain enemies about their necks.

The use of parts of the human body for fetichistic purposes is common. Mr. Spencer says the primitive idea that any property characterizing an aggregate inheres in all parts of it, implies a corollary from this belief. The soul present in the body of a dead man preserved entire is also present in preserved parts of his body: hence the faith in relics. The Crees carried bones and hair of dead persons about for three years. Several Guiana tribes had their cleaned bones distributed among the relatives after death. The Eskimos, when a whaler died, cut his body into small pieces and distributed them among his fellow-craftsmen. These were dried and preserved as fetiches; they rubbed the points of their lances upon them to bring them luck.[3] Such a weapon would reach a mortal spot in a whale where another would fail. The Caribs thought that the bones of the dead were the abiding-place of his soul. They took bones of the dead from the grave and carefully wrapped them in cotton, and thought they could answer questions. The Mexicans had a grand master of such relics.[4] They thought the left arm and hand of a woman who had died in childbed had special talismanic virtue.[5]

The fear that some part of the body might be used by others in sorcery and witchcraft led to the custom of preserving all of its parts during life and also after death, lest it should get into the possession of others. This superstition will be referred to again in burial customs.

Cannibalism was fetichistic in its nature, and originated in

---

[1] Kohl, 345–46. [2] Ib., 344. [3] 1 Bancroft, 76.
[4] 2 ib., 202. [5] 2 ib., 269.

the same superstitious idea that instigated scalping and cutting off the heads and limbs of enemies. Its prevalence among all primitive peoples is probable.

Among the Northern tribes of Indians there are evidences of a limited cannibalism. It was practised at religious festivals to some extent, and I am fully persuaded, after investigating the subject pretty thoroughly, that the practice, except in a few isolated cases, was based upon religious superstition. All primitive peoples thought that by eating anything animate they became endowed with the qualities of the thing eaten. This superstition was the result of their theories of transmigration. We have the very best evidence that in those cases where the dead have been buried in the stomachs of their living relatives, which will be noticed in the chapter on burial, the superstitious idea of the transmigration of the soul into their bodies urged them to the act.

Mr. Keating says the Ojibways, the Miamis, the Potawatomies, and all the other Algonkin tribes are cannibals. The most frequent cause of cannibalism among them is their belief that by eating an enemy they acquire a charm that makes them irresistible. There is a common superstition with them that he who tastes of the body of a brave man acquires a part of his valor, and if he can eat of his heart, the centre of all courage, his share of bravery is greater. Mr. Barron saw the Potawatomies feast on the bodies of white men and Cherokees, instigated by the same superstition. Captain Wells, who was killed in the vicinity of Chicago in 1812, and was celebrated for his valor among the Indian tribes, was divided into many parts and sent to all the allied tribes, that all might have an opportunity to get a taste of the courageous white man.[1] The Thlinkeets devoured those killed in battle, in the belief that the bravery of the victim thereby enters into the nature of the partakers.[2] The Californian tribes ate human flesh, not as food, nor for the purpose of wreaking vengeance on, or showing

---

[1] 1 Keating, 101–3.   [2] 1 Bancroft, 106.

hate to, a dead adversary, but because they thought by eating part of a brave man they absorbed a portion of his courage.[1] Mr. Dall says some of the natives of Alaska practise cannibalism, but it was not instigated by starvation.[2]

Traces of cannibalism are found among all the tribes of America. Mr. Parkman mentions a family of the Miamis whose duty it was to devour the bodies of prisoners. The act had a religious character, and was attended with ceremonial observances. The Hurons had cannibal feasts, and when remonstrated with by the Jesuit priests they threw a hand of a victim in at their door. The Mohawks ate those captured in war: the chiefs ate the head and heart, the common people the arms and trunks. Among the Blackfeet, when war is declared against other nations, the manner of expressing it is, "to hang the kettle on the fire," which has its origin in the barbarous custom of eating the prisoners and those that were slain, after they had boiled them. Traces of cannibalism are found among the Winnebagoes, Sauks, and Comanches.[3]

Pyrlæus says "the Five Nations formerly did eat human flesh; they at one time ate up a whole body of the French king's soldiers."[4]

Heckewelder mentions the same custom among the Iroquois. He says, "Aged French Canadians have told me, many years since, while I was at Detroit, that they had frequently seen the Iroquois eat the flesh of those who had been slain in battle, and that this was the case in the war between the French and English, commonly called the War of 1756."[5]

Says Megapolensis of the Delawares, "They eat captives, after having burned them with a slow fire."[6]

Says Roubaud of the Ottawas, "The first object which presented itself to my eyes, on arriving at the encampment of the Ottawas, was a large fire, while the wooden spits fixed in the earth

---

[1] 1 Bancroft, 380. [2] Alaska, 49.
[3] 1 Keating, 233; 1 Schoolcraft, 135. [4] Heckewelder, 235.
[5] Ib., 37, note.
[6] Megapolensis and De Vries, N. Y. Hist. Coll., 2d Series, vol. iii. 155-59.

gave signs of a feast. There was indeed one taking place. But, oh, Heaven! what a feast! The remains of the body of an Englishman was there, the skin stripped off, and more than one-half the flesh gone. A moment after, I perceived these inhuman beings eat with famishing avidity of this human flesh. I saw them taking up this detestable broth in large spoons, and apparently without being able to satisfy themselves with it. They informed me that they had prepared themselves for this feast by drinking from skulls filled with human blood, while their smeared faces and stained lips gave evidence of the truth of the story."[1]

Says Josselyn, " At Martha's Vineyard, certain Indians whilst I was in the country seized upon a boat that put into a by-cove, killed the men, and ate them up in a short time before they were discovered."[2]

The following description of a cannibal feast among the Ojibways is given by Henry: " An invitation to a feast is given by him who is the master of it. Small cuttings of cedar wood of about four inches in length supply the place of cards, and the bearer, by word of mouth, states the particulars. Seven prisoners were killed, and shortly after two of the Indians took one of the dead bodies which they chose as being the fattest, cut off its head, and divided the whole into five parts, one of which was put into each of five kettles hung over as many fires kindled for this purpose at the door of the prison lodge. An invitation came to Wawatam to assist at the feast. Wawatam obeyed the summons, taking with him, as is usual, his dish and spoon. After an absence of about half an hour, he returned, bringing in his dish a human hand and a large piece of flesh. He did not appear to relish the repast, but told me that it was then and always had been the custom among all the Indian nations when returning from war to make a war feast from among the slain."[3] There was a lake in the Red River country

---

[1] Roubaud, in Kip., 155.   [2] Josselyn's Two Voyages to New England, 125.
[3] Henry's Captivity.

called Lake Windigoostigon, or Cannibal Lake, in commemoration of deeds of cannibalism committed there by Ojibways in 1811.

Among the Ojibways early cannibalism appears to have passed into their traditionary history embodied in a myth. They had an imaginary being whose deeds were horrible in the extreme. The ghostly man-eater, a species of vampire, had his residence on an island (imaginary) in the centre of Lake Superior. He had the appearance of the human form, yet intangible, with long nails with which he dug up dead bodies and devoured them, or robbed the burial-scaffold of its burden. He travelled with lightning speed from one place to another, and whenever the Indian heard strange songs above his wigwam, it was the ghostly man-eater hurrying upon the wings of the wind from a recent banquet to his mysterious island home. This spiritual monstrosity appears to have been doomed to this life as a punishment for an act of cannibalism, when he killed and fed upon the body of a youth who was the last remnant of a once powerful tribe. Having thus extinguished the last hope of an Indian race for perpetuation by this bloody act, the Ojibways have handed down his infamy in their folk-lore.[1]

Another mythological character which belongs to our subject was a giant, who came from the north and sought the hospitality of an Indian village bordering on the Lake of the Woods. He was entertained at their expense, and when the feast was ready the giant, disdaining the wild rice and game, destroyed with one exception the inhabitants who had gathered at his feast, and devoured their dead bodies. The youth who escaped carried revenge in his heart, and when he became a great hunter he invited the cannibal giant to a feast, and into his bowl of soup he placed a bitter root, which soon deprived him of his strength. He prepared to sleep, and under him was spread his robe of weasel-skins, and over him was thrown his

---

[1] Lanman's Haw-Hoo-Hoo, 195-96.

net woven by a mammoth spider. When deep sleep had fallen upon him, the guests despatched him with their clubs, and his flesh became alive very soon with little animals and birds, who fed upon it.[1] Truly he was a fit companion for the giant Ymer of the Norse folk-lore.

The Indians of Brazil and Paraguay formerly delighted in human flesh. They confessed, after the introduction of Christianity, that the flesh of animals tasted insipid to them in comparison with that of men.[2] The Botecudos sucked the blood from living victims, thinking they would imbibe spiritual force.[3]

The Brazilians had human flesh salted and smoked and hung up in their houses. One man boasted that he had partaken of the bodies of three hundred enemies. But it was a stronger passion than hunger that gave these accursed banquets their highest relish.[4] Children were raised by their captives from tribal women for the express purpose of being eaten. In their great cannibal feasts the women were the most ravenous cannibals, and even the children had the brains and tongue allotted to them. Every part of the body was devoured.[5] One of the children raised from captives, whom the Portuguese offered to redeem and save from a feast to which she was dedicated, preferred, she said, to be buried in the bellies of her lords and masters whom she loved.[6]

Among the Brazilians, the first food given a child when weaning it from its mother's milk was the flesh of an enemy.[7] The bones of those eaten were laid up in piles before their houses, and the rank and estimation of a family were in proportion to the size of its heap.[8]

Prisoners dedicated to a cannibal feast were treated well, had attendants appointed for them and women given them. They were fattened, and paraded up and down with great ceremony. Every guest invited to the feast came and touched the prisoner,

---

[1] Lanman, 235.   [2] 2 Dobriz., 26.   [3] 3 Southey, 808.
[4] 1 Southey, 17.   [5] 1 ib., 218-22.   [6] 1 ib., 640.
[7] 2 ib., 289.   [8] 1 ib., 655.

who was treated like a god.[1] Mr. Southey thinks the motive for their cannibalism was some savage notion of superstition.[2]

The priests of Guatemala ate the bodies of those who were sacrificed. It was considered sacred meat.[3]

Cieza, speaking of the Peruvians, says, "All the Indians of this country eat human flesh."[4] Cieza saw them eat in one day more than a hundred men and women they had taken in war.[5] Drawing blood from the nose of a child in Peru was a relic of cannibalism. The more uncivilized Peruvians always ate the flesh of those whom they sacrificed to their gods;[6] and the bodies of the victims were cut up and exposed for sale, and sold in the public markets.[7] Peruvian mythology had its giants who were cannibals, who were exterminated by a resplendent young man who came riding upon the clouds, shining like the sun, and hurling flames of fire.[8]

Cannibalism prevailed among the Mexicans. The bodies of those slain on the field of battle were devoured by those voracious cannibals who followed the armies to feed on the dead bodies.[9] The towns had wooden cages where they kept and fattened, for the purpose of eating, the captives in war.[10] Human flesh, exquisitely prepared, was found upon the table of Montezuma, and was eaten by the Mexicans, not for the purpose of allaying appetite, but from religious motives.[11] All the Nahua nations practised this religious cannibalism. That cannibalism as a source of food, unconnected with religious rites, was ever practised, there is little evidence. Sahagun and Las Casas regard the cannibalism of the Nahuas as an abhorrent feature of their religion, and not as an unnatural appetite. They ate the flesh of their sacrificed foes only.[12]

The Mayas also ate the flesh of human victims sacrificed to the gods. In Nicaragua, the high-priest received the heart, the king the feet and hands, the captors took the thighs, and the

---

[1,2] Southey, 370.   [3] ib., 709.   [3] Ximenez, 183.
[4] Cieza, 46.   [5] Ib., 78.   [6] Ranking, 89.
[7] Ib., 77.   [8] 1 Zarate, 17.   [9] 1 ib., 267.
[10] Diaz, 496.   [11] 2 Bancroft, 176.   [12] 2 ib., 357-58; Diaz, 66.

tripe was given to the trumpeters. The natives of Honduras said the Spaniards were too tough and bitter to be eaten.¹ "The Mosquito men never gave quarter to any but women; but as many men and children as they take they tie and throw upon a barbecue, as they call it, which is a rack of stakes doing the office of a gridiron, and make a good fire underneath, which, with the help of the sun overhead at noon, soon dresses their bodies fit for their teeth, which food they esteem best of any. But before this cookery, whilst the prisoner lives, they draw out his finger and toe nails, and knock out his teeth with stones, which teeth and nails they wear about their necks like a necklace." ²

Many Brazilian tribes manifested their love for the dead by reducing the bones to powder, and mingling it with a bread which they then ate. Love, as well as hatred, leads to cannibalism, and an Artemisia could be found in every Tapuya widow.

Among the Tapuyas, when an infant died it was eaten by the parents. Adults were eaten by the kindred, and their bones were pounded and reserved for marriage-feasts, as being the most precious thing that could be offered.³ When they became old they offered themselves to their children, who devoured them after putting them to death. They thought their spiritual substance became incorporated.⁴

The Xomanas and Passes burned the bones of the dead, and drank the ashes, and in this way, they thought, they received into their bodies the spirits of their deceased friends.

The Maypuris devoured their sick and infirm.⁵

The Arawaks pounded the bones of their dead lords into powder, and drank them.

The ancient Peruvians ate their deceased parents.

I have dwelt longer upon the painful subject of cannibalism than might seem desirable, in order to show its religious char-

---

[1] 2 Bancroft, 725.
[2] Descrip. Mosquito Kingdom, Churchill's Coll. Voy., vol. vi. p. 291.
[3] 1 Southey, 379. [4] Denis, Brésil, 9. [5] 1 Southey, 590.

acter and prevalence everywhere. Instead of being confined to savage peoples, as is generally supposed, it prevailed to a greater extent and with more horrible rites among the most civilized. Its religious inception was the cause of this.

The origin of a religious rite among the aboriginal Americans similar to the eucharistic among Roman Catholics is undoubtedly based upon the primitive superstition, that by eating a part of any animate body, or body supposed to be animate, the partaker is endowed with the qualities of that body. This superstition was very prevalent among the various tribes who thought they became endowed with the qualities of the animal eaten. It developed itself in cannibalism, which had a strangely protracted life in the semi-civilization of America, and it manifested itself in the eucharistic idol and feast of the Aztecs. This singular rite was called Teoqualo,—that is, "the eating of the god." A figure of Huitzilopochtli was made in dough, and after certain ceremonies they made a pretence of killing it and dividing it into morsels, which were eaten by the worshippers as a sacred food.[1]

The superstition underlying idolatry explains this apparently meaningless rite. They supposed their idol was animate, and the spiritual substance inhered in the material of the idol and passed into their bodies with it and was assimilated. Thus a transmigration of a portion of the spiritual substance of a god was accomplished. One of these eucharistic ceremonies is thus described by Herrera : " An idol made of all the varieties of the seeds and grain of the country was made and moistened with the blood of children and virgins; this idol was broken into small bits, and given by way of communion to men and women to eat, who, to prepare for that festival, bathed and dressed their heads and scarce slept all the night. They prayed, and as soon as it was day were all in the temple to receive that communion, with such singular silence and devotion that though there was an infinite multitude there seemed to be nobody. If

---

[1] Tylor's Anahuac, 280.

any of the idol was left, the priests ate it. Montezuma went to this ceremony attended by abundance of quality and richly dressed."[1] Mendieta mentions the same ceremony, and says, "Gods were eaten in this way; they made idols of seeds, and ate them as though they were the bodies of their gods."[2] These seed idols have a special significance, because the mysterious vitality of a seed and its germinating power impressed itself on all the American tribes, and manifested itself in many rites and ceremonies. The tobacco-plant was supposed to be imbued with the spiritual body of the goddess Ciuacoatl, and was eaten in the eucharistic ceremony to her. The Totomacs had a communion in the following way. Every three years they killed three boys and took out their hearts. From their blood, mixed with certain seeds, they made a paste which was considered a eucharist and a most sacred thing, and was partaken of every six months by men above twenty-five and women above sixteen. They called the paste, food of our souls.[3]

The significance of this rite consisted in a supposed afflux of spiritual life. A transmigration was the explanation of the mystery.

Another fetichistic superstition arose from the animistic beliefs of primitive peoples. Consequent upon their belief in the omnipresence of spirits was a superstitious fear of having their own names spoken aloud or of using the names of the dead.

The superstition prevailed among all the tribes that the utterance of a word at any distance had a direct effect on the object which that word stands for. They thought they could be bewitched through their names as well as their images or parts of their bodies.[4]

The Araucanians would not allow their names to be told to strangers, lest these should be used in sorcery.[5]

The New Mexican tribes never made known their own names or those of friends to a stranger. The Indians of British Co-

---

[1] 2 Herrera, 379.   [2] Mendieta, 108.   [3] Ib., 109.
[4] Tylor's Researches, 124.   [5] 2 Wood, 564.

lumbia had a strong prejudice against telling their own names. Among the Ojibways the name-superstition prevailed. Husbands and wives never told each other's names, and children were told they would stop growing if they repeated their own names.[1] Their names were considered sacred, and were generally kept secret. The names by which the Indians were called were generally not their true names, but were given them for some characteristic peculiarity. The secret name of Pocahontas was Matokes, which was concealed from the English out of superstitious fear.[2] In the mythical story of Hiawatha the same was true, his real name being Tarenyawagon. The Abipones of Paraguay had the same superstition. Mr. Dobrizhoffer says they would knock on his door at night, and when he would ask who was there no answer would come; they were afraid to utter their names. Among some tribes the names of all the acquaintances of a person were changed at his death, to avoid, as far as possible, the recognition of the living by the ghosts of the dead. The Chinooks changed their names when a near relative died, under the impression that spirits would be attracted back to earth if they heard familiar names.[3] The Lenguas of Brazil changed their names on the death of any one, for they believed that the dead knew the names of all whom they had left alive, and might look for them; for this reason they changed their names, hoping that if they returned they could not find them.

The Indians also refrained from mentioning the names of dead persons. Among the New England tribes, if any man bore the name of the dead, he immediately changed his name.[4]

A superstitious fear of pronouncing the names of the dead prevailed everywhere. It was a crime among the Abipones to utter the name of a dead person. A mistake in doing this led to bloody quarrels.[5]

The Fuegians never mentioned the name of the dead.[6]

---

[1] Jones's Ojibways, 162.
[2] 2 Schoolcraft, 66.
[3] 1 Bancroft, 248.
[4] 1 Arnold's Rhode Island, 77.
[5] 2 Dobriz., 444-45.
[6] Darwin's Nat. Voy., 214.

The Indians of Virginia, says Blome, did not mention the name of a dead person, and those having the same name changed it. Among the Western tribes they never mentioned the names of their relations after they were dead.[1]

Among the Northern tribes, when a death occurred, if a relative of the deceased was absent they hung along the road by which he would return something to apprise him of the fact, so that he would not mention the name of the dead on his return. Among the Northwestern tribes the Indians considered it a sacrilege to mention the name of a person after he was dead.[2]

This superstition is found in the Shawnee myth of Yellow Sky, who was a daughter of the tribe, and had dreams which told her she was created for an unheard-of mission. There was a mystery about her being, and none could comprehend the meaning of her evening songs. The paths leading to her father's lodge were more beaten than those to any other. On one condition alone at last she consented to become a wife. That condition was, that he who became her husband should never mention her name. If he did, she cautioned him, a sad calamity would befall him, and he would forever thereafter regret his thoughtlessness. After a time Yellow Sky sickened and died, and her last words were that her husband should never breathe her name. The widower for five summers lived in solitude. But, alas, one day as he was upon the grave of his dead Yellow Sky an Indian asked him whose it was, and he forgot and uttered the forbidden name. He fell to the earth in great pain, and as darkness settled round about him a transformation scene began, and next morning near the grave of Yellow Sky a large buck was quietly feeding. It was the unhappy husband.[3]

The Connecticut tribes never pronounced the names of the dead. If the offence was twice repeated, death was not regarded as a punishment too severe. In 1655, Philip, having

---

[1] Parker's Journal, 251. [2] Harmon's Journal, 349.
[3] Lanman's Haw-Hoo-Hoo, 231–32.

heard that another Indian had spoken the name of a deceased relative of his, came to the island of Nantucket to kill him, and the English had to interfere to prevent it.[1] Among the California tribes the name of the departed was never breathed by the living. If spoken accidentally, a shudder passed over all those present.[2] The Atuas never mentioned the name of the dead. Such an act would have been considered the greatest rudeness.[3] Among the Iroquois, upon the death of a person, his name could not be used again in the lifetime of his oldest surviving son without the consent of the latter.[4]

Tattooing is fetichistic in its origin. Among all the tribes, almost every Indian has the image of an animal tattooed on his breast or arm, which can charm away an evil spirit or prevent harm to them.

It is quite remarkable to find this superstition as prevalent as it was among the more civilized tribes.

The Central Americans tattooed their breasts, arms, and thighs with figures of eagles, serpents, and other animals.[5]

The Nicaraguans practised the same custom. Herrera mentions the custom of tattooing the skin with stags and other such creatures among the natives of Honduras.[6]

The Isthmians tattooed their bodies with the figures of animals and trees.[7]

The Mexicans thought themselves perfectly safe from all harm when their bodies were anointed or painted with an unction, called the divine medicament, composed of a mixture of poisonous insects, such as scorpions and spiders.[8]

Tattooing will be further noticed under animal worship.

All fetiches are supposed to have spiritual intelligent beings who reside in them. In its broadest definition, therefore, fetichism would include the whole subject of primitive religion; but in order to deal with it as a separate subject it is limited to those material objects which are worn or kept about the

---

[1] Beach, 301.   [2] 4 Schoolcraft, 226.   [3] Dall's Alaska, 524.
[4] Morgan's Ancient Society, 79.   [5] Cogolludo, book 4, chap. 5.
[6] 1 Herrera, 262.   [7] 1 Bancroft, 753.   [8] 1 Clavigero, 273.

person for individual use. Fetichism, being dependent on the ghost theory, has of course succeeded it in point of time.

In America we find fetichism among the rudest tribes, but among the civilized Peruvians it became immensely elaborated.

It is plain that a good deal of mental activity has been present among a people that have elaborated the doctrine of fetichism to any extent, as was the case among the Peruvians.

A barren mind could not conceive of an inanimate object having in it some existence besides that which his senses acquaint him with. He could not imagine an invisible entity within a visible one, but showing no evidence of its existence. He has not the mental power to grasp such a conception.[1]

A rude fetichism prevailed among the Eskimos, who loaded themselves with amulets dangling about their necks and arms. They consisted of bones, bills, and claws of birds, which, according to their opinion, had a wonderful virtue to preserve those that wore them from disease and misfortune.[2] The men always kept some part of the seal they had killed, lest they should forfeit their luck. They were very anxious to get a rag or shoe of a European, to hang about their children's necks, that they might acquire European skill and ability thereby. They requested Europeans to blow upon them. The prows of their boats were always adorned with a fox's head, and their harpoons with an eagle's beak. They piled the heads of their seals before their doors, that the souls of the seals might not get angry. The kayak was often adorned with a dead sparrow or snipe, or the feathers or hair of some animal, to ward off danger. Eagles' claws were a great fetich.[3]

It must be borne in mind that the souls of animals among savage peoples were more potent than those of men, and animal fetiches prevailed as early man depended upon the animal world and most of his associations were with it.

The natives of the Yukon territory wear bears' claws and teeth, sables' tails and wolves' ears, porcupine quills and ermine

---

[1] 1 Spencer, 345.   [2] Egede, 198.   [3] 1 Crantz, 200.

skins, beavers' teeth, and the bright-green scalps of the mallard. They pierce the nose to insert shells therein.[1] The Innuits wear beluga teeth. Ear-rings are much worn among them, and the ceremony of boring the ear is a religious one. They also wear images of animals.[2] The Haidahs used small owls and squirrels as amulets. Amulets made of the tusks of some animal akin to the mastodon were found in many of the graves of Tennessee.[3] An Indian who possessed a tooth pronounced by Professor Marsh, when in the Black Hills, to be that of a brontotherium, said it belonged to a big horse struck by lightning.[4] He thought it was a great fetich. The New Mexicans wore feathers of birds, antelopes' toes, and cranes' bills as charms.[5] The Isthmians wore around their necks the figures of animals, and carried about their persons the claws of wild beasts and feathers.[6] The Abipones wore crocodiles' teeth suspended from their neck, and believed they would defend them from the bites of serpents. The Haytians also used such fetiches.[7] In the tombs of all the more civilized American nations small images of animals intended as fetiches were found. The eyes of the cuttle-fish were very popular fetiches in Peru.[8]

The Brazilian savages wore bones in their ears and cheeks as fetiches. One of the tribes wore a parrot's feather through the nose. Animal fetiches were more used than any other, on account of the prevalence of the system of animal manitous hereafter noticed. Among the Northern tribes, boys, when arriving at puberty, selected an animal as a patron, and always wore a piece of the skin or bone of that animal as an amulet, and used every precaution against its loss, which would have been regarded as a great calamity. The young Indian, after having chosen his patron or manitou, yielded to it a sort of worship, propitiated it with offerings of tobacco, thanked it in prosperity, and upbraided it in disaster. The superstition be-

---

[1] Dall, 95. [2] Ib., 140–41. [3] Smithsonian Rep., 1877, 274.
[4] Beach, 259. [5] 1 Bancroft, 522. [6] 1 ib., 752.
[7] 1 Rafinesque, 191. [8] Bollaert, 151.

came mere fetich-worship.[1] If the animal would admit of its skin being made into a bag, it became his medicine-bag. The medicine-bag and its meaning and importance should be understood, as it may be said to be the key to Indian life and Indian character. These bags were constructed of the skins of animals, and ornamented in a thousand different ways as suited the taste or freak of each person. Every Indian carried his medicine-bag, to which he paid the greatest homage, and to which he looked for safety and protection through life. Feasts were often made and dogs and horses sacrificed to a man's medicine-bag, and days and even weeks of fasting and penance of various kinds were often suffered to appease this fetich, which he imagined he had in some way offended. He looked upon this as a supernatural charm or guardian, on which he depended for the preservation of his life. In death it was buried with him, and was thought to be as useful in the next world as in this. If an Indian should sell or give away his medicine-bag, he would be disgraced in his tribe. If it was taken away from him in battle, he was forever subjected to the degrading epithet of "a man without medicine," and he could only restore his honor and replace his medicine by capturing one from an enemy in battle. He could institute his medicine-bag but once in life, and then by a dream.[2] They did not dare touch the medicine-bags of each other, for they would injure any who dared to examine their sacred contents.[3] Before they went to war they examined these as carefully as our soldiers would their cartridge-boxes.[4]

The Tupinambas of Brazil carried their devotion to their maracas farther than the North American to his medicine-bag. These maracas were worshipped. They were supposed to give oracles. They sacrificed human beings to them. They were supposed to be inhabited by a spirit.[5]

These maracas were gourds with pebbles in them. They

---

[1] Parkman's Jes., lxxi. [2] 1 Catlin, 36-37. [3] 1 ib., 154-55.
[4] Kohl, 314. [5] 1 Southey, 202.

were so sacred none but their owners could look at them. Offerings of game and honey were made to them.[1] They performed sacred dances to them. The maraca was made of a fruit so called, was hollow, and had a stick running through it, and on the top of this stick was a tuft of human hair, which undoubtedly gave it its sacred character. Every man of those tribes on the Orinoco had one of these.[2]

The medicine-bag, or maraca, did not exclude the use of other fetiches. Sometimes as many as twenty amulets were found within a medicine-bag. Among the Northern tribes a child's cradle was hung with fetiches to ward off evil.[3]

The Iroquois wore amulets as a defence against witchcraft and sorcery. They were worn on the breast, or suspended from the neck or ears. They were sometimes representations of a human face, but generally a part of some animal.[4]

A great part of their philosophy of medicine consisted of amulets. They believed the possession of certain articles about the person rendered the body invulnerable. Some of them were kept in the medicine-sack, some worn as ornaments. Seashells have always been very popular amulets. The sea appears to have been invested with mystical powers, and any of its inhabitants shared the mystery,—a very reasonable superstition, it would appear, when we look at these colored, glittering, and beautifully-formed objects. Their wampum-strings were always sacred in their eyes, and were a token of the sacred character of treaties. Amulets used in life were buried with the dead.[5]

Among the Peruvians the conopas were the individual deities. If a person found anything that was of peculiar color or figure, it was a conopa, and became a fetich to them. They worshipped them. The bezoar stones, which were very popular conopas, were often found with blood on them, implying a bloody sacrifice. These conopas descended from father to son.[6] They protected their estates against thieves by laying down tortoise-

---

[1] 1 Southey, 379.   [2] 1 ib., 187-88.   [3] Kohl, 8.
[4] Schoolcraft's Iroquois, 137-38.   [5] 1 Schoolcraft, 86.   [6] Arriaga, 14-15.

shells. No one dared enter an estate where there was one of these shells.[1] Flamingoes were used to preserve dwellings from harm. Each Peruvian might have as many fetiches as he pleased. The number was not restricted, as in Mexico, where the king might have six, a noble four, and a plebeian only two. They made little images of llamas, alpacas, vicuñas, huanacas, deer, monkeys, parrots, lizards, and other animals, and carried and worshipped them. Some of them had little cavities in the back, in which sacrifices were placed.[2]

Among the Mexicans, "travellers carried a black stick which was a fetich, for they thought it preserved them from all harm, and when they made a halt they worshipped it."[3]

The Northern tribes used banners as fetiches, on which was a picture of the totemic animal of the tribe. Many heraldic devices, which will be noticed under animal worship, were sketched on skins of animals. An animal chosen as a crest must not be killed or ill treated in the presence of any wearing its figure.

The supposition that the animate creation could be subjected to the control of any who possessed a part has survived even among the most civilized of the American peoples. The superstition has been extended to include a belief which has developed therefrom, that by keeping in possession the bones of an individual of a species, the other members of the species could be influenced thereby.

The natives of Honduras kept the bones of deer in their houses, thinking it gave them power over the deer. If they lost them they would kill no more deer.[4]

The prevalence of these superstitions relating to parts of the bodies of animate creation would develop a desire to preserve with sacred care the bones of the dead, for by obtaining a part of the body of a deceased person the possessor had control over the spirit of the deceased.

---

[1] Oliva, 118-19.
[3] 1 Clavigero, 388.
[2] Rivero and Tschudi, 171-74.
[4] 4 Herrera, 142.

Again, it was the universal desire of primitive peoples to have their bodies kept intact, with the expectation of reanimating them at some future time. The perfection of this reanimated body was prevented, they thought, if the parts were separated. Hence we are led to the consideration of the mortuary customs of the aborigines, and the ceremonies connected therewith, which will elucidate their worship of the dead.

CHAPTER V.

RITES AND CEREMONIES CONNECTED WITH THE DEAD.

Burial-customs—Care of the dead—Interment—Suspension—Cremation—Tombs the primitive altars—The mounds, their builders and uses—Burial-towers—Resurrection of the dead—Sacrifice—Food-offerings the primitive form—Human sacrifices—Tombs the primitive temples.

BURIAL-CUSTOMS and ceremonies are closely connected with the subject of the worship of human spirits. In the performance of this "last act" we can find valuable evidence to aid in our researches on primitive religion. The rites and ceremonies attending the disposition of the dead were religious in their nature, and religious rites are unconscious commentaries on religious beliefs.

The great care of primitive peoples in preserving the bodies of the dead has been instigated by many of their superstitions, prominent among which was their belief in a resurrection. The doctrine of the resurrection was the most deeply-rooted and wide-spread conviction of the Indian mind. It is indissolubly connected with their highest theories of a future life. The Delawares told Loskiel, " We Indians shall not forever die. Even the grains of corn grow up and become living things." The Indians thought the soul would return to the bones and be clothed again with flesh.[1]

Their belief that dreams were produced by the soul's departure from and return to the body was akin to their belief in resurrection. The only difference between sleep and death to the primitive mind consisted in the extent of time the soul was absent. In both the soul would return; in both the body

---

[1] Brinton, 272-73.

would reawake. The custom which we have noticed of burying the dead quickly after death in many tribes, and with no medical skill to know whether life was extinct, resulted often in the return of the supposed dead man to life, and thus afforded practical proof of a resurrection to the savage mind. This doctrine of a resurrection manifested itself in Oriental art in the production of the topes. In Egypt the pyramids are an evidence of it. In Greek literature Antigone is an expression of this thought.

The same superstitious care of the bodies of the dead which has inspired so many classical tales is found among even the rudest of the American tribes. Says Del Techo of those tribes inhabiting Brazil and its vicinity, "They carefully keep the bones of their relatives; nor is there any affront they avenge with so much war and slaughter as when you upbraid them that the bones of their ancestors have been lost for want of looking after."[1] Mr. Humboldt says, in speaking of the cave of Ataruipe, in Guiana, which he thought to be the grave of an extinct tribe, "We counted about six hundred well-preserved skeletons placed in as many caskets formed of the stalks of palm-leaves. These skeletons were so perfect that not a rib or finger was wanting."[2] Among the Northern tribes the bones of the dead were preserved with scrupulous care, and if one was missing it would be looked for till found. Even the comfort of the body was looked after. Says Arriaga of the Peruvians, "They are convinced that corpses feel, eat, and drink, and will rise again, and are much better satisfied with vaults, where they do not suffer with a load of earth placed upon them."[3] They so skilfully embalmed the bodies of their deceased Incas that they were as successful as the Egyptians in perpetuating the existence of the body beyond the limits assigned to it by nature.[4]

Among the tribes of North America, unless the rites of burial

---

[1] 4 Churchill, Coll. Voy., 705.
[2] Views of Nature, 171.
[3] Arriaga, 40–41.
[4] 1 Prescott's Peru, 33–34.

were properly performed, many of them thought the spirits of the dead wandered upon the earth in great unhappiness. Hence arose their solicitude to get possession of the bodies of the slain.[1] Among the Ottawas a great famine was thought to have been produced on account of the failure of some of their tribesmen to perform these burial-rites. After having repaired their fault they were blessed with an abundance of provisions.[2]

Many of the nomadic tribes carried their dead with them in their migrations. Heckewelder gives a curious instance of this in the following words:

"These Nanticokes had the singular custom of removing the bones of their deceased friends from the old burial-place to a place of deposit in the country they now dwell in. In earlier times they were known to go from Wyoming and Chemenk to fetch the bones of their dead from the Eastern Shore of Maryland, even when the bodies were in a putrid state, so that they had to take off the flesh and scrape the bones clean before they could carry them along. I well remember having seen them between the years 1750 and 1760 loaded with such bones, which, having flesh on them, caused a disagreeable stench as they passed through the town of Bethlehem."[3]

This disposition of each tribe to cling to the earthly remains of their kindred would originate the custom of burial in gentes or families. We find a good deal of evidence to show that this was done in early times. Mr. Morgan thinks that formerly a tendency existed to bury in this way. This practice he discovered at Lewiston among the Tuscaroras, where the beaver, bear, and gray-wolf gentes buried separately. The Choctaws and Cherokees kept separate and apart the bones of each gens, and the ark containing the bones had the family totem marked upon it. Among the Onondagas and Oneidas the practice survived to recent times.[4] Among the Hurons the same practice prevailed. In the Jesuit Relations an elaborate annual cumula-

---

[1] Morgan's League, 175.
[2] Kip's Jesuit Missionaries, 33.
[3] Heckewelder, 75, seq.
[4] Morgan's Ancient Society, 83–84.

tive burial of the bear gens of the Hurons is described. Among the tribes of South America, where hut-burial was so prevalent as it was, the house of each family became its burial-place.

The place of sepulture and the manner of disposing of the dead vary greatly according to locality. The influence of climate is apparent, also the occupation of the people, also the degree of progress they have made from savagery. The Eskimos prefer an elevated and remote situation for the tomb, and a woman waving a light follows the corpse, which has been taken out of the house through a window, and not the usual entrance; or, if living in tents, an opening is made in the back part of the tent. On the way to the place of interment she cries, "Here thou hast nothing more to hope for!"[1] A superstitious fear of the spirit of the dead is here plainly shown in the custom of carrying the body out of another beside the ordinary exit, and also in their address to the dead, which is not certainly very hospitable. Sometimes the body is buried in the ground, beneath a covering of fur or sods, over which heavy stones are placed as a protection against foxes and birds.[2] The Eskimos do not generally, however, inter the dead, but elevate them above the earth. In the Yukon territory the body is doubled up in a box, and elevated above the ground on four posts.[3] Sometimes it is enclosed in a standing posture in a circle of sticks, looking much like a cask.[4] The Ingalik graves sometimes look like an old-fashioned bedstead, with four posts supporting the box or coffin. The Tuski carry the dead out through a hole cut in the back of the hut, which is immediately closed up, that the spirit may not find its way back. Cremation sometimes occurs among them, but the dead are generally suspended above ground, because if buried the bears would dig them up.[5] Some are, however, buried with the head above the surface.[6]

The external surroundings have had much influence among

---

[1] 1 Crantz, 217.
[2] Lyon's Journal, 371.
[3] Dall's Alaska, 17.
[4] Ib., 95.
[5] Ib., 382.
[6] Hooper's Tuski, 221.

wild tribes upon their burial-customs. Where there is no soil, as in many places, interment is impracticable. Where there are no trees and but little drift-wood, cremation is impossible, and the natives are compelled to expose their dead on some hill-side. In the Yukon valley, just below the surface, the soil is permanently frozen and excavation extremely difficult, but timber abounds, and the bodies are placed in wooden coffins and suspended on posts out of the reach of wild beasts. Where the soil is unfrozen and there are no obstacles to digging, interment is practised. Among the Kaniag and Aleut branches of the Eskimos the dead were mummified. The body was prepared by making an opening in the pelvic region and removing the internal organs, and the cavity was stuffed with dry grass and placed in running water to wash away the fatty portions, and the body after preparation wrapped in several folds of skins and furs, and then consigned to caves and rock shelters, which were shunned by the living. There was a cave on the Four Mountain Islands, which was the mausoleum of a chief and three children, since which the place has been abandoned by the natives. Those Kadiaks who hunted the whale formed a caste by themselves, and their bodies were preserved with religious care and secreted in caves only known to the possessors, because if not kept secret they would be stolen by other whalers to cut up for fetichistic purposes. The Aleuts often laid the dead in the clefts of the rocks, but they were generally placed in boat-shaped coffins and suspended to poles. Children were sometimes kept in the house, where the fond mother would continue to watch carefully over them and wipe away the mould.[1] The Thlinkeets suspended their shamans in boxes, but, with that exception, buried their dead. Before burning a warrior, however, they cut off his head and kept it in a box, which was placed over the box containing his ashes.[2]

The Santees made rude attempts at embalming, but usually exposed the body until the flesh could be scraped off, when the

---

[1] Dall's Alaska, 390.   [2] 1 Bancroft, 113.

flesh was burned; then the bones were carefully preserved in a wooden box and oiled every year. They have preserved them in some instances for many ages. When an Indian was slain in battle, however, the body was generally covered with a tumulus of stones and sticks.[1] The Root-diggers seem to have practised cremation,[2] which appears to have been almost universal among the California tribes. They assigned as the reason for this custom the prevention of putrefaction and destruction of the body by insects.[3] A few mummies in remarkable preservation have been found among the Chinooks and Flatheads. They were generally placed in canoes on elevated ground, with all their implements around them.[4]

The Mandans never bury the dead, but place the bodies on scaffolds just out of the reach of wolves and dogs. Near the village there was always a group of these scaffolds, resembling a city of the dead. The body was carefully and thoroughly bandaged, and then placed upon a scaffold facing the east. The mourners spent much of their time under these scaffolds. When the scaffolds fell, all the bones but the skulls were buried. These were collected and placed in circles of a hundred or more on the prairie.

Among the tribes about the Santa Fé trail suspension in high trees is very common. If buried, the wolves dug them up.[5] The same practice prevails among the Dacotahs and Western Ojibways. The bones and hairs are gathered, after the flesh is gone, and interred. Suspension was practised by many of the tribes on the Columbia River, the body having first been placed in a canoe.[6]

Although the Dacotahs practise suspension usually, they sometimes inter, and in a sitting posture, as a sign that the man has been killed in war. The common practice among the Indians of relating the brave deeds of such and addressing the corpse probably suggested the placing them in a convenient pos-

---

[1] 4 Schoolcraft, 156. [2] 4 ib., 225. [3] 5 ib., 217.
[4] 5 ib., 693. [5] 1 ib., 262. [6] 1 ib., 217.

ture for these ceremonies. Once a year the Dacotahs gather the bones of the dead for general burial. When they inter, they say that the little red squirrel sometimes devours the corpse, and for this reason they will not eat that animal. Of this curious reason for the abstention from animal flesh I will speak further under the head of animal worship. A remarkable mode of burial was seen in the neighborhood of Kenosha, Wisconsin. Two Indians were set in the ground in a standing or upright posture, and all of their bodies above their waists protruded above the surface of the ground, where they could see what was going on. The progress of decay had already deprived one of the bodies of its head when seen by the whites.

When a Comanche warrior dies, he is buried on the summit of a high hill in a sitting posture, with his face to the east, and his buffalo robe and all his scanty wardrobe with him. His best horses also are killed, and the remainder of his animals have their manes and tails shaved close, and the women of the family crop their hair, as a symbol of affliction and mourning. After the death, the relatives and friends of the deceased assemble morning and evening outside the camp, where they cry and cut themselves with knives for half an hour or more, and this sometimes lasts for a month. When an ordinary person dies, the corpse is buried immediately. The death of a young warrior is always greatly lamented, and the mourning ceremonies continue a long time; but when an old man dies they only mourn for him a few days.[1]

Says La Hontan of the Northern nations, "As soon as a savage dies he is dressed as neatly as can be, and his relations and slaves (captives) come and mourn over him. When the corpse is dressed, they set it upon a mat in the same posture as if the person were alive, and his relations being set around him, every one in his turn addresses him with a harangue, recounting all his exploits as well as those of his ancestors. He that speaks last expresses himself to this purpose: 'You sit now

---

[1] Marcy's Army Life on the Border, 56.

along with us, and have the same shape that we have; you want neither arms, nor head, nor legs, but at the same time you cease to be, and begin to evaporate like the smoke of a pipe. Who is it that talked with us but two days ago? Sure 'twas not you, for then you would speak to us still. It must therefore be your soul, which is now lodged in the great country of souls along with those of our nation.' After they have made an end of their harangues, the male relations remove to make room for the female friends, who make him the like compliment. This done, they shut the corpse up twenty-four hours in the hut for the dead, and during that time are employed in dances and feasts, which are far from being a mournful show. After the twenty-four hours are expired, the slaves of the deceased person carry his corpse upon their backs to the burying-place, where it is laid upon stakes that are ten feet high, in a double coffin of bark, with his arms and some pipes, with tobacco and Indian corn put up in the same coffin. When the slaves are carrying the corpse to the burying-place, the male and female relations accompany them, dancing all the while, and the rest of the slaves of the deceased person carry some baggage, which the relations present to the dead person and lay upon his coffin."[1]

The Assiniboins, like several other tribes of the great American deserts, never bury their dead, but suspend them by thongs of leather between the branches of the great trees, or expose them on scaffoldings sufficiently high to place the body out of reach of the voracious wild animals. The feet of the corpses are turned toward the rising sun, and when the trees or scaffoldings fall through old age, the bones are collected and buried religiously within a circle formed of heads. This sacred deposit is guarded, as among the Mandans, by medicine-trees or posts, from which amulets or medicine-bags are suspended.

The practice of suspension undoubtedly arose from a desire to prevent animals from devouring the dead. Carelessness

---

[1] 2 La Hontan, 54.

about the preservation of the dead seldom occurs among the Northern tribes. There are only a few instances mentioned among all the tribes of America where an attempt was not made to prevent the destruction of the dead by animals.

The Chippewyans had a great aversion to being buried in the ground. The idea of being eaten by the worms was horrible to them. They enclosed the body in hollow wood, which they hung to trees. The widow was obliged to remain near the body for one year, to keep away animals. When nothing but the bones were left they were burned, and the ashes kept in a small box.[1] If their dead had been wicked or unpopular in life, then such care would not be bestowed upon them, but they would be burned forthwith.[2]

The Ojibways interred with the head toward the west, and built a tomb of poles placed lengthways. If the deceased was a husband, the widow ran zigzag toward home, dodging behind trees to elude the spirit of her dead husband. For several nights they rattled at the door, in order to frighten away his spirit. Some hung up scarecrows to flutter in the wind, imagining the spirit to be as timid as themselves.[3] When the ground was frozen and it was almost impossible to penetrate the surface, they wrapped the corpse in skins or bark and hung it on a tree beyond the reach of wolves and foxes. When the bones fell to the ground they were gathered and buried.[4]

It will thus be seen that among the Northern tribes all the various kinds of burial were resorted to, yet interments were less frequent, because during many months in the year they could not be made. In many cases those accustomed to inter in the summer would burn or otherwise dispose of the dead in winter. Cremation appears to have been the most usual method of disposing of the dead among most of these Northern tribes. The reasons that led to this were that it was the easiest and quickest mode of disposing of the more destructible parts

---

[1] Smithsonian Rep., 1866, 319.
[2] Ib., 326.
[3] Jones's Ojibways, 98–100.
[4] Ib., 100.

of the body, and the indestructible were reduced to less bulk, so that they might be disposed of or carried more easily. Their flesh was thus saved from the devouring worm, or from being eaten by the birds or other animals. The curious custom prevailed to some extent of drinking the ashes of relatives, by which superstitious practice the spirit of the deceased, or a part of it, was supposed to be absorbed and assimilated by the spirit of the person drinking the ashes. For the same reason these ashes were often smeared, when moistened, over the bodies of the living. Among the California tribes cremation was almost universal. The weird and showy spectacle undoubtedly added much to the interest taken in cremation, as I find among tribes using this method that the attendance was generally large at these ceremonies. Another advantage of cremation was that thereby the personal effects of the deceased, which were generally sacrificed, were so disposed of that they could not be stolen, as they frequently were when deposited with the body in exposed places.

Passing to the customs of the Southern tribes, we find them vary much from those of the North, where a rude fear of spirits exists but has not developed into worship.

The Mosquitos deposit the body in a canoe, in which they place a spear, bow, and paddle. If a widow survives, she supplies her dead husband with food for a year, after which she carries his bones on her back in the daytime and sleeps with them at night for another year. After this they are deposited in the house.[1]

Among the wild tribes of Central America interment and cremation were both practised. The custom prevailed to some extent of placing the body in a hut or primitive temple and there offering sacrifices to it as long as anything but the bones remained. In the higher civilizations of America a more elaborate system of sacrifices was gradually being developed, and great monuments and temples were built over the remains of

---

[1] 1 Bancroft, 744.

dead heroes. In Peru, embalmment was a common mode of preserving the dead caciques. It was also practised to some extent in the provinces of Central America, where slow fires of herbs were built under the body; it was thus gradually dried, until only skin and bones remained. These were then dressed and adorned with ornaments of gold, jewels, and feathers, and placed in an apartment of his palace, where the remains of his ancestors were kept. Quinantzin, monarch of Tezcuco, who died after a long and prosperous reign, in the thirteenth century, was burned with great pomp and ceremony, and his ashes placed in an emerald urn. The Aztecs were very particular about the disposal of their dead. The monarchs were often embalmed by taking out the bowels and replacing them with aromatic substances. The process was not complete, and only served temporarily while the tedious ceremonies of having the dead equipped properly for the long journey were being performed. Hence no remains of mummies are found.[1] The body was then burned. Cremation was a very ancient custom among the Nahua nations. It appears to have been practised in the early times by the migrating tribes. The ashes could thus be easily carried, and the bodies preserved from desecration. The Chichemecs burned their kings who were killed in battle, and thus their ashes were carried home with convenience and safety. There is much evidence to show that the Toltecs practised interment in ordinary cases, and that the Aztecs introduced the general use of cremation. The later usage was to burn all except those who died a violent death or of certain diseases, and those under seventeen years of age. The Tlascaltecs and Aztecs practised cremation.[2] The altar devoted to the burning was doubtless one attached to the temple of the deity who presided over the dead.[3] Upon this altar the body was laid in full array, with all those things set apart to him for his future use, and the funeral pyre was started. A few devoted themselves to following the deceased into the other world, to

---

[1] 1 Bancroft, 779.   [2] 2 ib., 609.   [3] Ib.

minister to his wants. The number continually increased during the bloody rule of the Aztecs, until, at the funeral of Nezahualpilli, royal sage of Tezcuco, in 1515, two hundred males and one hundred females were immolated. After the body had been burned, the ashes, bones, and jewelry were placed in an urn with the hair of the deceased.[1] They were often, however, placed in an image of the deceased.

Among the Toltecs, where the practice of interment was common, large vaults of stone and lime were used. Among the Aztecs the funerals of the subjects were attended with less pomp than those of the rulers and privileged classes. They were wrapped in mantles bearing the image of their professional deity upon them,—the warrior with the mantle of the war god, the merchant and artisan with that of the patron deity of his trade. The drunkard would, in addition, be covered with the robe of the god of wine, and the adulterer with the robe of the god of lasciviousness. If burned, the robes were generally given to the temples; but if buried, placed with the body. People who had died a violent death, or with leprosy, tumors, itch, gout, dropsy, and women who died in childbed, were not burned, but interred in special graves.[2] These exceptions to the general rule of cremation were probably due to the impure condition of the body, which was not in a fit condition to be so soon spiritualized. A trader who died on a journey was placed in a basket and hung on a pole or tree.[3] When the death was reported, however, to his family, the funeral ceremonies were conducted with full pomp over the image of the deceased, which was made for the occasion. Among those people who differed from the Aztecs in funeral ceremonies were the Teo Chichemecs, who interred their dead. In Goazacoalco it was the custom to place the bones in a basket as soon as the flesh was gone and hang them up on a tree, so that the spirit might have no trouble in finding them.[4] Suspensions were, however, rare among the Nahua nations. The Miztecs, in Oajaca, where

---

[1] 2 Bancroft, 610–11.   [2] 2 ib., 615–16.   [3] 2 ib., 616.   [4] 2 ib., 619.

cremation does not seem to have obtained, after much ceremony, interred the dead in natural or artificial caves. The bones in most such cases appear, however, to have been removed to the house and temples when the flesh was gone. The Mayas disposed of the bodies of their dead by both burial and cremation. In Vera Paz, and probably throughout Guatemala, the body was placed in the grave in a sitting posture, with the knees drawn up to the face. Their lords of provinces were gorgeously dressed for the ceremony and burial. Their interment was generally on the top of a hill, and a mound raised over them. The common people had mounds raised over them also, and the height of these mounds was proportioned to the rank of the defunct.[1] This last fact will be enlarged upon when those monuments of the American tribes which appertain to their religious life are examined. Among the Yucatecs, only the poorer classes buried their dead. Their bodies were generally interred in the house, which was then forsaken by its inmates.[2] Such a custom as this would impoverish and retain in poverty the people who practised it, and it is probable that the absence of the ruins of all buildings except the temples and palaces of the lords, which has so puzzled the antiquary, is due to this custom, which was so common among the nomadic tribes, but can be looked upon only as a survival from barbarism among the civilized nations of Central America. The Pipiles interred the dead in the house they lived in, and the high-priest was buried in a vault of his own palace.[3] Among the higher classes in Yucatan, cremation was practised, and the ashes deposited in the image of the deceased, which was then placed in a temple.

The Tupinambas of Brazil tied their dead fast, that they might not be able to get up and annoy their friends with their visits. The body was placed in a pit dug in the hut. Here it was swung in a hammock, and surrounded with provisions which the soul could eat when it pleased.[4] In the case of chiefs

---

[1] 2 Bancroft, 800.   [2] Ib.   [3] Ib.   [4] 1 Southey, 248.

the body was generally anointed with honey and clothed with a coat of feathers. The vault was roofed over, and the family continued to live over it as before.[1] One burial-place was found among them where they were interred and their long hair left above ground.[2] The Xomanas and Passes burned the dead and drank the ashes, thinking they received the spirit of the deceased by this act.[3] The Guaranies buried their dead in urns, which were generally placed underneath the cabin floor. When they buried outside the cabin, a mound was raised over the place.[4] The Retoronos, Pechuyos, and Guarayos interred the dead, but when the flesh had decayed dug up the bones and reduced them to powder, which was mingled with maize in a cake, which was then eaten.[5] The Tapuyas buried their dead in their own stomachs. The infant was eaten by the parents, the adult by all his relatives. The bones were reserved for marriage-feasts, when they were powdered, and taken as the most precious thing that could be offered. The reader will probably infer the incentive to this custom. Whilst this species of cannibalism among the Tapuyas was the last demonstration of love, among the Tupis it was confined to their enemies, whom they devoured as the strongest mark of hatred.[6] The tribes on the Orinoco preserved the bodies of their dead in baskets, after having placed them in the river over-night for the purpose of having the carib-fish strip off the flesh.[7] Urn-burial was used by those skilled in pottery. Some of these urns were large enough to receive these bodies erect.[8] The Mbayas interred the dead, unless the death happened at a distance from home, when they hung the body in a tree for several months, where it became as dry as parchment and was then removed.[9] Among the Patagonians the customs vary considerably, but interment was the most common practice. The body was wrapped up and carried to the grave, which was a hole dug in the earth. If a warrior, this was made so that the grave

---

[1] 1 Southey, 248. [2] 3 ib., 318. [3] 3 ib., 722.
[4] 3 ib., 165. [5] 3 ib., 204. [6] 1 ib., 379.
[7] 1 ib., 631. [8] 1 ib., 165. [9] 1 ib., 392.

could be opened yearly and the skeleton cleaned and reclothed by an old matron whose special duty it was to perform this office for the dead. Suspension of the body on platforms, however, was not uncommon until the flesh separated from the bones.[1] The Mapuches interred the dead, and with the face to the west, their spirit-land.[2]

The Abipones pull out the heart and tongue of the dead and boil them and feed them to the dogs, that the author of his death may soon die also, for they think death is always produced by sorcery. The body is then wrapped in a hide and bound with leather thongs, and carried quickly out of the house and interred in a grave, which is covered with prickly boughs to keep off tigers. Around the grave are placed various useful articles. Their favorite place of burial is a wood, whose umbrageous shade is thought to be delightful. The sacred character of woods and groves in warm countries is a subject of deep interest if connected with this custom of burial, as it undoubtedly is. The forests on the banks of the Parana, when re-echoing the sounds of their voices, are thought by the Abipones to be haunted by the spirits of the dead. They are very zealous in preserving the bones of those slain on the field of battle, and, having obtained the body, strip off the flesh, which they bury in the ground, and carry the bones home with reverence. They venerate the burial-places of their ancestors.[3]

The caves of Hayti were much used in early times for burial of the dead, and afterward as temples;[4] cremation, however, succeeded this mode of burial, the second Bohito having, according to the legends, introduced this custom, which was considered an improvement.[5]

Many of the Guiana tribes carefully preserved the bones of the dead after the women had picked off all the flesh. Sometimes the body was immersed in the water until the bones had

---

[1] 2 Wood, 542. [2] 2 ib., 565. [3] 1 Dobrizhoffer, 271.
[4] 1 Rafinesque, 170. [5] 1 ib., 191.

been picked clean by fish, when they were carefully dried and suspended in the roof of the habitation.[1] Sometimes the body was buried in the house and a wide plank put over the place.[2] Those slain in war were interred by heaping over them a mound.[3] The high-priests of the Pipiles were buried sitting on stools in their own houses.[4]

In Florida the natives buried in the temples, in which there were wooden chests containing the bodies of the dead.[5] In one mausoleum at Talomeco, which was one hundred paces in length and forty in breadth, with lofty roofs of reed, there were benches upon which were placed the wooden chests, skilfully wrought, in which reposed the bodies of the priests and chiefs.[6] The same custom prevailed among the Southeastern tribes of the United States, where the temples were dedicated to the preservation of the bodies of their chiefs. Early temples arose in this way, and the survival of such sacred burials in our day is seen in the Catholic altar, built upon and sanctified by the bones of saints, and also in the Mohammedan shrine. Among the natives of Alabama, temples were discovered in their chief towns, in which the dead were deposited in baskets and boxes.[7] Says Mr. Pickett, "These bone-houses were the miniature temples of the Indians."[8]

Among some of these Southern tribes a mound was erected over chiefs and priests. On the sea-coast even the common people had a shell-mound thrown over them. In the interior shell-mounds were not used, but large earth mounds take their place, which were dedicated to the inhumation of the general dead. Many small mounds occur, in which one or more bodies were found. These were undoubtedly used for the burial of a single chief or priest, as above stated. The erection of large mounds has been gradually discontinued since the advent of Europeans. Some of the tribes, however, have continued the practice. The Yemassees slain by the Creeks in their last de-

---

[1] Brett, 154.   [2] Ib., 188.   [3] Ib., 341.   [4] 4 Herrera, 155.
[5] 5 ib., 315, 318.   [6] Jones's Antiquities, 26.
[7] 1 Pickett's Alabama, 169.   [8] 1 ib., 170.

cisive battle were interred, and many small mounds raised over them.[1]

The Carolina tribes interred the dead at first in an artificial vault. When the flesh was gone they took up the bones and placed them in the temple. A fee was charged for this admittance to the temple. These bones were carried with them on their journeys.[2] The Choctaws placed their dead upon scaffolds until the flesh decayed, when the bones were taken down and put in a chest, which was deposited in a bone-house, with which each town was provided.[3] When the bone-house was full, the boxes were taken out and piled up, and a mound raised over them, forming a pyramid.[4] The chiefs of the Cherokees were placed in a sitting posture on the surface of the earth, and a mound erected over them.

Thus it will be seen that many of the mounds among these Southern tribes were erected over the dead by the Indians inhabiting the country after the discovery. So materially have the customs and institutions of the Indians been changed since the discovery, that it has been not only doubted, but even denied by many writers, that these mounds were constructed by the immediate ancestors of the present Indians. It appears, however, from many respectable authorities, that many tribes still continue to raise a tumulus over the dead, the magnitude of which is often proportioned to the rank and celebrity of the deceased. These mounds are scattered at intervals over the surface of both Americas, and neither by their size nor by their contents impress us, says Mr. Bradford, " with a high opinion of the civilization of their authors."[5]

" Some have supposed that the number and magnitude of the mounds would indicate the existence of a race of men more industrious than our modern Indians. A little reflection will show that the amount of labor required in their erection did not surpass the common industry of the savages. Suppose a

---

[1] Bartram's Travels, 139.   [2] Lawson's Carolina, 181.
[3] Roman's East and West Florida, 89–90.   [4] Bartram, 516.
[5] Bradford's Antiquities, 18.

mound to be forty feet in diameter at its base, and to rise by steps one foot in height and a foot and a half in depth to the height of thirteen feet, with a level surface on the summit four feet in diameter. It would contain about six thousand two hundred and thirty-three cubic feet of earth, or a fraction less than two hundred and thirty-one cubic yards. To deposit on the mound one cubic yard of earth would be a moderate day's labor for one man. Therefore the erection of the mound under consideration would employ two hundred and thirty-one persons one day only. Among the Indians the women would perform as much of this kind of work as the men. Within the Indian territory we have ninety-four thousand inhabitants. One-fifth of these or more are competent to labor. This gives eighteen thousand eight hundred laborers. If each of these would, in the course of twelve months, bestow only as much labor on the erection of mounds as would amount to one day, eighty-one mounds would be built in one year. And if the work should progress at the same rate with an equal number of inhabitants for three centuries, twenty-four thousand three hundred mounds would be constructed within the Indian territory. A few reflections of this kind must satisfy any one that the Indians could have erected these mounds."[1]

M. Malte-Brun, speaking of the earthworks in Ohio and the Northwest, says there is nothing to indicate on the part of the people who originated these works a greater degree of power than we should find possessed at this very day by the Iroquois or Ojibways, if they enjoyed entire liberty and were at a distance from the Anglo-Americans. Says Mr. Melish, "I saw no reason to refer the erection of the mounds to a different race or a different state of civilization than what is found among the Indian tribes at present in North America. As to their ingenuity, I really see nothing to lead us beyond the present race of Indians."[2]

The mounds show no more art than might be expected from

---

[1] McCoy's Baptist Missions, 27.   [2] 2 Melish's Travels, 104.

the present Indians. They are mere erections of earth, exhibiting no other trace of skill than that most of them are of regular forms contained under circular or right lines. Iron tools were not used in the formation of them. The only circumstance which strongly discredits their having been formed by the progenitors of the present Indians is the immensity of the size of some of them beyond what could be expected from the sparse population and the indolence of the present race.[1]

La Trobe says, "The degree of civilization necessary for construction of mounds has always been falsely estimated. Their being constructed of the superficial earth thrown into a heap, the rare occurrence of stone-work of the rudest kind, the comparative insignificance of implements and ornaments in them, all militate against the idea of their having been erected by a people much more civilized than the present Indians, and no more civilized than the Natches."[2]

Mr. Brown, in the "Western Gazetteer," says, "We obtained ample testimony that these masses of earth [meaning the mounds] were the work of a savage people."[3] The mounds at Butte des Morts were of recent origin. The great hill of the dead was raised by their survivors over the bodies of one thousand warriors who perished in a battle in 1706.[4] Each of the other mounds was raised over the grave of some renowned chief who fell in that battle.[5]

Mr. Lapham is of opinion that the skeletons in the mounds could not be very old, and that all traces of a skeleton would be gone in a few centuries, and hence concludes that there is no probability that the mounds have an antiquity of many hundred years.[6]

The present tribes continued after the discovery the practice of mound-building so far as to erect a conical tumulus over their dead. Among the natives of South Carolina, the bones of the dead, with the articles to be interred with them, were

---

[1] 1 Flint's Geography.
[2] 2 La Trobe's Rambles N. A., 241–43.
[3] Western Gazetteer, 58.
[4] Allouez, 3 Smith's Wisconsin, 262.
[5] 1 Wis. Hist. Coll., 192.
[6] 1 ib., 29.

placed upon the surface of the ground; then they were covered to the depth of several inches with a mixture of charcoal and ashes, which was covered by clay, piled upon it until a mound was formed several feet in height. The storms of centuries would only serve to beat more firmly together the mass of clay and indestructible carbon, which thus formed a protection to its contents.[1]

Mr. Battey says that whilst among the Indians on Sulphur Creek, he noticed a small mound of fresh earth surmounted by a buffalo's skull, which had just been erected over the grave of a young child.[2]

Mr. Brinton thinks the Florida mounds and all those in the Atlantic States, and most of those in the Mississippi Valley, were the production of the identical nations found there by the whites.[3] Many cases of mound-burial occurred after the discovery. It was customary among the tribes on St. John's River, when a chief died and his corpse was interred, to raise a mound above the grave, and place upon its summit the conch-shell from which he used to drink.[4] A good many instances are found of the prevalence of the same custom among the tribes of the Northern United States after the advent of whites. The Indians of Canada erected a sort of pyramid over an illustrious personage.[5] Those Indians dwelling in the country now embraced within the territory of the State of New Jersey and its vicinity buried their dead in a sitting posture and covered the grave with a pyramid, or mound of earth.[6] Within a short time the Leavenworth *Ledger*, Kansas, announced the death and burial of a young Indian chief twelve years of age. He was placed in a sitting posture upon the surface of the earth, surrounded by all his personal effects, and a mound was then thrown over the whole. Mr. Featherstonhaugh noticed a mound among the Osages which had just been raised over a chief, and enlarged from time to time till

---

[1] 1 Logan's Upper South Carolina, 222.
[2] Quaker among the Indians, 142.
[3] Brinton's Florida, 176.
[4] Basanier, Hist. Not., 10, seq.
[5] 1 Jes. Rel., 19.
[6] Smith's N. J., 13.

very large.¹   Mr. Squier also noticed one of modern date in Belmont County, Ohio.²

Mr. Bierce mentions another recent case of mound-construction,—an Indian named Nicksaw, who was buried where he was killed and a mound raised over him.³

The Dacotahs erected a mound ten feet high over the body of the son of one of their chiefs, who was recently killed in trying to make the famous leap at the Red Pipe-Stone Quarry.⁴

One of the largest mounds in the country of the Osages, says Mr. Beck, " has been thrown up on the Osage River within the last thirty or forty years by the Osages in honor of one of their deceased chiefs." This fact proves conclusively the original object of these mounds, and refutes the theory that they must necessarily have been erected by a race of men more civilized than the present tribes of Indians. Were it necessary, numerous other facts might be adduced to prove that many of the mounds are no other than the tombs of their great men, and are of recent origin.⁵

It is related by intelligent Indian traders that a custom once prevailed among certain tribes, on the burial of a chief or brave of distinction, to consider his grave as entitled to the tribute of a portion of earth from each passer-by, which the traveller sedulously carried with him on his journey. Hence the first grave formed a nucleus, around which, in the accumulation of the accustomed tributes of respect thus paid, a mound was soon formed. It also became an honorable distinction for the dead to be buried by the side of the chiefs so deposited in the first mound; and as the custom of earthy tribute continued, the mound increased in size, and the irregularity in the shape and size of the burial-places may thus in a measure be explained.⁶

After a battle the slain are collected in one spot, and a large mound of earth is heaped over them. Some of these mounds are very large. There was one on the road from St. Augustine

---

¹ Travels, 70.   ² Aboriginal Monuments of N. Y., 107.
³ Summit County, 138.   ⁴ 2 Catlin's Illus., 170.
⁵ Beck's Gazetteer, 308.   ⁶ 3 Smith's Hist. Wis., 245, seq.

to Tomaka, which must have covered two acres of ground. Barrows of this kind are numerous over the whole American continent,[1] and contain vast numbers of the dead. The custom of burying the remains of many individuals in one spot and heaping over them a mound of earth was common in remote times among the wandering tribes around Lakes Huron and Superior. The dead were laid upon the bare rock, and covered with stones to protect the body from wild animals. After a certain number of years the tribe made a gathering of their dead and bore the bones to a suitable resting-place, where earth existed in sufficient abundance to admit of a mound being made without difficulty. This would be easier in the valleys of rivers.[2]

Cumulative burials instigated the erection of many of the large mounds. A mound at Vincennes, Indiana, showed undoubted signs of cumulative burial. In it was found a bed of human bones closely packed and pressed together and promiscuously mingled. A mound at Merom, Indiana, had three layers of human bones. This cumulative burial was very prevalent among the different tribes. We have already noticed it among the tribes of the Southern United States. It was the custom also among those of the Northern States, especially the Hurons and Iroquois, to gather together annually the bones of the dead from the scaffolds, trees, houses, temples, rock shelters, or any other places where the bodies may have been deposited, and bury them all in one place. This has undoubtedly been the cause and occasion of erecting many of the large mounds. In a mound in the township of Beverly, Upper Canada, a tumulus was discovered containing the remains of about one thousand Indians, with all their arms and cooking-vessels.[3] A mound at St. Louis thirty-five feet high was thrown over a trench containing many human bones.

It was the custom among the tribes of Georgia, when the

---

[1] Prince of Econchatti, 70-72.   [2] 1 Hind's Nar., 90-91.
[3] McIntosh's Book of Indians, 312.

accumulation of bones was great, to have a general inhumation, when a mound was erected over them.[1]

The shell-mounds along the coast appear to have been extensively used as tumuli for the dead. One of these on Stalling's Island in the Savannah River, fifteen feet high and three hundred long, contained hundreds of skeletons.[2]

In Shenandoah County, on Mr. Steenburger's land, are the remains of an Indian mound. When first seen, it was eighteen or twenty feet high and fifty to sixty yards in circumference. This mound was literally filled with human skeletons.[3] On the land of Mr. Noah Keyser, near the mouth of the Hawksbill Creek, stand the remains of a large mound. This, though reduced by ploughing, is yet some twelve or fourteen feet high and sixty yards round at the base. It is found to be literally filled with human skeletons, and at every fresh ploughing a fresh layer of bones is brought to the surface.[4]

In Chile, the bones of the dead are kept until the time of yearly burial, when the skeletons are placed in a sitting posture in a row, with all their weapons around them, and earth is then thrown over them. Sacrifices are brought by the people to this mausoleum, where a priestess offers them to the dead.[5]

Many instances are given of the erection over the dead of small mounds of stones, commonly called cairns. Miantonnomah is buried in the east part of Norwich, at a place called Sachem's Plain, from the event of his death, and is buried on the spot where he was slain. But a few years since, a large heap of stones, thrown together by the wandering Indians, according to the custom of their country, and as a melancholy mark of the love the Narragansetts had for their fallen chief, lay on his grave.[6]

The Patagonians raised stone-heaps over the dead, the size of which depended upon the importance of the deceased.[7]

Sometimes the tumuli were made of dried twigs arranged

---

[1] Jones's Antiquities, 191-92. [2] Ib., 197-98.
[3] Kercheval's Valley of Virginia, 50. [4] Ib., 57.
[5] 2 Molina, 380-81. [6] Gardener's Pequot War. [7] Musters, 91.

in a conical pile, which was occasionally ten feet high and twenty-five in circumference. The Pimos buried their dead in the sitting posture, and raised a mound of sticks and stones over them.[1]

Mr. Macauley says the Iroquois raised heaps of stones over the bodies of distinguished chiefs.[2]

Thus it will be seen that many burial-mounds of earth or other material have been erected among the tribes of the United States since the advent of whites. There is much evidence to show that in Mexico, Central America, and South America mounds have been erected over the dead by the natives inhabiting those countries within the historic period and since the discovery. In Guatemala they buried their dead by raising over them mounds of earth corresponding in height with the importance of the deceased.[3]

The Indians of Quito, says Ulloa, threw so much earth on the body as to form a tumulus in imitation of nature with its mountains and eminences. The magnitude of these indicated the dignity or riches of the person interred.[4] Within the jurisdiction of Antioquia they piled up such masses of earth in making their tombs that they looked like small hills.[5] Other Peruvian tombs were mounds of conical or quadrilateral shape heaped up during the mourning period. The size of the tumulus shows the fortune of the deceased.[6] Says Mr. Prescott of the Peruvians, " Vast mounds of an irregular or more frequently oblong shape, penetrated by galleries, were raised over the dead, whose dried bodies have been found generally in a sitting posture."[7]

Most of the graves near Truxillo externally exhibit the figure of a loaf of sugar and are hollow within.[8]

Graves similar to these are found in the valley of Espiritu Santo, which have been erected in recent times.

---

[1] Brown, Apache Country, 113.
[2] 2 History of New York, 239.
[3] Ximenez, 213.
[4] 1 Ulloa, 461.
[5] Cieza, ch. 63.
[6] Joaq. Acosta, 126.
[7] 1 Prescott's Peru, 90.
[8] 2 Biblioteca Peruana, 160.

The general erection of tumuli over the dead, the construction of vast terraced pyramidal piles for sacred purposes, seem to have marked the steps of that primitive people vaguely denominated the Toltecs, whose more imposing monuments still rear their spectral fronts among the dense tropical forests of Central America and Yucatan, but whose ruder — because earlier — structures throng the fertile alluvions which border the great Mississippi and its giant tributaries, — silent but most conclusive illustrations of the grand law of development.[1]

Peru, Mexico, and Yucatan contain so many sepulchral mounds it would be tedious to describe them. A large group in Yucatan, near the ruins of Ichmal, extended for miles around in every direction as far as the eye could reach. Some were forty feet high. When several of them were opened, they were found to contain rooms in which were sitting the skeletons of the dead.[2] Near Otumba, Mexico, around the pyramid of the sun, were grouped many small conical burial-mounds.[3] The plains near Cayambe, Peru, are covered with sepulchral tumuli. The Indians laid a body without burial on the ground, and after protecting it with a cover of stones dirt was heaped over it.[4]

In three Kentucky mounds evidences of cremation appear. They seem to have been erected over the ashes and calcined bones of the dead. A large mound at Marietta, Ohio, covered blackened earth, charcoal, and a stone coffin, dark and stained with smoke, which demonstrated that the funeral obsequies had been celebrated with fire. Another near Marietta enclosed calcined human remains.[5]

It is extremely doubtful whether a great error has not been made by many able American archæologists in denominating a class of artificial mounds altar-mounds. Many things have tended to lead them into this error. The burial-customs of the aboriginal Americans have not been thoroughly investigated.

---

[1] Squier's New Mexico and California.   [2] Norman's Yucatan, 146.
[3] Bullock's Mexico, 411.   [4] 1 Ulloa, 266.
[5] Bradford's Antiquities, 52–53.

A supposed great antiquity has been ascribed to them; and a special race of mound-builders has been created to furnish builders for these great monuments of what has been called an extinct race. Whence they came, and where they have gone, has puzzled the brain of many an antiquarian. This imaginary people, with an elaborate ritual of sacrifice offered on the altars so carefully covered with an abundance of earth to protect them from the sacrilegious hands of barbarian intruders, will, however, eventually be resolved into a very primitive people, and their sacrificial altars turned into cremation-pyres, where the bodies of the dead were burned with their worldly effects, and a tumulus erected over their remains. Upon most of these supposed altars human bones have been found; in a few, however, their absence is noted by explorers. They may have been reduced to ashes; but it is not necessary to account for their absence in this way alone, for the custom, as we have seen, was very prevalent of preserving the bones after cremation and removing them, and among many of the tribes they were reduced to a powder, which was used in some liquid as a drinking potion for the relatives. The altar-mound theorists have had to account for the presence of human bones by the horrible rite of human sacrifice. The conclusion that the mounds of this class were devoted to this superstitious rite does not appear to be satisfactory. They rather appear to indicate that cremation was practised. The sacrificial origin of these mounds has been inferred from the fact that articles of only one class occur in them. This would only indicate that a division of labor was established; because with their belief in a future life, and a continuance of all the employments of the present life, many of the products of any skilful person and material for new labor would be deposited with such a person. On this subject of sacrifice, running as it does through all their ceremonial life, I would refer the reader to that part of this work devoted to that subject. Evidences have been found of cremation in Florida mounds.

Quite a number of mounds near Mount Carroll, Carroll

County, Illinois, were opened, and calcined human bones with charcoal and ashes found in each of them. There was an Indian tradition that they were cremation-mounds.[1] In Virginia, a number of stone-heaps are found, oven-like, containing the bones of the dead and bearing evident marks of fire. The stone-heaps are covered with earth. There is a tradition that it was the universal custom at one time to consume the bodies of the dead with fire. This may account for the existence of nothing but ashes in some of the mounds that have been opened.[2] Quite a number of such have been found in Minnesota, some also with calcined human bones and clay, showing marks of intense heat.[3] Sometimes the bodies were burned, and the ashes placed in urns and deposited in mounds. In Dubuque County, Iowa, an urn was taken from a small mound containing ashes; another, from a mound near the State line of Illinois and Wisconsin, contained about a half-bushel of ashes. Urn-burials are rare in this part of the country, however.[4]

A mound in Wisconsin contained much charcoal and burnt clay, and stones almost calcined into quick-lime by the great heat. Some of the bones of a human being were found, but most of the skeleton had evidently been consumed at the time of the interment.[5]

Near Red River settlement a burial-mound was excavated, and four or five skulls found on a floor of hard mud which showed evidences of fire.[6]

Says Mr. Atwater of the Western mounds, "Nearly all the bodies buried in the mounds were burnt first, before the mounds were reared."[7]

Mr. Evans, who appears to have spent much time in investigating this matter, says, "I have penetrated the centres of many mounds, and the ashes and charcoal and human remains lying in successive strata in the mounds, showing the action

---

[1] Smithsonian Rep., 1877, p. 255.
[2] Da-coo-dah, 57.
[3] Ib., 83.
[4] Ib., 204–10.
[5] Lapham's Ant., 28.
[6] Smith. Rep., 1867, p. 399.
[7] Atwater's Antiquities, 381.

of fire, have induced me to believe that the mound-builders practised cremation, and after the rites were performed the remains were covered with earth, each succeeding funeral pyre adding to the height of the mound. The strata of ashes and charcoal which I found in all the mounds I examined indicated that successive fires had been kindled, and when the substances were reduced to ashes they were covered with earth."[1]

In some of the burial-mounds the presence of a layer of baked clay above the human remains leads to the conjecture that fires were sometimes built for the purpose of hardening this layer of clay.[2]

In a mound at Cincinnati, human bones were found imbedded in ashes and charcoal, the unfailing signs of the burning of the deceased.[3]

A large cremation-furnace, eighteen feet long and six feet wide, was found in a mound, fifteen feet high, near Lancaster, Fairfield County, Ohio. In a huge vessel upon this furnace twelve human skeletons were found, surrounded with ashes and charcoal. In the Chilhowee valley, Tennessee, cysts were found containing human bones and ashes, so placed as to indicate that fire had been used at the burial. In some of the mounds near New Harmony, Indiana, the same unmistakable evidences of cremation appeared. There can be no doubt that many of those mounds called altar-mounds in the books on the antiquities of America are none other than cremation-mounds.

It will thus be seen that the custom of raising mounds over the dead survived the advent of Europeans, and that many of those mounds denominated altar-mounds were thrown over the remains of those dead that had been burned, according to the prevailing custom among a large part of the aboriginal tribes. Cumulative burials necessitated the magnitude of many mounds, and the multitude of those thus cared for inspired the labor necessary.

Among the American sepulchral monuments, the chulpas, or

---

[1] Chicago Tribune.   [2] Short, 37–39.   [3] Bradford's Ant., 53.

burial-towers of Peru, are among the most interesting of all the antiquities of this continent connected with sepulture. Primarily these chulpas consisted of cysts or excavations walled with stones, over which was built a tower with an opening barely large enough to admit the body of a man on a level with the surface of the ground. This opening was toward the east. These chulpas varied in height from ten to twenty-six feet, and were often ornamented with stucco-work. Some are round and some square,[1] but the interior plan is pretty much the same in all. Upon the floor human bones and remains of pottery are found. These tombs are common in the Titicaca region, and usually stand in groups of from twenty to one hundred. There is a large group of them at Sillustani. Fig. 12 is one of these chulpas, from Rivero and Tschudi's "Peruvian Antiquities." These chulpas resemble the Oriental topes. In some of them an entire family appear to have been buried, as many as twelve skeletons being found in them. Some of them, however, which had never been opened before, were opened by Mr. Squier and only one skeleton was found.[2] He describes them as follows: "In some provinces they have for sepulchres high towers, hollow below. In some parts they are round, in some square. They are built half a league or more from their towns, so that they appear like other and very populous villages. The dead, wrapped up in skins of the llama, are deposited in them in a sitting posture. The doors of the tombs are then closed." Mr.

FIG. 12.

---

[1] Squier's Peru, 243-44.   [2] Ib., 388.

Squier thinks the chulpas were built and used by the Aymara race only.[1]

The rock-tombs of Peru are another interesting feature in its antiquities. The faces of many of the high cliffs in the mountainous parts are full of ancient tombs excavated in the rock, within which the dead were placed, and then walled up with stones and stuccoed over and painted. The region of Ollantaytambo is rich in these rock-tombs. In many a niche and crevice tier on tier of these tombs are seen plastered up like nests of the mud-swallows. The "steeps of Lamentation are literally speckled with the white faces of these tombs. Some are solitary cells, others populous chambers. In this dry atmosphere the bodies are preserved surrounded with a few rude household-utensils."[2] At Chimu is found a necropolis consisting of chambers or vaults enclosed in a mound, each vault containing niches wherein were found skeletons elaborately clothed and plumed. The tombs of men of note "were above the ground, built with unburnt bricks, and round, like little pigeon-houses, five or six feet in diameter and twelve or fourteen in height, arched like the top of an oven, in which the dead were placed sitting and then they were walled up. In travelling through the country there are still many to be seen, even of those before the conquest by the Spaniards."[3]

The kings of Quito were buried in a pyramid, in which their embalmed corpses were arranged in order, with their earthly effects around them. The manner of burying the vassals was different. In the south the nobles and magnates were placed in urns, and these urns deposited in the woods and forests. The common people were interred, or left in caves or rock protections. The openings to all the sepulchres are to the west. In some the opening is small, and only made as a conduit for drink and food leading to vases placed in the sepulchre for their reception. Embalmment of the dead was confined to the Inca class. The mummified bodies so numerous throughout

---

[1] Squier's Peru, 389. [2] Ib., 531–32. [3] Frezier's Voyage, 178.

Peru owe their preservation to atmospheric and other influences.[1]

The object among all the American tribes, in all their various burial-customs, was to preserve the bones of the dead. The belief underlying all these customs was that the soul, or a part of the soul, dwelt in the bones. Language illustrates this theory. The Iroquois word for bone is *esken;* for soul, *atisken*,—literally, that which is within the bone. In an Athapascan dialect, bone is *yani*, soul is *i-yani*. Mythology adds more decisive testimony. In one of the Aztec legends, after one of the destructions of the world, Xolotl descended to Mictlan, the realm of the dead, and brought thence a bone of the perished race. This, sprinkled with blood, grew on the fourth day into a youth, the father of the present race. Among the Quiches, the hero-gods Hunahpu and Xblanque succumbed to the darksome powers of death. Their bodies were burned, and their bones ground to powder and thrown into the waters; but these ashes, sinking to the bottom of the stream, were, in the twinkling of an eye, changed into handsome youths, with the same features as before. Among many of the tribes the practice of pulverizing the bones of the dead and mixing them with the food was defended by asserting that the souls of the dead remained in the bones and lived again in the living. Even the animals were supposed to follow the same law. Hardly any of the hunting tribes, before their manners were vitiated by foreign influence, permitted the bones of game to be broken or left carelessly about the encampment. They were left in heaps or thrown into the water. The Yuricares of Bolivia carried this superstition to such an inconvenient extent that they preserved even small fish-bones from harm, saying the fish would desert the rivers unless this was done. The traveller on our prairies often notices the buffalo-skulls arranged in circles and symmetrical piles by the careful hands of the native hunters. Among the Peruvians, so careful were they lest any

---

[1] Rivero and Tschudi, 200–9.

of the body should be lost, they preserved even the parings of the nails and clippings of the hair. Among the Choctaws the spirits of the dead will return to the bones in the bone-mounds, and flesh will knit together their loose joints, and they shall again inhabit their ancient territory. The Peruvians expected the mummified body to be again inhabited by its soul.[1]

This belief can be traced among all the primitive peoples of the world. Among the Tartars the pyramid of horses' heads found by Pallas is analogous to bone-pyramids of the buffalo and deer in America. The Hebrew rabbis taught that the coccyx remained at death the germ of a second life, and would develop into the purified body as the plant from the seed.

Among the Iroquois the spirit stayed near the body for a time, and, unless burial was performed, was very unhappy; and among the Brazilian tribes the spirits of the dead were not at rest when the body was unburied, and, if they had had a Creon, an Antigone would have undoubtedly arisen to perform the sacred rites of burial. It will be noticed, then, that there was no uniform custom prevalent among the American nations in their mode of burial, but that diversity of custom prevailed in many instances in the same tribe,—that climate and the nature of the soil, and other natural influences, together with the pursuits of the various peoples, had their effect on the formation of burial-customs, and these a reflex action again on their religious beliefs and superstitions. Yet through it all there are plain indications of a belief that the preservation of the bones of the dead in their integrity was necessary to the peace and happiness of the departed spirit. Hence the security of these was sought in all their various customs. In the suspension of the bodies in trees or on scaffolds or otherwise, their preservation, after the dissolution of the flesh, was attended to. In cremation, the residuum of calcined bones was preserved by interment or a deposit in urns or images of the deceased, or by heaping a mound over them. Interment in the earth had

---

[1] Brinton, 276-80.

the same object in view, as also in caves and other secret and protected places. Thus security is sought in secrecy or by inaccessibility, or both. Among the Chibchas, sepulchres were concealed by trees planted for that purpose. The greatest danger to the remains of the dead arose from the depredations of animals, yet enemies outside or inside the tribe or clan or family were much feared, the possession of any part of a living or dead person by one seeking revenge being looked upon with exceeding great superstitious fear. The origin and progress of sorcery are traceable to this superstition. Among all primitive peoples, where a belief in the renewal of life or the resurrection exists, the peace and happiness of the spirit, which remains in or about the body, depend upon success in preventing the body or any part of it from being devoured or destroyed in any manner. Of course, among peoples to whom the art of preserving the bodies of the dead by embalming or other means was unknown, the destructibility of all but the skeleton or bones was recognized as unavoidable, and their superstition must be modified to that extent. It maintained itself and increased in strength as to the indestructible parts, even including the nails and hair, through all the stages of savagery and barbarism and into our modern civilization. The caciques of Bogota were protected from desecration by diverting the course of a river and making the grave in its bed, and then letting the stream return to its natural course. Alaric, the leader of the Goths, was secretly buried in the same manner. The imposing pyramids of Mexico, Peru, and the sepulchral mounds of both Americas were intended for, and became, obstacles to the desecration of the remains of distinguished dead, as well as memorials of their greatness; but the temples of the more civilized nations mark the highest stage of the progress of this idea in America, as elsewhere. In these temples the interment of heroes took place, and a priestly hierarchy arose to guard and attend at the sacred precincts of their shrines, and offer sacrifice to their idol likenesses stuffed with their ashes and bones. In addition to their religious care in the preservation of the dead, their comfort was also regarded. Hence protections against pressing earth or stones were provided for; also a way for the spirit to have access to the body was considered of vital importance by most of the aborigines. Embalming and the other customs have the same purpose in view, namely, the arrest of decay. It is quite curious to find embalmment and its antithesis, cremation, practised in the same tribe; yet, since the principal idea underlying both practices is the same,—namely, the preservation of all the parts of the dead,—there is no inconsistency here. In both, the destructible parts of the body are preserved to a great extent, for what fire destroys is supposed to be dematerialized and ushered quickly into the world of spirits. Hence it became a very common instrument in sending to the dead the sacrifices offered by their living friends, and the Algonkin would throw his choicest bit of venison into the fire and send it to his hungry spirit-relative, before a morsel had been touched by the living, with as much religious fervor as would the Greek offer a bullock on the sacrificial altar or the Chinaman of our day burn paper houses and money for use in the spirit-world. It must be borne in mind that this spirit-world was in earlier times in and among the living world, and not banished, as in our modern civilization, to some unknown far-off country "from whose bourn no traveller returns." Thus, whether cremation or embalmment took place, the spirit was ready and waiting for a rehabitation of its fleshly tenement-house, none the less real because the flames had wafted it into the shadow-land. With the belief that reanimation will be prevented if the other self finds a mutilated corpse, or none at all, there goes the belief that to insure reanimation putrefaction must be stopped. Naturally there arises the inference that if destruction of the body by animals or otherwise prevents revival, decomposition of it may prevent revival. That this idea is not found among men in very low states is undoubtedly due to the fact that no methods of arresting decomposition have been discovered by them. Hence cremation is found among lower tribes, and survives when this more approved method is discovered; and even among those who are acquainted with the process much greater care is taken to preserve the bodies of kings and distinguished men than the mass of the people. Hence the latter are often carelessly looked after. Distinctions of caste, which are apt to arise in the higher stages of human progress under certain conditions of development, tend to destroy the belief in the immortality of the lower class. Such glaring examples of this are found in some of the more advanced American nations that immortality has been denied to all but a few of the upper class. Hence, while great care is taken in the preservation of their bodies by the erection over them of pyramids and temples, the common people die with "none so poor as to do them reverence."

The belief in the resurrection of the body was universal among primitive peoples, and owed its origin often to cases of resuscitation. Among the tribes of the West there was a superstition against touching dead bodies, or those supposed to be dead; and hence there have been many cases where the natives have been buried alive. Two cases of this kind are mentioned by Lee and Frost among the natives of Oregon.[1] Among these tribes there are a few resurrection-traditions, growing undoubtedly out of this careless habit. The Virginians had fictions concerning the resurrection of certain persons from the dead. Hariot gives two instances of this. He says, "They told me that a wicked man having been dead and buried, the next day the earth of the grave was seen to move, whereupon, being taken up again, he told where his soul had been, and that he was very near entering into Popogusso, had not one of the gods saved him and given him leave to return again and teach his friends what they should do to avoid that terrible place of torment. Another revival from the dead occurred the same year, and it was told me for strange news that one being dead, buried, and taken up again as the first, showed that although his body had laid dead in the grave, yet his soul was alive, and

---

[1] Ten Years in Oregon, 321.

had travelled far in the long, broad way, on both sides whereof grew most delicate and pleasant trees, bearing more rare and excellent fruits than ever he had seen before. He at length came to most fair houses, near which he met his father that had been dead before, who gave him great charge to go back again and show his friends what good they were to do to enjoy the pleasures of that place."[1]

In cases of the falling sickness, catalepsy, or any diseases where the person is in a lethargic state, the savage believes that the soul has left the body and returns to it again when revival takes place. This has perhaps suggested in many cases their belief in a resurrection. The Ojibways say of such cases that the soul could not get into the spirit-land and had to come back. They conceive the person to be dead, and the revival is a resurrection. The savage believes that the insensibility of death is, like all the other insensibilities, only temporary.[2]

Among the Eskimos, if a man wished to become of the highest order of priests, it was requisite that he should be drowned and eaten by sea-monsters; then, when his bones were washed ashore, his spirit, which had spent all this time gathering information about the secrets of the invisible world, would return to them, and he would rejoin his tribe.[3]

There are curious traditions of resurrections among them. An Eskimo female carried home a bird, and, having cut it up, found in its crop the bones of her lost brother. She singled these all out and kept them together, when, behold, they moved. The brother quickly revived, and seemed entirely unhurt.[4] An Eskimo man and wife who were old and unable to provide for themselves, in their extremity decided to go to the tomb of their dead foster-son. The grave was opened and the body appealed to, when, lo, it began to move. The son arose from the dead, went home with them, got a kayak, and

---

[1] Hariot, ap. 3 Hakluyt, 277, seq. [2] 1 Spencer, Soc., 167.
[3] Brinton, 299. [4] Rink's Trad., 260.

thereafter provided for his aged parents.[1] Many stories are told of such resurrections among the Eskimos. In one case a son revived three times, after as many burials.

The natives of Canada had a universally received tradition that their dead bodies were to rise again.[2]

The Peruvians thought the bodies of the dead arose from their graves. Some of them asserted that they had seen them walking about after burial.[3] Atahuallpa requested the Spaniards that he might be hanged instead of burned. He said then his body would rise again.[4] The Chibchas also believed that the dead would be raised.[5] The natives of Quimbaya thought that the bodies of the dead would come to life again.[6] Those of Guazacualco thought the dead would rise again, and therefore hung their bones to the bough of a tree, that they might be easily found.[7] Among many of the tribes of South America it was within the power of the sorcerers, they thought, to bring the dead to life.[8]

The Bois Brulé tribe carried their belief in the resurrection so far that if a leg or a foot should be separated from the rest of the body the stray member would be hunted for till found.[9] All of the aborigines preserved with almost as much care the bones of animals. They said these bones contained the spirits of the slain animals, and that some time in the future they would rise, reclothe themselves with flesh, and stock the earth anew.[10]

The Minetarees believe that the bones of the bisons which they have slain and divested of flesh rise again with new flesh and life the succeeding June. They have a curious myth bearing upon this subject of animal resurrection. They say one of their boys, supposed to have been killed, was found in a buffalo. He had killed it, and, as a refuge against an inclement night,

---

[1] Rink's Trad., 298.
[2] 1 Warburton's Canada, 196.
[3] Cieza, 160–61.
[4] Pizarro (Rep., 247).
[5] P. Simon, 243.
[6] 5 Herrera, 202.
[7] 4 ib., 126.
[8] Müller, Amer. Urreligionen, 287.
[9] 2 Beltrami, 394.
[10] Brinton, 278.

took shelter within its body in place of the viscera which he had taken out. During the night the flesh of the bison grew over the side, the animal came to life, and the boy had lived there for one year before he was found.[1]

So thoroughly are the Minetarees convinced of the truth of the resurrection, that they have a tradition that the tribe came from under ground. These traditions of underground origin are very common among the American tribes, and have originated on account of their belief in the resurrection, accompanied by the tribal custom of interment. Some of the Southern tribes of the United States had traditions of underground origin. The most curious instance is that of the Muscogees, who thought that they had emerged from two mounds in the forks of Red River.[2]

The Navajos had a tradition of underground origin. When confined under the surface of the earth, they were aided in emerging therefrom by the locust, who bored the first hole, which was so small, however, that the badger had to make it larger. The badger was the first to crawl out, in a miry spot, and his fore-legs were so covered with mud that they have remained stained ever since. After arriving on the surface of the earth, they had to call the wolf, the bat, and the squirrel to their aid in procuring fire. The wolf tied some inflammable wood to its tail, and held it over the crater of a volcano until it ignited. The bat then fanned the flame with its wings, while the squirrel carried the fire to the Navajos.[3]

The Zuñis vary the legend about their emerging from the earth. The woodpecker attempted to peck a hole through for them, but failed, when an eagle, with a blow of its beak, broke the crust of the earth, and the bear forced its way through, leaving a hole for the Indians.[4]

Sacrifice was the most interesting rite attending the burial of the dead, and is illustrative of the worship of spirits. All

---

[1] 1 Long's Exp., 257.
[2] 1 Stevens's Ga., 51.
[3] Cozzens's Marvellous Country, 132.
[4] Ib., 346-48.

primitive peoples make offerings of meat, drink, and all other useful things to the dead. The Coras of Mexico, after a man's death, placed meat upon sticks about the burial-place. The Nootkans burned salmon and venison at the graves of the dead. Among the Mosquito Indians, the widow was compelled to supply the grave of her husband with provisions for a year after his death. The Pueblo Indians placed corn-bread and meat in places supposed to be haunted by the dead. Blankets were burned at the funerals of the Ahts, that the soul might not be sent shivering to the next world.[1] The Ukiahs and Sanels of California placed food in those places supposed to be the favored haunts of the dead.[2] Among the Algonkin tribes the female relatives went to the grave frequently, and made offerings of bread, meat, clothing, tobacco, and even watermelons, for as long a period as a year after interment.[3] The Illinois buried corn with their dead, together with a pot to boil it in. They thought they might be hungry without a supply of provisions.[4]

Mr. Riggs says the idea of sacrifice was at the foundation of all the ancient ceremonies of the Dacotahs. Sacrifices were universally made to the spirits of their dead. Food was given for their use. The offerings were often left on the graves. There was no sacrificial priesthood among them, but each one made his own offerings. Among the Iroquois, when an Indian was about to die, they cut the throats of all the dogs they could catch, that the souls of these animals might accompany him. They stripped themselves of everything that was most valuable, to adorn the dead. They deprived themselves of food to carry it to their sepulchres or other places which they fancied were haunted by their souls. When a post was set up on the grave adorned with the portrait of the deceased, they hung their offerings upon it. They carried fresh provisions to the grave every morning, and when the dogs devoured them they imagined they had been eaten by the souls of the deceased. The

---

[1] 3 Bancroft, 521.   [2] 3 ib., 524.   [3] 1 Loudon's Narratives, 341, 350.
[4] Joutel's Journal, 164.

Potawatomies left food at the grave when they visited it. A fire was lighted at the head of the grave.[1]

The idea among all the tribes was that the sacrifices were used. The Algonkins told Father Le Jeune that they found meat which had been left for souls that had been gnawed by them. The Caribs said they heard the spirits moving the vessels and champing the food set for them, and this they believed though nothing appeared to be touched.[2] Mr. Müller says they thought the spirit of the food was appropriated by the spirits of the dead, though it had no appearance of having been touched.

Among the tribes of South America sacrificial offerings of the same kind were made to the dead. The Araucanians supplied provisions to the dead for their supposed journey. The natives of Brazil carried provisions every day to their dead.[3] The natives of Panama presented food to the dead, and carried a yearly sacrifice of maize to their graves.[4] The Chibchas placed food in the graves with their dead.[5] Among some of the tribes of Peru, wives stayed several days at their husbands' graves to cook for them. They poured chicha on their bodies.[6] The children would carry stores of food and clothing to the tombs of their parents.[7] In Peruvian graves, corn, potatoes, cocoa, and nuts were found in abundance.

At the time of the discovery, the Mayas of Yucatan offered animals of all kinds and provisions of every sort to the dead.[8] The mouths of their dead were stuffed with ground maize. In their religious festivals food was always offered the dead. Among the mountain-tribes of Yucatan, chocolate and large maize tortillas were placed about the dead when buried.[9] The Zapotecs placed food in the grave or in its immediate vicinity.[10] The Isthmians filled the graves of their dead lords with jars of maize, fruit, and wine; even flowers were offered.[11]

---

[1] 1 Keating, 113.   [2] 2 Tylor, 388.
[3] 4 Herrera, 97.   [4] 3 Picart, 175.
[5] Bollaert, 14.   [6] Frezier's Voyage, 58.
[7] Markham's Cuzco, 126.   [8] Landa, 28.
[9] Cogulludo, bk. 12, ch. 7.   [10] 1 Bancroft, 667.   [11] 1 ib., 783.

The periodical renewal of these sacrifices that were supposed to supply the wants of the dead is found among nearly all the tribes. At the annual cumulative burial-ceremony of the Northern tribes, when the bodies have been ranged in order, broth is offered to these skeletons, and many presents are offered them. The Peruvians often opened the tombs of the dead and renewed the offerings of food and clothing.[1] At certain seasons of the year the bodies of their chiefs were carried to the fields and sheep offered to them.[2]

Among the Mexicans a daily sacrifice of food and flowers was placed on the tombs of the dead for twenty days after death.[3] The honors paid their dead ancestors continued for many years after their death, and did not cease with their funerals. An annual feast was celebrated for the dead, when the houses were richly decorated and food of all kinds prepared, as though the spirits would come and partake of it. The members of the family carried torches during this ceremony. The spirits were thought to extract all the nutritive qualities of the food.[4] The continuance of this custom for three centuries after the conquest is noticed by the Abbé Brasseur. Even recently the Indians in the interior of Yucatan place out-of-doors, under a tree, a portion of their food for their deceased friends to eat, and they say that the portion thus set apart is always eaten.[5]

Thus among these more civilized races we find the same primitive ideas of sacrifice as among those in savagery and barbarism; but it was supplemented by an elaborate sacrificial ritual in the worship of their monarchs and heroes.

Of all the food-offerings made to the dead, those of mothers to their children were the simplest and showed the primitive idea of sacrifice. Among the Iroquois, mothers have been known to keep the dead bodies of their children by them for years and continually feed them with their milk.[6]

---

[1] Cieza, 228–29. [2] Ib., 227. [3] Motolinia, 31.
[4] 3 Brasseur, Hist., 23–24. [5] 1 Stephens's Yucatan, 45.
[6] 2 Charlevoix, Journal, 185, seq.

Among the Californian tribes, mothers dropped their milk on the lips of their dead children, that they might have sustenance till they reached a place of rest.[1] They sprinkled nourishing milk on the graves of their dead babes for some time after their burial.[2] The Nicaraguan mothers withheld their milk from other children for four days after the death of their own babe, that it might be supplied.[3] Among many tribes, when a child died a dog was sacrificed, to guide its wandering steps to the spirit-land. They thought children did not have sufficient understanding to find the way.

These simple offerings were not acts of worship, but illustrate the primitive forms of sacrifice before it became an act of homage. Fear soon became the instigating cause of these offerings, and many tales are told among all the tribes of the punishments inflicted upon those who failed to make the offerings, whether intentionally or not. They generally put them in the fire. Occasionally they visited the graves of the dead and made their offerings there.[4] They thought a neglect of this duty brought upon them the vengeance of the spirits. Whenever a burying-ground or grave was passed, something was offered; and it was considered a wicked act to neglect this attention to the dead. The following is an amusing illustration of the origin and strength of this religious sentiment. An Ojibway was once passing an Indian burial-ground at dusk with a kettle of whiskey in his hands; he felt his duty to his ancestors, but, rather than part with his precious drink by pouring out a small libation, he grasped his whiskey the firmer and hurried on. His guilty conscience worked on his imagination, and a ghostly pursuer was after him and gaining rapidly. He determined to make a desperate struggle to keep his whiskey, and he turned to grasp his pursuer. But, lo! he did not hold in his arms his ghostly pursuer, but a tall bunch of rushes into which it had transformed itself. When an Indian falls into the fire and gets burned, he believes

---

[1] 1 Bancroft, 590.
[2] 3 ib., 524.
[3] 3 ib., 543.
[4] Jones, Ojibways, 101.

that the spirits of the dead have pushed him in, to punish him for neglect of those pious offerings due to them.[1]

Among all primitive peoples the doctrine of sacrifices is based on utilitarian principles : the things offered are supposed to be used by the dead and to be necessary to their happiness. Among the more uncivilized American tribes all or nearly all the property of the deceased was offered in sacrifice, or, more correctly speaking, was sent to him in the next world. Gitchi Gauzini, an Ojibway chief, after a severe illness, was thought to be dead. He, however, revived after four days, and gave an account of his journey to the spirit-land, in which he met hosts of spirits travelling thither laden with pipes, kettles, and provisions. Women had basket-work, paddles, and other female utensils.[2] This indicates the nature of their faith in the utility and existence of these sacrificial offerings in the spirit-world.

The natives of Canada think the souls of their kettles and other utensils follow the dead into the next world.[3]

> "Do not lay such heavy burdens
> On the graves of those you bury;
> Not such weight of furs and wampum,
> Not such weight of pots and kettles;
> For the spirits faint beneath them;
> Only give them food to carry,
> Only give them fire to light them."
>
> LONGFELLOW.

In a Peruvian tomb, alongside of a female there lay an unfinished piece of weaving stretched upon its frame and with its yarn of various colors still bright. The needle of thorn was in it, and beside it several balls of yarn. It was laid beside her under the belief that she would resume her task in a future life.[4]

The natives of the West India islands put all the wealth of the dead into their tombs, and women and servants sacrificed themselves. Among the Patagonians all the property of the

---

[1] 1 Schoolcraft, 139.
[2] 2 Tylor, 481–82.
[3] 3 Picart, 99.
[4] 2 Wilson's Prehist. Man, 141.

deceased is laid with him in the grave. If he has horses, they are killed, stuffed, and held up on sticks around the grave.[1] The Araucanians buried with the dead all their property.

Among the Mosquitos the hatchets, harpoons, and lances of the dead, with plenty of provisions, were buried with them. Even the boat of the deceased was cut up and placed over the grave.[2]

The Omahas sacrificed to the dead their bison robes and moccasins.[3] The Western tribes always placed the weapons of the deceased with him, thinking that he would use them.[4] Mr. Winslow said that the Narragansetts offered nearly all their riches by casting them into a great fire.

Among the Delawares, says Gabriel Thomas, kettles and all the property of the deceased were buried with them.[5] The natives of West New Jersey, says the same author, buried all the house-utensils of the deceased, and even money, with him, thinking he would use it in the next world.[6]

All of the tribes admitted that the bodies, skins, dishes, and other articles offered to the dead remained in this world, but the spirit went to the next world. The phantoms of the articles left at the grave entered the spirit-land.[7]

Those tribes which practised cremation thought the flames spiritualized their sacrifices.

Many of the Indians during their life provided for an abundance in the next world. A Potawatomie requested that he should be deposited in a log in the forks of a road between Detroit and Chicago, in order that he might receive plenty of tobacco from travellers.[8]

The Hurons thought that at the annual collection and inhumation of the bones of those who had died during the year, the souls of the dead started for the land of shades, carrying with them the spirits of the wampum-belts, beaver-skins, bows

---

[1] 2 Wood's Uncivilized Races, 542.
[2] 6 Churchill's Coll. Voy., 295.
[3] 2 Long's Exp., 2.
[4] Lyon's Journal, 374.
[5] Gabriel Thomas, Penn., 50.
[6] West New Jersey, 2.
[7] Dodge's Plains, 284.
[8] McCoy's Baptist Missions, 136.

and arrows, pipes, kettles, and beads buried with them in their graves.[1]

This belief in the delay of the departure of the spirits for a spirit-land was due to the lingering hope and expectation that the dead might return to the living, until the disintegration of the body dispelled that hope.

In addition to their own property, provisions of all kinds were supplied. Seeds were often tied to the dead by tribes who practised agriculture to any extent: these he was expected to plant in the spirit-land and raise a crop therefrom. Numerous flocks of llamas were pastured and raised in Peru for the purposes of sacrifice. About two hundred thousand of these animals were sacrificed annually in the city of Cuzco alone. Alpacas, vicuñas, and guanacos were also offered in large numbers. Among wild animals, foxes, rabbits, apes, deer, tapirs, tigers, serpents, lizards, humming-birds, parrots, cuckoos flamingoes, and even flies were offered, and also all the useful vegetable products.[2]

If anything which could be of use to the dead was retained, it was thought to be a great wrong done to the deceased. This destruction of property at death was a serious check to the progress of early peoples toward civilization.

The extravagance manifested in the sacrificial destruction of property reached its height among the nations of Central America and Mexico.

The Guatemalans made costly sacrifices whenever they dedicated a house to the guardian spirit or spirits thereof, and sprinkled the blood of animals on the door-posts and walls.[3] The one who offered the most sacrifices at one of the Mexican festivals was especially honored all the year after.[4] The Mexicans would not even pluck leaves or foliage without offering a portion of them to spirits.[5] In Granada, their idols, representing men, were found with their mouths full of flowers, which

---

[1] Parkman, Jesuits, lxxxi.   [2] Rivero and Tschudi, 196–98.
[3] Ximenez, 188.   [4] 3 Herrera, 121.
[5] Worsley's View, 175.

were offerings from the natives.[1] This æsthetic worship was uncommon, and affords a pleasing contrast to most of their ceremonial.

In Peru, the substitution of the images of the things sacrificed was displacing to some extent their human and animal sacrifices. These sacrifices were, however, continued to the time of the conquest and long thereafter. When sacrifice degenerated into an act of homage, it became a ceremonial rite of worship. This was not its primitive meaning. The sacrifice of property that was of little or no use gradually supplanted the primitive sacrifice, and even systematic efforts to defraud the dead and reduce sacrifice to a mere formality prevailed among the civilized American aborigines as well as among the ancient peoples of the Old World, where cheap imitations of expensive articles were made for the purposes of sacrifice.

Human sacrifices prevailed to a certain extent in both Americas. It is quite a remarkable fact that they prevailed to a much greater extent among the civilized races than among the uncivilized; yet there are some traces of it among the latter. Mrs. Eastman mentions a case of human sacrifices among the Dacotahs, and Mr. Keating says there were traditions about human sacrifices among the Ojibways, among whom the cruel rite seems to have expired in a myth. An epidemic appears to have swept over their tribe, which they ascribed to the punishment sent by spiritual influences on account of their wickedness. All other efforts failing, it was decided that the most beautiful girl of the tribe should enter a canoe, push into the channel just above the Sault, and throw away her paddle. The morning of the day appointed for the solemn sacrifice dawned, and loud and dismal was the wail of sorrow which broke upon the silent air. The beautiful sacrifice was surrounded with her long-loved companions, who decked her hair and neck with the brightest shells and most beautiful feathers. The time appointed for the sacrifice was the sunset hour, and, as the day

---

[1] Boyle's Camp Notes, 84.

rapidly waned, the gloom which pervaded the entire village increased. The time approached; the Indian maiden was led to the canoe, when, lo! a strange echo came over the waters, and a black speck was seen coming from the setting sun. It was a small canoe, which swept mysteriously over the watery waste. It contained a fairy-like being who stood with her arms folded and her eyes fixed upon the heavens. As she moved directly toward the rapids, her song was, "I come from the spirit-land to stay the plague and save the life of the beautiful Ojibway." The canoe and its spirit voyager passed into the foam of the cataract and were lost forever.[1]

Human sacrifice was practised among the Miamis, for we are told by Mr. Drake that Little Turtle, the famous Miami chief, "did more than any other to abolish human sacrifices among his people."[2]

There are many evidences of the practice of human sacrifice among those tribes living on the Ohio, Cumberland, and Tennessee Rivers.[3] Father Jogues mentions the sacrifice of a woman among the tribes of New York, and De Vries mentions another instance of this practice among them.[4] The tribes of British America practised human sacrifice to a limited extent. The Pawnees offered human victims at their annual ceremony immediately preceding their horticultural operations.[5] It was among this tribe that Petashaleroo struck the final blow at human sacrifices, by rescuing his intended bride, who had been chosen as a victim.

Human sacrifices never prevailed to any extent among the barbarous tribes of the North. Very few cases of compulsory human sacrifice are found. Among these primitive tribes voluntary sacrifice was more frequent. Suicides often occurred, that the person committing this self-sacrifice might follow the deceased into the next world. The Carriers sometimes burned the widow at the funeral ceremonies of her husband.[6]

---

[1] Lanman's Haw-Hoo-Noo, 227–28.   [2] Indian Biography, 1st ed., 158.
[3] Haywood's Ab. Hist. Tenn., 140.   [4] 3 N. Y. Hist. Coll., 56, 203.
[5] 3 Long's Exp., 80.   [6] West's Journal, 141.

Among some of the tribes west of the Rocky Mountains the sacrifice of the wife took place at the funeral of her husband.[1] Sutteeism was also practised among the Tlascalans.[2]

Among the tribes farther south, human sacrifice prevailed to a greater extent. When De Soto died, two young men were killed to wait upon him in the spirit-world.[3] Among the Floridians slaves were burned with their chiefs, to wait upon them in the next world. The Gent of Elvas mentions human sacrifices among the Calloosas, and also among the tribes around St. John's River. Says Charlevoix, describing the human sacrifices among the Natches at the obsequies of a female chief, "The husband of this woman not being noble, that is to say, of the family of the great chief, his eldest son strangled him according to custom; then they cleared the cabin of all it contained, and they erected in it a kind of triumphal car, in which the body of the deceased woman and that of her husband were placed. A moment after, they ranged round these carcasses twelve little children, which their parents had strangled. This being done, they erected in the public place fourteen scaffolds, adorned with branches of trees and cloths, on which they had painted various figures. These scaffolds were designed for as many persons who were to accompany the woman chief into the other world. They apply sometimes ten years beforehand to obtain this favor. They appear on their scaffolds dressed in their richest habits, holding in their right hand a great shell. During the eight days that precede their death, some wear a red ribbon around one of their legs, and during all this time everybody strives who shall be the first to feast them. . . . On the occasion I am speaking of, the fathers and mothers who had strangled their children took them up in their hands and ranged themselves on both sides of the cabin; the fourteen persons who were also destined to die placed themselves in the same

---

[1] 1 Bancroft, 440.   [2] 2 Herrera, 303.
[3] Foster's Prehistoric Races, 316.

manner. At last they began the procession. The fathers and mothers who carried the dead children appeared first, marching two and two, and came immediately before the bier, on which was the body of the woman chief, which four men carried on their shoulders. All the others came after, in the same order as the first. At every ten paces the fathers and mothers let their children fall upon the ground; those who carried the bier walked upon them, then turned quite round them; so that when the procession arrived at the temple these little bodies were all in pieces. While they buried the body of the woman chief in the temple, they undressed the fourteen persons who were to die; they made them sit on the ground before the door, each having two savages by him. Then they put a cord about his neck and covered his head with a roebuck's skin. They made him swallow three pills of tobacco and drink a glass of water, and the relations of the woman chief drew the two ends of the cord, singing till he was strangled. After this they threw all the carcasses into the same pit, which they covered with earth."[1]

Among the rude tribes of South America voluntary sacrifices were common. Many of the Brazilians killed themselves on the graves of their chiefs. Among the Itatines a number of the relatives of the deceased person would commit suicide by throwing themselves from a precipice, in order to accompany the deceased to another world. A Mbaya woman, when she found that a chief's daughter received no sacrifices at her funeral, celebrated by a Catholic priest, whose faith she had espoused, asked a fellow-savage to knock her on the head, that she might go and serve the damsel. This he did quickly and without hesitation.

The Guaycurus of South America butchered a certain number of men and women on the death of a person of distinction, in order that they might bear him company into the other world. It is evident that human sacrifices were made that the

---

[1] 2 Charlevoix's Journal, 162.

spirits of the victims might serve the spirits of those to whom they were offered.

A New Mexican king, mentioned by Gage, had a cup-bearer, cook, and laundress sacrificed at his death.[1]

In Mexico, the chaplain of a great magnate who died was killed to officiate for him in the other world.[2] This was a very extraordinary piece of self-sacrifice on the part of a pagan priesthood, who have generally arranged religious worship in such a way that they are not sacrificed to the people, but the people to them. The usual victims at their sacrifices were captives, slaves, and criminals.

The sacrificial system of the Mexicans was very elaborate. They were more civilized in one sense than the Northern tribes, but more inhuman in the sacrifice of human beings. They sacrificed slaves to the dead on the fifth, twentieth, fortieth, sixtieth, and eightieth days after burial.

The manner of conducting human sacrifices in Mexico was revolting in its details. The victim was stretched upon the altar and held by four priests, while a fifth placed an instrument in the shape of a coiled serpent about his neck. The high-priest then approached, cut open his breast, tore out the bleeding heart while still palpitating, and offered it to the idol. The head was then cut off, and, after some preparation, placed in a charnel-house of skulls, and the body was thrown down the stairway leading to the temple. The bodies thus thrown down were picked up and carried away to be eaten. In some of the provinces these bodies were cut up and sold in the meat-markets.[3] The idols were daily sprinkled with the blood of human beings.[4] Clavigero says that twenty thousand human beings were annually sacrificed throughout the Mexican empire.[5] Herrera estimates the number much higher.

The Mayas of Yucatan offered human sacrifices in times of distress. Among them, however, the substitution of figures of

---

[1] New Survey, 158.   [2] 3 Herrera, 220.
[3] 1 Clavigero, 279.   [4] Gage, New Survey, 115.
[5] 1 Clavigero, 281.

the heart seems to have begun to receive favor in the place of human sacrifices. With them the sacrifice of human beings appears to have been associated in many instances with the idea that they would act as intercessors, and they were sent as messengers to the spirit-world to make known the wants of the people. In Yucatan, where Cukulcan opposed human sacrifice, his influence operated as a check upon this inhuman rite; but they sent young virgins occasionally into the presence of the gods to intercede for needed blessings. That they were intended as intercessors only is shown by a curious incident. One of the intended victims threatened to invoke the most terrible evils upon the people, instead of blessings, if they sacrificed her against her will. The perplexed priests let the girl go.[1] Slaves were sacrificed in large numbers.[2]

Holocausts of victims were sacrificed in the sanguinary funeral rites of the Incas. On the death of Huayna Capac the human victims numbered over a thousand.[3] The Inca Yupanqui shut up a great many women and servants in the tomb of his father, to die there, as a sacrifice to him.[4] The Yuncas of Peru buried with a chief his wives and other persons with whom he had much friendship. If there was no room in the tomb, his companions had to be buried in holes around the tomb. They would often commit suicide on his grave.[5]

Among the coast people of Peru, human sacrifices were offered at the sepulchres of the dead.[6] Human sacrifices were made to the animal deities of the Peruvians.[7] It was the custom when they gave the borla to the new Inca to sacrifice two hundred boys from four to ten years old. Girls also were taken from the monasteries for sacrifice. It will thus be seen how prevalent human sacrifices were throughout Peru, many authors to the contrary notwithstanding. Huascar became very unpopular among his subjects because, being tired of

---

[1] 3 Bancroft, 471.
[3] Ranking's Peru, 229–30.
[5] Cieza, 223.
[2] Fancourt's Yucatan, 116.
[4] 4 Herrera, 298.
[6] Xeres, Rep., 32.
[7] Ranking, 89, 94.

seeing the great part of his empire in the hands of the dead, he ordered that all corpses should be buried. The easy conquest by the Spaniards is ascribed to this alienation of the people[1] because the worship of the dead was interfered with and human sacrifices prevented.

The Quiches of Guatemala offered human sacrifices to their idols.[2] The intercessory character of many of their sacrifices is evident from their sculptures.[3]

The Pipiles of Salvador had human sacrifices annually, and with the blood of the victims they sprinkled the walls of the temples. If any blood was left over, they poured it back into the body of the victim. For success in war, captives were sacrificed.[4]

The custom of offering captives as sacrifices was prevalent among all those guilty of human sacrifices. The Araucanians of Chile sacrificed prisoners of war to the manes of their warriors killed in the war.[5] The Peruvians, before the Incas, sacrificed men and women who were captives taken in war. "They opened their breast while yet alive, and took out heart and lungs, and anointed the idol with their blood, and watched the omens in the heart and lungs to see whether it was accepted. They then ate the sacrificed Indian with relish and delight."[6]

The sacrifice of children prevailed among both the civilized and uncivilized peoples. Among the latter they were seldom sacrificed, except when the death of the mother occurred when the child was so young that its care was considered a burden, and it was sent into the next world to receive maternal care. The sacrifice of children grew, however, into great proportions among the more advanced nations.

The following description of these sacrifices in Culhuacan is taken from Martyr:

"Let every godly man close the mouth of his stomake, lest

---

[1] P. Pizarro, 238-40. [2] Ximenez, 183.
[3] See Habel's Sculptures. [4] Palacio, 65.
[5] 2 Molina's Chile, 78. [6] 1 Garcilasso, Commentaries, 50.

he be desturbed. They offer younge children of bothe kyndes to their Idoles of marble and earth. Amonge their Idoles of marble there standeth a lyon havynge a hole throwgh the necke, into the whiche they poure the bludde of the miserable sacrifice, that it maye from thence runne down into a syncke of marble. They cutte not their throtes, but open the very brestes and take owtt their hartes yet pantynge with the hotte bludde, whereof they anoynte the lyppes of theyre Idoles and suffer the resydue to faule into the synke. This doone, they burne the harte and bowels, supposynge the smoke thereof to be acceptable to their Goddes. Of their Idoles one is made to the shape of a man bowynge downe his head and lookynge toward the synke of bludde, as it were acceptyng the offeringe of the slayne sacrifyce. They eate the fleshe of the armes, thighes, and legges. They founde a streame of congealed bludde as thoughe it had runne from a bouchery."

The inhabitants of Cozumella "sacrifyce children of both kyndes to theyr Zemes, which are the images of their familiar and domesticall spirites whych theye honour as Goddes."[1]

Children were sacrificed, says Molina, at all the chief huacas of the provinces of Peru.[2] Young children and boys were sacrificed to two huacas at Hunoyan.[3] When the Indians were ill, their own children were sometimes offered as a sacrifice to Viracocha.[4]

The sculpture of the ruined temples at Palenque presents many representations of the sacrifice of children. Female figures erect, adorned with jewels and ornaments, are found, each figure with a child in her arms, not in the attitude of receiving a mother's nourishment, but held by the parent in such a manner as if in sorrowful contemplation of her infant victim. Other female figures are represented seated and in the most melancholy postures, with downcast heads and looks as if mourning for that loss which had made them motherless.

---

[1] Martyr's Decades, 156.
[2] Narrative, 58–59.
[3] Arriaga, 265.
[4] Jos. D'Acosta, bk. 5, chap. 19.

In an inner apartment, believed to be the sanctum of a temple, is sculptured (in basso) the resemblance of the dread altar, portraying the entrance of the fiery furnace, for even the bars and grating are distinctly visible. A large and monstrous mask, or demoniac face, is directly above the fire-grating, representing that of the remorseless deity. On either side of the altar-furnace are stationed a young and an elderly priest of sacrifice, both standing erect upon crushed and prostrate human beings; the priests have their hands and arms elevated, and each holds an infant raised up toward the demon deity, as if in the act of presenting the victims. The sculptured mask has a hideous face, distorted eyes, a ravenous and distended mouth, and its tongue hanging out, as if athirst for infant blood, thus presenting a perfect portraiture of the child-craving appetite of the god. The sculpture described is, as we have stated, upon the stuccoed walls of Palenque, and we believe was placed there as a record of a religious custom practised anterior to the walls being stuccoed.[1]

The Chibchas of Bogota offered sacrifices of children to the sun. Their caciques had a receptacle on the beams of their houses, into which they placed a boy who had been killed for a sacrifice. His blood trickled down the posts of the house.[2]

A few instances of the sacrifice of children as an act of worship appear among the tribes of the territory now embraced within the United States. "The Florida savages sacrificed their first-born."[3] The Eskimos sacrificed the favorite child on the grave of its deceased parent.[4]

Self-mutilation was another form of sacrifice. The funereal mourners, generally the relatives of the deceased, cut off fingers, knocked out teeth, punctured flesh, and did many other acts wholly unutilitarian, but which manifested the great sorrow felt by the survivors, and thus were supposed to be pleasing to the dead.

---

[1] Jones, Ancient America, 141, seq.
[2] P. Simon, 248–49.
[3] 3 Picart, 129.
[4] Chappell's Voyage, 190.

Describing the death of A-ra-poo-ash, chief of the Crows, and the exhibitions of grief on the part of his nation that followed, Bonner, in his life of Beckworth, says,[1] quoting Beckworth's language, "Every warrior immediately set up the most dismal cryings that I have ever heard in my life. I despatched a herald to the village to inform them of the head chief's death. When we drew in sight of the village, we found every lodge laid prostrate. We entered amid shrieks, cries, and yells. Blood was streaming from every conceivable part of the bodies of all who were old enough to comprehend their loss. Hundreds of fingers were dismembered; hair torn from the head lay in profusion about the paths. A herald having been despatched to our other village to acquaint them with the death of our head chief and request them to assemble at the Rosebud, in conformity with this summons over ten thousand Crows met at the place indicated. Such a scene of disorderly, vociferous mourning no imagination can conceive nor any pen portray. Long Hair cut off a large roll of his hair,— a thing he was never known to do before. The cutting and hacking of human flesh exceeded all my previous experience: fingers were dismembered as readily as twigs, and blood was poured out like water. Many of the warriors would cut two gashes nearly the entire length of their arm, then, separating the skin from the flesh at one end, would grasp it in their other hand and rip it asunder to the shoulder."

Among the Dacotahs, "when a death happens in a family, no matter how well they are clothed, the good clothes are stripped off and given away, and the worst old rags substituted in their place. They gash their legs and arms, and leave them to get well without the least attention. Some of them carry their grief so far as to raise the skin of their arms and pierce holes with their knives and put pegs through them. They continue their mourning about a year."[2]

Says Belden, "The practice of disfiguration prevails exten-

---

[1] P. 264, seq.   [2] 2 Wis. Hist. Coll., 180.

sively among nearly all the Western tribes. One day an Indian boy was thrown from his pony with such violence that he died. His mother and sisters, as a sign of their grief, cut off a finger each at the first joint. I have seen the Crows gash their arms, legs, bodies, and faces when their friends died. At Fort Phil Kearney it is said that hundreds of fingers were cut off, and gashes innumerable made on their persons, by the friends of the dead. When a warrior is killed, his pony is gashed in the sides and on the legs with knives, to make him feel sorry for the death of his master."[1]

The same custom prevailed among all the Northern tribes. Among the Mexicans their self-mutilations were as cruel as their bodies would bear, for, in their pious fanaticism, "they mangled their flesh as if it had been insensible, and let their blood run in profusion." They pierced themselves with the sharp spines of the aloe, and then bathed their bloody bodies in a pond at the great temple, which was called Ezapan, because always discolored with blood.[2]

In the pictographs in Lord Kingsborough's "Antiquities of Mexico" there are many representations of mourners thrusting a weapon through their tongues; and among the uncivilized tribes of South America the same practice prevailed. Among all the Brazilian tribes mutilations were a part of the funeral ceremonial. Some cut off fingers at the death of a kinsman,[3] others toes. The Mumanes, if all their fingers had been cut off, began on their toes.[4]

The most common mutilation in these mourning ceremonies was cutting the hair. Among the Peruvians, even the plucking out of an eyebrow and blowing it into the air was thought to be an acceptable offering.

Under the head of sacrifices and burial-ceremonies we have seen that the tombs of all of the American tribes have been their temples. Said Prudentius, the Roman bard, " there were

---

[1] Belden, 160, seq.   [2] 1 Clavigero, 283-85.
[3] 1 Southey, 345.
[4] 1 ib., 417; D'Orbigny, L'Homme Américain, 238.

as many temples of gods as sepulchres," implying that they were the same and identical among the ancient classical nations. The Collas of Peru took more care of their tombs than of the houses of the living. These tombs were small towers, the magnitude of which depended on the rank and wealth of the deceased.[1]

Many of the Peruvian tombs were places of worship. The burial-towers of Peru were often sprinkled with the blood of sacrifices, and most of the huacas, or sacred places, were the tombs of the dead. Many of the tribes of South America built a rough hut for the reception of the skeletons of the dead, and these were their temples. Mr. Stedman mentions one which contained four hundred skeletons, which were hung up therein.[2]

Columbus mentions a sepulchre as large as a house, built on a mountain and elaborately sculptured. A body lay therein, which was uncovered.[3]

"De Soto," says Biedma, in his narrative, "opened a large temple built in the woods, in which were buried the chiefs of the country."

The Virginia kings, after their bodies were prepared by a species of mummification, were laid upon a shelf in the temple, where a priest remained in constant attendance night and day.[4]

"The traditional name of the ancient burial-mounds among the Choctaws was Nanne-Yah,—the hills or mounts of God, a name almost identical, it is said, with that of the Mexican pyramids. Who can fail to perceive that the same principles of architecture have governed the construction of both, and that the temple-mound of Kentucky is but a ruder form of the Mexican teocalli?"[5]

The tribes in the United States were well acquainted with the character of the sepulchral mounds. These mounds were regarded with great reverence, and were frequently resorted

---

[1] Cieza, 364. [2] 1 Surinam, 400.
[3] Select Letters, 192. [4] Beverly, 47.
[5] 1 Collins's Kentucky, 385.

to by the Indians as places sacred to their devotional exercises.[1]

In Mexico and the States of Central America, and in Peru, where the temples had attained a magnitude and beauty of architecture rarely surpassed anywhere among the pagan peoples, their use as tombs had not become obsolete. In the great temple at Cuzco, an array of Incas, seated in all their rich vestments, was the most striking feature of its interior. In Mexico, the kings and lords, after having been prepared for burial, were placed in some temple. Even the idols found in these temples were generally the images of the dead, and often contained their ashes. Among the Iroquois a fire is built at the head of the grave of the dead, immediately after the burial, around which the relatives and friends sit for nine successive nights.[2] Thus tombs have always been regarded as sacred to religious devotions.

The utilitarian view of sacrifice has now almost passed away. The God of the Christian world asks naught but the sacrifice of a broken and contrite heart. But the method of worshipping him in the Roman Catholic Church by the sacrifice of the mass has its prototype in the funeral rite of the savage. The fire on the grave of the savage for the spirit to warm itself by and cook its food survives in the light on the graves of Catholic Europe on All Souls' day and in the light on the sacrificial altar of the Roman Church. The mutilation in the primitive funeral ceremony now appears in the cropped hair and lacerating garments of religious devoteeism. Among the more civilized races of America, the simpler forms of sacrifice survived amid an elaborate sacrificial ritual.

---

[1] Hunter's Memoirs, 307, seq. [2] Life of Mary Jamison, 107.

CHAPTER VI.

ANIMAL-WORSHIP.

Its animistic origin—Immortality of the spirits of animals—Transmigration of human souls into animals—Omens—Manitology—Totemism—Animal names given to human beings—Traditionary descent of tribes from animals—Totemism in art—Heraldry—Totemic writing—Tattooing—Probable totemic origin of the animal mounds—Traditionary descent of animals from the human race—Metamorphosis—Animal dress—Worship of animals—Fabulous animals—Animals in the rôle of creators.

THE worship of animals has been supposed by many mythologists to have originated in symbolism. This explanation of it is wholly unsatisfactory. Symbolism is unknown to a very primitive people, and it is among them that animal-worship is universal. Again, this symbolism, which is used as an explanation of animal-worship among the advanced nations, such as the Egyptians, must itself be explained. The basis of the science of Naology, as the derivation of the word implies, must be the representation of an idea by a sign; the origin of animal symbolism in mythology can be found in totemism. Among the natives of America, animal-worship has originated in animism, or spirit-worship. Among primitive peoples all animals are supposed to be endowed with souls. In many cases the souls of human beings have transmigrated into animals. Hence among many of our wildest tribes a likeness has been recognized between an animal and some deceased relative or friend, and the animal has been addressed as the person would have been, and has been honored on account of such resemblance with an adoration which, among primitive peoples, is equivalent to worship. In the cosmogony of many of the tribes, animals have figured as the progenitors of the tribe, and in a few tribal traditions they appear as creators. This creation in some cases is fiatic in its nature, but usually it can be traced to a belief in a natural descent from the animal which stands as a progenitor of the tribe and is therefore held in great veneration as an ancestor. Here we have a point of contact with ancestral worship. This very curious and primitive belief in descent from animals has originated from the totemic system upon which their social system rests. The division of a tribe into the families of the bear, turtle, crane, etc., indicates a time when families claiming descent from ancestors bearing those names have banded themselves together for their common interest, generally for defence. That an ancestor should be named the bear or turtle or crane, indicates a time still farther back when the name was given him for some good reason. A great many ethnologists have supposed those names were given to designate a quality or characteristic of the individual: a very slow man would be called a turtle; a man with very long legs, a crane. Although there is no doubt that such nicknaming as this has occurred, and has originated many such names, yet the totemic system has a much broader and deeper foundation than this, upon which their social structure is built. Totemism is explained by manitology, or the worship of manitous. The manitou is a personal deity,—almost always an animal,—chosen by each individual at that most important period of his life—when he becomes of age. This animal manitou is always pointed out to the individual in a dream which is produced by the greatest religious act of his life,—the first fast. The animal then becomes an object of worship, and its skin or stuffed body is carried about the person as a fetich, or its likeness painted on the body or sculptured on the weapons. Heraldry, animal dress, tattooing, and the metamorphoses of men to animals and animals to men thus originate. The prevalence of the animal forms in primitive art can here find explanation. Hence the animal appears as the manitou, or personal fetich, and then develops into the totem, or sacred animal of the gens or family which descends from that person. Under favorable conditions it then appears as the creator, in which capacity it gradually assumes a fabulous nature, and is the author of all changes in the economy of the universe as far as known to the peoples among whom the myths occur. From animals the natives have descended, according to tradition. Upon animals they depend for their earthly blessings, and look to them in a worship which will be noticed throughout this chapter. In the future life they also figure in as important a rôle as in this. In art they appear as idols. Their figures are sculptured and painted on houses, temples, and natural rocks. They are tattooed upon the bodies. Their skins are worn as medicine-sacks and also as garments. In this latter capacity they have tended to produce the curious legends of metamorphosis noticed in this chapter and elsewhere. Their cries and actions, voluntary and involuntary, become the omens of the savage tribes, and originate the divination and augury of the more civilized. Dreams are their revelations to man. Disease is produced by their angry spirits, which are everywhere present and ready to avenge an act of impiety to their kind. Hence all the tribes worshipped the commonest animals. They supposed that all animals of land, air, and water were endowed with immortal spirits and could punish those who maltreated them. When they worshipped any of these they imagined that they would obtain the aid of their spirits.

The immortality of the souls of all animals is as thoroughly and universally believed as that of human souls. The subject has received so much consideration in other parts of this work that only a few authorities will be introduced here. Among the natives of Canada the spirits of animals were thought to be immortal.[1] Among the Western tribes, says Mr. Dodge, the phantoms of all animals are supposed to go to the happy hunting-grounds. The Indians have not yet separated themselves from the whole animated creation, and do not exclude animals from their world of spirits.[2] Says Mr. Buchanan, "The Knis-

---

[1] 1 Jes. Rel., 13.   [2] Buchanan, 181.

tenaux have a place assigned to animal spirits, and on this side of the land of the dead Knistenaux. Their spirits have to pass through the land of animal spirits, when the shades of the animals can avenge their wrongs."[1] Chateaubriand says that all the Indians granted immortality to the spirits of insects, reptiles, fishes, and birds.[2]

All of the Indians fancied that the souls of animals came to see how their bodies were treated, and afterward acquainted both the living and the dead with the facts; and that if they were ill treated they would not suffer themselves to be any longer taken, either in this world or the next.[3]

The intelligence of these spiritual agents and their interest in human affairs, according to the theories of the aborigines, were demonstrated in omens, animal oracles, and augury.

The Aztecs, in their migration, appear to have received their oracles from a bird, crying *tilini, tilini,*—" let us go, let us go." This led them from place to place. The importance of the little bird tilini-tochan, whose note is still heard in Mexico, tends to show how great an influence the animal world has had in the history of primitive peoples. The Aztecs founded Tenochtitlan in obedience to an oracle bidding them go until they found an eagle on a tuna-tree. The conditions were met when they came upon the site of the above city, for there sat an eagle upon a tuna-tree growing out of a rock, with her wings displayed facing the sun, and with a beautiful bird in her talons. They prostrated themselves before this eagle, which bowed her head in recognition of them. Their arms and those of the Mexicans at this day are an eagle in a tuna-tree.

Among hunting tribes the cawing of a crow at night would cause a large party of warriors to run for home and give up an expedition. The Comanches regarded the wolf as a brother, and said that it warned them of danger. If one sprang up before them in their journeys and barked or howled, they

---

[1] Buchanan, 275. [2] 2 Chateaubriand's Travels, 38.
[3] 2 Picart, 85.

would turn aside, and travel no more in that direction that day.[1] The Pecos said an eagle conversed with them and foretold the arrival of the white men.[2] The Ojibways believed much in omens. The barking of foxes and of wolves, the bleating of deer, the screeching of owls, the flight of uncommon kinds of birds, the moaning noise of a partridge, were ominous of ill. The two last were certain omens of death. But the sailing of an eagle to and fro, and the noise of a raven, were omens of good.[3] The inhabitants of St. Catherine's Island, on the coast of California, had two crows in the court of their temple, which were their oracles. They were thrown into great alarm because they were killed by the Spaniards.[4]

When the mankawis, a species of quail, perch at night upon a cabin belonging to a Seminole, the inhabitant of that cabin prepares for death. If a white bird sports aloof in the air, this indicates a storm. If it flies in the evening before the traveller, throwing itself from one wing upon the other, as if frightened, it forebodes danger.[5]

Among the Mayas the songs of birds and cries of animals were omens.[6]

Among the Northern tribes the march is regulated by a sorcerer according to good or bad omens. If the sorcerer but cries out at night that he has seen a spider on a willow-leaf, the army must break up.[7] If they hear the howling of a large wolf which they call the medicine-wolf, when travelling, sadness is at once visible in their countenances, for it is considered as foreboding some calamity near at hand.[8]

Small ducks, among the Abipones, which flew about together at night, making a loud hiss, were omens of evil, and were believed to be spirits of the dead.[9] Among the Brazilian tribes the screaming of vultures was an omen of death. The Para-

---

[1] Battey's Quaker, etc., 333. [2] Davis, El Gringo, 153.
[3] Autobiography of Kah-Ge-Ga-Bow, 48. [4] McCulloh, Ant., 112.
[5] 1 Chateaubriand's Travels, 246. [6] 2 Brasseur, Hist. Mexico, 51.
[7] 2 Chateaubriand's Travels, 21. [8] Parker's Journal, 243, seq.
[9] 1 Dobrizhoffer, 331; 2 ib., 270.

guayans consulted the songs of birds and cries of animals as auguries to guide their conduct.[1]

The Peruvian priests inspected the entrails of beasts for omens.[2] When the animals were opened and the lungs were palpitating, it was favorable.[3]

The llama was used at the sacrifice at the feast of Raymi, to get the auguries. When the body was opened, the priest sought, in the appearances which it exhibited, to read the lesson of the mysterious future.[4]

Let us now pass to the consideration of the subject of manitology, or the worship of manitous among the tribes, and make it introductory to the subject of totemism. After our consideration of these two subjects we will understand their animal-worship.

The most prominent belief in the Indian religion was their doctrine of manitous, or what may be denominated manitology. All the tribes had some equivalent for this, although the word used is Algonkin. The word manitou did not mean the Deity or Great Spirit, as has been erroneously asserted: it was confined to a spiritual and mysterious power thought to reside in some material form. The Potawatomie had his tutelary spirit, generally in the shape of some animal he had met in his dreams. To this animal he addressed his prayers and stated his wants; he consulted it in all difficulties, and frequently conceived that he had derived relief from it. Of course he abstained from eating the animal, and would rather starve than sacrilegiously feed upon his animal idol. He knew that others had different manitous, and did not feel bound to protect his animal from his companions, for he thought there was no virtue in the animal for anybody but himself.[5] Among the Illinois, each man had a manitou, which was some animal about which he had dreamed, and in which he placed all his confidence for success.[6]

---

[1] Caddell's Hist. Missions, Japan and Paraguay, 30.
[2] 1 Zarate, 52.
[3] 2 Garcilasso, 161.
[4] 1 Prescott, Peru, 106.
[5] 1 Keating, 118.
[6] Marquette, Récit de Voyage, 57.

The power of these manitous to deliver them from danger is well illustrated in the following tale:

A canoe full of Ojibways was once pursued by enemies. They endeavored to escape, but found the enemy gaining on them rapidly. At last they began calling on their manitous. One called upon the sturgeon, and their speed was soon equal to that fish's, and the enemy were left far behind. But the sturgeon was a short-winded fish, and soon became tired, and the enemy gained on them. All the manitous but one were tried in vain, and they began to give themselves up for lost, when a young man whom they had disregarded called upon his manitou, which happened to be the saw-bill (duck), and held its skin by the neck in the water. Immediately the canoe began to glide swiftly away at the usual speed of a saw-bill, and the enemy were left far behind and gave up the chase.[1]

The initial fast at the age of puberty which every Indian underwent was for the purpose of individually becoming aware of this personal manitou. When revealed in dreams, his purpose was accomplished, and he adopted that revelation, which was generally some bird or animal, as his personal or guardian manitou. There was no exigency in life in which it could not help him. The misfortune was that these manitous were not of equal power. Hence the Indian was never sure that his neighbor was not under the guardianship of a manitou stronger than his own.[2]

Each primitive Indian had his guardian manitou, to whom he looked for counsel, guidance, and protection. These spiritual allies were gained by the following process. At the age of fourteen or fifteen the Indian boy retired to some solitary place and remained for days without food. Superstitious expectancy and the exhaustion of abstinence rarely failed of their results. His sleep was haunted by visions, and the form which first or most often appeared was that of his guardian manitou (almost always an animal). An eagle or bear was the vision of a des-

---

[1] Jones, Ojibways, 89, 90.   [2] 1 Schoolcraft, 34.

tined warrior; a wolf, of a hunter; a serpent, of a medicine-man. The Indian henceforth wore about his person the object revealed in his dream, or some portion of it, within which was thought to reside its spirit. The Indian yielded to it a sort of worship and made offerings to it. The superstition now became mere fetich-worship.[1]

It is astonishing what an influence this superstition had on the daily life of the Indian. Mr. Cass knew an old Dacotah chief who had never been to war because he had dreamed of an antelope, the peace spirit of his people.

When the tribes pitched their tents they took very little care to guard against a surprise, because they placed great confidence in their manitous, which they always carried with them, and which they were persuaded took upon themselves the office of sentinels, and they slept very securely under their protection. These manitous were called by some tribes wakons,—that is, spirits.[2]

The Arkansas, next to the Natches the most civilized of the aborigines of the United States, had manitous which they always consulted. Their manitou was sometimes an animal, sometimes a bird, and to it they attributed all their good or bad luck.[3]

The early missionaries found great difficulty in inducing the natives to give up these guardian spirits, which they thought visited them and gave them valuable information.[4]

These manitous often had sacrifices offered to them. Says Marest, " The Illinois worship manitous, which are the skins of beasts or birds. They hang them up in their wigwams and offer to them sacrifices."[5] A famous sagamore of a tribe in Maine had a marten's skin for his manitou, which if laid under the head brought dreams at night, and to which he offered sacrifices.[6]

After an animal had become a manitou the individual would

---

[1] Parkman, Jesuits, lxxi.
[2] Lewis and Clarke, Lond. ed., 81.
[3] 3 French's Hist. Coll., 127.
[4] Jones's Ojibways, 270.
[5] Kip's Jes. Mis., 200.
[6] 2 Maine Hist. Coll., 94.

not kill it. Beltrami gives an incident illustrative of this. He says, "One day when I was fishing, a Sioux was greatly offended at my asking him to get me some frogs for bait. The frog, it appeared, was his manitou. . . . If an Indian does kill his manitou by accident, he begs for pardon, and says, 'It is better that you should have been killed by me than by any other man, for he would sell your skin, whereas I shall keep it with the greatest devotion;' and accordingly it takes its station among the divinities in the medicine-bag."[1]

The Californians had about the same system of manitology as the tribes east of the Rocky Mountains. At an early age they were placed under the protection of a tutelar divinity, which was supposed to take the form of some animal. To discover the particular beast which was to guide his future destinies, the child was intoxicated by a plant called *pibat*, and kept three or four days without food until he saw his divinity, which was immediately tattooed on the breast and arms of the novitiate.[2]

The Zapotecs had a very curious manner of selecting a manitou for a child at its birth. When a woman was about to be delivered, the relatives assembled in the hut and commenced to draw on the floor figures of different animals, rubbing each one out as fast as completed. The one that remained at the time of the birth was called the child's second self, and as soon as grown up he procured the animal, and believed his health and existence bound up with it.[3] Another manner of obtaining a manitou among the Zapotecs was to assign to the child the first bird or beast that appeared after the birth of the child.[4]

In Yucatan it was customary to leave an infant alone in a place sprinkled with ashes. Next morning the ashes were examined, and if the footprints of any animal were found on them, that animal was chosen as the deity of the infant.[5]

It will be noticed that the manner of choosing the manitou

---

[1] 2 Beltrami, 229. [2] 1 Bancroft, 414. [3] 1 ib., 661.
[4] 2 ib., 277. [5] 2 ib., 181.

or guardian spirit has changed a little among the civilized tribes, but the same faith in their power as spiritual agents survived. The natives of Honduras thought their destiny was so leagued with these guardian spirits that whenever anything happened to the animal it happened to them also.[1]

The Quiches of Guatemala, Herrera quaintly enough writes, "are deluded by the devil to believe that their life dependeth upon the life of such and such a beast which they take with them as their familiar spirit, and think when the beast dieth they must die. When he is chased, then their hearts pant; when he is faint, they are faint."[2]

The Indians could see no difference between their system of manitous and those of the white race, for they say the Boston people have for their manitou the eagle, and the English people a lion.

From the selection and worship of manitous by the individual we will pass to the subject of totemism. We will not look upon the subject from the social stand-point, except as far as may be necessary to explain the religious nature of the subject. The totemic social system has been most ably elucidated among the natives of America by Mr. Morgan, who has pursued the study of the subject among other races sufficiently to point to a time when all the races of the earth have had this primitive social system among them. As introductory to the subject of totemism, let me say that among all those tribes which had not emerged from barbarism, names of animals were given to many members of the tribes. There is some evidence to show that this habit has survived even among the more civilized, and there are traditions which point to the prevalence of the custom in the past history of all the American tribes.

Among the Lenape legends, warriors named White Eagle, White Owl and Snow-Bird, Strong Buffalo, Big Owl, White Crane, Strong Wolf, White Lynx, Blue-Bird, Big Beaver, Water Turtle, figure in their early history.[3] Many of the

---

[1] 4 Herrera, 138.   [2] 4 ib., 334.   [3] 1 Rafinesque, 131–34.

Northwestern Indians were named after beasts.[1] In Chile, as among the North Americans, each family was distinguished by the name of an animal, among which were the tiger, lion, guanaco, and ostrich.[2]

In Brazil there was a tribe called Achkeres, who took their name from the cayman, an animal of which they stood in strange fear. They thought it killed with its breath, and killed all with its sight, and the only way it could be killed was by holding a reflector before it, when it killed itself.[3] The natives of Guiana gave animal names to many of their children: Red and Blue Macaw were favorites.[4] Many of the Zapotecans were named after animals.[5] The cacique of Coatlan was called Dog.[6] These names were sometimes given from the personal manitou, and sometimes from the possession by the person of qualities similar to those of the animal. Mr. Bates, while on the Amazon, had two attendants named Tortoise, who were descended from a father who had received that nickname on account of his slowness. Here we see the first step toward the formation of a tortoise family and tribe. Let the tradition of the ancestor fail to keep clearly in view the fact that he was a man called after some animal, let him be habitually spoken of just as when alive, and the natural mistake of taking the name literally will bring with it the belief in descent from the actual animal.

It is in this way that we can find an explanation of the mythical descents of so many of the tribes from animals; and I will introduce here a few of these traditionary descents. Falkner describes the Patagonians as possessing a multiplicity of animal deities, each of whom they believe to preside over a family of Indians of which he is supposed to have been the creator. Some are of the caste of the tiger, some of the guanaco, and others of the ostrich. Ross says the tribes north of the Columbia pretend to be derived from a musk-rat. The Haidahs stead-

---

[1] Harmon, 347. [2] 2 Molina, 378. [3] 1 Southey, 156–57.
[4] Brett, 290. [5] 3 Herrera, 267. [6] 3 ib., 268.

fastly maintain that they are descended from the crows, and the Ahts say that men first existed as birds, animals, and fishes. The Chippewyans derive their origin from the dog, and at one time were so strongly imbued with respect for their canine ancestry that they ceased employing dogs in drawing their sledges.[1]

The California Indians, who claim to have descended from the prairie-wolf, explain the loss of their tails by saying they have been erased and destroyed by the habit they acquired of sitting upright. Those of them who claim descent from the bear assert that bears in old times walked on their hind legs like men.

The Kickapoos thought their ancestors had tails, and when they lost them the impudent fox sent every morning to ask how their tails were, and the bear shook his fat sides at the joke.[2]

The Flat-Heads believed in animal descent, and peopled their paradise with their grandfathers the spiders, who were exceedingly useful, according to their conception, for they spun threads to let the dead down to earth again.

The Chinooks are descended from a large bird, which they called Hahness. When one of their old men was cutting a salmon across the side, it was metamorphosed into an immense bird, which flew away and alighted on the Saddleback Mountains, near Columbia River, where its nest was made and eggs laid, and from these eggs sprang mankind.[3]

The Crane tribe of the Ojibways have the following legend of their origin. Two cranes flew down to the earth and spent a long time visiting different parts of the continent. They went over the prairie, and tasted buffalo-meat, but came to the conclusion it would not last. They passed over the forests, and tasted the elk, deer, and other animals, but were afraid the sources would fail. When they came to the rapids at the out-

---

[1] 1 Spencer, Soc., 363.   [2] 3 Jones, Traditions, 176.
[3] Swan's Washington Territory, 203-4.

let of Lake Superior, and found fish in abundance in the noisy waters, which could be taken with ease, they were satisfied, and folded their wings close to their bodies, alighted on the chosen spot, and were at once transformed into a man and woman.[1]

The Delawares thought that their ancestors lived for a time in certain terrestrial animals, such as the ground-hog, the rabbit, the tortoise.[2] The tortoise gens claimed a superiority and ascendency over all the others, because their ancestor the great tortoise, who had become a fabled monster in their mythology, bore their world on his back.[3] Upon this subject Mr. Heckewelder says, "That the Indians, from the earliest times, considered themselves in a manner connected with certain animals, is evident from various customs still preserved among them, and from the names of those animals which they have collectively as well as individually assumed. They are as proud of their origin from the tortoise, the turkey, and the wolf as the nobles of Europe are of their descent from the feudal barons of ancient times."

The Ottawas claimed their origin from three families. Some were from the family of the great hare. They pretended that the great hare was a man of prodigious size ; that he could spread nets in the water at eighteen fathoms' depth, while the water scarcely came to his armpits. The second family of the Ottawas claimed to be derived from the carp. Their tradition was, that a carp having deposited its eggs on the borders of a river, and the sun having darted its rays upon them, they were formed into a woman, from whom they were descended. The third family of the Ottawas attributed their origin to the bear, but without explaining in what manner they were derived.[4]

The Iowas thought they were descended from animals. The Mandans had an Indian name of great length, which when translated would be " people of the pheasants." The Choctaws

---

[1] Beach, Mis., 175.
[2] Heckewelder, 241.
[3] 1 Yates and Moulton's N. Y., 31–32.
[4] Rasles, in Kip's Jes. Mis., 32.

have a crawfish gens, which believe they came up out of the mud and were a species of crawfish, and they went on their hands and feet at first. When the Choctaws chased them, they would run down through the mud and get away from them. Finally some of them were caught and treated kindly by the Choctaws, and they became the present crawfish family.[1] The Potoyantes believe they are descended from the coyotes.[2]

The natives in the neighborhood of Mt. Shasta have a tradition that the grizzly bears formerly walked on their hind feet like men, and talked, and were the ancestors of the Indians; and the Indians will not kill them; but if an Indian is killed by a bear the spot becomes memorable, and each one casts a stone on the spot till a monument is reared.[3] The Cayuses, Nez Perces, and Walla Wallas sprang from the beaver.[4]

A tribe of Lacandones, near Palenque, was named the Snakes, and the great mythical hero, Votan, declared himself a snake and descendant of the snakes.[5] Many of the Indians of Peru claimed descent from animals, some from the bear, others from the tiger, eagle, condor, or other animal.[6]

Among the natives of Brazil, belief in descent from animals survived in the curious custom of cutting a stick at a wedding. The father performed this ceremony, imagining that he cut off the tails of any future grandchildren.[7]

Mythologies are full of stories, says Mr. Spencer, where beasts, birds, and fishes have played intelligent parts in human affairs, and have befriended human beings by giving them information, by guiding them, or by deceiving them. Belief in actual descent from an animal, strange as we may think it, is one by no means incongruous to the savage.[8]

The traditionary unions of animals and human beings were common in the folk-lore of all the tribes. In a great deluge, an Ojibway woman was saved by catching hold of a large bird

---

[1] 2 Catlin, 128. [2] 3 Bancroft, 88. [3] 3 ib., 93.
[4] 3 ib., 95. [5] 3 ib., 451. [6] 1 Garcilasso, 75.
[7] 1 Tylor, 384. [8] Spencer, Recent Discoveries, 42.

that was flying over. She was carried to the top of a high cliff, near which she had twins by her savior the war-eagle.[1]

The Osages believe the first man of their nation married a beaver, by whom he had many children, from whom the Osages have descended. They never kill the beaver, for they would think they were killing their own people.[2]

The Quiches had a legend that mankind descended from a woman and a dog who could transform himself into a handsome youth. The Apaches have a tradition that a bear went into the palace of Montezuma and stole one of his daughters and had children by her.[3]

These myths of descent from the union of an animal and a human being are very common. Some of the composite forms of animal and human beings to be found among their fabulous animals, which will be noticed hereafter, and which are common subjects chosen for representation by their artists, are explicable by this theory of descents.

The Aleuts claim descent from a dog of the female sex which was visited by an old man from the North. The result was the birth of two creatures, male and female, each half man, half dog.[4] Many of those composite figures which appear in the mythology of savage as well as civilized races of the pagan world, and which have been represented in their art, undoubtedly have their explanation in the totemic social system. To illustrate: if a member of a wolf gens should marry and have offspring with a member of a crawfish gens, and the offspring should attain celebrity and pass into their traditionary history with his parentage unforgotten, yet growing more indistinct as the twilight of time gathers around it and all recollections merge themselves in the prominent figure, soon there would be a hero tale, transparent with the characteristics of the wolf and the crawfish. Among the Indians men and animals were closely akin, and a belief prevailed that men themselves owed their first parentage to beasts, birds, or reptiles, and the names

---

[1] 2 Catlin, 168.   [2] 2 ib., 319.   [3] 5 Schoolcraft, 211.   [4] 3 Bancroft, 104.

of the totemic clans, borrowed in nearly every case from animals, are the reflection of this idea.

Papago traditions reach back to a time when men and beasts talked together and used one language. In early times men and beasts associated together in friendly intercourse. A famous chief of the Kootanies had a beautiful daughter, and all the young warriors, hunters, and fishers came courting her, but the father would only give his child to one who should split the tines of an elk-horn asunder with his hands. The story is told in the following language. The news went forth, and the competitors began to assemble, until the lodge was full. The bears sat growling in one corner, and the wolves in another. The raccoons and deer tried in vain, and went back disheartened. The salmon finally came along, while the lodge resounded with jeers and laughter at the bare idea of his attempting it after the flower of Indian athletes had failed; but Kewuk (salmon) was the girl's sweetheart, and her prayers had gone forth in his behalf. The tines split asunder, and she was Kewuk's bride. The rivals were bitter with envy, and skulked away to their lodges; but the wolf was determined to effect by foul means what he could not accomplish by fair. Watching his opportunity, he seized her and fled; but she tore pieces from her dress and left them on the bushes, marking the path, along which Kewuk pursued in hot haste and recovered his bride. The young wolf's father, however, set out with his son to seize again the bride, and they gaining rapidly on Kewuk, overloaded with his precious burden, he jumped into a river at hand and was turned into a salmon, and thus escaped.[1] This myth shows evident traces of totemism, and the animals therein are human beings bearing animal names. There is a tradition among the Neeshenams which illustrates this subject. It is the tradition of the coyote's elopement. The coyote and the bat were one day gathering the soft-shelled nuts of the sugar-pine, when there came along two women who were the wives of pigeons. The

---

[1] 1 Brown's Races, 138.

coyote upon this took a handful of pitch and besmeared the bat's eyes so that it could not see; meantime, the coyote eloped with the two women.

The supposed descent from animals has originated many superstitions found among all the tribes about killing and eating animals. The Indians of Queen Charlotte's Island believe they are descended from crows, and never kill one. They besmear themselves with black paint to preserve the native tradition of descent.[1]

Many tribes on the Pacific slope ate no flesh, but regarded everything of the meat kind with a superstitious fear.[2] They carried the superstition of abstaining from flesh about as far as the Brahmins. The Yakuts were divided into eight tribes, each of which had a bird or animal which they regarded as sacred and would not eat.[3] The Dacotahs dared neither kill nor eat their totemic animals. The Navajos never ate the flesh of the gray squirrel.[4] The Crow Indians would not trap or hunt the bear, and would not touch its flesh for food.[5] The Sioux would not kill the prairie-dog. If they saw anybody kill one, they ran away.[6] The Apaches had a superstitious prejudice against eating bear's meat,[7] as had also the Navajos.[8] The Kaluschians of the Northwest coast will not eat the whale. It seems to be forbidden them.[9] When, through necessity or accident, one of those animals from which they should abstain is killed, religious ceremonies are performed to appease its spirit.

Manitology and nicknaming have both tended to develop totemism. The totem is a symbolic device, generally an animal, which represents that all those having it have descended from one common ancestor. It has developed into the heraldic device of the family. It is not generally the object of religious

---

[1] Poole's Queen Charl. Islands, 136. [2] 1 Thatcher's Indian Traits, 71, seq.
[3] Dall's Alaska, 522. [4] 4 Schoolcraft, 214.
[5] Belden, 137. [6] Ib., 138.
[7] 1 Bartlett's Personal Narrative, 321. [8] 2 Domenech, 402.
[9] McCulloh, 79.

worship, because each member has chosen his own manitou on arriving at age. The totem has, however, great religious significance, and should have a prominent place in the study of their superstitions.

The totemism of the American tribes has manifested itself in much of their art. Among the Haidah, Sitka, and Chimsean Indians, a pillar elaborately carved out of a cedar-tree, or occasionally of stone, and sometimes fifty feet high, is built before each house, and represents the totems or manitous of all those living within the house. Since several families generally inhabit one of these houses in common, the totem of each family is represented, and hence we obtain those curious combinations of figures that characterize much of the architecture of this region. The same peculiarity is noticed in other parts of America, especially in the remains of the Central American States, where the complex system of configuration in the pillars and also the walls of their ruins has undoubtedly had the same origin, with perhaps the additional pictographic representations that may be descriptive of them.

At Fort Tongas, in Alaska, Rev. Dr. Jackson mentions the existence of a whole forest of crest- or totem-poles. "Many of them were from sixty to seventy feet high, and carved from top to bottom with a succession of figures representing the eagle, wolf, bear, frog, whale, and other animals."[1]

The Nootkans also have a rude system of heraldry, by which some animal is adopted as a family crest, and its figure painted on canoes and paddles or embroidered on their blankets. The Thlinkeets adorned the fronts of their principal dwellings and their canoes with figures representing the heads of crows, sea-lions, and bears.[2] These are their totems, and each family adorned their house and canoe with the bird or beast designating their clan. Hence we see how the medicine-bag or manitou, at first a personal fetich, expands till the idea of a family or tribe manitou, or totem, exhibits itself, and the tribal fetich

---

[1] Alaska, 263.   [2] 1 Bancroft, 107.

manifests itself in primitive decorative art, which began with ornamenting household utensils, canoes, and huts with heraldic devices. The use of the totem in art prevailed among the Southern as well as the Northern tribes. The coyote, which figures so extensively in the myths of the savage tribes west of the Rocky Mountains, appears in Nahua art. An image of a coyote hewn from the rock was found at the country residence of King Nezahualcoyotl, whose name signified hungry fox. Near this was the colossal figure of a winged beast, bearing in its mouth a sculptured portrait of the king.[1]

The figures or emblems connected with the signatures of the Indians were called totems, and were the signs of the gentes or families into which the nations were divided. They were not the personal emblems of the chiefs. These figures were generally some bird, beast, or reptile. The Indians in their earliest intercourse with the whites resorted to the use of hieroglyphics. Some of those made use of in the treaty made at Falmouth with the Penobscot, Norridgwock, and other Indians in 1649 were very curious. They signed with the figure of the body of the totemic animal; Nattoonos by the representation of a fish, Seboowosset by that of a fly, and others by various other strange and uncouth drawings. The treaties and petitions of tribes were a species of such hieroglyphic representations, as represented on Plate IV., which was a petition sent to Congress by a Western tribe, which was divided into the totemic families represented by the bear, marten, and other animals therein figured. Totemism is thus seen to be closely connected with the pictography and hieroglyphic writing used in America by the natives.

Tattooing, or painting the figures of animals upon their bodies, was an almost universal custom throughout both Americas. It is probably the most primitive form of decorative art, and is fetichistic in conception. The tattooing, of which the Indians were so fond, and which had a religious

---

[1] 2 Bancroft, 170.

significance among them, was gradually given up as they adopted the dress and customs of the whites. Yet there were many instances of their clinging to the idea, by ornamenting their dress with the pictures of animals. The famous Philip wore a belt curiously embroidered with figures of birds and beasts, and the band of his cap was adorned in the same manner. The Dacotahs were tattooed with animals, which they thought charmed away all evil.[1]

The tattoo-marks of the Haidahs appeared to be both totemic and connected with their manitology. Occasionally a fabulous being with no prototype in natural history will be selected, undoubtedly the product of a dream or of a very fanciful imagination. Animals are the subjects tattooed generally, and of these the bear, frog, codfish, and mythological thunder-bird are the most common.

The same custom prevailed among the Canadian tribes, whose breasts, arms, and legs were tattooed with sharp needles or pointed bones, the colors being carefully rubbed in. "The manitou and the animal chosen as the symbol of his tribe are first painted on the person, then all his most remarkable exploits and the enemies he has slain or scalped: so that his body displays a pictorial history of his life."[2] Among the New England nations "the better sort of Indians bear on their cheeks certain portraitures of beasts, as beavers, deer, moose, wolves, eagles, hawks, etc."[3] A woman of Queen Charlotte's Island had half her body tattooed with fish, beasts, etc., and said that the representation of a halibut would protect her and her kin from drowning at sea.[4] The first objects delineated on the skin of the Indian in tattooing were his guardian spirit and the guardian spirit of his tribe.[5] These spirits were then supposed to be enlisted in his behalf.

The natives of Yucatan and Nicaragua, who were naked,

---

[1] Eastman's Legends of Sioux, 74.　[2] 1 Warburton's Conq. of Can., 200.
[3] Wood's N. E. Pros., 74.　[4] Poole's Queen Charl. Islands, 311.
[5] 1 Hugh Murray's British America, 54.

tattooed the body with serpents and birds.[1] Tattooing was a profession among them.[2]

Tattooing was a form of animal-worship. Mr. Agassiz says that tattooing was a religious institution among the Brazilians.[3]

Among the Mexicans and other civilized nations, who were not naked, the custom of tattooing survived in the banners, flags, armorial bearings, crests, and other insignia, upon which appear animal forms. They had flags upon which were inscribed animals. The armorial ensign of the Mexicans was an eagle, with its wings spread, in the act of darting on a tiger; that of Tlascala, an eagle; that of Ocotcholco, a green bird on a rock; that of Tizatlan, a heron on a rock; that of Tepeticpac, a wolf.[4]

The connection of the animal-mounds of Wisconsin with the existing totemic system of the Indians is too strong to escape attention. By the system of names imposed upon the men composing the Ojibway, Iroquois, Cherokee, and other nations, a fox, a bear, a turtle, is fixed on as a badge or stem from which the descendants may trace their parentage. To do this the figure of the animal is employed as an heraldic sign or surname. This sign, which by no means gives the individual name of the person, is called in the Algonkin languages town mark or totem. A tribe could leave no more permanent trace of an esteemed sachem or honored individual than by the erection of one of these monuments. The fox, bear, wolf, and eagle are clearly recognizable in the devices of these mounds,[5] and, besides these, among the animal-mounds of Wisconsin are lizards and turtles, serpents, elks, elephants, buffaloes, and cranes. We may therefore suppose that Red men formerly occupied Wisconsin whose superstitious ceremonies and belief required the erection of the mounds delineated. Among the Ottawas there was a tradition that a mountain, shaped like a beaver, on the northern shore of Lake Nipissing, contained buried beneath it the great beaver. They never passed it with-

---

[1] 2 Bancroft, 733.   [2] Ib.   [3] Brazil, 318.
[4] 1 Clavigero, 368–69.   [5] 1 Schoolcraft, 52.

out offering something.[1] Animal-shaped mounds are found elsewhere.

There are huacas in Peru which represent animals.[2] In Putnam County, Georgia, there is a bird-shaped structure composed of boulders of quartz rock, none of them so large that an individual could not have carried them. It represents an eagle with its head turned toward the east. Another similar one is found in the same county, one hundred and two feet in length, and from tip to tip of wings one hundred and thirty-two feet. Mr. C. C. Jones thinks both of them are monuments of the dead.[3] In the Newark, Ohio, works, a bird-mound was found with length of body one hundred and fifty-five feet and two hundred feet from tip to tip of spread wings.[4]

The general drift of many of the myths of descent of man from animals would indicate a wide-spread belief in the theory of an evolution of mankind from animals. The process of evolution is thus described by an Iroquois myth, which says that men were metamorphosed from little worms, into which entered spirits. The worms, with the spirits in them, grew, putting forth little arms and legs, and moved the light earth that covered them.[5]

It will be seen, however, that traditions are not wanting whose teaching is precisely the reverse. The Salish, Nisquallies, and Yokimas all hold that beasts are descended from human originals.[6]

In an Iroquois tradition, a woman brought forth a deer, bear, and wolf, and again cohabited with these animals. She thus became pregnant, and bore divers sorts of creatures at one birth. From this arose the variety not only of animals, but also of men, in color either black, white, or sallow, in disposition either timid as the deer, revengeful as bears, or rapacious as wolves.[7]

---

[1] 3 Jones, Trad., 69.
[2] A. Oliva, 121; Arriaga, 12.
[3] Smithsonian Report, 1877, 281–82.
[4] McLean, Mound-Builders, 35.
[5] Miner's History of Wyoming, 22.
[6] 3 Bancroft, 97.
[7] Montanus, Tr. in Doc. Hist. N. Y., vol. iv., 83.

Connected closely with the subject of the traditionary descent of Indians from animals, and the superstitions growing out of such belief, is the traditionary descent of animals from the human race.

The Indians living around Lake Pepin thought the animals and fish were once human and endued with speech, and held counsel together until they began to prey upon each other; the otter brought the discord by eating a few fish.[1] The Dacotahs believed that beavers were once people and endowed with language, but lost their speech. The Black-Feet Indians also believed that the beavers were a fallen race of Indians.[2] The Moquis, who were divided into gentes bearing animal names, thought that after death they would change back into their original forms, and become bears, deer, and prairie-wolves.[3]

The belief in the descent of animals from human beings has received an impetus from their various tales of metamorphosis. In the animal kingdom the metamorphoses which actually occur are at first sight more marvellous than many which are only supposed to occur. The contrasts between the maggot and a fly, an egg and a bird, a tadpole and a frog, are greater than the contrasts between human beings and many animals, or between many different varieties of animals. The savage mind yields therefore unhesitatingly to anything which suggests that a creature has assumed a different shape. In Brazil, the people universally believe that the humming-bird is transmutable into the hawk-moth. The belief that human spirits disguised themselves temporarily as brutes was very prevalent. The Thlinkeets of North America would kill some animals only in case of great necessity, for they supposed human spirits assumed these animal forms at pleasure and frequently.

Myths of descent and metamorphosis are found in the folk-lore of both Americas.

The Potawatomies claimed descent from a wolf. By meta-

---

[1] McLeod's Wisconsin, 277. [2] Slight's Researches, 103.
[3] Marcy's Army Life on the Border, 109.

morphosis the bones of a dead wolf were transformed into a woman, the mother of their race.[1]

In Algonkin mythology, the animal creation is supposed to have been metamorphoses of human beings. The Ojibways think the white-fish sprang from the brains of a woman who dropped into the water.[2]

The Flat-Head Indians (a tribe on the Columbia River) entertain a curious tradition with respect to beavers. They firmly believe that these animals are a fallen race of Indians, who were metamorphosed to their present shape and state, but that in due time they will be restored to their humanity. They allege that beavers have the power of speech, and that they have heard them talk with each other.[3]

The Ojibways remembered the name of the member of the human race who was changed into a beaver. It was Amik.[4]

The Flat-Heads have a tradition that a warrior of the early day found his wife unfaithful, whereupon she fled away, was turned into the speckled duck, and dives at the sight of a human being.

Those tribes that have progressed and remember a former condition of greater savagery always describe that condition as one wherein they were animals. Of course the language is metaphorical at first; but this metaphorical language, in connection with the many animal superstitions that have survived their lower state, tends to make fiction grow into reality. A number of travellers have acknowledged that they never clearly understood whether the Indians believed that at one time all men were in the form of beasts or whether they were in the form of men, but with the nature, habits, and disposition of animals.

The Eskimos have many stories of metamorphoses of human beings into animals.[5] The dolphins are supposed to be a family of metamorphosed brothers. Their folk-lore abounds in stories

---

[1] Haw-Hoo-Noo, 242.
[2] 3 Schoolcraft, 526.
[3] 2 Turner's Traits, 87.
[4] 3 Schoolcraft, 562.
[5] Rink's Trad., 145.

of reindeer, foxes, and hares which have assumed human form and then changed back again when their object was accomplished.[1]

The Thlinkeets have a tradition that when the sun first shone on the earth, human beings ran into the mountains, woods, and waters, and became animals and fish.[2] They think their shamans can metamorphose themselves into animals at pleasure.[3]

Quawteaht, an apotheosized man of the Northwest, metamorphosed all who refused him what he asked. He converted a canoe-man into a beaver for refusing to ferry him over a lake. A fisherman on the Coquitlan River was turned into a pillar of stone for refusing him salmon, and there the rock stands to this day, the monument of an inhospitable man. A woman was transformed into a raven for refusing him berries, and a boy was swallowed by a whale, vomited up again, and changed into a mink, because he refused him sea-eggs. He turned a whole tribe of Indians into wolves in a fit of anger.

Among the Ahts, the loon and the crow were metamorphosed fishermen, who quarrelled and were thus changed by Quawteaht, who put an end in this way to their quarrel; and the only complaint is the mournful voice of the loon across the silent lake, as the poor fisherman tries to make his wrongs known.

The natives of Vancouver's Island will not kill the ogress squirrel, on account of the following tradition of metamorphosis. There once lived an old woman with finger-nails like claws. She ate children; and many were the broken hearts and empty cradles produced by her depredations. At the prayer of a red mother, says the tradition, her little child slips from the ogress's grip, not a child, but metamorphosed into the loveliest little squirrel, bearing those four dark lines along its back where her cruel claws made their mark.[4] After death, the Pimos believe that their souls go to the banks of the Colorado, their ancient dwelling-place, and there take refuge in

---

[1] Rink, 450. [2] Dall's Alaska, 422. [3] Ib., 423. [4] 3 Bancroft, 130.

the great sand-hills, where they are metamorphosed into owls, bats, wolves, and other animals.[1]

Lycanthropy was common among many tribes of the Northwest.

> "Ah, ye wolves, in all your ranging
> I have found you kind and true,
> More than man, and now I'm changing,
> And will soon be one of you."

Many traditions of metamorphosis of men into wolves appear in the folk-lore of the Northwest. The Ahts have victims of a lycanthropy. They say that men go into the mountains to seek their manitous and associate with wolves, and after a time turn into wolves.[2] In British Columbia many a wolf-circle gathered around a fire on the mountain-side, with their skins hung up to dry on sticks, has been seen by the imaginative savages inhabiting that region.[3] The folk-lore of all the tribes is full of the traditions of changes of human beings into various animals.

An ogress in the folk-lore of the Northwest coast, who lived on children and went about with a basket to gather them up and take them home to roast, was circumvented by a parcel of youngsters, who pushed her into the fire she had prepared for them. Her ashes were turned into mosquitoes, who now eat mankind.[4] This tale probably represents all that is left of cannibalism among the tribes whose folk-lore it adorns.

Among the Nisqually folk-tales is one of a man and his wife who were metamorphosed, the man into the heron, which is called grandfather by them, and the woman into the horned grebe.[5]

The Ojibways thought the robin was a metamorphosed woman, who painted her breast and flew away laughing for joy and telling her friends she would be back in the spring.[6]

---

[1] 2 Bartlett's Nar., 222.   [2] Sproat, 173.
[3] 1 Brown's Races, 118.   [4] 1 ib., 140.
[5] 1 ib., 150.   [6] Jones's Ojibways, 65.

Another tradition says that an Indian lad who was fasting for his manitou reduced himself to such a pass that life was so nearly extinct that the only sign it showed was the gentle heaving of his breast. His father came with food, but, alas! too late; for he found, on looking up, a beautiful robin-redbreast, which looked at his father and said, "Mourn not my change; for I shall be happier now and always the friend of men. My food is now in the fields, and my path is in the air;" and away he flew to the woods.[1]

The voluntary assumptions of new forms by amphibious animals are frequently found, and are suggested by their mysterious adaptation to the different elements.

A mythical female character among the Ojibways was a beaver who assumed the form of a woman and married an Ojibway named Otterheart. They lived happily together, but Otterheart did not know why his wife would not eat the beaver he brought to the lodge. But, alas! the beaver woman stumbled and fell into the water one day, and was immediately changed back into a beaver. Her child on her back underwent a like metamorphosis. In despair, Otterheart followed the course of the stream till he reached a beaver-pond, and there he saw his wife, who had her beaverling bound to her back. Otterheart pleaded with her to return to him, but she could not.[2]

The Zuñis have a tradition of an Indian who was turned into a fish because he had desecrated their sacred spring by bathing in it.[3]

Many metamorphoses appear among the Haytian folk-tales. A number of fishermen were turned into plum-trees; a chief of the Hiana became a nightingale; a messenger of the king of Caziba was turned into a singing-bird. The change of children into opossums is mentioned; but, as there are no opossums in Hayti, the myth must have had its origin among the Caribs of South America.[4]

---

[1] 2 Schoolcraft, 230.
[3] Cozzens, 310.
[2] Kohl's Kitchi-Gami, 100–104.
[4] 1 Rafinesque, 179–82.

Among all the tribes, their wizards and witches are supposed to be able to turn themselves into bears, wolves, foxes, owls, bats, and snakes. Such metamorphoses they pretend to accomplish by putting on the skins of these animals and howling in imitation of the creature they represent. They say they often pursue a witch, but all at once they will see an animal walking along as innocently as a lamb.[1]

We find here the germ of many metamorphoses in the aboriginal mythology. That great body of impostors among all primitive peoples, called sorcerers, doctors, medicine-men, witches, etc., have practised upon the credulity of the masses by assuming the animal dress and appearance and imitating them in action and voice. They were enabled, of course, to practise this imposture successfully only because the savage mind was predisposed to believe in the transmigration of souls. They thought it no strange thing for the spirit of man or animal to enter into anything in nature it chose; that they always entered into the bodies of the living when sickness came upon them. That a sorcerer for whom they had great superstitious reverence, clad in the skin of a bear, and imitating it with great success and practising upon the deluded many tricks of the trade, should be transformed into that animal, would require no great stretch of the imagination, and was a metamorphosis in ideality. That he should suddenly doff his animal skin and appear as a man would be a metamorphosis in reality.

The Eskimos thought they could get inside of a walrus-skin and then they could lead the life of a walrus.[2]

The Iroquois thought their wizards could turn into a fox or wolf and run very swiftly, or into a turkey or owl and fly away, when they wished to escape their pursuers.[3]

The same belief is found among the more civilized tribes. The Nicaraguans thought their sorcerers could assume animal forms, and they were much feared on this account. To

---

[1] Jones's Ojibways, 145. [2] Rink's Traditions, 124.
[3] Schoolcraft's Iroquois, 87.

strengthen this belief they disguised themselves in the skins of beasts.¹

Mendieta says that among the Mexicans there were sorcerers and witches who were thought to transform themselves into animals. Herrera tells us that the people of Honduras said that sorcerers ranged on the mountain like tigers, killing men, till they were taken and hanged. Piedrahita says the Chibchas pretended to have great sorcerers, who might be transformed into tigers and bears and devour men. The same power of metamorphosis was thought to be possessed by the sorcerers of Peru, who could take upon themselves whatsoever shape they chose, and fly through the air whithersoever they pleased.² The same mysterious power was ascribed to potentates among the civilized nations. Malivalxochitl, a famous Chichemec princess, is said to have had the power of transforming herself into any shape at will.³ A certain Chibcha ruler was believed to have had a long tail, which he dragged on the soil after the manner of a tiger.⁴ The power of metamorphosing others was ascribed to many kings. The whole line of Tunja kings had the power of changing men into animals, and their sorcerers transformed themselves into bears and tigers.⁵ Xolotl, the Chichemec culture-hero, changed himself into a fish in order to escape death, but was at last killed by the god of the air.⁶ The wife of Yappan, a famous Mexican anchorite, was metamorphosed into a scorpion by Jaotl, a messenger of the gods, who was himself metamorphosed into a locust for exceeding the bounds of his commission.⁷

As the subject of animal dress is closely connected with that of metamorphosis, and as the custom of arraying themselves in the skins of animals has survived from the primitive custom of dressing themselves in the skins of beasts, and appears in most of the religious exercises of the tribes in all stages of progress,

---

¹ 3 Bancroft, 496. ² 4 Herrera, 353.
³ 4 Bancroft, 327. ⁴ 1 Spencer, Soc., 348-50.
⁵ P. Simon, 245. ⁶ 4 Schoolcraft, 561.
⁷ 1 Clavigero, 260.

I will give a few of these customs. At many of their religious ceremonies the Peruvian tribes arrayed themselves in the skins of various animals. At the Capac Raymi festival they put on the skins of animals, arranging the head and neck so as to cover their own.[1] Falcons were worn on the heads of the dancers and singers in nearly all their festivals.[2] The Chugatshes make a conical hat of wood, in representation of the head of some fish or bird.[3] The Thlinkeets wear wooden masks a great deal, ingeniously carved and painted in colors to represent the head of some bird or beast. They were always worn in battle formerly, but now their use is generally confined to festive occasions. In rainy weather they wear a hat ornamented with painted figures and pictures of animals.[4] The Lacandones, when going to war, wore on their shoulders the skin of a tiger or some other fierce animal. In Chiapas, the natives wore deer-skins, and also the Mijes.[5] The Mosquitos wore armor of tigers' skins in war.[6] The natives of Honduras disguised themselves with the skins of animals, whose actions and cries they imitated.[7]

Herrera says the Mexicans clothed themselves in skins of tigers, lions, and other fierce creatures.[8] The Mexican warriors usually encased their heads with a wooden covering, fashioned in the shape of tigers' or serpents' heads, with the mouth open and large teeth to inspire terror, and very animated in appearance.[9] The eagle tribe among the Aztecs wore a helmet in the form of an eagle's head, and the tigers wore armor spotted like the skin of the animal whose name they bore.[10] Many of the warriors had monsters and other heraldic devices painted on their backs,[11] and upon their heads the representation of some animal, bird, or serpent.[12] They wore arm and leg guards made to represent the head of a tiger, serpent, or monster.[13]

---

[1] Molina, Nar., p. 45. [2] Avila, Nar., 131. [3] 1 Bancroft, 74.
[4] 1 ib., 101. [5] 1 ib., 648. [6] 1 ib., 723.
[7] 1 ib., 736. [8] 3 Herrera, 225. [9] 1 Clavigero, 366.
[10] 2 Bancroft, 403. [11] 2 ib., 405. [12] 2 ib., 406.
[13] 2 ib., 407.

In many of their animal-dances, all the tribes are accustomed to clothe themselves in animal dress and assume animal characters.

The Sioux have a bear-dance previous to starting on a bear-hunt, in which they sing to the bear-spirit.[1] This dance has religious significance, and may properly be termed a worship. They are clothed in bear-skins, or at least some portion of one, and imitate closely the movements of that animal. They never neglect this ceremony, for if they did they would have no success.

The eagle-dance among the Choctaws is a very pretty scene gotten up in honor of that bird, for which they have religious regard. They are decorated with eagles' feathers, and the dance is different from any other, consisting in hops and jumps, in imitation of that bird.[2]

"The Tonkawas," says Marcy, "like all the aborigines of this continent, likewise had their national dances for different important occasions, and among these ceremonies was one which seemed very curious and entirely different from any other I had heard of. It was called the wolf-dance, and was intended to commemorate the history of their origin and creation. Their traditions have handed down to them the idea that the original progenitor of the Tonkawas was brought into this world through the agency of the wolves. The dance is always conducted with the utmost solemnity and secrecy. . . . About fifty warriors, all dressed in wolf-skins from head to foot, so as to represent the animal very perfectly, made their entrance upon all-fours in single file, and passed around the lodge, howling, growling, and making other demonstrations peculiar to that carnivorous quadruped. After this had continued for some time, they began to put down their noses and sniff the earth in every direction, until at length one of them suddenly stopped, uttered a shrill cry, and commenced scratching the ground at a particular spot. The others immediately gathered

---

[1] 1 Catlin, 245.   [2] 2 ib., 127.

around, and all set to work scratching up the earth with their hands, imitating the motions of the wolf in so doing, and in a few minutes . . . they exhumed from the spot a genuine live Tonkawa, who had previously been interred for the performance. As soon as they had unearthed this strange biped, they ran around scenting his person and examining him throughout with the greatest apparent delight and curiosity. The advent of this curious and novel creature was an occasion of no ordinary moment to them, and a council of venerable and sage old wolves was at once assembled to determine what disposition should be made of him. The Tonkawa addressed them as follows: 'You have taken me from the spirit-land, where I was contented and happy, and brought me into this world, where I am a stranger, and I know not what I shall do for subsistence and clothing. It is better you should place me back where you found me, otherwise I shall freeze or starve.' After mature deliberation, the council declined returning him to the earth, and advised him to gain a livelihood as the wolves did; to go out into the wilderness and rob, kill, and steal whenever opportunity presented. They then placed a bow and arrows in his hands, and told him with these he must furnish himself with food and clothing; that he could wander about from place to place like the wolves, but that he must never build a house or cultivate the soil; that if he did he would surely die."[1]

"The Nootkans have," says Cook, "a truly savage and incongruous appearance when they assume what they call their monstrous decorations. These consist of an endless variety of carved wooden masks or visors applied on the face or to the upper part of the head or forehead. Some of these resemble the heads of birds, particularly of eagles, and many the heads of land and sea animals, such as wolves, deers, porpoises, and others; but in general these representations much exceed the natural size."[2]

Boller describes the religious dances of Western tribes, in

---

[1] Marcy's Army Life on the Border, 174, seq.   [2] 6 Cook's Voyages, 281.

which they appear as bulls, antelopes, and frogs, and appearing with as much resemblance to those animals as possible.[1]

Processions of masked men among the Brazilian tribes are described by Denis, in which they assumed as a head-dress the head of some animal. They also wore the entire skins of animals.

In addition to the custom of arraying themselves in animal skins and imitating the animals, I would attribute as another cause for the origin of myths of metamorphosis the superstition that by eating an animal the partaker was endued with the qualities of the animal eaten. A few myths are found to substantiate this theory. I will notice only one of them, that of the priests of Xaratanga, who in a drunken frenzy ate a serpent that was brought them in the place of fish, and were immediately turned into serpents and plunged into a lake and disappeared.[2]

Fear of the avenging spirits of animals has instigated much of their worship. They think the souls of animals are ready in the next world to take revenge upon those who have killed them, and must be appeased. The Dacotah hunter will pay religious devotions to the spirit of the beast whose body lies dead at his feet, and on which he and his family will feast that night.[3] Among all the Algonkin tribes, when a bear was killed, the hunter put the end of his lighted pipe between his teeth, blew into the bowl, and, thus filling the mouth and throat of the beast with smoke, conjured its spirit to bear him no malice for what he had done to the body, and not to oppose him in his future huntings. A remarkable illustration of this appears in the following account by Henry. He says, "A bear having been shot, all my assistants approached, and all took his head into their hands, stroking and kissing it several times, begging a thousand pardons for taking away its life, calling it their relation and grandmother. As soon as we reached the lodge, the bear's head was adorned with all the trinkets in

---

[1] Boller's Eight Years, 102–8.   [2] 5 Bancroft, 517.   [3] Riggs, 59.

the possession of the family, such as silver arm-bands and wrist-bands and belts of wampum, and then laid upon a scaffold set up for its reception within the lodge. Near the nose was placed a large quantity of tobacco. The next morning no sooner appeared than preparations were made for a feast to the manes. The lodge was cleaned and swept, and the head of the bear lifted up, and a new blanket, which had never been used before, spread under it. The pipes were now lit, and tobacco-smoke was blown into the nostrils of the bear, telling me to do the same, and thus appease the anger of the bear on account of having killed her." An address to the bear and a feast closed the ceremony.

The Southern Californians have a curious illustration of this superstitious fear of the spirits of animals, which compels them to hunt in pairs. Many believe that if a hunter should eat meat or fish he himself procured, his luck would leave him, and so they go in pairs and exchange their game when the day is over, each taking what the other has killed.[1] They think they will escape the vengeance of the slaughtered animals by this bit of trickery. At the annual fishing-season the mikon, a small silvery fish which fills the Nasse River in March, is propitiated by annual ceremonies. After these religious ceremonies to the fish, the slaughter begins without further scruple.[2]

An imaginary transmigration of a human soul into an animal renders it an object of worship. The souls of wicked men were supposed by the Brazilians to have entered those birds that inhabited the cavern of Guacharo and made a mournful cry,[3] and these birds were religiously feared. The coast tribes of the Del Norte country think the tarantula contains a malicious human spirit. The Moquis, who were divided into the deer, the bear, the hare, the prairie-wolf, and the rattlesnake gens, believed that their families descended from these animals, and that after death they transmigrated into the form of that animal

---

[1] 1 Bancroft, 417-18. [2] 1 ib., 485.
[3] 2 De Pons, Travels, 254-55.

from which they originally sprang.[1] Hence they worshipped these animals. The Ahts believed that the birds and beasts of old had the spirits of the Indians dwelling in them,[2] and, hence, were worthy of reverence. The Indians dwelling about the Falls of St. Anthony supposed the spirits of their dead warriors inhabited the eagles which frequented the place,[3] and these eagles were objects of their worship. The most beautiful woman of the Knistenaux, named "Foot of the Fawn," died in childbirth, and the babe with her. Soon thereafter two doves appeared, one full-grown and one a little one. They were the spirits of the mother and child. The Indians would gather about the tree on which they were perched, with reverential love, and worship them as the spirit of the woman and child.[4] The Tapuyas thought evil spirits appeared in the shape of flies, toads, cats, and they worshipped the most inferior animals on account of this supposed transmigration.[5] Thus it will be seen that the supposed transmigration of souls is the reason for animal-worship in many cases. If this belief has originated animal-worship, it explains the worship of every variety of the animal life.

It has been thought by most mythologists that only those animals that have been useful to mankind have been objects of worship. We find, however, in America that no animal is too insignificant to escape the superstitious fear of savages. Among some of the Western tribes a little bird called the road-runner is an object of reverence.[6]

The Virginia Indians had great reverence for a small bird called Pawcorance, that flies in the woods and in its note continually sounds that name. This bird flies alone, and is heard only in twilight. They say, says Beverly, that "this is the soul of one of their princes, and on that score they would not hurt it for the world; but there was once a profane Indian in

---

[1] Cozzens's Marvellous Country, 465.
[2] Sproat, 210.
[3] 3 Jones's Traditions, 117.
[4] 3 ib., 370-71.
[5] Vasconcelles, 72.
[6] Dodge's Plains, 279.

the upper parts of James River who, after abundance of fears and scruples, was at last bribed to kill one of them with his gun, but the Indians say he paid dear for his presumption, for in a few days after he was taken away and never heard of again."[1] Among the Peruvians the little bird alma perdida is an object of superstitious reverence.[2]

The hare was an object of superstitious reverence among the Indians of the North, and around it cluster many myths in the Old World. The superstition about the evil omen of a hare crossing your path, for instance, is very ancient. The ancient inhabitants of Ireland killed all the hares they found among their cattle on May-day, believing them witches who had designs on the butter. A Calmuck regards the rabbits in the same light, and many primitive people use them for divinations and refuse to eat their flesh. Cæsar gives account of the horror in which this animal was held by the Britons of his day. The animal was sculptured on the sacrificial stone in ancient Mexico, and was the "sign" of the divine years in the Mexican calendar, while the celebrations and sacrifices in its honor were the most numerous of all. Superstitions, therefore, seem to have been attached to this little beast from the lowest state of primitive savagery up to the present height of civilization. Wabasso, who fled to the north as soon as he saw the light, and was changed into a white rabbit, under that form became canonized.

The Indians on the Orinoco rendered honors of divinity to toads in order to obtain rain. The animals were beaten if the prayers were not answered.[3] Among the Araucanians of Chile the land toad was called lord of the waters. The Creeks and Cherokees had a great annual festival, the prominent feature of which was the tadpole dance. A small tribe in Guiana were named Maopityans, or Frog Indians, from *mao*, frog, and *pityan*, people. Their illustrious ancestor, the frog, was worshipped. Among the Chibchas the frog had its place in their heaven.

---

[1] Beverly's Virginia, 184.   [2] Markham's Cuzco, 267.
[3] 1 De Pons, 198.

The Chibchas had an annual ceremony connected with their calendar, in which the toad had a prominent place. It held a prominent place among their divinities. When springing, it represents the sign Ata; when engraved with a tail, it represents 12, because it has left the rest of the months behind. On some stones the toad is seen without feet, and probably represents the sign Gurta. The toad is used often in composite figures, such as a man with the head of a toad, a tailed toad, and the body of a toad with a tunic.[1]

The frog also held a place among the divinities of the Toltecs. Frog-shaped idols were found at Tulla, the ancient capital of the Toltecs. These croaking annoyers of some marshy neighborhood were undoubtedly raised to the dignity of divinities, and propitiated by the offer of an occasional sacrifice. And so, perhaps, was the grasshopper, images of which, cut out of red marble and beautifully polished, were found. It was said to be the god of Chapultepec.[2]

The Peruvians near the sea-coast worshipped sardines; also the golden fish, on account of its beauty, and crabs and crawfish where they were abundant.[3] Every small insect was an object of superstitious fear.

The Omahaws worshipped a sacred shell which was enveloped in the skin of an elk. This shell, which descended from their ancestors, was not suffered to touch the earth. It had a temple and a person to take care of it. Those who should happen to see the shell became totally blind. They offered sacrifices to it and consulted it before making expeditions. It was carried on a man's back to national hunts.[4] Their ascription of human spirits to shells has found expression in that mythical character Aisemid, the little shell man of Indian lodge-lore, who carried on his back a curious little shell that had magic powers. The sorcerers often ascribed their powers to sea-shells, and no small part of their paraphernalia

---

[1] Bollaert, 47–49. [2] Mayer's Mexico As It Was, 275–76.
[3] 1 Garcilasso's Com., 49, 50. [4] 2 Long's Exp., 47, 48.

was found in conchology.[1] Sea-shells were found in many of the graves, and were undoubtedly objects of a superstitious worship.[2] Thus it will be seen that even shells shared the superstitious reverence entertained for animals, and that the most worthless and diminutive animals have been objects of superstitious worship.

Among all the tribes, animals of an unusual size were supposed to be inhabited by powerful spirits, and were objects of worship.[3]

Beltrami gives the following instance of such worship. He says, "The Tortoise Lake," so called by the Indians, "took its name from a tortoise of extraordinary size which the Indians found there about a century ago. They fed it with everything they could offer it most delicious, and long worshipped it as a great manitou."[4]

Buffaloes were objects of worship among those inhabiting the buffalo country. Among the savages of the West every one had one or more buffalo heads, which they worshipped.[5] A buffalo's head on a mound of earth was a place where incantations took place.[6] Their lodges had an elevation on which were placed buffalo heads.[7] Says Bradbury, "On some bluffs in the Mandan country I observed fourteen buffalo skulls placed in a row. The cavities of the eyes and the nostrils were filled with a species of artemisia common on the prairies. On my return I caused our interpreter to inquire into the reason for this, and found that it was an honor conferred on the buffaloes which they had killed, in order to appease their spirits and prevent them from apprising the living buffaloes of the danger they ran in approaching the neighborhood."[8] The Indians of South Carolina worshipped the panther, and called it the cat of God, and selected it as one of their great religious emblems. Their male children were made to sleep upon its

---

[1] 4 Schoolcraft, 490.
[2] Bollaert, 179.
[3] Harmon's Journal, 364; Lewis and Clarke, 107.
[4] 2 Beltrami, 417.
[5] Brackenridge's Views, 71.
[6] Ib., 244.
[7] Ib., 248.
[8] Bradbury's Travels, 125.

skin from infancy to manhood, that they might imbibe from it some portion of the cunning, strength, and prodigious spring of the animal to which it belonged. For the same superstitious reason their female offspring were reared on the soft skins of fawns and buffalo calves, that they might become gentle and obedient.[1]

The Moxos of Brazil worshipped the jaguar. It was necessary for their priests to have been attacked and wounded by a jaguar before they could be initiated to their office. When scratched or wounded by this animal, they were supposed to have its mark set upon them, and were thus designated for its service. It was not even necessary for the aspirant to have a witness to the assault.[2]

The Brazilians believed that a garment made of the skin of a jaguar was impenetrable and that they could not be hurt when clothed with one.[3]

This was a fetichistic superstition, as the skin could be easily penetrated by their weapons.

The Peruvians worshipped all the animals they were acquainted with. In the great temple of Pachacamac they held a fox in great veneration and worshipped it.[4] The Indians before the Incas would not fly if the fierce animals they worshipped crossed their path, but went down on the ground and worshipped them, and even allowed themselves to be killed and eaten.[5]

The early Peruvians fought many battles to maintain the privilege of worshipping their animal deities, and only adopted the worship of the sun after conquest.

The Mexicans had chapels to the tiger, eagle, and serpent, and a tomb to the bones of a wolf, which were discovered therein deposited in a coffin. The Mexicans worshipped the horse of Cortez and made an image of it, and this god was named Tziminchak.

---

[1] 1 Logan's Hist. of Upper South Carolina, 54.
[2] 3 Southey, 202.
[3] 3 ib., 669.   [4] Cieza, 183.
[5] 1 Garcilasso, 47.

The builders of Copan worshipped monkeys. Fragments of colossal apes were found upon monuments.[1]

White animals were special objects of superstitious fear. The Lipans revered with superstitious fear a white wild stallion on a prairie of Texas. The Peruvians regarded white sheep as sacred animals and objects to be worshipped. Judge Henderson, in his article before the Anthropological section of the American Association for the Advancement of Science, says, "Among the Apaches of the West white birds were regarded as possessing souls of divine origin, and to the Indians of the plains the white buffalo is a sacred object, like the white elephant of Siam; while some of the California tribes consider a white wolf-skin a badge of chieftainship. This was carried to a great extent in the robes of the high-priests of the Cherokees, and they also wrapped their dead in pure white deer-skins." The Dacotahs believed that the white buffalo, not often seen, possessed a supernatural power. They cut off its head and placed it in their lodge, making of it a household deity.[2]

"Long before whites set foot in the Housatonic Valley, the Indians used to notice a deer of spotless white which came to Onota to drink. Against this gentle creature no red man's arrow was ever pointed, for in their simple faith they believed she brought good fortune to the dwellers in the valley. So long as the snow-white doe came to drink at Onota, so long famine should not blight the Indian's harvest, nor pestilence come nigh his lodge, nor foe lay waste his country. He who had dared harm her would have met swift punishment. Year after year, soon as the white blossoms clothed the cherry, the sacred deer came to drink at her chosen fountain, bringing good omens to all, especially the maiden who first spied her. Finally, she brought with her a fawn of more faultless purity and grace than herself, and that year more than the usual plenty and happiness reigned around the lake. After the coming of the whites, a desire seized a Frenchman to present the skin of the

---

[1] 1 Stephens's Central America, 136. [2] Eastman's Chicora, 67.

white deer to the French king, and, after many fruitless endeavors to procure it through the Indians, it was at last obtained by a large price offered to one while under the influence of fire-water, who, when discovered, suffered speedy punishment. Many were the efforts to avert punishment, but prosperity departed, and the Indians slowly wasted away."[1]

Beyond all others two subdivisions of the animal kingdom have riveted the attention of men by their unusual powers, and entered into their mythology. These are the bird and the serpent. "The bird has the incomprehensible power of flight. It floats in the atmosphere, rides on the winds. It flies proudly over the mountains and moors, where he toils wearily along. He sees no more enviable creature. All living beings, say the Eskimos, have faculty of soul, but especially the birds. The flight and note of birds have ever been anxiously observed as omens of grave import. In Peru and Mexico there was a college of augurs, who practised divination by watching the course and professing to interpret the songs of fowls."[2] The eagle was everywhere worshipped. Among the Araucanians the namcu, or sea-eagle, was the object of much of their worship.[3]

Mr. Cass says of the natives of Michigan, "the calumet eagle is held in great veneration by the Indians, and a horse is sometimes given for a feather."[4]

The eagle was considered by many tribes as their sacred bird. Its images carved in wood, or its stuffed skin, surmounted their council lodges. None but an approved warrior dare wear it among the Cherokees; and the Dacotahs allowed such an honor only to him who had first touched the corpse of the common foe. The Natches and Arkansas seem to have paid it religious honors and installed it in their most sacred shrines. The Californians worshipped one with great ceremony yearly.[5]

The Delawares believed that a guardian spirit in the form of

---

[1] Taghconick, 113–16. [2] Brinton's Myths, 105–6.
[3] 2 Wood's Uncivilized Races, 564. [4] Cass, Indians, 69.
[5] Brinton, 110.

a great eagle watched over them, hovering in the sky far out of sight. Sometimes, when well pleased with them, he would wheel down into the lower regions, and might be seen circling with wide-spread wings against the white clouds. At such times the seasons were propitious, the corn grew finely, and they had great success in hunting. Sometimes, however, he was angry, and then he vented his rage in the thunder, which was his voice, and the lightning, which was the flashing of his eye. The Delawares made sacrifices to this spirit, who occasionally dropped a feather from his wing in token of satisfaction. These feathers made the wearer invisible and invulnerable. The Indians generally considered the feathers of the eagle as possessed of occult and sovereign virtues. At one time a party of Delawares were driven by the Pawnees to the summit of a high hill in their hunting-grounds. Here the chief warrior, driven almost to despair, sacrificed his horse to the tutelar spirit. Suddenly an eagle, rushing down from the sky, bore off the victim in his talons, and, mounting into the air, dropped a feather from his wing. The chief caught it up with joy, and, leading his followers down the hill, cut through the enemy without any one of his party receiving a wound.[1]

Owls were often worshipped. The Lummi, inhabiting the mainland opposite Vancouver's Island, will never kill an owl.[2] The owl among the Aztecs, Quiches and Mayas, Peruvians, Araucanians, and Algonkins was thought to have some relation to the dead. The Ojibways called the bridge they thought the spirits of the dead had to pass, the owl bridge. The Creek priests carried a stuffed owl with them as the badge of their profession. The Arickaras placed one in their council lodge, and the culture-hero of the Monquins of California was represented, like Athene, as having one for his companion. The natives of the Antilles wore tunics with figures of these birds embroidered on them.[3]

---

[1] Irving, Tour on the Prairies, 92, seq.   [2] 1 Bancroft, 219.
[3] Brinton, 110-11.

Among the Zuñis, owls of pottery were very common objects of worship. Says Brinton, the Indians were of opinion that there were great numbers of inferior deities, and that the irrational animals were engaged in viewing their actions. The eagle for this purpose with her keen eye soared about in the day, and the owl with her nightly eye was perched on the trees around their camp. Therefore when they observed the eagle or the owl near, they immediately offered sacrifice or burned tobacco.

Other birds shared in the worship of the tribes. The Aztecs reverenced a bird called Quetzal, a variety of paroquet. Neither Hurons nor Mandans would kill doves, for they believed they were inhabited by the souls of the departed.[1] The Floridians had a sacred bird called Tonatsuli.[2] The name denoted a sweet singer. It was probably the mocking-bird.[3] Crows were held in veneration by the Indians of Rhode Island, and were rarely killed. They had a tradition that a crow first brought to them a grain of corn in one ear and a bean in the other from the southwest, and from that seed came all their corn and beans.[4] The Kutchin would pray to a passing crow for meat.[5] The Caribs thought that bats were deities whose office it was to watch during the night.[6]

"Of all animals," says Brinton, "the serpent is the most mysterious. Alone of all creatures it swiftly progresses without feet, fins, or wings. Said wise King Solomon, ' There be three things which are too wonderful for me, yea, four which I know not, and the chief of them are the way of an eagle, and the way of a serpent on a rock.' It seems to be associated in its winding course to rivers. The Kennebec, a stream in Maine, in the Algonkin means snake, and the Antietam, in Maryland, in Iroquois has the same significance. How easily might savages, construing the figure literally, make the serpent a

---

[1] Brinton's Myths, 111–12. [2] Brinton's Florida, 107.
[3] 1 Bancroft, 520. [4] 1 Arnold's Rhode Island, 80.
[5] Smithsonian Rep., 66, 325. [6] 3 Picart, 137.

water-god!" This they did to a certain extent. Among several tribes the words for spirit and snake are similar, as among the Dacotahs, Shawnees, and Sauks. In the Crow dialect of the Dacotah *Iahise* is snake, *Isahe* spirit.[1] It has in association of ideas become connected with the lightning. The Algonkins thought the lightning was an immense serpent. The Shawnees called the thunder the hissing of the great snake; and Tlaloc, the Toltec thunder-god, held a serpent of gold in his hand to represent the lightning. The Caribs spoke of the god of the thunder-storm as a great serpent, and in the central region of the volcanic island of Dominica dwelt a monstrous serpent. Racumon, the great serpent, was brother of Lavacon, the elemental bird.[2] In the Ojibway mythology the serpent robs the thunder-birds' nests.

The Potawatomies entertained a high degree of veneration for the rattlesnake. They seldom killed one, and if they did it was accompanied with forms and ceremonies, and a sacrifice was left near the carcass. The fang was said to be a charm against rheumatism.[3]

Says Henry, "I once saw a rattlesnake which, as I was about to kill, the Indians [Ojibways] surrounded, addressing it by turns and calling it their grandfather. During this part of the ceremony they filled their pipes, and now each blew the smoke toward the snake. After remaining coiled and receiving incense for the space of half an hour, it stretched itself along the ground in visible good humor. At last it moved slowly away, the Indians following it and still addressing it by the title of grandfather, beseeching it to take care of their families during their absence. They further requested that he would remain and inhabit their country. The next day, a storm arising while we were out on the lake, the Indians prayed and offered sacrifices to the god-rattlesnake. One of the chiefs took a dog, and, after tying its fore-legs together, threw it overboard, at the same time calling on the snake to preserve us from being

---

[1] Brinton, 114-15.   [2] Ib., 120-21.   [3] 1 Keating, 127.

drowned, and desiring him to satisfy his hunger with the carcass of the dog. The wind increased. Another chief sacrificed another dog, with the addition of some tobacco. In the prayer which accompanied these gifts he besought the snake, as before, not to avenge upon the Indians the insult which he had received from myself in my design to put him to death."

Carver says he was told a remarkable story concerning one of these reptiles. An Indian belonging to the Menomonee nation, having taken one of them, found means to tame it, and, when he had done this, treated it as a deity, calling it his great father, and carrying it with him in a box wherever he went. This the Indian had done for several summers.[1] The Winnebagoes reverenced and never killed the rattlesnake. The Indians of Florida venerated the rattlesnake, and would not kill one, for fear its spirit would incite its kindred to revenge its death. The Cherokees worshipped the rattlesnake. This worship paid to the rattlesnake was universal among all the tribes; but worship was not conferred exclusively upon that serpent. All the snakes of the country enjoyed a share of it, though in a less degree. The Indians suffered them all to live unmolested, on which account they became very numerous.[2] In Brazil, in a large town of eight thousand cabins, Don Alvarez found a tower which contained a serpent twenty-seven feet long, with a very large head. The Indians worshipped this serpent as a divinity, and fed it with human flesh. The Peruvians worshipped adders.[3] Many images of serpents were found in South America, before which the inhabitants knelt in adoration.

In Mexico, many sculptured images of serpents are found. There is one noble specimen of the great serpent idol, almost perfect, and of fine workmanship. This monstrous divinity is represented in the act of swallowing a human victim, which is seen crushed and struggling in its horrid jaws.[4] In the town of Tenayuco, Diaz found so many enormous figures of serpents

---

[1] Carver's Travels, 47.
[2] 1 Logan's Upper South Carolina, 89.
[3] 1 Garcilasso, 188.
[4] Bullock, 328.

which the inhabitants worshipped as gods that he named it the town of Serpents.[1]

It is evident that although some animals may have received a preference, yet all animals shared in the superstitious worship of primitive peoples, and this broad universality of their worship militates against any other theory of its origin except that based upon the transmigration of souls. If all animal life was accounted for by transmigration, then all animal life would be surrounded with superstitious fear,—which was the fact. The religious ceremonies of the Ojibways consisted chiefly in songs and speeches to birds and beasts. The Cœur-d'Aleins rendered divine worship to all the animals they knew.[2] The Wyandots and Ottawas thought that all the animals were divinities, who watched the actions of men, and should receive worship.

Among all the tribes of both Americas the animal form is a prominent feature in their primitive art.

In the mounds are found many animal images; the sculptured figures of birds, serpents, and frogs are most common.[3] Nearly every animal known to natural history is represented. The tortoise, which was a symbol of the Tyrian colony of Thebes, in Greece, and the serpent, are ever recurring upon American ruins. At Uxmal is a building called "the house of the turtles," from a row of tortoises around the cornice. Divers turtles in stone have also been discovered among the ruins. In a large box filled with terra-cotta antiquities once offered to Mr. Wilson, about three-fourths of the whole collection were serpents and turtles.[4]

In the vases found in the sacred spring of the Zuñis, a vast amount of labor was found to have been spent in decorating their interior and exterior with animals. Horned frogs and tadpoles alternate on the inner surface. Several of the figures would serve as spirited specimens of diablerie. In a large vase,

---

[1] Diaz, 260. [2] De Smet, Ind. Sketches, 16.
[3] Squier and Davis, Aborig. Mon., 259, 268.
[4] Wilson's Conquest of Mexico, 161–62.

which was an offering to the spirit of the spring, a frog was in the act of leaping from the vessel as if disturbed by some one's approach. The outline of this vessel is identical with that of the classical caldrons of antiquity and of our own times. This introduction of figures of water-animals on vases dedicated to the genii of fountains is peculiarly appropriate. In another vase are figures of crested serpents, probably representing some water-snake, and very similar to those found in the ruins of Pompeii. In still another vase the figures of butterflies appear.

The elephant appears in American art three times: once in the elephant head of Palenque, where its head forms the head-dress of a bas-relief figure; again in the large animal mound of Wisconsin, and again in the pipe recently discovered in Iowa. On the stem of this pipe a very perfect representation of this animal appears.[1]

Among the most civilized nations transmigration and metamorphoses filled their pantheon with animal gods and mythical beings which assumed animal or composite forms. All of these aided to give color and form to the art of those races which, emerging from the primitive condition that originated and fostered these ideas, had not thrown them off. Animal forms appear everywhere in their art. About one-third of the Nicaraguan statues in stone represent animals and monsters. A very remarkable feature of the art of the civilized nations of Mexico, and especially Nicaragua, is that most of their statuary exhibits the human form connected with the animal. The human form clothed in animal dress is very frequently found.

In many of the bas-reliefs and pictographic representations the head-dress is the head of some animal, and occasionally a composite figure surrounded by much ornamental work. There can be little doubt that these designs were intended to represent and satisfy the primitive styles which we have found among the barbarous tribes, and surviving to some extent

---

[1] Short, 530–31.

among the civilized races. These styles of animal dress had their origin in real life. The warrior donned the skin of the tiger or other animal to render himself terrible in war. The sorcerer clothed himself in the skin of some animal revered by his tribe to inspire them with reverence for himself. Each individual carried his personal manitou, generally the skin of some animal. Each gens was represented by a totemic badge, generally some animal. In the pictography of the Codices in Lord Kingsborough's Mexican Antiquities, we have composite figures of tigers with human hands, and other combinations of animal and human form frequently occurring.

The same superstitious ideas that in art found representation in composite forms would in tradition find expression in myths of fabulous animals. Some of these animals assumed unnatural forms, others did unnatural acts. Among many of the American tribes animals have taken an important part in their cosmogony. In the cosmogony of the Gallinomeros of California, animals were in existence before there was light. One of the catastrophes that happened in this darkness resulted in light being produced. The hawk happening by chance to fly into the face of the coyote, there followed mutual apologies, and afterward a long discussion on the emergency of the situation. The coyote got ready a ball of inflammable material and some pieces of flint, which the hawk took and flew with them into the sky, where he struck fire with the flints and lighted his ball, and sent it whirling along in a fierce red glow, as it continues to the present day, for it was the sun.[1] In the Chibcha cosmogony the blackbird plays a prominent part in scattering light all over the world.[2]

The great hero-deity of the Thlinkeets, Yehl—the crow, their creator—brooded over dark chaos, and beat back its waters with its black wings. A myth of the Tolowas, in accounting for the manner in which the tribe obtained fire, said that the spiders wove a gossamer balloon out of their webs

---

[1] 3 Bancroft, 85, 86.   [2] P. Simon, 241; Bollaert, 11.

and started on a perilous journey to the moon, from which they expected to obtain the fire and return to the earth with it. The Cahroc folk-lore is full of the good deeds of the coyote. It was he that opened up the Klamath for the salmon at the solicitation of the starving people, and when the dam was opened the green waters rushed through all ashine with salmon. "The adulations of flatterers and sycophants puffed up the coyote to such a degree that he determined to have a dance through heaven itself; and whom should he choose as his partner but a star, which, after much solicitation, engaged with him in the dance. But its giddy mazes were too much for the poor coyote, who slipped his hold. Terrible was the fall, but after ten long snows he strikes the earth, and is smashed as flat as a willow mat."[1] The following myth of the origin of fish in Clear Lake makes the coyote play the rôle of creator again. He filled himself with the water of Clear Lake, after eating a great quantity of grasshoppers, and lay down to sleep, when he was thrust through with a spear, and all the water and grasshoppers ran out and down into the lake basin, and the insects became fish.[2]

A Shasta legend makes a ground-mole the creator of the world, which was heaved into existence by the "rooting underneath somewhere" of that animal.[3] The Pima creator was the butterfly, the prettiest fancy of all. It was a metamorphose, however, that gave the little creature such power. Their evil spirit seems to have been the eagle, to whose instrumentality they ascribed the deluge. The only man saved took revenge when the waters subsided by climbing to the eagle's nest and slaying it. About its nest he found the bodies of a great multitude of those the eagle had destroyed. He found a woman the monster had taken to wife, and a child, from whom descended the ancient people called Hohocam, who were led in their wanderings by an eagle and passed into Mexico.[4]

In Indian folk-lore, the winds are generally produced by

---

[1] 3 Bancroft, 138–39. [2] 3 ib., 86, 87. [3] 3 ib., 547. [4] 3 ib., 79.

birds. The owl creates the north wind, the butterfly the south.[1] Among the Iroquois, the wind was thought to be produced by a water-lizard which crawled out of its pool.[2] The Piutes had a fabulous serpent deity in Pyramid Lake. The wind, when it swept down among the nine islands of the lake, drove the waters into the most fantastic swirls and eddies in localities when the rest of the lake was placid. This, said the Piutes, was the snake causing the lake to boil like a pot. Among the Northern tribes about the Great Lakes, the god of water described by Perrot was of composite form, lived in a cavern, and produced the winds by shaking his monstrous tail.[3] Pre-eminent in the Ojibway tales about water-animals was the toad (frog), by which they said a deluge was produced. A huge toad had a quarrel with some land-animal with horns. The toad had the whole management of the waters, and appears to have presided over them with great satisfaction to the Indian race until this fight arose, when, failing to swallow its antagonist, the latter rushed upon it and pierced a hole in its side, out of which the waters gushed in floods and overflowed the earth. Manabozho, the great hare, who was living at that time, fled for refuge to the mountains, carrying some animals with him. When the mountain-tops were flooded, he took to a tree, and with the aid of various animals he recreated the earth. The most useful of these animals was the musk-rat, which went to the bottom of the waters and brought him earth.[4] The traditional deluge of the Crees was caused by a quarrel of a large fish with one of their demi-gods, in which it attempted to drown the god.[5]

Traditions of the production of convulsive changes in the earth's surface by fabulous animals are frequent. There is a legend of Aputaput Fall, Oregon, in which a beaver of enormous size, when pursued by the hunters, tore away the banks of Pelouse River, and in its final struggle produced the cataract.[6]

---

[1] 5 Schoolcraft, 420.
[2] Parkman's Jesuits, lxxxviii.
[3] Memoirs, 20.
[4] Jones, Ojibways, 33-35.
[5] Hartwig's Polar World, 325.
[6] 4 Wilkes, Ex. Exp., 467.

A fabulous animal of the Algonkins was the great beaver, which was one of the most powerful of the manitous. It was he who formed Lake Nipissing. The cataracts in the Outaway River, which issues from the Nipissing, are the relics of dikes thrown up by the great beaver to form that lake; but he died in the midst of the undertaking. He is buried at the top of the mountain to which he has given his form. No native passes the foot of his tomb without smoking in honor of him.[1] The Kaniagmuts say that the island of Kadiak was separated from Alaska by a large otter which pushed its way through from Cook's Inlet.[2] The Salish Indians have a fabulous toad, which, when pursued, in its efforts to escape destruction played havoc with terrestrial objects, but succeeded in springing upon the face of the moon.

Among some of the Western Indians there is a tradition of an immense eagle which hovers in the air out of sight, and carries a lake on his back, full of water. When this aërial monster flaps his wings, loud peals of thunder roll over the prairie. When he winks his eyes, it lightens. When he wags his tail, the waters of the lake overflow and produce rain.[3]

In the myths of nearly all the tribes the thunder and lightning are thought to be produced by either a bird or a serpent. In many of them a fabulous animal, by the name of the thunderbird, becomes a well-defined personality. In some myths the thunder and lightning are the result of a struggle between the serpent and the thunder-bird. The serpent produces the lightning's flash from its forked tongue, whilst robbing the thunderbird's nest. The thunder is the flapping of the wings of the bird in the struggle. These fanciful myths about animals can be referred generally to a simpler germ from which they have sprung, and have gradually been clothed with the imagery of an uncultivated mind, to which nothing is incredible.

In a Thlinkeet myth, the soul of an ancestor appears in the thunder-bird. In the Thlinkeet deluge, a brother and sister were

---

[1] 2 Chateaubriand's Travels, 41.   [2] Dall's Alaska, 405.   [3] Boller, 257.

forced to separate by the flood, and the parting word of the brother was that his sister should never see him again, but should hear his voice. He then clothed himself in the skin of a great bird and flew away southwest. "The sister was swallowed in a great hole or crater near Sitka; but when the storm sweeps down over the country about her subterranean home, the lightning of the thunder-bird's eyes gleams down her crater window, and the thundering of his wings re-echoes throughout all her subterranean halls."[1] Fig. 13 is a representation of the thunder-bird of the Haidahs.[2]

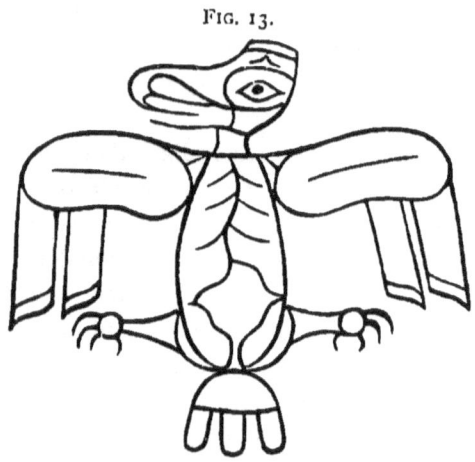

Fig. 13.

The Ojibways had their thunder-bird. When seen flying by day, it foreboded misfortune. These fabulous birds were supposed to have their nests somewhere. A great Ojibway warrior was returning late one night from the hunt, when one of these monstrous birds caught him, and arose and flew westward to a high hill, where he was left in the nest of the young birds. They immediately began to peck at this delicate morsel that had been provided for them. The warrior summoned up courage, and determined to defend himself from these young thunder-birds; but whenever they winked a flash of lightning

---

[1] 3 Bancroft, 103-4.   [2] Swan, Haidah Indians, Smith. Contrib., No. 267.

would pass from their eyes and burn him. By the most wonderful deeds of valor known to Indian folk-lore, he mastered the tender birds, took their hearts, and when he got home made a delicious broil of them. Since this experience with the warrior these birds do not trouble the Indians, but live on snakes and fish. Their nests are now in the Rocky Mountains, but they are heard at times passing east to the sea.[1]

There are among the different families of a tribe different ideas of the size of this mythical bird, for among the Ojibways another tradition says that the thunder-bird is about as large as the end of the little finger, and cannot reproduce her own species, and is eternal. Her mate is a serpent, whose fiery tongue destroys the young ones as they are hatched. She sits on her eggs during fair weather and hatches her brood at the approach of a storm.[2] We have here a very pretty mythological sister for the halcyon of the Greek mythology.

A large bird, according to tradition, used to slay the buffaloes of early day, and sit on the ledge of the Red Rocks, on top of Coteau des Prairies, and eat them. Their blood ran down the rocks and made them red. This bird had its nest near by, and when serpents crawled in to molest the eggs they would hatch out in a clap of thunder.[3]

According to Dacotah tradition, they won a battle against the Iowas by aid of a thunder-bird. Their thunder-bird was a winged monster, which bore down on the Iowa village in a most terrible and godlike manner. Tempests howled, lightnings flashed, the thunder uttered its voice, and the earth trembled. A bolt was hurled at the Iowas, which ploughed the earth and formed that deep ravine near the village of Oak Grove.[4]

"A bird of thunder was once killed, the Dacotahs assert, near Kaposia. Its face resembled the human countenance. Its nose was hooked like the bill of an eagle. Its wings had

---

[1] Copway's Ojibways, 109–13.
[3] 2 ib., 168.
[2] 2 Catlin, Ill., 164.
[4] 1 Minnesota Hist. Coll., 145.

four joints, and were zigzag like the lightning. About thirty miles from Big Stone Lake, near the head-waters of the Minnesota, there are several small lakes bordered with oak-trees. This is the supposed birthplace of the thunder-bird, and is called the nest of thunder."[1] The Dacotahs show at this place the footprints of the thunder-bird twenty-five miles apart.

Tupan, the thunder-bird of the Tupi tribe of Brazil, flapped his celestial wings and flashed light therefrom, and his name still stands among the Christianized natives as the equivalent of God.[2] The Caribs thought the thunder-cloud was a bird, and that it produced the lightning in true Carib fashion by blowing it through a hollow reed, just as they do their poisoned darts.[3] The thunder-bird appears upon the Guatemalan sculptures. The natives of the Isthmus of Darien have a tradition of two birds with maiden faces that came with a storm from the east. They seized men and women and carried them off to their mountain nest. At last they made an image of a man and fastened it into the ground. One of the birds swooped down upon this, and fastened its talons so that they could not be released, and they killed it.[4]

A tradition very similar to this was found among the Illinois, which I will give in the language of Mr. Jones. "In the reign of the illustrious Owatoga, chief of the Illinois, they were terrified with a fearful visitation from a thunder-bird. There appeared upon the inaccessible cliffs, where it made its home, an immense and hideous animal, half bird, half beast, which, from the circumstance of its having wings, they called the Piasau bird. This name, like all Indian names, is significant of the character of the monster which it designates: it means the man-destroying bird. This bird is described as being of gigantic size, capable of bearing off with ease in its talons a horse or buffalo. Its head and beak were like those of the vulture, with eyes of the most dazzling brilliancy; its wings black as the raven and

---

[1] Neill's Minnesota, 58.   [2] 2 Tylor, 262–63.
[3] Brinton, 108.   [4] 3 Bancroft, 500.

clothed with thunder, making a most fearful noise in its heavy flight; its legs four in number, and talons like those of a mighty eagle; its body similar to that of the dragon, ending with a tail of huge dimensions like a scorpion's. Its body was gorgeously colored with every hue, and in its flight it made a most imposing spectacle, inspiring terror, awe, and wonder. Such was this strange visitor which had taken up its abode in their sacred cliffs; and while their priests were studying the omen, whether it should be for good or for evil, all doubt was dissipated by the sudden descent of the bird into their midst, which seized one of their bravest warriors in its talons and bore him as a prey to its wild eyrie in the rocks. Never again was the unfortunate victim seen by his friends. But the sacrifice was not complete. Brave after brave, and women and children not a few, were borne off in succession by the fierce devourer, whose appetite seemed but to be whetted to a keener set the more it tasted of human blood. Such was the fearful state of things, when the brave Owatoga, chief of this mighty tribe, sought out his priests, and with them, retiring to a secret place, fasted many days and with all the mummery of their religion. At length, in a trance, it was revealed to Owatoga that the terrible visitant who had hitherto eluded their utmost sagacity might be destroyed. The mode was this. First, a noble victim was to be selected from among the bravest warriors of the tribe, who, by religious rites, was to be sanctified for the sacrifice. Secondly, twenty equally brave, with their stoutest bows and sharpest arrows, were to conceal themselves near the spot of sacrifice. The victim was to be led forth and singly to take his stand upon an exposed point of the rock, where the ravenous bird would be likely to notice and seize upon him. At the moment of descent the concealed warriors were to let fly their arrows, with the assurance that he would fall. . . . Owatoga appeared at the head of his tribe as the voluntary victim. . . . Soon was the ill-omened bird seen hovering over the place, and, after wheeling about for a few moments high above the head of the devoted chief, nearing at each gyration the unquailing victim, suddenly he came thundering down toward his prize. In an instant the barbed arrows from twenty sure bows buried themselves to the feather in the body of the common foe, and he fell quivering and dead at the feet of the noble chieftain, himself escaping unscathed. . . . It was determined to perpetuate the event by engraving the picture of the Piasau bird upon the smooth-sided limestone cliffs which tower above the river. There it was done, and stained with the fast and fadeless colors whose subtle compounding the Indian only knows, and which remain plainly visible to the present day. The spot became sacred from that time, and no Indian ascended or descended the Father of Waters for many a year without discharging his arrow at the image of the warrior-destroying bird."[1]

Of the worship of compound monsters, impossible hybrid animals and forms that are half human, half brutal, Mr. Spencer says, "When a chief nicknamed the wolf carries away from an adjacent tribe a wife who is remembered either under the animal name of her tribe or as a woman, it will happen that if her son distinguishes himself, the remembrance of him among his descendants will be that he was born of a wolf and some other animal, or of a wolf and a woman. We need not be surprised, then, at finding among the Egyptians the goddess Pasht represented as a woman with a lion's head, and the god Month as a man with the head of a hawk." Gods having the form of a man with an eagle's tail, or uniting a human bust to the body of a fish, no longer appear such unaccountable conceptions.[2]

Many nondescript animals are pictured on the exposed surfaces of rocks throughout the length and breadth of both Americas. Where they are isolated and not a part of a pictographic system of writing, they are probably drawn as objects of worship. Specimens of these are described by Father Marquette and Hennepin in the following language: "As we

---

[1] Jones's Illinois and the West, 53-59.   [2] Spencer's Rec. Dis., 46, seq.

coasted along rocks frightful for their height and length, we saw two monsters painted on one of these rocks which startled us at first, and on which the boldest Indian dare not gaze long. They are as large as a calf, with horns on the head like a deer, a fearful look, red eyes, bearded like a tiger, the face somewhat like a man's, the body covered with scales, and the tail so long that it twice makes the turn of the body, passing over the head and down between the legs, and ending at last in a fish's tail. Green, red, and a kind of black are the colors employed. On the whole, these two monsters are so well painted that we could not believe any Indian to have been the designer, as good painters in France would find it hard to do as well; besides this, they are so high up on the rock that it is hard to get conveniently at them to paint them."[1]

Says Hennepin, "I had quite forgot to relate that the Illinois had told us that toward the cape which I have called in my map St. Anthony, near the nation of the Messorites [Missouris], there were some tritons and other sea-monsters painted, which the boldest men durst not look upon, there being some enchantment in their face. I thought this was a story; but when we came near the place they had mentioned, we saw, instead of these monsters, a horse and some other beasts painted upon the rock with red colors by the savages. The Illinois had told us likewise that the rock on which these dreadful monsters stood was so steep that no man could climb up to it; but had we not been afraid of the savages more than of the monsters, we had certainly got up to them. There is a common tradition among that people that a great number of Miamis were drowned in that place, being pursued by the savages of Matsigamea; and since that time the savages going by the rock use to smoke and offer tobacco to those beasts, to appease, as they say, the manitou."[2]

Mermaid-myths are found in some localities. The Ottawas

---

[1] Marquette's Narrative, in Shea's Discovery, 39.
[2] Hennepin's New Discovery, 135-36.

had a mermaid which was a woman from the waist up, but two fishes below. Her hands and arms were covered with scales. Her face was very beautiful. She was named "the daughter of the flood."[1] The natives of the Arctic regions have a female spirit who is the protectress of sea-animals. She can make them plenty or scarce as she pleases. The sorcerers say, however, that they are able to compel her to let go the sea-animals by cutting off her nails. Whole herds of walrus rise to the surface when a knuckle is detached. Her name is Nooliayoo, and she represents the mermaid-myths of those Northern parts. The Indians are said to be descended from her union with a malformed dog which watched the door of her house.[2]

FIG. 14.

Many of these composite forms appear in the mythology of the Haidahs. Oolala was half man and half bird, that lived in the mountains, and was greatly feared by the natives. Tchimose was a mythological creature supposed to live in the ocean, and was represented as in Fig. 14, taken from the book entitled "Swan's Haidah Indians," published by the Smithsonian Institution. The Ojibways have a composite mythological figure called Ne-ban-a-baig, partaking of the double nature of man and fish, a notion which, except as to sex, has its analogy in the mermaid of Western Europe. These animals, according to their traditions, inhabit the upper lakes. A gens claim descent from this fabulous animal, and they have made a totem of it: their word for it might be translated the man-fish totem. It is represented on Plate IV. The sacred animal of the Winnebagoes was a nondescript and composite figure, seen only by medicine-men after severe fasting. Fig. 15 is a representation of this animal.

---

[1] 3 Jones, Traditions, 126.   [2] Lyon's Journal, 362–63.

The finding of the bones of the mastodon, or of those of other animals akin to it in size, by the Indians from time to

FIG. 15.

time, has not had the tendency to check their disposition to make for themselves fabulous animal gods. On the contrary, they looked upon all relics of this nature with superstitious reverence. The Dacotahs had legends of large animals which they had preserved to keep away sickness and dangers.[1] Mastodons' bones have been found in Wisconsin mounds. The natives of British America preserved the bones of mammoths found on Shell Creek, and regarded them as the bones of a manitou.[2]

A meagre acquaintance with these large animals has tended to produce superstitious feelings in the minds of these uncultured peoples, and has originated undoubtedly many of their myths about fabulous animals. There can be but little doubt that the mastodon had existed within the recollection of the oldest members of some of the present tribes, or their ancestors, at the time of the advent of the whites. Mexican sepulchres have been opened containing the skeletons of the mammoth or of some similar animal. These tombs appeared to have been specially prepared for their reception, and they were buried apparently with the same care as men. Says Mr. Winchell on this subject, "I have observed the bones of the mastodon and

---

[1] Eastman's Legends, 228.   [2] 1 Hind's Narrative, 313.

elephant imbedded in peat at depths so shallow that I could readily believe the animal to have occupied the country during its possession by the Indians."[1] "Judging from geological data, the appearance of man in America was later than in the Old World, but even in America the race has probably looked upon the later representatives of the mastodon and mammoth tribes. I have myself exhumed mastodon bones from a bed of peat not more than three feet deep, which could be easily accumulated in five hundred years. The Indians have traditions of the same."[2] Says Du Pratz, "Some years ago the skeletons of two large elephants and two small ones were discovered in the marsh near the river Ohio, and they were not much consumed."[3] The discovery by Mr. Koch of a mastodon, which had near it weapons and other evidences of having been attacked and killed by Indians at a not very distant day, bears evidence to the same effect. There are many traditions, among different tribes, of these monstrous animals. The tribes of New York had a tradition of a remarkable and ferocious animal, the Yagesho, which existed in the northern parts of New York about three centuries ago. "It was much superior to the largest bear, remarkably long-bodied, broad down by its shoulders, but narrow just at its hind legs. It had a large head and fearful look. Its legs were short and thick. Its paws (with claws nearly as long as an Indian's finger) spread very wide. It was almost bare of hair, except the head and the tender part of its legs. Several of these animals had been destroyed by the Indians, but the one of which the following account is given had escaped them, and for years had destroyed many Indians. It would catch and kill the largest bears and devour them. The men assembled to deliberate on the plan of killing him. This beast lived near Lake Hoosink, and got the scent of the party detached to decoy him, and rushed upon them. Arrows and stones were discharged at him until he dropped down and died. His head was cut off and carried in triumph

---

[1] Winchell's Sketches, 350. [2] Ib., 240. [3] 2 Louisiana, 130.

to their village and exalted on a pole. The Mahicanni claim the honor of this act."[1]

The tradition of the flying heads among the Iroquois, which greatly disturbed their quiet and defied all human power successfully to combat, may be enumerated among their singular fancies. These heads, of monstrous size, enveloped in beards and hair of flaming fire, rushed through the air like shooting stars or falling meteors, threatening the destruction of their nation. The priests, prophets, and medicine-men were alike unsuccessful in subduing these supernatural monsters. The frontispiece is a representation of one of them. The Quis-Quis, or great hog, was another monster which gave the Onondagas great trouble, as did also the great bear, the horned water-serpent, and many other equally fabulous inventions.[2] There is a myth that a young Iroquois found a two-headed serpent when he was out hunting and brought it to his lodge and fed it. After some time it grew so large it rested on the beams of the lodge, and the hunters had to feed it with deer. It at last went out-doors and maintained itself on a hill. Finally it surrounded the nation with its folds, and, as they attempted to escape, devoured them all but one man and his sister. In a dream it was revealed to him that if he would fledge his arrows with the hair of his sister and shoot at the heart of the monster he would conquer. He obeyed, and the wound was mortal, and the serpent rolled down the hill into the lake, where he vomited up all the people he had eaten.[3]

All animals with which they were unacquainted would produce superstitious fear among the Indians when seen for the first time. A very curious illustration of this is told by Catlin. In a Minnitaree village a great sensation was produced by the appearance (to use the language of the Indians) of "a small animal not far differing in size from a ground-squirrel, but with

---

[1] Yates and Moulton's New York, Pt. 1, notes, pp. 9-10.
[2] Plate in Cusick's Six Nations; 1 Clark's Onondaga, 143.
[3] Schoolcraft's Iroquois, 61.

a long, round tail." This unknown animal showed himself slyly about a chief's wigwam, peeping out from under the pots and kettles. They looked upon it as great medicine, and so sacred no one dared kill it; but hundreds came to watch and look at it. After councils had been called and solemn decrees issued for its countenance and protection, a fur-trader came among them and pronounced it a rat, which had been introduced by whites.[1] At the mouth of the Q'Appelle River, an Indian, in June, 1858, set his net and caught a large fish of a kind different from any with which he was familiar. He immediately pronounced it to be a manitou, and, carefully restoring it to the water again, at once sacrificed five valuable dogs to appease the anger of the supposed deity.[2]

No doubt many of the fabulous animals of uncultured peoples are the appearances of their disordered imaginations in dreams. An Ojibway, in obedience to a dream which recurred ten successive nights, arose on the eleventh and issued forth with his magic staff to the side of a stream, whose waters he touched. They began gradually moving beneath the influence until a violent whirlpool arose, which drew into its coils the fish and other water-animals, such as frogs, toads, lizards, and aquatic birds and insects, which passed before the astonished eyes of the enchanter. At length he stood in the midst of the commotion, like Goethe's apprentice to the magician, and, although a strange horror crept over him, he insisted that the king of fishes should appear. Forced by the magic spell, he came, and, emerging from the lake in the shape of a mighty serpent, it gave him a powder like the vermilion with which the Indians paint their faces. This powder cured all diseases, and made him a mighty doctor among his nation. But his distinction was purchased at the price of his children, who were sacrificed one by one to the water-god in accordance with his promise.[3] The following is a Mexican tradition: "Certain fishermen near the Lake of Mexico took a monstrous fowl of

---

[1] 1 Catlin's Ill., 194-95.   [2] 2 Hind's Nar., 134-35.   [3] Kohl, 422-25.

extraordinary make and bigness. Its deformity was horrible, and on its head was a shining plate like a looking-glass, from which the sun reflected a dim light. Montezuma, drawing near, saw within it a representation of night and a heaven covered with stars. Looking a second time in the glass, he saw an army of men, coming from the east, making a terrible slaughter of his subjects. When the magician priests came to examine and had tried experiments, it escaped with astonishing flight."[1] One of the fabulous animals of the Mexicans was Xochitonal, a great crocodile, who guarded the path to the spirit-land.[2]

Local manitous generally assume a monstrous form, and might be called unnatural gods. The figure of a large bird is the most common. The spirit of Rock Island was a white bird with wings like a swan, but ten times larger.[3] In Cox's Recollections of Wabash Valley we find the following account of one of these fabulous animals of the Potawatomies. "There was a tradition existing among the Potawatomie Indians that there was a monster in the shape of a serpent in Lake Manitou. Their superstitious dread of this lake was such that they would not hunt upon its borders nor fish in its waters, for fear of incurring the anger of the evil spirit that made its home in this little woodland lake. . . . When the government officers were about erecting the Potawatomie mills, the Indians strenuously objected to the erection of a dam at the outlet of the lake, lest its accumulated waters might disturb and overflow the subterranean chambers of the serpent, and the exasperated demon rush forth from his watery dominions and take indiscriminate vengeance on all those who resided near the sacred lake."[4]

Among the South American nations these unnatural forms of man and beast are represented in their art. Numerous idols were found everywhere with the form of man and animal com-

---

[1] 1 De Solis, Conq., 144. [2] 3 Bancroft, 537.
[3] Autobiography of Blackhawk, 70.
[4] Cox's Recollections of Wabash Valley, 136.

bined, and were the objects of a degrading worship that often descended to human sacrifice. A scene illustrative of this is represented in Fig. 16, which is taken from Zarate's Peru.

Fig. 16.

The Araucanians of Chile have fabulous creatures called ulmenes, which are the genii of their mythology. They are male and female, and attach themselves to individuals as guardian spirits.[1] Among the Brazilian tribes curious fables of animals are related, from which we can readily see that they ascribe to them monstrous forms and unnatural deeds. The tortoise figures extensively in races and other athletic sports. They have a bird of evil eye which kills with a look. The ground under its nest is white with human bones. There is a myth that a hunter once killed one of these and cut off its head without the eye being turned upon him. He killed his game thereafter by turning the evil eye upon it. His wife, not dreaming of its destructive power, however, once turned it toward her husband and killed him, and then accidentally turned it toward herself and died. They believe in the existence of an enormous water-serpent, whose track marked out the lakes

---

[1] 2 Molina, 86.

and channels.[1] A mythical monster called the Curupira (probably a man-shaped ape) is the dread of the timid. These fabulous animals are the guardian deities of the forests, and go about beating on the trees just before a tempest to see if they are strong enough to withstand it.[2] Mr. Tylor mentions a tradition among the Brazilians of an ape which had been found to be an extinct species.[3] The natives living near the river Casanare had a tradition of a serpent with numerous heads which had devoured many of the inhabitants.[4] The natives living near the river Huallaga had a tradition of a vulture-like animal who preyed upon wanderers.[5] The Peruvians named their sacred Titicaca from *titi*, a cat, and *caca*, a rock. They have a myth that on the rock in the island of the same name there lived and sat in ancient times a cat with fire shooting from its eyes.[6]

Occasionally a myth pretends to account for the form and color of different animals. The two following myths are curious illustrations of this. The red fox got its black legs by being thrown into a cauldron where the food was cooking for a grand feast, to which he was invited by a host whom he had formerly insulted. He got out with his legs burnt.[7] The mythical hero Manabozho was walking along the banks, and, seeing a flock of ducks enjoying themselves on the blue waters, he called them. Some favored going to him, some not; but at last they all trooped after him with many pleasant quackings and entered his lodge. Placing himself in the centre, he ranged the ducks in a circle around him. He had a sack around his neck. "Now," said he, "you must all shut your eyes tight and not open them under any circumstances. I will take my Indian flute and play upon it, and when I give the word you may open your eyes and commence dancing." The ducks shut their eyes and waited, all impatient for the dancing to

---

[1] Smith's Brazil, 559-60. [2] Ib., 564.
[3] Researches, 314. [4] Ursua and Aguire's Ex. Int., 10.
[5] Ib., 45. [6] Markham's Travels, 114.
[7] Kinzie's Waubun, 368-70.

begin. Presently a sound was heard like a smothered quack, but the ducks did not dare to open their eyes. Again the sound of the flute would be interrupted by the gurgling cry of "quack." There was one duck at this juncture that could not resist opening one eye, when, lo! the deity was seen seizing each duck nearest him, throttling it, and stuffing it into the bag on his shoulder. Edging a little out of the circle, it cried, "Open your eyes," and flew. Manabozho grasped her back with his hand, but she escaped with her back shaped as now, and her neck unnaturally stretched forward. The same plight came upon many others at the same time.[1]

---

[1] Kinzie's Waubun, 312-14.

CHAPTER VII.

WORSHIP OF TREES AND PLANTS.

Worship of trees—Their supposed vitality explained by animism—Supposed descent of human beings from trees—Worship of plants—Personality ascribed to them—Origin of plants from human bodies—Those having medical properties supposed to be endowed with supernatural powers.

THE worship of trees and plants is found in America. The vegetable kingdom shared with other natural objects the superstitious belief in the animation of all nature by spirits. One of the causes that probably led to the prevalence of the superstition as to trees is the primitive custom of burying or suspending the dead in trees. We have heretofore noticed this custom among many of the tribes. The probabilities are that under certain conditions they have all practised this custom more or less. In nature-worship, the precipice, waterfall, or dangerous locality of any kind, which has become a place of Indian devotion, has connected with it a story of being haunted by the spirit of some unfortunate tribesman who has lost his life there. The spirits of the dead remain about the place where death has overtaken them, or where the body or any portion of it is placed. Customs such as that of the Nicaraguans, of suspending the heads of sacrificed captives in trees,[1] would tend to induce a superstitious fear of such trees. Some of the Northwestern Indians thought that those who died a natural death would be compelled to dwell among the branches of tall trees.[2]

The Ojibways believed that trees had souls, and in pagan times they seldom cut down green or living trees, "for they thought it put them to pain. They pretended to hear the wail-

---

[1] 2 Bancroft, 746.   [2] Barrett Lenard's Travels, 54.

ing of the trees when they suffered in this way."[1] On account of these noises, real or imaginary, trees have had spirits assigned them and worship offered to them. A mountain-ash in the vicinity of Sault Ste. Marie, which made a noise, had offerings piled up around it.[2] If a tree should emit from its hollow trunk or branches a sound during a calm state of the atmosphere, or should any one fancy such sounds, the tree would be at once reported, and soon come to be regarded as the residence of some local god.[3] Mr. Kohl mentions an Ojibway Indian who had chosen a tamarack-tree for his protector because he fancied he heard a remarkable rustling in its branches.[4] This was ample evidence that a spirit was domiciled in the tree. Mr. Schoolcraft mentions a hollow tree from the recesses of which, Indian tradition said, there issued on a calm day a sound like the voice of a spirit or manitou. It resembled the sounds of their own drum. It was therefore considered as the residence of some powerful spirit, and deemed sacred. To mark their regard for the place, they began to deposit at its foot boughs and twigs of the same species of tree as they passed it from year to year on their way to and from their hunting-grounds.[5]

Roman Pane says of the West India tribes "that if an Indian going through a wood would perceive a motion in the trees which he thought supernatural, frightened at the prodigy, he would address himself to that tree which shook the most. The trees generally did not condescend to confabulate with them, but ordered them to go to a boie, or priest, who would order them to sacrifice to their new deity." He also says, "The natives of the Antilles used to believe that certain trees sent for sorcerers, to whom they gave orders how to shape their trunks into idols, and then, being installed in temple huts, they received prayer and inspired the priests with oracles."

---

[1] Jones's Ojibways, 104.
[2] Schoolcraft's Oneota, 191.
[3] 2 Schoolcraft, Ind., 224-25.
[4] Kohl's Kitchi-Gami, 59.
[5] Schoolcraft's Thirty Years, 99.

This mysterious spiritual vitality ascribed to trees has even led to a belief in the descent of the human race from trees. The natives about Saginaw had a tradition of a boy who sprang from a tree within which was buried one of their tribe. A descent from trees can be traced among the traditions of many tribes. The founders of the Miztec monarchy descended from two majestic trees that stood in a gorge of the mountains of Apoala.[1] The Zapotecs attributed their origin to trees, and their cypresses and palms often received offerings of incense and other gifts.[2] The Caribs had a gens called the cabato-tree.[3] The Chiapanese had a tradition that they sprang from the roots of a silk-cotton-tree.[4]

In the pictography of the Indians the trees supposed to be inhabited by a spirit find representation in anthropomorphic forms. In a folk-tale of the Ojibways the maiden Leelinau, whenever she could leave her father's lodge, would fly to remote haunts and recesses in the woods, or sit in lonely reverie upon some high promontory of rock overlooking the lake. In such places she would often, with her face turned upward, linger long in contemplation of the air, as if she were invoking her guardian spirit and beseeching him to lighten her sadness. But, amid all the leafy haunts, none drew her steps toward it so often as a forest of pines on the open shore, called Manitowok, or the Sacred Wood. It was one of those hallowed places which are the resort of the little wild men of the woods and of the turtle-spirits, or fairies, which delight in romantic scenes. Owing to this circumstance, its green retirement was seldom visited by Indians, who feared to fall under the influence of its mischievous inhabitants; and whenever they were compelled by stress of weather to make a landing on this part of the coast, they never failed to leave an offering of tobacco, or some other token, to show that they desired to stand well with the proprietors of the fairy-ground.

---

[1] 5 Bancroft, 527.
[2] 3 ib., 459.
[3] 1 Rafinesque, 195.
[4] 5 Bancroft, 605.

It had been her custom to pass many of her hours in her favorite place of retirement, under a broad-topped young pine, whose leaves whispered in every wind that blew, but most of all in that gentle murmur of the air at the evening hour, dear to lovers, when the twilight steals on. Thither she now repaired, and, while reclining pensively against the young pine-tree, she fancied that she heard a voice addressing her. At first it was scarcely more than a sigh; presently it grew more clear, and she heard it distinctly whisper, "Maiden! think me not a tree, but thine own dear lover, fond to be with thee in my tall and blooming strength, with the bright green nodding plume that waves above thee. Thou art leaning on my breast, Leelinau; lean forever there, and be at peace. Fly from men who are false and cruel, and quit the tumult of their dusty strife for this quiet, lonely shade. Over thee I my arms will fling, fairer than the lodge's roof. I will breathe a perfume like that of flowers over thy happy evening rest. In my bark canoe I'll waft thee o'er the waters of the sky-blue lake. I will deck the folds of thy mantle with the sun's last rays. Come, and on the mountain free, rove, a fairy bright, with me!" Leelinau drank in with eager ear these magical words. Her heart was fixed. No warrior's son should clasp her hand. She wasted away until she disappeared from her father's lodge forever; but her figure is frequently seen, accompanied by her fairy lover, gliding through the forest of young pines. Such stories as these are frequent in Indian lodge-lore, and represent that phase of their imagination which gives a spiritual life and form to plants and trees.

The Ojibways considered curious trees as gods.[1] A converted Ojibway confessed that at one time, when in danger of perishing in the woods with cold, he prayed to the trees standing around him to save him, but the trees stood still and made no effort in his behalf. He was glad that he had been brought to know the vanity of such things.[2] On Grand River stood a

---

[1] Jones's Ojibways, 85. [2] Ib., 88.

lofty pine-tree with a large, spreading, closely-matted top. This tree was taller than any other in view, and made a great god for one of their Indians, who with his family made periodical visits to it, with prayer and sacrifice. The best of his game was offered at the foot of this tree, and it was boiled for the convenience of this god.[1]

Many trees were worshipped by the Dacotahs, and among them the medicine-wood, which gets its name from a superstition that it was a genius to protect or punish them according to their merits or demerits.[2] They hung small red capotes upon trees as a sacrifice.[3] Mr. Pike, speaking of an immense plane-tree seen by him, says, "This plane, which is perhaps the colossus of the whole vegetable kingdom, the Indians adored as a manitou."[4]

Charlevoix mentions an instance of tree-worship. He says, "Formerly the Indians in the neighborhood of Acadia had in their country, near the sea-shore, a tree extremely ancient, of which they relate many wonders and which was always laden with offerings. After the sea had laid open its whole root, it still supported itself a long time almost in the air against the violence of the winds and waves, which confirmed those Indians in the notion that this tree must be the abode of some powerful spirit, nor was its fall even capable of undeceiving them, so that as long as the smallest part of its branches appeared above the water, they paid it the same honors as whilst it stood."[5]

The natives of Carolina, says Lawson, held the yaupon, or tea-plant, in veneration above all plants they were acquainted with, and they say the discovery thereof was by an infirm Indian that labored under the burden of many rugged distempers and could not be cured by all their doctors. One day he fell asleep and dreamed that if he took a decoction of the tree that

---

[1] Jones's Ojibways, 254. [2] 6 Wisc. Hist. Coll., 205.
[3] Pike's Expedition, 31. [4] Ib., 396.
[5] 2 Charlevoix's Voyage, 149.

grew at his head he would be cured. Upon this he awoke, and saw the yaupon, or cassena-tree, which was not there when he fell asleep. He followed the direction of his dream, and became perfectly well in a short time.[1] On the banks of the river Chata Uche stood a wild fig-tree, which the Indians had consecrated as an object of worship. The Creeks had a sacred tree on which they hung strips of buffalo flesh.[2]

The cult existed in Mexico and the Central American states. The Mayas recognized divinities in trees.[3] A gigantic ancient cypress in Mexico had offerings attached to its boughs, of teeth and locks of hair in great numbers. The Tepanees worshipped and offered sacrifice to trees.[4] The ticara or wild calabash-tree was an object of religious veneration to the Guatemalans.[5] Darwin saw a tree near Siena de la Ventana which the Indians reverenced as the altar of Walleechu. Offerings of cigars, bread, and meat were suspended upon it by threads. There was a little hole to pour libations in. The tree was surrounded by bleached bones of horses that had been sacrificed. The tree was a landmark in a dangerous passage.[6] The Chibchas had a tree called huaycan (holy wood). It is a large tree, and its wood does not rot under water. According to their traditions, the earth was supported by pillars of this wood. The Peruvians used this wood for making their idols.[7] Tree-worship was found among the Brazilian tribes. The Calchaquis of Brazil worshipped certain trees, which were trimmed with feathers.[8] The Indians frequently adorn them with feathers. The same is true of many tribes inhabiting those parts of Brazil in which trees obtain a magnitude that inspires them with veneration.

A western tribe of North America, called the Achonawi, ascribed a fabulous origin to trees, for they thought that the feathers of eagles, when they dropped and stuck in the earth,

---

[1] Lawson's N. C., 359–60. [2] Lubbock, Origin, 196.
[3] 2 Bancroft, 688. [4] 2 ib., 330.
[5] Boyle's Camp Notes, 49. [6] Darwin's Nat. Voyage, 68–69.
[7] Bollaert, 13. [8] 3 Southey, 395.

grew tall trees. They thought all trees were mysterious, because fire proceeded from their wood when rubbed.[1]

The transmigration and presence of spirits in plants explain the worship of this subdivision of the vegetable kingdom. Many traditions illustrate this subject. The Brazilians have a mythological character called Mani: she was a child who died and was buried in the house of her mother. Soon a plant sprang out of the grave, which grew, flourished, and bore fruit. This plant was the mandioca, named from *mani*, and *oca* (house). They thought they saw the body of Mani in the root.[2] The Ojibways have a legend in which one of their number, in a dreamy state, saw a handsome young man dressed in green robes with green plumes on his head, who returned thrice and wrestled with him. In the last struggle the visiting youth was thrown and killed, and his body was buried. The Indian watched the grave and kept it clean, not letting even the wild flower grow there. Soon he saw the green plumes coming out of the ground, at first in spiral points, and then rising in green stalks, and soon silken fringes and yellow tassels appeared. The majestic plant waved its taper leaves and displayed its bright plumes. Its name was Mondamin, the Indian corn.[3]

Among the Virginia tribes the red clover was thought to have sprung from and be colored by the blood of the red men slain in battle. The pantheistic tendency of the transmigration theory is shown in many of the agricultural ceremonies of the tribes. One of these illustrates the far-reaching extent of their philosophy. When a child's umbilical cord was cut, it was over an ear of corn, which was immediately sown and cultivated as a sacred thing. The perpetuity of this spiritual life and force, and its never-ending circle of existence, is the secret of this primitive superstition.

The Pawnees sacrificed a female slave at their agricultural

---

[1] 3 Ethnology of Powell Exp., 273, 287. [2] Smith's Brazil, 586.
[3] 2 Schoolcraft, 231–32.

ceremonies, and, while the flesh was warm, stripped it from the bones in small pieces, which were put into a basket and carried to the corn-field, where a drop of blood was squeezed upon the grains of corn that were deposited in the ground.[1]

A personality was ascribed to plants. Mr. Kohl tells a very interesting traditionary story. One year there was an extraordinary abundance of corn, and they let it lie about and rot, and the children fought each other with the stalks and then threw them in the mud. Very soon want overtook them, and a famine threatened them, and in their distress one of the tribe, who had taken no part in the indignities offered the corn, had a communication with the spirit of the corn, who consented to make a revelation to him. As he was walking alone he came to a meadow, and in its centre a mound, on which stood a birch-bark lodge, from which cries and groans issued. On entering, he found a poor dried-up manikin, who complained of his wretched condition, due to the ill-treatment of the Indians. He hurried to his tribe and told them, and they sacrificed to the spirit of the corn, which was appeased, and returned them good crops thereafter.[2]

The Miamis have a tradition similar to this, except that the corn-spirit was angry in their case because they had thrown corn-cobs at each other in play. The corn-spirit pretended to have suffered serious injury in his body on account of this cruel sport.[3]

The Iroquois acknowledged the existence of spirits in trees and plants, and had three mythological characters, who were sisters, the spirits of the maize, of the bean, and of the squash. The Iroquois say that the spirit of corn, the spirit of beans, and the spirit of squashes are supposed to have the forms of beautiful females.

Many tribes when they gathered herbs sacrificed to the spirit by leaving some in the place left vacant.[4]

---

[1] 5 Schoolcraft, 78.
[2] Kohl's Kitchi-Gami, 266-68.
[3] 5 Schoolcraft, 195.
[4] Harmon's Journal, 374.

Mr. Rafinesque has, as is his custom, put one of his large names on the plant branch of mythology, and called it Phytomorphy. Among the most prominent of the plants worshipped in the Antilles he mentions mushrooms, pines, opuntias, zapos, and zeybas.[1] Among the Virginia tribes the mysterious growth of toadstools was ascribed to supernatural agency, and they became objects of worship. The divinities supposed to reside in them were painted on the outside.

Among savage peoples, those plants that produce great nervous excitement, or a lethargic state, are supposed to contain a supernatural being. In Peru, tobacco has been called the sacred herb, and throughout all America it has been looked upon with reverence. In Peru, coca is another plant which they look upon with superstitious veneration. It has an invigorating effect. It is pretended that the use of the coca— that herb so famous in the histories of Peru—adds much to the strength of the Indians. Others affirm that they use it as a charm. When, for instance, the mine of ore is too hard, they throw upon it a handful of that herb chewed, and immediately get out the ore with more ease and in a greater quantity. Fishermen also put some of that herb, chewed, to their hook when they can take no fish, and they are said to have better success thereafter.[2] It sustained an important part in the religion of the Incas. In all ceremonies, whether religious or warlike, it was introduced for producing smoke at the great offerings, or as the sacrifice itself. During divine worship the priests chewed coca-leaves, and unless they were supplied with them it was believed that the favor of the gods could not be propitiated. It was also deemed necessary that the supplicator should approach the priests with coca in his mouth. It was believed that any business undertaken without the benediction of coca-leaves could not prosper, and to the shrub itself worship was rendered. During an interval of more than three hundred years Christianity has not been able to subdue the

---

[1] 2 Rafinesque, 208.   [2] Frezier's Voyage, 269.

deep-rooted idolatry, for everywhere we find traces of belief in the mysterious power of this plant. The excavators in the mines of Cerro de Pasco throw masticated coca on hard veins of metal, in the belief that it softens the ore and renders it more easy to work. The origin of this custom is easily explained when it is recollected that in the time of the Incas it was believed that the coyas, or the deities of metals, rendered the mountains impenetrable if they were not propitiated by the odor of coca. The Indians, even at the present time, put coca-leaves into the mouths of dead persons to secure to them a favorable reception on their entrance into another world; and when a Peruvian Indian, on a journey, falls in with a mummy, he, with timid reverence, presents to it some coca-leaves as his pious offering.[1]

The following religious ceremony to the Irish potato, which was first discovered in Peru, shows the regard entertained for it. Cieza, describing the ceremony, says, "About noon they began to sound drums. When the caciques were seated in the plaza, a boy, richly dressed, went up to each cacique. On the left hand of each boy walked a girl beautifully dressed. From their shoulders a lion-skin hung down. Behind them came many women as attendants; then came six Indian laborers, each with a plough on his shoulders. Then followed six others with bags of potatoes. When they were near the chiefs, the ploughs and potatoes were put on the ground, and a dance performed around them. Then a year-old lamb, all of one color, was brought and thrown on the ground, and its bowels torn out and given to the sorcerer, and the blood was poured quickly among the potatoes."[2]

In Oajaca, priests devoted themselves to the maize-god. At harvest-time, a procession ceremonially visited the corn-fields and selected the fairest and best-filled ear. This they bore to the village, placed it on an altar decked with flowers, sang and danced before it, wrapped it in a white cloth, then, with renewed

---

[1] Tschudi's Travels in Peru, 317, seq.   [2] Cieza, 412-13.

procession and solemn rites, the magic ear was buried in the midst of the corn-fields in a a small hole lined with stones. The next year this was dug up, and its decayed remains distributed to the populace as talismans against all kinds of evil.[1]

Among the Chibchas, plants that affected the system were objects of superstitious reverence: the coca was used as an inspiring agent by the priests, and the people chewed and smoked tobacco to produce the power of divination.[2]

The Americans have used plants in their totemic system, although these cases are rare. The Pueblos have a gens called the tobacco-plant, and also one called the red grass race. The Brazilian Indians have the mandioca race, and among the Arawaks individuals are named tobacco, tobacco-leaf, and tobacco-flower. One of the Peruvian Incas was called after the Peruvian name of the tobacco-plant. The Salish, Nisquallis, and Yokimas have traditions in which edible roots have descended from human ancestors,[3] which is explicable, of course, by their system of transmigration. The Potawatomics had five primitive men, one of whom was named smoking-weed, another pumpkin, another melon, another bean, and the other yellow maize.[4] The first four were rejected lovers, but the last was accepted by the primitive female from whom the Potawatomies were descended.[5] The Ojibways had many roots of virtue in disease, over which spirits were supposed to preside, and they were also fetiches, which they carried in time of war.[6]

The inhabitants of the province of Culhuacan have a great veneration for the hidden virtues of poisonous plants, and believe if they crush or destroy one some harm will happen to them. It is a common custom to hang a small bag containing poisonous herbs around the neck of a child, as a talisman against diseases or attacks from wild beasts.[7]

Sanchoniathon, in his historic fragment, thinks the order of

---

[1] 2 Bancroft, 350.   [2] 1 Spencer, Soc., 377-78.
[3] 1 ib., 383-84.   [4] Lanman's Haw-Hoo-Noo, 242.
[5] 1 Schoolcraft, 320.   [6] Copway, 149.
[7] 1 Bancroft, 587-88.

religious development shows that plants first received worship, next the sun, then man. Although the evidence we now have does not confirm his assertion, yet the worship of plants is perhaps synchronous with that of many other natural objects, animate and inanimate. It did not prevail to any extent until some medical knowledge had been acquired. Most of the plants for which the Indians had superstitious feeling were those with medical qualities. Many of their healing plants were held in religious veneration, such as snake-root (a sure remedy for the bite of rattlesnakes), sassafras, colt's-foot, ladyslipper, liverwort, milk-weed, white pond-lily (the origin of which is told in a beautiful myth hereafter), also lobelia, winter-green, butternut, slippery elm, hemlock, sumach, wild cherry, and especially the wild parsnip, a deadly poison. Many of these were kept in their medicine-bags as fetiches; but this superstition has arisen from their medicinal use. Many plants were supposed to possess the power of bewitching them and of performing extraordinary cures and of charming the pretty Indian girls.[1] They had a mixture called the hunter's medicine, which they would place in the track of an animal, and they had faith to believe that the animal would appear to them, influenced by the charm, even though two or three days' journey off. If put in their gun-barrel, the first shot would be sure to hit. The warriors also had an herb mixture which makes their bodies invulnerable. A love-powder brings into complete subjection to their wishes any of the opposite sex.[2]

The Creeks had seven sacred plants, including the yaupon and blue flag, which had intoxicating and narcotic effects. Among the Mexicans the snake plant was sacred, and among the Californians the chucuaco.[3]

The seneka and convolvulus of the Carolinas grow wherever there are rattlesnakes. The Indians say that a great spirit, taking compassion on the bare-legged warriors of the red skin, sowed those salutary plants, which are a remedy for their bite,

---

[1] Copway, 88.   [2] Jones's Ojibways, 153-55.   [3] Brinton's Myths, 292.

WORSHIP OF TREES AND PLANTS. 299

in spite of the remonstrances of the souls of the serpents. By rubbing themselves with the convolvulus they can handle these reptiles with impunity.[1] Athaensic planted the flea-bane in the islands of Lake Erie. If a warrior looked at that herb he was seized with a fever, and if he touched it a subtle fire ran upon his skin. The natives regarded it with superstitious fear. The Osages had an annual religious ceremony in which freshly-cut grass placed in bunches forming a magic circle received the worship of the men of the tribe.[2]

FIG. 17.

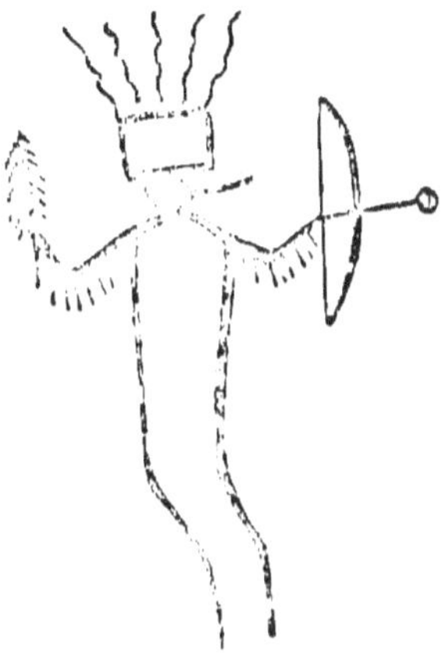

The buffalo grass of the Ojibways had magic properties; it preserved them in battle; they rubbed their bodies with a decoction of it. They carried the plant in their medicine-bags.

The god of the grass, represented in Fig. 17, was said to make them crazy. The figure suggests its anthropomorphic character. The manitou plant was venerated by the inhabitants of the distant provinces of Mexico,[3] and received its name from its supposed supernatural character. Bonpland mentions the same worship by the Indians of Toluca.[4]

It will thus be seen that the vegetable kingdom shared in the worship of all of the American tribes, savage and civilized. Trees and those plants having medical properties obtained most of their worship. The cause of their being held in veneration is found in their belief that they were animated by spirits.

---

[1] 1 Chateaubriand, 180.   [2] 3 Schoolcraft, 491.
[3] 2 Lyon's Mexico, 123.   [4] Plantes Equinox., 123.

CHAPTER VIII.

WORSHIP AT HAUNTED LOCALITIES.

The worship of remarkable natural objects—Worship of mountains and dangerous places—Their supposed frequentation by spirits—Worship of volcanoes—Echoes and other noises supposed to be the voices of spirits—Traditions of descents of tribes from mountains—Metamorphosis—Worship of islands—Traditions of the origin of islands—Origin of the belief that the world was supported on the backs of animals—Worship of springs and fountains—Traditionary tribal descents from them—Their healing properties supernatural—Worship of rivers and lakes—Places of refuge.

THE worship of natural objects, such as mountains, rocky defiles, valleys, streams, or other places in nature that were in any way remarkable, prevailed among all the American tribes: they were thought to be haunted by spirits. Among all the tribes any remarkable features in natural scenery or dangerous places became objects of superstitious dread and veneration because they were supposed to be abodes of gods. In former days, long before the sublime and stupendous Falls of Niagara became a place of fashionable resort, the Red men would draw near to this awful cataract with timid steps, invoking most solemnly the mighty spirit which they imagined must certainly reside there. When journeys by water were undertaken, sacrifices would be offered to the lake or river for a safe voyage.[1] The Sauks and Foxes rarely passed any extraordinary cave, rock, hill, or other object without leaving behind them some tobacco for the use of the spirit which they supposed lived there.[2] The Southern nations on the Mississippi River believed everything in nature had a spirit: one presided over the air. They invoked the rivers, floods, and dreadful cascades.

---

[1] Jones's Ojibways, 96.   [2] Drake's Life of Blackhawk, 39.

If they met with any torrent, they threw to it beaver-skins, tobacco, and other offerings.[1] The Quiches had a multitude of genii, who presided over the objects of nature. The places where they most loved to linger were dark, quiet spots in grottos, or at the foot of some steep precipice, or on the top of a mountain, or at some spring; and here the simple native came to offer his sacrifice.[2] Among the tribes of British America, rivers and mountains were supposed to be inhabited by spirits, says Mr. Harmon, and for this reason these objects were adored. The Chibchas of Bogota worshipped lakes, rivers, rocks, and hills, not because they regarded these objects as gods, but because some spirit was thought to be present at these places. Each man had such a place for his worship and offerings.[3] In the city of Cuzco there were four hundred sacred places, such as springs, fountains, and wells.[4] Throughout Peru, such places as springs, fountains, valleys, and hills were made objects of worship.[5] It was their custom, says Molina, when any natural object excelled its kind, to worship it. Arriaga says they made images of their mountains and worshipped them. He mentions their worship of the Snow Mountains. If a hill was so steep and inaccessible that its top could not be reached, the sacrifice offered to the hill was hurled to the top with a sling.[6] Snails were offered as sacrifices to the mountains.

Impassable or dangerous places had small temples erected to the spirit haunting the place, and in these temples offerings were made. Often the temples were so inaccessible that offerings were projected into them by various means. Fig. 18 is one of these rock temples. In Rivero and Tschudi's folio volume of plates, illustrations of these temples or fanes to the spirits of precipices are found. Mr. Squier is of opinion that these small round structures, perched like toy-houses on some of the rocks in the remarkable passes of the Andes,

---

[1] 3 Picart, 84. [2] 3 Bancroft, 481.
[3] P. Simon, 249. [4] Ondegardo, Narr., 154.
[5] Ib., 155. [6] Molina, Narr., 55.

near Ollantaytambo, were shrines erected to the spirit of the place to protect it from land-slides.[1]

FIG. 18.

Isolated rocks were held in great veneration by the ancient Peruvians, and had offerings made to them or the spirit supposed to dwell in them. Mr. Squier saw hundreds of such rocks on the highways of the sierra, to which the Indians took off their hats, and offerings of some kind were left generally.[2]

The popular religion of the Andean people consisted in the belief that all objects in nature had a soul which presided over them, and to which men might pray for help. This worship of nature was combined with worship of ancestors, the nature-gods being called Huaca, and the ancestral deities Pacamia.[3]

All sounds that issued from caverns were thought to be produced by their spiritual inhabitants. The Sonora Indians say that departed souls dwell among the caves and nooks of their cliffs, and that echoes often heard there are their voices.[4] The caverns or hollow rocks in the mountains which surround Burlington Bay were once noted as being the abodes of the gods. When explosions were heard, caused by the bursting of sulphurous gas from the rocks around the head-waters of Lake Ontario, the superstitious Indians attributed them to the breathing of the manitous.

Mountains have always been favorite places of worship. The Choles of Itza kept a perpetual fire burning on the largest of their mountains. The Mexicans had many great peaks which were hedged about by a divinity.[5] In the Yosemite

---

[1] Squier's Peru, 509–10. [2] Ib., 520.
[3] Markham's Introduction to Narratives, 11, 12.
[4] Alger's Doctrine, 208. [5] 3 Bancroft, 122–23.

country one of the lofty peaks was named after a mythical heroine,—the beautiful Tisayac. Their once famous chief, Totokomila, when hunting, met a spirit maid, the guardian angel of the locality. A passionate love arose in his heart, but when he reached forth his hand for hers she was lifted above his sight. Totokomila wandered here and there seeking that wonderful vision that had made all else worthless in his sight. All was allowed to go to waste by him, and the fair valley was desolate, and even the waters were dried up. But Tisayac visited her valley again. Lighting upon the dome, the granite was riven beneath her feet, and a beautiful lake was formed between the cloven walls, and a river issued to feed the valley forever. Then sang the birds as of old, and the odors of flowers rose like a pleasant incense, and the trees put forth their buds. Tisayac went away, but the people called the dome by her name. Totokomila never returned from a hopeless search for her, but a high rock guarding the entrance to the valley was named after him.[1] The Chinooks have a mountain named Ikanam, after one of their gods who lives there and inspires in their minds superstitious reverence for the place. Among some of the tribes thunder was supposed to be produced by the spirits of the mountains.[2] Almost all the mountains and high places throughout both Americas are supposed to be the dwelling-places of spirits and spirit forms, and their tops are the scene of much fairy revelry. Among the Aricaras, near the mouth of White River, in the midst of an extensive plain, stood a hill called the mountain of spirits, which were little devils in human shape eighteen inches high, armed with bows and arrows, with which they defended their mountain home. A sacred place among the Western tribes was the Red Pipe-Stone Quarry. They always offered prayers before approaching this sacred place, which was guarded by two female spirits. A celebrated rock in Oregon was a place of pilgrimage for all the surrounding tribes.[3]

---

[1] 3 Bancroft, 125–26. [2] Loskiel, 31. [3] Peschel's Races, 249.

"Dead Mountain stands at the head of the Mojave Valley, and is regarded with reverence by the Indians, who believe it to be the abode of their departed spirits. They thought any one who dared visit it would be instantly struck dead.[1] The Indians seat themselves and earnestly observe the Dead Mountain. When its hoary crest is draped in a light floating haze, and misty wreaths are winding like phantoms among its peaks, the wondering watchers see the spirits of departed Mojaves hovering about their legendary abode, and gaze reverently at the shadowy forms that circle around the haunted summit."[2]

The enchanted mountain in Georgia was a place held in superstitious fear by the Indians. They had many traditions about it. It was thought to be the sanctuary of a great spirit that controlled the world from its lofty summit. The tracks of man and beast imbedded in the rocky top of this mountain were regarded with awe.

The following tale is told of a haunted hill in the country of the Assiniboins. Many summers ago, a party of Assiniboins pounced on a small band of Crees in the neighborhood of Wolverine Knoll. Among the victors was the former wife of one of the vanquished, who had been previously captured by her present husband. This woman directed every effort in the fight to take the life of her first husband, but he escaped and concealed himself on this knoll. Wolverine—for this was his name—fell asleep, and was discovered by this virago, who killed him and presented his scalp to her Assiniboin husband. The knoll was afterward called after him. The Indians assert that the ghosts of the murderess and her victim are often to be seen from a considerable distance struggling together on the very summit of the height.[3]

The worship of mountains was prevalent among the natives of Victoria, and pilgrimages were made to them at stated times in the year.[4]

---

[1] Ives's Rep., 75; Newberry's Rep., 32.
[2] Ives's Rep., 80.
[3] Simpson's Overland Journey, 52.
[4] Jackson's Alaska, 305.

"The Black Hills are chiefly composed of sandstone, and are in many places broken into the most fantastic forms. The wandering tribes of the prairies, who often behold clouds gathering around the summits of these hills, and lightning flashing and thunder pealing from them when all the neighboring plains are serene and sunny, consider them the abode of the genii or thunder-spirits, who fabricate storms and tempests. On entering their defiles, therefore, they often hang offerings on the trees or place them on the rocks to propitiate the invisible lords of the mountains."[1]

Says Mr. Brinton, "Strange as a fairy-tale is Bristock's description of the rites of the religion of the holy mountain Olaimi, among the Appalachians. It had two sacred caverns, the innermost two hundred feet square and one hundred in height, wherein were the emblematic vase, ever filled with crystal water that trickled in the rock, and the grand altar of one round stone, on which incense, spices, and aromatic shrubs were the only offerings."

The Guanches worshipped the mountain of Tirmak, and enthusiasts offered themselves as sacrifices to it.[2]

Metamorphosis accounts for some of the superstitions about mountains. Two mountains in Oregon, called the Old Man and the Old Woman, were supposed to be two Indians changed into these mountains by Talapus, one of their gods, in a fit of anger.[3]

One of the loftiest summits of the Rocky Mountains had a personality assigned to it which can only be explained by metamorphosis, for the natives have a tradition that it gave birth to the progenitor of all the bisons.[4]

An illustration of the origin of this curious belief can be found among the natives of Maine, for the following tradition of metamorphosis was found among them. They had a tradition that Mount Kineo had anciently been a cow-moose,

---

[1] Astoria, 285.
[2] Peschel's Races, 250.
[3] Lee and Frost's Ten Years in Oregon, 202.
[4] Eastman's Chicora, 55.

and that a mighty Indian hunter succeeded in killing this queen of the moose tribe with great difficulty, while her calf was killed somewhere among the islands in Penobscot Bay. This mountain still had the form of the moose in a reclining posture, its precipitous side presenting the outline of her head.[1]

Another tradition of metamorphosis is told by Mr. Irving. "In one part of the great salt plains of the Saline River is a large rock of pure salt of dazzling whiteness, which is highly prized by the Indians, and to which is attached the following story. Many years since, long before the whites had extended their march beyond the banks of the Mississippi River, a tribe of Indians resided upon the Platte near its junction with the Saline. Among these was one, the chief warrior of the nation, celebrated throughout all the neighboring country for his fierce disposition. . . . They gloried in him as their leader, but shrank from all fellowship with him. His lodge was deserted, and even in the midst of his own nation he was alone; yet there was one being that clung to him and loved him in defiance of the sternness of his rugged nature. It was the daughter of the chief of the village, a beautiful girl, and graceful as one of the fawns of her own prairie. . . . She became his wife, and he loved her with all the fierce energy of his nature. It was a new feeling to him. It stole like a sunbeam over the dark passions of his heart. . . . Her sway over him was unbounded. He was as a tiger tamed. . . . She died; he buried her; he uttered no wail, he shed no tear. He returned to his lonely lodge and forbade all entrance. No sound of grief was heard from it; all was silent as the tomb. The morning came, and with its earliest dawn he left the lodge. . . . A month elapsed, and he returned, bringing with him a large lump of white salt. In a few words he told his tale. He had travelled many miles over the prairie. The sun had set in the west, and the moon was just rising above the verge of the horizon. The Indian was weary, and threw himself on the grass. He had not slept long when he was awakened

---

[1] Thoreau's Maine Woods, 176.

by the low wailing of a female. He started up, and at a little distance, by the light of the moon, beheld an old and decrepit hag brandishing a tomahawk over the head of a young female who was kneeling imploring mercy. He approached them, but they seemed unconscious of his presence. The young female, finding her prayers unheeded, sprang up, and made a desperate attempt to get possession of the tomahawk. A furious struggle ensued, but the old woman was victorious. Twisting one hand in the long black hair of her victim, she raised the weapon in her other, and prepared to strike. The face of the young female was turned to the light, and the warrior beheld with horror the features of his deceased wife. In an instant he sprang forward, and his tomahawk was buried in the skull of the old squaw. But ere he had time to clasp the form of his wife the ground opened, both sank from his sight, and on the spot appeared a rock of white salt. He had broken a piece from it and brought it to his tribe. This tradition is still current among the different tribes of Indians frequenting that portion of the country. They also imagine that the rock is still under the custody of the old squaw, and that the only way to obtain a portion of it is to attack her. For this reason, before attempting to collect salt, they beat the ground with clubs and tomahawks, and each blow is considered as inflicted upon the person of the hag. The ceremony is continued until they imagine she has been sufficiently belabored to resign her treasure without opposition."[1]

Potosi was an object of veneration to the Peruvians, and a smaller hill near by, called Little Potosi, was thought to be its son. This personification of material natural objects, and the tendency to ascribe to them the power of producing their kind, has grown out of traditionary metamorphosis and descents of human beings from these objects. Such traditions are very common among all of the tribes. The Greenlanders thought they sprang from little hillocks,[2] and hence

---

[1] 1 Irving's Indian Sketches, 117, seq.   [2] Egede, 198.

peopled them with spirits and had many superstitious traditions about them.

The tradition of the Seneca Indians in regard to their origin is that they broke out of the earth from a large mountain at the head of Canandaigua Lake, and that mountain they still venerate as the place of their birth.[1] They had a superstitious reverence for this mountain.

Volcanoes have always been objects of superstitious fear. They were supposed to be produced by subterranean gods who reside in the interior of the earth. The Koniagas think that when the craters of Alaska send forth fire and smoke the gods are cooking their food and heating their sweat-houses.[2] Mount Hood was supposed to be an extinct volcano, and native traditions peopled it with men destitute of the powers of vision.[3] The Indians in the neighborhood of Mount Shasta say that their great spirit hollowed out that mountain, and used it for a wigwam for himself, and the smoke used to be seen curling out of the mountain-top, but his hearth-fire is alight no longer, now that the white man is in the land. Many thousand snows ago, a storm arose, shaking the huge lodge to its base. The spirit commanded his daughter to go up and bid the wind be still. The eager child hastened up to the hole in the roof, but, venturing too far out, the storm caught her by her long hair, and blew her down the side of the mountain. From her sprang the human race. Her wigwam was Little Mount Shasta; but the spirit of the big mountain at last found his daughter, shut the door of her wigwam, the Little Mount Shasta, and they passed away, and have never been seen since.[4]

The Indians of Nicaragua offered human sacrifices to their volcano Masaya, flinging the bodies into the crater; and it has been convenient for their Roman Catholic teachers to turn it into a hell and send their penitents to the top to catch a glimpse of it. Around the edge of the crater were placed

---

[1] Life of Mary Jamison, p. 95, seq.
[3] Lee and Frost, 57.
[2] 3 Bancroft, 120-22.
[4] 3 Bancroft, 91-93.

earthen vessels of food. They did not worship the volcano itself, but a deity residing in it, who occasionally appeared in the form of a hideous old woman.[1] Those inhabitants of Valdivia living near volcanoes offered sacrifices to them, and the Quiches had an annual religious festival to their volcano Quetzaltenango.

Ravines and mountain-recesses share this superstitious fear. There is a curious myth about one of the gorges of the Colorado. It was supposed to have been made by the trail of one of their gods, who afterward rolled a river into the gorge, that no one might follow his track. They do not dare enter this gorge now, on account of this myth.[2] Among the Western tribes, the Rocky Mountains were the limits of their known world, and their vast recesses are the abodes of gods and spirits. It is the paradise of many of the tribes.[3]

A famous place of sacrifice among the New England tribes was a rocky cavern of an unsearchable profundity, into which offerings were thrown.[4]

Islands are places of resort for spirits, and generally have connected with them traditions which inspire fear among the natives.

The Indians would not venture near Manitobah Island. The origin of their superstition in relation to this place was due to the sounds produced by the waves as they beat upon the beach at the foot of the cliffs near its northern extremity. During the night, when a gentle breeze was blowing from the north, the various sounds heard on the island were quite sufficient to strike awe into the minds of the superstitious Indians. These sounds frequently resembled the ringing of distant bells: so close, indeed, was the resemblance that travellers would awake during the night with the impression that they were listening to chimes. When the breeze subsided, and the waves played gently on the beach, a low wailing sound would be

---

[1] 2 Tylor, 207. [2] Powell's Exploration, 7.
[3] 1 Domenech's Deserts, 283. [4] Joslyn's Two Voyages, 133.

heard three hundred yards from the cliffs. The Indians always objected to land or remain on this fairy island.[1]

Father Dablon tells the following legend: "Certain Indians, lost in a fog, landed on the island Missipicooatong, supposed to be a floating island. When departing, they were going to take with them lumps of copper which they had found, when a loud and angry voice, ascribed to Missibizzi, the goblin spirit of the waters, was heard exclaiming, 'What thieves are these that carry off my children's cradles and playthings?' One of the Indians died immediately from fear, and two others soon after. The fourth only survived long enough to reach home. After this the Indians steered far off the site of the haunted island."

The Isle of Yellow Sands derives its chief interest from the traditions and fanciful tales which the Indians relate concerning its mineral treasures and their supernatural guardians. They pretend that its shores are covered with a heavy, shining, yellow sand, which they are persuaded is gold, but that the guardian spirit of the island will not permit any to be carried away. To enforce his commands, he has drawn together upon it myriads of eagles, hawks, and other birds of prey, who, by their cries, warn him of any intrusions upon the domain, and assist with their claws and beaks to expel the enemy. He has also called from the depths of the lake large serpents of the most hideous forms, who lie thickly coiled upon the golden sands and hiss defiance to the steps of the intruder. A great many years ago, they say, some people of their nation, driven by stress of weather upon the enchanted island, put a large quantity of the glittering treasure in their canoes and attempted to carry it off; but a gigantic spirit strode into the water and in a tone of thunder commanded them to bring it back. Terrified, they obeyed, and were suffered to depart, but have never since attempted to land upon the island.[2]

---

[1] 2 Hind's Narr., 70, 71.
[2] Schoolcraft's Nar. Jour., 197; Carver's Travels, 98.

> "Listen, white man, go not there!
> Unseen spirits stalk the air;
> Ravenous birds their influence lend,
> Snakes defy, and kites defend. . . .
> Touch not, then, the guarded lands
> Of the Isle of Yellow Sands."

The little island of Hennepin was looked upon with veneration on account of a legend that it is the abode of a spirit. Sometimes in the morning may be seen above the great falls the ghost of an Indian woman carrying an infant in her arms, whom she presses to her breast; meanwhile she sings and steers a skiff made of bark, which is soon swallowed up in the foaming waters.[1]

The islands of Titicaca and Coati were both sacred, one to the sun, the other to the moon.[2] There is a tradition that formerly a puma appeared at night on the crest of Titicaca that had a jewel in its head so bright it flashed light far and wide over the lake.[3] There is also a gate through which pilgrims have to pass, called Puma-punco, or Puma door.[4] On the northern end of the island, high up where the fret of the waves is scarcely heard and the eye ranges over the broad blue waters and from the glittering crests of the Andes to those of the Cordillera, is the spot most celebrated and sacred in Peru. No bird would light or animal venture upon this rock, nor would a human being dare set his foot thereon. It is plated with gold and silver, and a veil of the richest cloth was thrown over it.[5]

Even animation is ascribed to some islands, and this conception survives in the many myths, the world over, wherein islands and even the earth are supported on the back of some animated being. The following curious tradition illustrates this subject among the American tribes. The island of Mackinac is named from a mammoth turtle, which, according to tradition, while on its travels was killed by ice, and was left a black spot on the waste of frozen waters. When spring returned, earth gathered around the shell of the turtle, and an island was born

---

[1] Domenech's Deserts, 332-33. [2] Squier's Peru, 359.
[3] Ib., 332.   [4] Ib., 334.   [5] Ib., 336.

and nursed in the bosom of the beautiful blue waves. Some Delaware Indians imagined that the earth swam in the sea; others, that an enormous tortoise carried the world on its back.[1] There was an island on the northeast shore of Lake Huron which presented the appearance of a turtle with its head toward the west. The Indians made offerings to it as they passed, and placed them near its head.[2] This, perhaps, induced the Ojibways in their pictography to adopt the turtle as the symbol of land. The West India Islands were thought to be animated. The island of Hayti was a turtle with its head toward the east.[3] There was the same tradition of Porto Rico; and this idea was represented in many of their sculptured stones. The Tlascaltecs believed that the world was borne up by certain divinities, who, when tired, relieved each other. When they were shifting the burden from shoulder to shoulder, earthquakes were liable to occur. The Mayas of Yucatan also thought the world was held up by four brothers. The Southern Californians increased the number to seven.

It is an interesting fact that in the New World as well as the Old, untutored man was moved by the same principle of gratitude to express his thankfulness for water, and, as he knows not to whom he is indebted, he imagines spirits preside over fountains, lakes, and streams of water. The Peruvians worshipped those great fountains and rivers which supplied water for irrigating their crops.[4]

The tribes of Central America, Mexico, and New Mexico had their sacred springs, which played as prominent a part in their mythology as they did in that of Greece and Rome, and many sacrifices were offered to the naiads of the New World. At the sacred spring of Zuñi, vases were kept in which offerings were placed, and death would overtake any one touching these or their contents. Into the water of this sacred spring frogs, tortoises, and snakes alone must enter,—animals sacred

---

[1] Loskiel, 30. [2] Jones's Ojibways, 255.
[3] 1 Rafinesque, 169–70. [4] 1 Garcilasso, 49.

to water.[1] Any desecration of its sacred precincts would be punished by the spirit presiding there.

We find in America the worship of streams of water, but among savage worshippers their ideas had not been generalized sufficiently to arrive at the conception of a deity presiding over water as an element. No Neptune appears even among the most civilized nations. Sacred springs are frequent. In Nebel's plate of a fountain in the living rock at Tusapan we have an image of the spirit of the spring. The statue is seventy-nine feet high, sculptured in the living rock, through which formerly ran the waters of a natural spring.

Near Fort Defiance, in the country of the Navajos, is a spring which the natives approach with much reverence, and at which they perform certain mystical ceremonies. This spring, they say, was once a boiling spring, but at present it boils only when approached by bad men, or when its ceremonies are neglected. They say the water will sometimes leap twenty feet from its bed to catch and overwhelm a bad Indian. The ceremonies consisted in making an offering of vegetable or mineral substances. They knelt by the spring-side, placed their closed hands in the water up to the elbows, and after a brief interval opened the hands and dropped their contents. Then the hands were slowly withdrawn.[2]

In Idaho there is a famous soda spring, of whose origin the Snakes have the following tradition. A Shoshone and Comanche chief quarrelled, and the Shoshone was knocked into the water when he stooped to drink. The murdered man fell forward into the spring, and immediately great bubbles and spirts of gas shot up from the pool, and amid a cloud of vapor appeared the great ancestor of the Comanche and Shoshone nations, Waukanaga, and with curses on his lips dashed out the brains of the Comanche, who fell beside his victim into the spring. Since that the spring has been as it is now.[3]

The Indians of Colorado regard the springs that bubble up

---

[1] 1 Bell's New Tracks, 165.   [2] 4 Schoolcraft, 213.   [3] 3 Bancroft, 94.

from the ground two miles from Colorado City with awe and reverence. They believe that spirits trouble the waters by breathing in them. An abundance of sacrifices were found in the waters and were hung to the adjacent trees,[1] as offerings to the springs. A charmed spot to the natives of this region of country was that which includes the medicinal springs and seething geysers. They brought their sick thither to be cured. The whole region was enchanted ground. Water that bubbled and boiled without visible cause was a mystery to them.[2]

The Arapahoes regard with awe the medicine-waters of their fountains, as being the abode of a spirit who breathes through the transparent water and thus causes the perturbations of its surface. Says Ruxton, "At the time of my visit the basin of a spring was filled with beads and wampum, while the surrounding trees were hung with strips of deer-skin and moccasins."[3]

The spring at Saratoga, now called the Deep Rock, was regarded with superstitious reverence in the early days by the natives inhabiting the neighborhood. It was supposed to have a healing power that was the gift of supernatural agents, and the sick were brought to it in large numbers.

One of the remarkable myths of the New World was that of the fountain of life. From the tropical forests of Central America to the coral-bound Antilles, the natives told the Spaniards marvellous tales of a fountain whose magic waters would heal the sick, rejuvenate the aged, and confer an ever-youthful immortality. It may probably have originated from the adoration of some of the very remarkable springs abundant upon the peninsula, round which were found signs of a dense early population. The later Indians of Florida seem to have preserved certain relics of a superstitious veneration of the aqueous element. That such magnificent springs as occur in Florida

---

[1] Richardson's Beyond the Mississippi, 276.
[2] 3 Amer. Ethnol. Powell's Ex., 200–203.
[3] Ruxton's Adventures, 243; 3 Bancroft, 94.

should have become objects of especial veneration is a most natural consequence of such belief.[1]

"Many of the tribes visit the spring whence they have been supplied with water, during the winter, at the breaking out of the ice, and there offer up their grateful worship to it for having preserved them in health and safety and having supplied their wants. This pious homage is performed with much ceremony and devotion."[2]

The Mayas had sacred springs supposed to be inhabited by divinities who had children through union with human beings. Traditions of tribal descent from springs and fountains appear among some of the tribes. The Caddos thought they sprang from the Hot Springs of Arkansas.[3] The Collas of Peru traced their descent from fountains; the natives of Xauxa, from the spring of Garibalia.

The worship of lakes and rivers was prevalent among all the tribes. Each remarkable feature, such as a great cataract, or a difficult and dangerous pass in a river, possessed a spirit of the spot, whose favor they were fain to propitiate by votive offerings.

Wherever a cataract was found, offerings were also found, which were made to the spirits which presided in these places. Waterfalls were the home of invisible spirits and mermaids. At many localities in all the rivers malevolent spirits were supposed to preside.

At the mouth of the Missouri a powerful manitou was supposed to prevent a safe passage in early days.[4]

There was a tradition that a vast serpent lived in the Mississippi near Fox River, but he finally took a notion to visit the Great Lakes, and the trail he made passing thither is the basin of that stream.[5]

The following tradition was told of the migration of an Ojibway river-deity. Near the Credit village, at the foot of a pointed hill, was a deep spot beneath the water which was said

---

[1] Brinton's Floridian Peninsula, 99, seq.
[2] 1 Warburton's Conq. of Can., 189.
[3] 5 Schoolcraft, 682.
[4] 2 Far West, 145.
[5] Kinzie's Waubun, 80.

to be the abode of a water-god. Here he was frequently heard to sing and beat his drum. When the whites came, he took his departure during a tremendous flood caused by his power, and went down the river into Lake Ontario.[1]

The rapids at the mouth of Old Man's River were, according to tradition, presided over by an evil spirit.[2]

The Crees had the following tradition about the Qu'Appelle. A solitary Indian was coming down the river in his canoe many summers ago, when one day he heard a loud voice calling to him. He stopped and listened, and again heard the same voice as before. He shouted in reply, but there was no answer. He searched everywhere around, but could not find the tracks of any one, so that from that time forth it was named the "Who Calls River."[3]

In passing the mouth of Devil's River, the Sauks, as soon as they came in sight of it, dropped their paddles. When they were opposite the entrance, they strewed the water with tobacco, feathers, and painted hair, then chanted a hymn and resumed their oars.[4]

Hennepin gives the following instance of river-worship: "As we were making the portage of our canoe at St. Anthony of Padua's Falls, we perceived five or six of our Indians who had taken the start. One of them was up in an oak opposite the great fall, weeping bitterly, with a well-dressed beaver robe, whitened inside, and trimmed with porcupine-quills, which he was offering as a sacrifice to the falls, which is in itself admirable and frightful. I heard him, while shedding copious tears, say, as he spoke to the great cataract, Thou who art a spirit, grant that our nation may pass here quietly without accident, may kill buffalo in abundance, conquer our enemies, and bring in slaves, some of whom we will put to death before thee."[5]

---

[1] Jones's Ojibways, 255. [2] Kane's Wanderings, 149.
[3] Morse's Ind. Rep., Appendix, 144.
[4] Hennepin's Louisiane, Tr. in Shea's Discovery, 133, seq.
[5] 1 Hind's Narrative, 370.

Father Marquette tells the following myth: "Before we arrived at the mouth of the Wabash we passed by a place dreaded by the Indians, because they think that there is a demon there who devours all who pass, and of this it was that they had spoken when they wished to deter us from our enterprise. The devil is this: a small bay full of rocks, some twenty feet high, where the whole current of the river is hurled back and checked by a neighboring island; the mass of water is forced through a narrow channel; all this is not done without a furious combat of the waters, tumbling over each other, nor without a great roaring, which strikes terror into Indians, who fear everything."[1] Joutel mentions the offering to this river, by way of sacrifice, of tobacco and beefsteaks, which they fixed on forks and left them on the bank, to be disposed of as the river thought fit.[2]

Many myths embody the animistic conceptions of the natives. The river-spirits had romances told of them. There was a tradition among the Indians on the Penobscot of a family who had a daughter accounted so great a beauty that they could not find for her a suitable consort. At length she was missing, and her parents could learn no tidings of her. After much time and pains spent and tears showered in quest of her, they saw her diverting herself with a beautiful youth, whose hair, like her own, flowed down below his waist, swimming and washing in the water of the Penobscot; but they vanished upon their approach. This youth they imagined to be one of those kind spirits who inhabit the place, and, according to their custom, they called upon him for moose, bear, or whatever creature they desired, and if they did but go to the water-side and signify their desire the animal would come swimming to them.

Many of the water-deities had musical tastes. "While among the Pascagoulas, Governor Périer was invited to go to the mouth of the river of that name, to listen to the mysterious

---

[1] Marquette's Narrative, Tr. in Shea's Discovery, 41.   [2] Joutel, 163.

music which floats on the waters, particularly on a calm moonlight night, and which to this day excites the wonder of visitors. It seems to issue from caverns or grottos in the bed of the river, and sometimes oozes up through the water under the very keel of the boat which contains the inquisitive traveller, whose ear it strikes as the distant concert of a thousand Æolian harps. On the banks of the river, close by the spot where the music is heard, tradition says that there existed a tribe different in color and in other peculiarities from the rest of the Indians. Their ancestors had originally emerged from the sea where they were born, and were of a light complexion. They had a temple in which they adored a mermaid. Every night when the moon was visible they gathered around the beautifully carved figure of the mermaid, and, with instruments of strange shape, worshipped that idol with such soul-stirring music as had never before blessed human ears. One day a priest came among them and tried to convert them from the worship of the mermaid. One night, at the solemn hour of twelve, there came a rushing on the surface of the river, as if the still air had been turned to a whirlwind by myriads of invisible wings sweeping onward. The water seemed to be seized with convulsive fury; it gathered itself up into a towering column of foaming waves, on the top of which stood a mermaid, looking with magnetic eyes that could draw almost everything to her, and singing with a tone which fascinated into madness. The Indians and the priest, their new guest, rushed to the bank of the river to contemplate this supernatural spectacle. When she saw them, the mermaid turned her tones into still more bewitching melody, and kept chanting a sort of mystic song. The Indians listened with growing ecstasy, and one of them plunged into the river, to rise no more. The rest, men, women, and children, followed in quick succession, moved as it were with the same irresistible impulse. When the last of the race disappeared, the river returned to its bed. Ever since that time is heard occasionally the distant music, which the Indians say is caused by their musical brethren, who still keep up their revels at the bottom of the river in the palace of the mermaid."[1]

The favorite places of resort for malevolent spirits were the dangerous passes in rivers, such as cataracts or rapids. Father Brebeuf relates that the Indians, before running a dangerous rapid in their frail canoes, would lay tobacco on a rock where the deity of the rapid was supposed to reside, and ask for safety in their voyage.

"The Brear-beaux Falls were the largest on the Wisconsin, and the Indian name, translated, signifies the Long Falls. These falls were two miles in length, having three perpendicular falls of several feet each in that distance. The Ojibways had a tradition that there was a great spirit that presided over these falls, to which they made an appropriate offering. In 1849 these falls were navigated in a bark canoe for the last time by two Indians,—the Black Nail and the Crow. At the head of the falls, before starting, Crow held the canoe by a rock projecting from the shore, while Black Nail made a prayer and an offering to the spirit of the falls. The offering consisted of two yards of scarlet cloth and a brass kettle. The prayer was in these words: 'O great spirit of the falls! I implore thee to extend thy protecting arm over us as we run these mighty waters. Mayest thou strengthen my arm and my paddle to guide my canoe safely down these dangerous waters.' Having finished his prayer, he threw the offering overboard and grappled his paddle, and the canoe went bounding over the billows and ran the falls in safety."

The Pohono Fall is a place for which the Indians have a superstitious fear. Many persons have been swept over and dashed to pieces there. No native of the vicinity will so much as point at this fall, nor will they sleep near it, for the ghosts of the drowned are tossing in its spray, and their wail is heard forever above the hiss of the rushing waters.

Lakes are also places of resort for ghosts. The Indians

---

[1] 1 Gayarre's Louisiana, 389, seq.

around Devil's Castle, in Siskiyou County, California, have a superstitious fear of its lake, and avoid the vicinity, thinking they are infested with malignant spirits.[1] The Chibchas threw very precious offerings into their lakes, which were intended for the spirits inhabiting them.[2] The principal temples of the Chibchas were the lakes where they made their offerings of precious things. Each village on the lake of Gualavita had a foot-path leading to it, worn by those who went to make their offerings. At the bottom of this lake lived the miraculous Princess Bachue and her daughter. Bachue was drowned in this lake by her husband, an ancient prince.[3]

Many traditions are found connected with the lakes of the Northwest. Manitou Lake is so named on account of the many superstitions connected therewith. Its waters were filled with forms monstrous and terrible, inhabited by evil spirits. There is a tradition that in a great drouth the sun shone so hot upon the surface of its waters that the rays penetrated to the horrible brood within its depths. The waters became troubled, and bubbles arose to the surface. The water boiled from its very depths, and the hot waves dashed wildly against the shores. A vast host of evil spirits emerged, and covered the banks with their foul, trailing carcasses. There is a whirlpool in this lake which carries the water around four times in every twenty-four hours. During the winter season this whirling motion is attended with noise and commotion beneath the ice, which adds greatly to the superstitious reverence of the Indians.

Those Indians dwelling about the great lakes of the Northwest thought that all the prominent points along the coast were created and guarded by monsters.[4]

"The savages living around Lake Superior respect the lake as a divinity, and offer sacrifices to it because of its size, for it is two hundred leagues long and eighty broad, and also in con-

---

[1] 3 Bancroft, 158.
[3] Rivero and Tschudi, 161-62.
[2] Bollaert, 14.
[4] Lanman's Michigan, 85.

sequence of its furnishing them with fish, upon which all the natives live when hunting is scarce in these quarters."[1]

The natives living about Lake Winnipeg account for the muddy condition of its water by a tradition in which one of their deities, after floundering about in mire, went into this lake to wash himself off, and has lived there since.

There are many places on Lakes Winnipeg and Manitobah which the Indians, who hunt and live on the shores of those inland seas, dare not visit. There is scarcely a cave or headland which has not some legend attached to it familiar to all the wanderers on these coasts. On the west side of Lake Winnipeg, in the long, dark, and gloomy chambers formed by fissures in the limestone, bad spirits are supposed to dwell, according to the belief of the Indians who hunt on the coast. The Indians never enter the abodes of these imaginary manitous. Near Limestone Cave Point, on Lake Winnipeg, are several of these supposed fairy dwellings. When an Indian approaches them in his canoe, he either lays an offering on the beach or gives them as wide a berth as possible. Steep-Rock Point, on Lake Manitobah, is also a noted dwelling-place for the little men.[2]

In Genesee County, New York, near the Tonawanda River, at the bottom of a steep hill, is a small lake, affording another instance of pagan superstition. The old Indians affirmed that formerly a demon in the form of a dragon resided in this lake, which frequently disgorged balls of liquid fire. To appease him, many sacrifices of tobacco had been made by the Indians.[3] The Mohawks had a superstition that some great misfortune would happen if any one spoke on Saratoga Lake.[4]

The lakes were thought to be thickly populated with spiritual forms. There is a remarkable lake in the country inhabited by the Spokanes, called "Never-freezing water," which is so completely surrounded by high and precipitous rocks

---

[1] Allouez, Tr. in Sheldon's Hist. Mich., p. 29. [2] 2 Hind's Nar., 133.
[3] Squier's Ab. Mon. N. Y., 48. [4] Lubbock's Origin, 23.

that it is impossible to descend to the water. It is said never to freeze, even in the most severe winters. The Indians believe that it is inhabited by the spirits of buffalo, elk, deer, and all other kinds of game, which, they say, may be seen in the clear, transparent element. There is a superstition respecting a point called Painted Rock in Pend d'Oreille Lake. The Indians, they say, do not venture to pass this point, fearing that a great spirit may, as related in the legends, create a commotion in the water and cause them to be swallowed up in the waves. The painted rocks are very high, and contain effigies of men and beasts, and other characters, made, as the Indians believe, by a race of men who preceded them as inhabitants of the land.[1]

The tribes of Guiana dreaded the water-mamma, or Orehu. This was a being which inhabited the water and sometimes appeared in the shape of a manati. The Orehu was a female spirit, generally malicious, and when in a bad temper was apt to rise close to the canoes and drag them and their crews under water.[2] The natives of Colombia thought that their lakes were the residences of deities, to which they offered yearly sacrifices of gold and jewels. Paths to these lakes were worn by the Indians in their ascent and descent in the performance of their idolatrous rites.[3] In Jalisco the towns about Chapala paid divine honors to the spirit of their lake, who was represented by an idol with a miniature lake before it.[4] The Mosquitos had a spirit of the water, called Lewin, which they feared greatly.[5] The Itzas thought that spirits haunted Lake Peten, into which they threw their dead.

The Peruvians had representations on their vases of water-deities, among which was the God of the Sea, represented in Fig. 19, which shows their anthropomorphic conception of such deities.

Those tribes who were fishermen always threw sacrifices into

---

[1] 12 Pacific R. R. Reps., 150.   [2] 2 Wood's Unciv. Races, 630.
[3] 1 Hamilton's Colombia, 192; Ursua and Aguirre, 3.
[4] 3 Bancroft, 447.   [5] 1 ib., 741.

the waters upon the approach of a storm. The Ojibways cast into the waters, during dangerous winds and storms that had overtaken them, sacrifices, and offered prayers to the spirits of the waters. The natives of Virginia living about Chesapeake Bay always practised such religious ceremonies.[1] Those living about Pamlico Sound also offered to the angry spirits of the waters during storms.[2] There is a tradition among the Pueblo

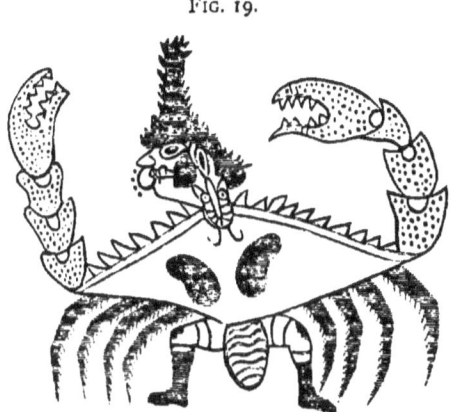

FIG. 19.

Indians that a young man and a maiden were thrown into a surging freshet as a sacrifice to the spirit that was threatening them with destruction.[3] Traditions of a flood appear among all the American tribes. These floods were, however, probably nothing more than local freshets, by which every region has been visited at some time within the memory of its inhabitants or their ancestors.

In the mythical deluge of the Chibchas, in answer to prayer, Bochica appeared seated on a rainbow, and quelled the floods by opening a breach at Tequendama, through which the waters poured down the precipice, leaving the plain more fertile than before.[4]

---

[1] Beverly's Virginia, 180.
[2] 1 Martin's N. C., 21.
[3] 1 Mollhausen's Journey, 95.
[4] Bollaert, 13.

Places supposed to be haunted by spirits gradually assume the character of sacred localities.

This sacred character of some localities has been the origin of places of refuge which were so common among the American tribes. Those escaping from the hand of an avenger fled to these sacred places in which their blood could not be shed. This gradually developed into lodges and cities of refuge. One of these is described by Mr. Bradbury, when among the Arickaras, as follows: "They have a sacred lodge in the centre of their largest village, within which no blood is to be spilled, not even that of an enemy, nor is any one taking refuge there to be forced from it."

These places of refuge were found by Mr. Adair among the tribes inhabiting the Southeastern States.

CHAPTER IX.

SABAISM.

Worship of the heavenly bodies—Their personality—Their anthropomorphic nature—Animistic conceptions of them—Their romantic attachments to human beings—Their vitality—Their occupation by translated heroes—Crude notions concerning them—Eclipses—Astrology.

THE worship of the heavenly bodies prevailed, in its various stages of progress, among all the aboriginal tribes. Natural objects that have made a serious impression upon the uncultivated mind on account of their supposed power of producing good or evil have always been subjects of reverence or fear.

All the various nature-myths that have been preserved for us by tradition have had very much added to them from age to age. The poet has used the folk-lore of prehistoric ages to create his epic, the priest to elaborate his theology, and even the early historian to bequeath to us his historic fragment. In this way metaphorical language has lost its signification, subsequent ages receiving as fact what preceding ages had only thought of as fiction. This excess of fancy has, however, produced too great an impression in the minds of a large school of mythologists, for they will no longer recognize any truth in the mythological stories of the ancients, and even the reality of the siege and destruction of Troy would have faded away in the twilight of a sun-myth had not Mr. Schliemann found its ancient treasures and described the city as it was described so many centuries ago. Nature-worship is wholly inexplicable, however, if we assume that the different objects were worshipped as inanimate, and even the personifications of former mythologists have a flavor of materialism about them that are not truthful to the nature of the primitive mind. The earliest conception of all of these objects of worship was, that they were not inanimate, but animated by a spirit, and thus assumed the character of a living being as real as the human body.

In the mythological lore of the Manacicas of Brazil, their culture-hero, born of a virgin, after spending a life in benefiting his people, soared away to become the sun. Their jugglers, who claimed the power of flying through the sky at pleasure, declared that the sun was a luminous human figure, although it was impossible for those upon the earth to distinguish his form.[1]

Some of the North American Indians believe their medicine-men have gone up through holes in the sky, have found the sun and moon walking about there like human creatures, have walked about with them, and looked down through their peep-holes upon the earth below. The Haidahs think the sun is a shining man walking round the fixed earth, wearing a radiated crown. The nations of Oregon had the same conception of the sun.[2] The Olchones of California worshipped the sun, but considered it the big man who made the earth. They offered to it the first-fruits of the earth. Many of the natives of Guiana thought that the sun and moon were living beings. The Kioways pointed out the Pleiades as having the outline of a man, and said it was the great Kioway, who was their ancestor and the creator.[3] The Guaycurus thought that the sun, moon, and stars were men and women that went into the sea every night and swam out by the way of the east. The Loucheux say the moon once lived among them as a poor ragged boy.

A supposed metamorphosis originates many of their traditionary stories about the heavenly bodies, and leads to their supposed anthropomorphic nature. The Atnas thought the moon was a metamorphosed man.[4] Chia, the female deity of the Chibchas, was transformed into the moon by Bochica, her husband.[5] The Tunjas had a tradition that a cacique of Soga-

---

[1] 3 Southey, 182.   [2] Dunn, 172.   [3] Battey's Quaker, 107.
[4] 2 Bancroft, 62.   [5] Bollaert, 13.

moso was metamorphosed into the sun, and another cacique into the moon. These they worshipped with much ceremony.[1] The Calchaquis were converted into stars, which were bright in proportion to their rank and bravery.[2]

The natives of Teotihuacan in their cosmogony had metamorphosed Nanahuatzin, a god of the early times, into the sun, and Mexitli into the moon. This great honor was conferred upon them evidently because of some self-sacrificing act on the part of these primitive heroes. The myths say that they cast themselves into a great fire built to illumine the darkness before the present order of things.[3]

Such myths are common among the Northern tribes. An Indian with his wife and two children was living in a wigwam on the great lake when the game of the country had nearly all disappeared. Everything seemed to go wrong with the poverty-stricken Indians, and starvation stared them in the face. Whole days did the father spend roaming through the forests, and returned without even a pair of snow-birds for a supper. On one occasion he shot a rabbit, and returned with the speed of the deer to his lodge, but his wife and children were gone, and he knew not where to find them. He turned off in search of them, and a noise resembling the wail of a loon came from the upper air. On raising his eyes, he beheld his family perched on the dry limb of a tall tree. They had been transformed into spirits, and announced that they would return the coming spring, when the time of his transformation would come. True to their word, they came, and all were changed into a family of shooting stars.[4] Another mythical character among the Ojibways went through a double transformation. Having been suddenly metamorphosed one night into a huge fire-fly, when he began to ascend into the air he was immediately transformed into the Northern star. These honors were heaped upon him as compensation for disappointment in love.[5] They called the

---

[1] P. Simon, 259. [2] 3 Southey, 395-96. [3] 5 Bancroft, 204.
[4] Lanman's Haw-Hoo-Noo, 180-91. [5] Ib., 260.

polar star No-adji-manguet, which, translated, means "the man who walks behind the loon-bird."

Translations of heroes and benefactors are very common among all people. Translation means the removal of the person to the heavenly bodies without death. The first mother of the Potawatomies was translated to a star, and was the first to take her station in the horizon after the sun had disappeared behind the distant hills. The Ottawas translated their male ancestor to the sun, and their woman to the moon, and thought that the man in the sun and the woman in the moon kept watch over all actions.[1] Two traditionary characters among the Ojibways were translated to the upper empyrean, and are called Pagak, or the flying skeletons. A noise as of rushing winds announces their flight overhead, and creates great fear among the people.

The Housatonic Indians believed that the Seven Stars were so many Indians translated to heaven, and that the stars in Charles's Wain were so many men hunting Ursa Major, the bear. They begin the chase in the spring, and it lasts all the summer, but by autumn they have wounded it, and the dripping blood turns red the leaves of the trees. The Cherokees thought that the morning star was once a sorcerer, who fled thither to escape those who pursued him to revenge necromantic murder. They also thought that the Seven Stars are inhabited by eight of their countrymen who were translated. The Ojibways saw in the face of the full moon the figure in faint outline of the beautiful maiden "Lone Bird," who was translated thither as a bride of that luminary. She now looked down upon the daughters of her nation, who traced her form in the disk of the moon and told her strange story of love by the light of the lodge-fire.

One of the guiding spirits of the Zuñis found a home in the sky without passing the portals of the grave, for he was taken by the Navajos, when visiting them, and placed upon a bow-string and shot into the clouds.

[1] Tanner's Nar., 320.

There is a tradition among the Algonkin tribes that the evening star was formerly a woman, and that three brothers travelling in a canoe were translated into a group of as many stars. The fox, lynx, hare, robin, and eagle had a place in their astronomy, and they had a tradition that a mouse was seen creeping up the rainbow. The Milky Way in their language was Tchibekana, which means "road of the dead."[1]

The notions the Greenlanders have, says Egede, of the origin of heavenly lights, as sun, moon, and stars, are very nonsensical, in that they pretend they have formerly been so many of their ancestors who on different accounts were lifted up to heaven and became such glorious celestial bodies. The moon, as they will have it, has been a young man called Aningait. His sister was named Malina, and was the sun. The reason why these two were taken up into heaven is this. The moon was in love with his sister, and stole to her in the dark to caress her. She, wishing to find out who her lover was, blackened her hands so that the mark might be left on him. This accounts for the spots on the moon. She, however, determined once to get rid of him, and flew up into the air, but the moon pursued her, and they have been going ever since. Their notion about the stars is that some of them have been men, and others animals and fishes. The three stars in the belt of Orion were three honest Greenlanders, who, being out at sea seal-catching, were bewildered, and, not being able to find the shore, were taken up to heaven. Canis Major is called Nelleraglek, which is the name of a man among them. Ursa Major is a reindeer. Taurus is a kennel of hounds.[2] Says Crantz, the Greenlanders consider the celestial bodies ancient Greenlanders or animals, who have mounted up thither and shine with a pale or fiery lustre according to the food they eat. The shooting stars are human souls on their travels. The moon, when not seen, has gone hunting seals, and gets enough to fatten to full moon. The moon has a demoniac hatred of women, and

---

[1] Baraga's Dictionary, 381.   [2] Egede, 206-10.

the sun of men. The Northern lights are the souls of the dead playing ball.[1]

The personality of the heavenly bodies was the subject of many traditions in which their personal acts are described.

The Aztecs said, when the sun had risen for the first time, at the beginning, it lay on the horizon and moved not, and when a deputation from the deities was sent to request it to move along its way, the answer was that he would never leave that place till he had destroyed them all, whereupon the god Citli immediately strung his bow and advanced against the glittering enemy, but by quickly lowering his head the sun avoided the first arrow, but the second and third pierced his body, and, filled with rage, he seized one of them and launched it back upon his assailant. The brave Citli laid shaft to string nevermore, for the arrow of the sun pierced his forehead.[2]

Among the remnants of the Iroquois living upon the northeastern shore of Lake Michigan there is the tradition that there are four meteors which have the power of shooting through the sky. These meteors were once Indians.

The Dacotahs say the meteors are men or women flying through the air. They have a tradition that an Indian once got on the back of one and took a ride. Coming to a pond full of ducks, which were quacking, the meteor went around and not over it; coming to a village where an Indian was playing the flute, he passed around that village.[3] The meteors were evidently not fond of earthly music, perhaps because their taste was too critical, having been cultivated by the music of the spheres. According to a legend of the Chippewyans, there was once a quarrel among the stars, when one of them was driven away from its home in the heavens and descended to the earth. It wandered from one tribe to another, and had been seen hovering over the camp-fires when they were preparing to sleep. It always attracted attention and inspired wonder and

---

[1] 1 Crantz, 212-13. [2] 3 Bancroft, 61.
[3] Eastman's Legends, xxvi.

admiration. Among all the people in the world, only one could be found who was not afraid of this beautiful star, and this was the daughter of a Chippewyan. She was not afraid of the star, but loved it, and was loved in return, for when she awoke at night she beheld it. In midsummer the girl went into the woods for berries, and lost her way, and a storm arose, and the only answers to her cries were those of the frogs, and the lonely, bitter night came, and she looked for her star, but no star could live in that storm. The Indian girl was caught by the rushing waters, and her body washed away so it could never be found. Many seasons passed away, and the star was seen, but its light was dimmed and never remained long in one place, but appeared to be looking for something it could not find. At last, with the leaves of autumn, it disappeared. A hunter chanced at night in one of the largest swamps of the land, when to his astonishment he saw a small light hanging over the water, but he could not follow in its dangerous path. On his return he told his people. The old men said it was the star that had been driven from heaven, and was now wandering in search of the beautiful girl, and was often seen by hunters as they journey by night.[1] One night the Ojibways saw a star that shone brighter than all others, and they doubted whether it was as far away as it seemed to be, and on examination they found it to be near the tops of some trees. A committee of the wise men was called to inquire into the strange phenomenon. At last a young warrior had the mystery revealed to him in a dream, for a beautiful maiden came and stood at his side, and told him she was charmed with the land of his forefathers, its flowers, its birds, its rivers, its beautiful lakes and mountains clothed in green, and she had come to dwell upon the earth, and asked that the great men should assign her a home. They could not select, and she was told to choose a place herself. She looked for a home in the flowers of the prairie, but feared the hoof of the buffalo. She next sought

---

[1] Lanman's Haw-Hoo-Noo, 240–41.

the mountain rose, but it was so high the children whom she loved most could not see her. At last she chose the white water-lily seen on the surface of the lakes, where she could watch the gliding canoe and see herself reflected in the peaceful waters.[1]

The personification of the heavenly bodies was so complete that romantic attachments to them sprang up in many cases. Many tribes have such traditions. Mrs. Jameson mentions an Indian woman who thought herself the bride of the sun, and lived alone in a lodge with its carved image.[2]

There is a legend of an Ojibway maiden whose name was Sweet Strawberry. "She was acknowledged to be the most beautiful maiden of her nation. Her voice was like the turtle-dove, and the deer was not more graceful in its form. Her eyes were brilliant as the star of the northern sky, and her dark hair clustered around her neck like vines around the trunk of the tree. The young men of every nation had striven to win her heart, but she smiled upon none. The snows of winter were all gone, and the pleasant winds of spring were blowing over the land. The wild ducks came and proceeded to build their nests in pairs. A cluster of early spring flowers peered above the dry leaves of the forest, and even these were separated into pairs and seemed to be wooing each other in love; all things whispered to her of love. She looked into her heart and longed for a companion whom she might love. The brow of the Sweet Strawberry continued to droop, and her friends looked upon her as the victim of a settled melancholy. She stood gazing upon the sky, and, as the moon ascended, her soul was filled with a joy she had never felt before. The longer she looked upon the brilliant object, the more deeply in love did she become with its celestial charms, and she burst forth into a wild joyous song. Her friends gathered around her in crowds, but she heeded them not. They wondered at the wildness of her words and the airy-like appearance of her form. They were

---

[1] Copway's Ojibways, 100-3.   [2] 2 Winter Studies, 149.

soon spell-bound by the scene before them, as they saw her gradually ascend from the earth into the air, where she disappeared as if borne upward by the evening wind. They soon discovered her clasped in the embraces of the moon, and the spots upon its surface are those of her robe, which was made of the skins of the spotted fawn."[1] Among the Ottawas the sun had a daughter on the earth whom a chief violated, whereupon tempests came upon the earth, the sun shot through the heavens with an unsteady motion, and suddenly stopped in its career and became fixed as if in astonishment at the red man's wickedness. It gradually changed to the color of blood, and with a dreadful noise fell upon the earth. It struck the northern shore of Mackinac, formed the cavity of the arched rock, entered the earth, from which it issued in the far east, and at an early hour the following morning resumed its journey. The Indians fear to approach the brow of the arched rock.[2] The Navajos have a tradition that one of their young women in ancient times had connection with the sun and brought forth a boy, who proved quite a hero.[3]

The Southern Californians trace their descent from the moon as their mother. Their god was roaming solitary and alone among his created works, and evidently in a disposition favorable to matrimony, when the moon came to that neighborhood. She was very fair in her delicate beauty, and kind. The god fell in love with her, and began to steal out of his lodge at dusk and spend the night-watches in the company of the white-haired moon. They soon eloped together to a home beyond the ether, where she may yet be seen, with her gauzy robe and silvery hair, treading celestial paths. They left, however, upon the earth a female infant, from whom the Indians claim descent.[4]

The legendary hero of the Chibchas of Bogota, Garanchaca, the first man to build a temple, assumed to be a child of the

---

[1] Lanman's Haw-Hoo-Noo, 192-94.
[2] Ib., 214.
[3] 4 Schoolcraft, 219.
[4] 3 Bancroft, 85.

sun by a damsel of the earth. The sumptuous temple which he prepared to build to his father was not commenced before death overtook him.[1]

There can be little doubt that the sun-worship of the Peruvians originated in such an assumption on the part of Manco Capac, their first Inca. Among the pre-Incarial tribes the primitive conceptions of the sun as animated prevailed among their other mythological traditions, and they may have progressed a step toward personification of this luminary, although there is no evidence that either Con, or Pachacamac, his successor at the head of the pre-Incarial pantheon, were connected in any way with the worship of the sun. On the contrary, Con was represented as a spirit without material covering, and in the process of creating flew rapidly from north to south, causing the mountains and valleys to appear in his wake, which form the main feature in their landscape. Pachacamac appears to have inherited the spiritual nature of his father, for their conception of him has not expressed itself in any image or representation. Yet there can be no doubt they are both culture-heroes. I have elaborated this view in the chapter set apart to that subject. About the year 1022 A.D., Manco Capac appeared, telling the people he was a child of the sun, and, in order to successfully usurp their place, also asserted that Con and Pachacamac had been children of the sun like himself,—that their common father had sent him on earth to teach and govern them. Manco was not wholly successful in his imposture, although all the civil power at the command of himself and his successors was used in his and their behalf, together with an ecclesiastical priesthood and a ritual as gorgeous and imposing as any that has ever existed. The intrusive religion of the sun was not, however, established for many generations after its founder, and then it was not exclusive, but a compromise was effected by which the worship of Pachacamac was tolerated, and in countries subjected by arms sun-worship never

---

[1] Bollaert, 21.

wholly supplanted the polytheistic religions, although their idols were carried captive to Cuzco.

The worship of Pachacamac was the most popular among the Peruvian people generally, whilst the religion of the sun was that of the court.[1] The priests of the sun consummated their persecution by constructing an idol of wood with a human face, horrible in its aspect, representing Pachacamac, and abusing the idol to subserve their purposes, causing it to pronounce feigned oracles, and enriching themselves at the cost of the nation's credulity.[2]

To the sun belonged the magnificent temples in all the cities and almost all the villages of the Peruvian territory,—temples resplendent with gold and jewels,—and to its ritual were consecrated priests, many of whom maintained a perpetual celibacy. There were also dedicated to the sun, virgins, who lived in cloisters secluded from the world. The most celebrated house of this character was located at Cuzco. This contained more than one thousand virgins famous for their beauty and lineage. They were taken in their most tender years from their families to be buried in this seclusion, under the superintendence of ancient matrons who had grown gray within the walls. Not even the Peruvian monarch dared tread within its precincts. But, like all other slaves of an ecclesiastical despotism, they were used by those who supported their institution, and were made to weave garments for the Incarial wardrobe, and even to prepare the chicha and bread for the monarch and his court, and the most beautiful of those in the convents outside of Cuzco were promoted to be the concubines of the reigning monarch, notwithstanding the death-penalty for those who lost their purity. Within the cloister-walls the morality of these institutions was not much better than that of the European monasteries during the papal supremacy.

When the evidence of their fall from the path of virtue was manifest, the child was sworn upon the sun, and was reserved

---

[1] Rivero and Tschudi, 153.   [2] Ib., 154.

for the priesthood,[1] and was a very appropriate resource for recruiting the ranks of that body. This same resort to a god to shelter the virtue of fallen women raised up the line of demi-gods in the ancient pagan religions.

The principle underlying Sabaism is the belief that all the heavenly bodies are inhabited and taken possession of by spiritual beings, which have migrated thither and made them their habitations. Ignorant as they were of astronomical knowledge, they did not see any absurdity in animating a sun, moon, or star with a brilliant hero. In very truth, a primitive people consider the stars as little spangles stuck on the sky as ornaments, and the sky itself as no farther off than the mountain that skirts their horizon. The sun, above all other natural objects, has become a mythical being among the most uncultivated tribes. "The original parent of the Comanches lives, they say, in the sun. The Chichemecs called the sun their father. The name for the sun in the language of the Salive, one of the Orinoco tribes, is, 'the man of the earth above.'"[2]

The Sauks looked upon the sun as the residence of a male deity. The souls of the dead journeyed toward the setting sun. The sun was a male and a beneficent being, whereas the moon was a female deity and delighted in evil.[3] The Dacotahs believed that a female spirit inhabited the sun, a male the moon. They were both considered benevolent.[4] Many of the Nahuas thought the sun was the abode of departed spirits.[5] The Guaycurus believed that their chiefs and jugglers lived among the stars, while the common people stayed about the place of interment.[6] The Abipones thought the Pleiades were their grandfather, and when that constellation disappeared at certain periods they supposed their grandfather was sick. As soon as they returned in the month of May, they welcomed him with joyful shouts and festivities. Among many tribes

---

[1] Rivero and Tschudi, 160.
[2] 1 Spencer, Soc., 404.
[3] 1 Keating, 215–16.
[4] 1 ib., 409.
[5] 2 Bancroft, 616.
[6] 3 Southey, 670.

the worship of the sun and moon was connected with ancestral worship. The caciques of the tribes of Chili were thought to become planets when they died. The starry heavens were peopled with dead Ojibways; the stars were the homes of the good; the brightest were ruling spirits; the constellations were council gatherings. Were all the stories related by them of the skies written, each star would be connected with some strange event.[1]

Many were assigned to a home in the sky as the reward of generous self-sacrifice. A great famine afflicted the Ojibways one severe winter, when the weather was so cold the white bear was afraid to leave his hiding-place. From one end of the country to the other came the cry of hunger and distress. In the midst of their council it was decided a human sacrifice should be offered. The lot fell upon three of the bravest men of the tribe. The spot selected was a neighboring hill, and on its summit at the hour of midnight the cruel duty was performed. On the following day the weather moderated, the hunter went forth, and an abundance of sweet game was brought to every wigwam. They gave way to festivity and dancing, but in the midst of it all eyes were fixed upon the northern sky, which was illuminated by a most brilliant light as changeable as the reflections upon the summer sea at sunset hour. Across this light were dancing three huge figures of a crimson hue. They were the ghosts of the three warriors who had given their lives for their people and had thus become great chiefs in the spirit-land.[2]

Mr. Schoolcraft is a very unwilling yet strong witness for the anthropomorphic conception of the Sabaism of the Northern tribes. He says that when the arcanum of their belief is reached, their monedo, or supreme spirit, is located in sun or moon or indefinite skies, and in their pictorial scrolls they paint the sun as a man's head and appear to confound the symbol with the substance. Iosco, who visited the sun, as their legends say,

---

[1] Copway, 147-48; 2 Keating, 150.   [3] Lanman's Haw-Hoo-Noo, 246-48.

found it to be a man, and walked a day's journey with him around the exterior rim of the globe.[1]

Among the Northern tribes Mr. Kohl found the representations of the sun to be anthropomorphic. One of these was a

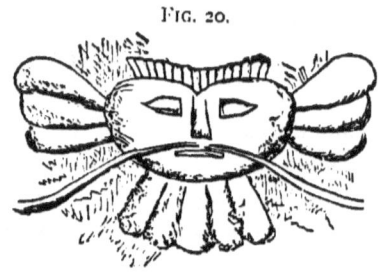

FIG. 20.

picture of the sun set on a man's shoulders. Fig. 20 is a representation found in Nicaragua and copied in Pim and Seeman's Dottings. It shows an anthropomorphic conception of the sun, which is the genesis of Sabaism. General Brown saw the Blackfeet pray hundreds of times to the sun, and yet upon inquiry they explained that they prayed not to the sun, but to the old man who lives there.

Among the more primitive peoples it was the habitation of one soul. Among the Natches and the Appalaches the sun was the bright dwelling-place of departed chiefs, and among the Florida Indians it was the heaven of all good spirits. Starting at first in the primitive mind as the habitable body of a spirit, it becomes the dwelling-place of a few privileged characters, and then the heaven of all good souls. Its capacity has thus been enlarged as the knowledge of its magnitude increases.

Mr. Tylor thinks it a very hard question to answer why some nations are sun-worshippers and others not, but says it is obvious that the sun is not so evidently the god of wild hunters and fishers as of the tillers of the soil. We have found in America sun-worship among all of the tribes. It has not become the predominant cult anywhere, except among the Peru-

---

[1] 5 Schoolcraft, 402–3.

vians and Natches. Among the other tribes it has simply coexisted with the worship of ancestors, kings, heroes, the moon, stars, mountains, springs, rivers, lakes, waterfalls, animals, and all else in nature animate or inanimate, for there was nothing into which a spirit might not penetrate and make it an oracle and a place of sacrifice and devotion. Among the Natches sun-worship had become the central doctrine of national religion. The Natches government was a solar hierarchy, at whose head stood the chief called the sun's brother. This assumed relationship with the sun of the Natches and Peruvian rulers is not as absurd as it would appear, when we consider that all sun-worship is based upon the primitive idea of its being a mere habitation or body for a culture-hero. This idea, carried to its logical conclusion, would necessitate admitting the relationship of the dead hero's family, who would also fall heir to much of his fame.

Such a sun-cult as that of Peru and the Natches would be impossible among fishers, for many reasons. Fishers will always find their deities in the sea, the river, the waterfall, the whirlpool, the eddy, the storm, and the wind, or the most dangerous or the most useful animals inhabiting water. The hunters will find theirs in inaccessible places on the mountains, or in the springs where they stop to slake their thirst, or in the tree that creaks in the rustling wind, in the thunder and the storm, and all animated nature which is filled with the spirits of their dead. The sun is no more to them than the ignis-fatuus that hovers around the wanderer's path at night, nor half as fear-inspiring. The moon is more of a favorite among hunters than the sun. Another condition necessary to such a sun-cult is a despotic power, and coincident with this there must be a sufficient amount of astronomical knowledge to assign to the sun its proper and important place in nature's economy. Sun-worship was ancient in Peru, but it was the Incas who made it the great state religion, and their heliolatry was organized for political ends.

When the sun has been recognized as the greatest of the

heavenly bodies, and the great producer of the earth's vegetation, and its size and distance from the earth are recognized, it becomes an object of reverence, and is then associated with a hero of pre-eminent and shining qualities.

The Mexicans worshipped the sun, and had a festival in which a human being was sacrificed to the sun, who ascended the stone steps slowly from the east, representing the course of the sun, placed his foot on the middle of the stone of the sun, was killed, and sent with a message of homage to that luminary, and his body was thrown down the steps to the west.[1]

In the Mexican worship of the sun it was sometimes represented by a human face surrounded with rays, at other times by a full-length human figure. Although the worship of the sun occupied a prominent place in the Mexican religion, yet it by no means occupied the first place, as assigned to it by many Americanistes. It was definitely worshipped under the name of Tonatiuh, and also under that of Naolin, names not very prominent in their pantheon. All of the Mexicans seemed to be very much distressed at eclipses of the sun and moon, and always made a great ado while they lasted, and generally offered up human sacrifices. Although the sun-cult is prominent among all the more civilized tribes, and even among the Natches, who had made little progress in civilization, yet the greatest devotion to the sun was found in Peru, where it became pre-eminently the ruling deity in the days of the Incas. In its exaltation we see a step taken toward monotheism. On the great altar of their greatest temple stood a representation of it in thick gold, richly set with jewels. The visage was round, environed with rays and flames. It was so large it nearly reached across the temple. It was so placed that the sun, on rising, cast its beams upon it, which were reflected with a grand refulgence. At the sides of this image were the bodies of the deceased Incas, ranged according to their antiquity, and

---

[1] Duran, 197–98.

so perfectly preserved they appeared to be alive. The visages of the Incas were as if looking on the floor of the temple, with the exception of Huayna Capac, the most adored of all the children of the sun, who, for his eminent virtues, was seated directly opposite the glorious orb.[1]

A reproduction of this in Mr. Brown's "Races of Mankind" shows the anthropomorphic character of the images, and indicates the origin of their sun-worship. In one of the pyramidal-shaped structures surrounding the temple of the sun was found the figure of the moon, with female visage, around which were ranged the deceased Incas' wives. Another was dedicated to the stars, another to thunder and lightning, and still another to the rainbow.[2] The Chibchas worshipped the sun with bloody rites. Human beings were sacrificed, and infants were slain, that their blood might anoint those rocks first touched by the rising sun.[3] The Lacandones worshipped the sun without the intervention of an image, and also the Pipiles. Among the Isthmians the heavenly bodies seem to have been very generally adored. The sun and moon were considered as man and wife. The thunder and lightning were thought to be instruments used by the sun to inflict punishment on enemies. Dabaiba, the goddess who received much of their worship, was a sun-goddess, and undoubtedly a native princess formerly.[4]

Mr. Tylor appears to be convinced of the animistic origin of nature-myths. In early philosophy throughout the world the sun and moon are alive, and as it were human in their nature, usually contrasted as male and female: they nevertheless differ in the sex assigned to them, as well as in their relations to one another.

Among the Mbocobis of South America, the moon is a man and the sun is his wife.

Moon-worship, naturally ranking below sun-worship in importance, ranges through nearly the same degree of culture.

---

[1] Ranking, 151–52.
[3] P. Simon, 248–49.
[2] Ib., 152–53.
[4] 3 Bancroft, 498.

There are remarkable cases in which the moon is recognized as a great deity by tribes who take less account, or none at all, of the sun. The rude savages of Brazil seem especially to worship or respect the moon, by which they regulate their festivals and draw their omens. The men would hold up their hands and women their babes to the moon. The Botecudos are said to give the highest rank among the heavenly bodies to the moon, which they say causes thunder and lightning and the failure of vegetables and fruits. The Caribs esteemed the moon more than the sun. The Ahts of Vancouver's Island regard the sun as the male and the moon as the wife, and their prayers are addressed to the moon as the superior deity and the highest object of their worship. Among the Hurons the moon is the maker of earth and man, and grandmother of the sun.[1]

The Iliscees ascribed an anthropomorphic nature to the heavenly bodies. They supposed the moon to be the wife of the sun, and the stars their offspring.[2]

The crude notions of savages concerning the heavenly bodies find expression in many fictions. Among the Zuñis their two oldest ancestors carry the sun and moon. At the time of their first construction, sun and moon were both alike, but the man who carries the moon has got so far away from the surface of the earth that we no longer feel the heat from that orb.[3] According to the unscientific creation of the Pueblo Indians, the sun, moon, and stars were not made as soon as their ancestors, but chaotic darkness prevailed, relieved occasionally by the glare of volcanic fire which burst from the mountain that had given them birth. Not satisfied with the condition of affairs as they found them, this ambitious adolescent people proceeded at once in the construction of sun, moon, and stars, and when made they were confided to the care of Indians, who are carrying them about on their backs.[4] It was not an unusual thing for the Northern Indians to dream of conversing

---

[1] 2 Tylor, 299.   [2] Ker's Travels, 105.
[3] Cozzens's Marvellous Country, 350-51.   [4] Ib., 346-51.

with the sun.[1] The Iroquois have a tradition in which Inigorio, their first man, is the creator of the heavenly bodies, and the material composing those bodies was taken from their great mother, the sun being created out of her head.[2] Among the California myths is one claiming that the coyote was once a partner of a star in the dance.[3] Among the Mbocobis the story is told that the sun once fell down in her course and an Indian put it up again, when it fell again and set the forest in a blaze of fire.[4] They have not had any trouble with it lately. This tradition is somewhat similar to the Phaeton myth of classical antiquity. Among the Mosquito Indians, Roman Catholic ingenuity introduced among their sun-myths that of the sun's standing still for a day. The Mosquito tradition starts him on his travels again in a very novel manner, showing their anthropomorphic idea about the great luminary. A mosquito scolded him roundly for his behavior, but, finding it of no avail, went up and stung him in the leg, which started him quickly on his course.[5] According to the Indians of Tlascala, the sun was a god so leprous and sick he could not move, whereupon the other gods, taking advantage of his helplessness, made an oven and lighted a fire and were engaged in cremating him. These absurd notions of heavenly bodies prevailed throughout America. Among the Northern tribes there is a tradition that the sun was caught in a trap set by a boy.

Thus it will be seen that Sabaism occupies a prominent place in the nature-worship of the Americans, and it can be found in all its stages of development from the purely anthropomorphic character that it assumes among the primitive peoples. It must always be borne in mind that the savage has no knowledge of the magnitude or distance of the heavenly bodies. Hence most of their myths are very absurd. To give the reader a proper conception of the astounding ignorance of savage and even partially civilized peoples about the heavenly bodies, a few

---

[1] Kohl's Kitchi-Gami, 206.   [2] Schoolcraft's Iroquois, 36.   [3] Ib., 400.
[4] 1 Tylor, 288.   [5] 5 Bancroft, 210.

illustrations will be given of their theory of eclipses and other celestial phenomena. Mr. Jones says, "The Ojibways, at an eclipse of the sun, think it is dying, and shoot coals of fire at it to rekindle it. They forbid their children pointing their fingers at the moon, considering it an insult."[1] The Chiquitos of Brazil called the moon mother, and during an eclipse they shot arrows into the air to drive away the dogs that attacked her.[2] They thought the moon was hunted across the sky by huge dogs, who caught and tore her till her light was reddened and quenched by the blood flowing from her wounds. The Indians rushed to her rescue, and by shooting arrows frightened away the antagonists, as they supposed.

Eclipses throughout the lower stages of civilization were omens of disaster and portents of dismay. The Indians of Tlascala thought the sun and moon were fighting when they were eclipsed, and were frightened, and offered human sacrifices to them. The reddest people they could get were sacrificed to the sun; albinos to the moon.[3]

"There was an opinion among the Seneca nation that eclipses of the sun and moon were caused by a manitou or bad spirit, who mischievously intercepted the light intended to be shed upon the earth and its inhabitants. Upon such occasions the greatest solicitude existed. All the individuals of the tribe felt a strong desire to drive away the demon, and to remove thereby the impediment to the transmission of luminous rays. For this purpose they went forth, and, by crying, shouting, drumming, and the firing of guns, endeavored to frighten him. They never failed in their object, for by courage and perseverance they infallibly drove him off. Something of the same kind is practised among the Ojibways even in our day when an eclipse happens. The belief among them is that there is a battle between the sun and moon, which intercepts the light. Their great object is, therefore, to stop the fighting and separate the combatants. They think these ends can be accomplished by withdrawing the

---

[1] Jones's Ojibways, 84, 85. [2] 1 Southey, 335. [3] Sahagun, bk. 7, ch. 1.

attention of the contending parties from each other and diverting it to the Ojibways themselves. They accordingly fill the air with noise and outcry."[1]

"The great eclipse of the sun on the 16th of June, 1806, occurred within a few days after the death of Little Beard, an Iroquois chief. This eclipse excited in the Indians a great degree of astonishment, for, as they were ignorant of astronomy, they were totally unqualified to account for the phenomenon. The crisis was alarming, and something must be done without delay. They accordingly ran together in the three towns near the Genesee River, and after a short consultation agreed that Little Beard, on account of some old grudge which he yet cherished toward them, had placed himself between them and the sun in order that their corn might not grow, and so reduce them to a state of starvation. Having thus found the cause, the next thing was to remove it, which could only be done by the use of powder and ball. Upon this every gun and rifle was loaded, and a firing commenced that continued without cessation till the old fellow left his seat and the obscurity was entirely removed."[2]

The Western Indians believe that when the moon is full, evil spirits begin nibbling at it to put out its light, and eat a portion each night until it is all gone. Then a great spirit, who will not permit the evil spirits to take advantage of the darkness and go about the earth doing mischief, makes a new moon, working on it every night until it is completed, when he leaves it and goes to sleep. No sooner is he gone than the bad spirits return and eat it up again.[3]

The Nootkans had no other way of accounting for eclipses except to ascribe them to the attacks of animals. The following is an illustration of this.

Says Mr. Jewitt, "On the 15th of January, 1805, about midnight, I was thrown into considerable alarm in consequence of

---

[1] Mitchell, in 2 Arch. Amer., 351 seq. [2] Life of Mary Jamison, 99.
[3] Beldén, 290.

an eclipse of the moon, being awakened from my sleep by a great outcry of the inhabitants. On going to discover the cause of this tumult, I found them all out of their houses, bearing lighted torches, singing and beating upon pieces of planks; and when I asked them the reason of this proceeding, they pointed to the moon, and said that a great codfish was endeavoring to swallow her, and that they were driving him away. The origin of this superstition I could not discover."[1] The Peruvians had very much the same idea, but shouted to frighten away the authors of the eclipse; some of them thought she was sick, and were afraid of her falling in total darkness. The sun in an eclipse was angry, and refused to show his face.[2] The natives of Cumana thought the sun and moon were man and wife, and they occasionally fell out, when an eclipse occurred.[3] The Opatas attempt to frighten by their yells the heavenly bodies during eclipses, that they may be prevented.

All the celestial phenomena are assigned to causes equally absurd. Many of the Indians of the British possessions believed that the Northern lights were the spirits of their departed friends dancing in the clouds, and when these were remarkably bright they said that their friends were making merry.[4] The Hurons were perfectly ignorant of the causes of celestial appearances, meteors, eclipses, and storms. They thought that thunder was the voice of men flying in the air, and eclipses were produced by the enemies of the sun and moon. The Patagonians said that the stars were their translated countrymen, and the Milky Way was the country where the dead Patagonians hunted ostriches.[5] The Ottawas thought the Milky Way was produced by a turtle swimming along the bottom of the sky and disturbing the mud.[6] The red clouds which adorned the rising and the setting sun were thought to be colored by the blood of men slain in battle.[7]

---

[1] Jewitt's Narrative, 134.
[2] 1 Tylor, 328–29.
[3] 3 Herrera, 309.
[4] West's Journal, 102.
[5] Alger's Doctrine, 79.
[6] Tanner's Nar., 320.
[7] Del Techo, in 2 Church. Coll. Voy., 701–2.

The seasons appear to have been considered as the productions of spirits. The Algonkins spoke of these spirits as the summer-makers and the winter-makers, and they tried to keep the latter at bay by throwing firebrands into the air.[1]

With such crude conceptions of the heavenly bodies the genesis of their anthropomorphic myths is not strange. Mr. Spencer thinks the identification of the heavenly bodies with persons who once lived has been caused by misinterpretation of names,—that the moon was used in primitive times as a complimentary name for a woman, and erroneous identification of object originated lunar myths. The use of such names has undoubtedly been a factor in the production of Sabaistic myths. A few such names were given heroes. "Chief of the Sky" was the name of one of the Ojibway chiefs. A chief bearing such a name with him into the spirit-land in primitive times would undoubtedly have the sun assigned him for a home, and the apparent worship of the sun in these early times was not a worship of that luminary as such, but merely worship of its inhabitant,—a famous spirit. Mr. Copway, himself an Indian and very familiar with the conceptions of his people on this subject, declares in very emphatic language, "Very few of the Northern Indians ever held the idea that the sun was an object of worship." The sun was the wigwam of a great spirit, and it was as the abode of this being that the Indians viewed that luminary.

Such cases of assigning names of sun, moon, or stars to human beings are rare, and are not sufficiently numerous to account for the universal worship of the heavenly bodies which we have found throughout America. Sabaism has not grown into such universal practice through an occasional accidental misinterpretation of names, but through animistic conceptions of the heavenly bodies.

If an ancestor, supposed to have migrated to the heavens, becomes identified with certain stars, we get a clue to the

---

[1] Parkman's Jes., lxxv.

fancies of astrology. A progenitor so translated will be conceived as still caring for his descendants, while the ancestors of others will be conceived as unfriendly. Hence may result the alleged good or ill fortune of being looked down upon at birth by this or that star. Supposed accessibility of the heavens makes similarly easy their identification with a man or woman. Every male Mexican burned marks upon his wrist in honor of certain stars, and no man would die without them. They worshipped Venus and drew many of their auguries from it. When it first rises they bar out its light from doors and windows, for its twinkle then is a bad augury.[1] Chasca, however, the Peruvian Venus, was always propitious, and was a youth with long and curling locks.

Astrology had not arisen as an occult science among any of the American nations. Traces of its embryonic condition among the Mexicans and Peruvians are found, however.

Thus it has been seen that Sabaism in all its forms prevailed throughout the New World. It was anthropomorphic in its character, and originated from the animistic superstition. Men and animals inhabited the celestial regions. It was as yet an unmapped country, as no tribe had constructed a chart of the heavens, but all the fancies of the Old World in reference thereto prevailed.

---

[1] 3 Bancroft, 113.

CHAPTER X.

ANIMISTIC THEORY OF METEOROLOGY.

Tempests produced by hostile spirits—Coercive measures used to prevent them—Winds the manifestations of spiritual agency—Anthropomorphic representations of aërial deities.

THE elements were objects of worship, not as being in themselves proper objects of adoration, but because they were manifestations of spiritual life. Many tribes ascribed tempests, rain, and hail to the agency of human spirits.[1] The land which the savage inhabits is always surrounded by an unknown country, which, as it becomes known, is found to be inhabited by tribes hostile to him, and who have a spiritual world whose borders become the borders of his spiritual world. The contests of the living are carried into the realms of the dead, and every wind that blows is laden with hordes of hostile spirits, and the elements wage war directed by shadowy warriors. The belief is very common that the convulsions of nature are but the fierce struggles of the hosts of the dead. Hence their future life was not void of incident, for their spirits followed the thunder-birds when the heavens were black and the lightning flashed, and they waged war in the elements against the hostile spirits of other tribes. The wind tore up the trees as they passed along, and those cloud-spirits who gained the victory hung out the bow of bright colors.[2] This is the poetic view taken of their spiritual life, in the midst of and controlling the elements. Every locality has been visited at some time within the memory of its inhabitants or their ancestors with destructive winds and storms. They were generally supposed to be pro-

---

[1] Jos. D'Acosta, bk. 5, ch. 4.   [2] Eastman's Legends, 228-29.

duced by demons or angry spirits. The storms and tempests were generally thought to be produced by aërial spirits from hostile lands.

The Guaycurus of South America, when a storm arose and there was much thunder or wind, all went out in troops, as it were to battle, shaking their clubs in the air, shooting flights of arrows in that direction whence the storm came.[1] The Araucanians thought storms, tempests, thunder, and lightning were the battles waged by the spirits of their dead with their enemies in the air.[2] The Indians of North America rushed with firebrands and clenched fists against the wind that threatened to blow down their huts.[3]

La Potterie says, "Certain savages to the north are of opinion that storms are raised by the spirit of the moon, when it lodges in the bottom of the sea. To pacify it, therefore, they sacrifice the most valuable things they have." Thunder, as we have seen, was produced by fabulous birds, according to the myths of many tribes. The Hurons thought that thunder was produced by a bird whose palace was in the sky. It left its home when the clouds began to gather. The lightning flashed whenever it opened or closed its wings.[4] The spirits of the dead were thought to transmigrate into the thunder-birds.

Mr. Brinton has elaborated quite a system of mythology in relation to the sacredness of the number four, associating it with the four cardinal points and the winds that blow from them. He traces many myths of origin from four brothers, and considers them personifications. He says, "Sometimes the myth defines clearly these fabled characters as the spirits of the winds. The simplest form is that of the Algonkins and Dacotahs. They both had four ancestors, concerned in various ways with the first things of time, not rightly distinguished as men or gods, but positively identified with the four winds. The Creeks told of four men who came from the

---

[1] Del Techo, in 4 Church. Coll. Voy., 732. [2] 2 Molina, 92.
[3] Farrar's Primitive Manners, 2. [4] Brebeuf, 2 Jes. Rel., 114.

four corners of the earth, and after rendering them service disappeared in a cloud. The ancient inhabitants of Hayti had a similar genealogical story, which Peter Martyr relates with various excuses for its silliness. Perhaps the fault lay less in its lack of meaning than in his want of insight. It was to the effect that men lived in caves, and were destitute of means to prolong their race, until they caught and subjected to their use four women swift of foot and as slippery as eels. The Navajos have an allegory that when they emerged from the earth the four spirits of the cardinal points were already there. In the mythology of Yucatan the world was supported by four mysterious personages at its four corners. Four mythical civilizers of the Peruvians are said to have emerged from a cave."[1]

In many of the myths found throughout America, one, two, or three winds figure in their cosmogony, and are perhaps enrolled in their pantheon of spirits. I think the effort to trace four winds through the mythological stories of the Americans would be futile, and whether there be one, two, three, or four is a matter of indifference. The number of these winds depends upon the locality of the tribe and the prevailing winds of that locality. The spirits of the dead were supposed to come riding upon the winds, and if angry could successfully assert their power in the tempest. The most delightful future the Indian could picture for himself after death was

> "To be imprisoned in the viewless winds
> And blown with restless violence round about
> The pendent world."

An Ojibway folk-tale of a great concourse of spirits that presided over nature and natural objects will illustrate our subject. "There were spirits from all parts of the country." Some came with crashing steps and roaring voice, who directed the whirlwinds which were in the habit of raging about the neighboring country. Then glided in gently a sweet little spirit which blew the summer gale. Then came in the old sand-

---

[1] Brinton's Myths, 77-85.

spirit, who blew the sand-squalls in the sand-buttes toward the west. He was a great speech-maker, and shook the lodge with his deep-throated voice as he addressed the spirits of the cataracts and waterfalls, and those of the islands, who wore beautiful green blankets.

The anthropomorphic character of the spirits that preside over the elements is aptly illustrated in Fig. 21, the god of

FIG. 21.

the air, as represented on a vase from South America, copied by Bollaert. The figure is painted red on a yellow ground.

A mythical Æolus was a prominent character in the folk-lore of many tribes. There was an Iroquois tradition connected with a rock in Corlear's Lake on which the waves dash and fly up to a great height. When the wind blew hard, the Indians believed that an old Indian living under this rock, who had the power over the winds, was angry, and therefore as they passed it, in their voyages over, they always threw a pipe or some other small present to this old Indian, and prayed for a favorable wind.[1]

The doctrine of spiritual agency is the explanation of the meteorological phenomena known and feared by uncultured man.

---

[1] Colden's Hist. Five Nations, ed. 1750, 32.

CHAPTER XI.

PRIESTCRAFT.

Priests—Sources of their influence—Medicine-men or doctors of rude tribes—Exorcism of evil spirits the method of curing diseases—Sorcerers—Miraculous powers ascribed to them—Rain-doctors—Witches—Rise of priestly hierarchies among the more civilized peoples—Priesthoods of Peru, Mexico, Yucatan, etc.—Monastic institutions of those countries—Educational institutions in the hands of the priests—Their influence in the State—Confessional—Priestly absolution saved criminals from legal penalties.

THE supposed power of priests over spirits has been the source of their influence in all religions, savage and civilized. The Tahkali priest lays his hand on the head of the nearest relative of the deceased and blows into him the soul of the departed, which is supposed to come to life in his next child. The survival of this superstition is found in the apostolic succession. Says the modern priest at ordination, "Receive the Holy Ghost for the office and work of a priest in the church of God now committed unto thee by the imposition of our hands."

In addition to the power of transmission of spiritual essence, primitive exorcism also survived to recent times. The power of the modern priest as an exorcist has about departed, although the Roman Catholic Church has always had a specially ordained body of exorcists, and retains the belief in the efficacy of exorcism. Even the Church of England adopted the superstition, exorcising infants before baptism in these words: "I command thee, unclean spirit, in the name of the Father, of the Son, and of the Holy Ghost, that thou come out and depart from these infants."[1]

---

[1] 1 Spencer's Sociology, 256, 260.

The priestly office is not found among primitive peoples. The predecessors of the priests in spiritual influence were the doctors, who practised their art by sorcery and knew little or nothing of medication. Sickness is a sign to the savage that his gods are against him, and therefore in all early stages of culture the office of priest and physician was one.[1] Among the Northern tribes there were in every tribe "medicine-men" who united in themselves the offices of priest, physician, and fortune-teller or prophet. They were supposed to possess unusual powers because of their constant communion with, and influence over, spirits. Various and extravagant were their incantations; their charms mysterious. They had a special dress for their profession. They thought that all distempers were caused by evil spirits; consequently none of their physicians attempted to effect a cure until they had conversed with their familiar spirits and ascertained whether their aid could be secured in the effort to exorcise the adverse demons. Violent gestures and noises were added to their other efforts for the purpose of frightening the spirits. Some used gourds with peas in them for a rattle; others a drum. They would scarify the patient, and then suck until they had gotten out, in the words of Lawson, "a great quantity of very ill-colored matter, and performing grimaces and antic postures which are not to be matched in Bedlam."[2]

Even in cases of fracture the same superstition prevailed. The following description of a surgical performance among the Pawnees is from Mr. Murray: "I learned that in the hunt already described a good many Indians had been bruised or wounded. Among those who were hurt was a chief of some distinction; he had a few ribs and one of his arms broken. The setting of this last, together with the completion of his wound-dressing, was to be accompanied with much ceremony: so I determined to be a spectator. I went accordingly to his lodge, where a great crowd was already assembled. A pro-

---

[1] Brinton's Religious Sentiment, 240.   [2] Jones's Antiquities, 28-33.

found silence was observed, and when all the medicine-men and relatives had arrived and taken their seats, a great medicine-pipe was brought and passed round with the usual ceremonial observances of a certain number of whiffs to the earth, the buffalo spirit, and other spirits. The pipe was not handed to the wounded man, probably because he was supposed to be for a time under the influence of a bad spirit and therefore not entitled to the privileges of the medicine. When this smoking ceremony was concluded, three or four of the doctors or conjurers and a few of the great medicine-men assembled round him; the former proceeded to feel his side and apply some remedy to it, while one of them set the arm and bound it very strongly round with leather and thongs. During this operation the medicine-men stooped over him and went through sundry mummeries which I could not accurately distinguish. As soon as the bandages and dressings were completed they began a medicine-dance around him. At first the movement was slow and accompanied by the low ordinary chant, but gradually both acquired violence and rapidity, till at length they reached the height of fury and frenzy. They swung their tomahawks round the head of the wounded man, rushed upon him with the most dreadful yells, shook the weapons violently in his face, jumped repeatedly over him, pretending each time to give him the fatal blow, then checking it as it descended, and, while once or twice I saw them push and kick his limbs, one of the most excited struck him several very severe blows on the breast. On inquiry, I learned that all these gesticulations were intended to threaten and banish the evil spirit which was supposed to have posesssed him."[1]

Among the New England Indians, says Roger Williams, "the priest was doctor, and came and conjured away their sickness with many strange actions."[2] "The greatest part of these conjurers do merely abuse the people, who commonly die under their hands, for, alas! they administer nothing but howl

---

[1] Murray's Travels N. A., 330, seq. [2] Williams's Key, 112.

and roar."[1] The method of cure of diseases was about the same among the medicine-men of the Northwest coast. They were supposed to possess the power of exorcising and driving away the ghosts or spirits of the dead and the evil spirits that were supposed to prey on the vitals of a sick person.[2] Among the tribes of the Northwest the medicine-men in their practice generally begin by singing, accompanying it with rattles or something that will make a great noise, and follow with mesmeric passes over the body of the patient. They get more excited as time passes, if quieter methods do not succeed. One of the most violent of their doctors around Shoalwater Bay was always called when the others failed. Mr. Swan gives an interesting account of his operations. " Old John came bringing with him his family of some half-dozen persons, who aided him in the cure by attacking the roof with long poles. Old John sat at the patient's feet with his head covered up with a blanket for some time. All at once he threw off his blanket and commenced to sing and throw himself about in the most excited manner, rattling large scallop-shells, the chorus in the mean time keeping up their pounding on the roof and also on a couple of tin pans and a brass kettle. He soon mesmerized his patient till she was asleep, when he pounced upon her breast with his whole weight and scooped his hands together as if he had caught something, which he tried to blow through his hands into the coals; but the skookum escaped by slipping out of his hands. He said he was sure he could get it in a day or two."[3]

The Loucheux and other Indians of British America had the same superstitious and implicit faith in the incantations of their medicine-men. Their influence exceeded even that of the chiefs. The conjurer ruled supreme when sickness prevailed. He pretended to dream of the death of certain persons, and when it became known to these persons they came to him with their offerings and begged his intervention to prevent their

---

[1] Williams's Key, 159.   [2] Swan's Wash. Ter., 176.   [3] Ib., 183-84.

doom. Many persons have fallen sick and actually died from the effects of such stories. An impious Ojibway who kicked a medicine-man received a severe punishment for his irreverence, for his leg was looped up to his thigh, according to tradition, and he had to hop all the rest of his life.[1] In this way the character and power of these cunning rogues reached a height where they were ever after looked upon with fear and respect.

"The medicine-men held the same relation to the Dacotahs as the Druids to the ancient Britons. They were the most powerful and influential of the tribe. They were looked upon as a species of demi-gods. They asserted their origin to be miraculous. At first they were spiritual existences, encased in a seed of some description of a winged nature, like the thistle. Wafted by the breeze to the dwelling-place of the gods, they were received to intimate communion. After being instructed in relation to the mysteries of the spirit-world, they went forth to study the character of all tribes. After deciding upon a residence, they entered the body of some one about to become a mother, and were ushered by her into the world."[2]

Among the Dacotahs, the doctor rattles his gourd, sucks the patient, and thrusts his face into a bowl of water to get rid of the disease by immersing it. If he decides it is some animal that is producing the sickness, he has an animal-shaped image made, and put in a bowl of water mixed with red earth and placed outside of the tent, where young men stand ready to shoot. When the doctor gets the disease he pops his head out of the tent and transfers it to the image, when the young men blow the little bark animal to atoms. All of the fragments of the image are then gathered together and burned.[3] The medicine-men are not infallible, and sometimes make mistakes in their diagnosis of cases and ascribe the trouble to a wrong animal. At the death of Iron Arms, a great warrior, it was

---

[1] 2 Algic Researches, 34. [2] 1 Minn. Hist. Coll., 269.
[3] Eastman's Legends, 23.

said he died because the doctor had made a mistake and thought a prairie-dog had entered him, when it was a mud hen.[1]

Such mistakes have tended to bring their conjurations into disrespect, and they were often treated with great severity by relatives of the dead. Women were allowed to practise medicine, and this custom also undoubtedly brought disrepute upon medical practice, since very little regard is shown women among uncivilized peoples. If they were unsuccessful in working a cure, they were very often killed. The following is told by Mr. Battey. "At the death of Ne-wah-kass-ett, chief of the Wichitas, his brother Keechi took his rifle, and, entering the lodge of the medicine-woman, without saying a word, deliberately shot her dead for having administered bad medicine. In all probability the woman had done the best she knew." Those in the village tore down her lodge and piled it with her effects upon her dead body, and set fire to the whole.[2] The following curious illustration of medical practice among the Piutes since the advent of the whites is very amusing. The medicine-woman who is the subject of the description bore the simple yet modest name of "Heap-Chokee," a name given to her in memory of the able manner in which, during her fifteenth year, she strangled two wounded emigrants whom her dear father had previously scalped. She became a widow at the age of sixty, and, having been duly examined by the chief men of the tribe and pronounced to be far too ugly for matrimonial purposes, she was duly licensed to practise medicine according to the tenets of the regular Piute medical school. Shortly afterward Dr. Heap-Chokee was called in to prescribe for a squaw who was in the last stages of consumption. Having made a careful examination of the patient by punching her in tender places with the handle of a hoe, the doctor decided that the case was one which did not call for drugs, but for "pow-wow." She therefore shut herself up in the patient's wigwam and danced and howled with much vigor for several hours, at

---

[1] Eastman's Legends, 41.   [2] Battey's Quaker among Indians, 57.

the expiration of which the patient was found to be dead. It so happened that the consumptive squaw was not a valuable one, and, in fact, her husband was rather glad that she was dead. Still, the death of the doctor's first patient was not adapted to give her a reputation for medical skill, and the affair was therefore investigated by a council of able warriors. The council decided that the doctor had committed an error in not prescribing medicine, and, while it was expressly conceded that it was not worth while to severely reprimand her for the death of a worthless squaw, she was affectionately warned that she would do well in future to prescribe a good dose of real medicine. A fortnight later a young warrior was brought into camp, suffering from an acute attack of grizzly bear, the leading symptom of which was the fracture of a dozen or two of his ribs and a general mashing of the internal organs. This time the doctor compounded a medicine that really ought to have worked wonders. It was made by boiling together a collection of miscellaneous weeds, a handful of chewing-tobacco, the heads of four rattlesnakes, and a select assortment of worn-out moccasins. The decoction thus obtained was seasoned with a little crude petroleum and a large quantity of red pepper, and the patient was directed to take a pint of the mixture every half-hour. He was a brave man, conspicuous for his fortitude under suffering, but after taking his first dose he turned over and died with the utmost expedition. Again the council of leading warriors investigated the case. They analyzed and tasted the medicine, and agreed that it was faultless in its way. While they fully approved of the prescription, they found that the doctor relied upon it alone and had omitted to dance and yell. This innovation was not passed over in silence, and Dr. Heap-Chokee was solemnly warned that she must either practise medicine properly or meet the consequences, and that young and valuable warriors could not be wasted with impunity. Soon after the daughter of the leading chief was attacked by what was undoubtedly an inflammation of the brain. Warned by experience, the doctor brought the entire resources of the medical art to bear upon the case. She not only administered large doses of her favorite decoction, but she took a large tin pan into the patient's wigwam and hammered it for twenty-four hours, during which time she never ceased to dance and to yell at the top of her lungs. Her zeal called forth the admiration of the whole tribe, and it was considered certain that the patient must recover; but, strange as it may seem, the doctor emerged from the wigwam in the morning of the second day, and sadly announced that the girl was dead. Once more the council met, but its deliberations were short. Dr. Heap-Chokee had attended three patients, and every one had died. There could be no doubt that she was an unsuccessful physician, and that if she continued to practise the tribe would soon be extinct. The course to be pursued was too plain to be ignored. The doctor was summoned, and was mildly but firmly told that her professional career was at an end. Three warriors then led her outside the limits of the camp, and administered to her six revolver-bullets, after which lots were drawn for the possession of her scalp, and the rest of her was quietly buried.[1] Although this account is written in a humorous vein, it represents fairly the methods of all the savage peoples in such circumstances.

Among the uncivilized tribes of South America the same system of medical practice prevailed. The Abipone physician was also prophet, sorcerer, and priest. Their method of cure was to suck the part in which the pain was located, and if the whole body was affected several of them were required. They would, after a while, produce a beetle or a worm, which they had previously put into their mouth, and said that it was the cause of the disorder.[2] Among the Patagonians the same notions prevailed. The sick were possessed with evil spirits, and the doctor went around with a drum intended to frighten them away.[3]

The principal employment of the American sorcerers was

---

[1] New York Times. [2] 2 Dobriz., 248-51. [3] 2 ib., 262.

the cure of disease by incantations; but the medicine-men did not inspire so much superstitious fear in the minds of the people by the practice of the healing art as by their other impostures, prominent among which was witchcraft. These sorcerers were also supposed to have the power of causing as well as of curing diseases, and were much dreaded by the people in consequence.[1]

The practice of witchcraft aided the American sorcerers in obtaining great influence. Most of the uncivilized tribes thought that a skilful sorcerer could kill any one in the space of twenty-four hours merely by means of the black art, and even at the distance of many hundred miles. They were also able to cause long and lingering disorders in any one they pleased.[2]

As the Indians in general believed in witchcraft, and ascribed to the arts of sorcerers many of the disorders with which they were afflicted in the regular course of nature, this class of men pretended to be skilled in a certain occult science, by means of which they were able not only to cure natural diseases, but to counteract or destroy the enchantments of wizards or witches. The Ojibway sorcerers were thought to have the power of transferring disease from the patient who paid them to his enemy. To effect this, he made a small wooden image of his patient's enemy. He pierced this image in the heart, and introduced small powders, which, accompanied with the proper incantations, were supposed to transfer the disease to the person represented in the image.[3] Mr. Tanner says the necromancers pretend to exercise an unlimited control over the body and mind of the person represented by these images, which they make of stained wood and rags, to which the name is given of the person they expect to control, and to the heart, eyes, or some other part of this image they apply their medicines, which have an effect upon the person represented. The sorcerers can work their injuries if they have a hair or any part of the person against whom they wish to direct them.[4]

---

[1] Brett, 284-89. [2] Loskiel, 118. [3] 2 Keating, 159.
[4] Tanner's Narrative, 190-91.

What a key we have here to the whole labyrinth of idolatrous and fetichistic superstitions! Among the Iroquois the belief in witchcraft was universal, and the effect upon their prosperity and population, if tradition is to be credited, was at times appalling. The witches constituted a secret association, which met at night to consult on mischief, and each was bound to inviolable secrecy. A witch had power to turn into a fox or wolf. In order to escape, they could transform themselves into a turkey and fly away. Sometimes they changed themselves into a stone or rotten log until their pursuers passed by. These witches could blow hairs and worms into a person and produce disease.[1]

"It is incredible to what a degree the superstitious belief in witchcraft operates on the mind of the Indian. The moment his imagination is struck with the idea that he is bewitched, he is no longer himself. Of this extraordinary power of their conjurers, of the causes which produce it, and the manner in which it is acquired, they have a very indefinite idea. The sorcerer, they think, makes use of some deadening substance, which he conveys to the person he means to 'strike' in a manner which they can neither understand nor describe. The person thus 'stricken' is immediately seized with an unaccountable terror. His spirits sink, his appetite fails, he is disturbed in his sleep, he pines and wastes away, or a fit of sickness seizes him, and he dies at last a miserable victim to the workings of his own imagination."

The supposed familiarity of the Indian sorcerer with the inhabitants of the spiritual world gave him his influence. Most of his official duty consisted in calling on his familiar spirit or spirits, whose attention and aid having been once secured, miraculous power was supposed to be conferred upon him. Some of these sorcerers claimed to influence several of these spirits. An Eskimo sorcerer had as many as ten of these spirits under his control. Chusco, an acquaintance of Mr. School-

---

[1] Schoolcraft's Iroquois, 87.

PLATE V.

craft, claimed to influence the spirits of the turtle, swan, crow, and woodpecker.[1] Plate V. will illustrate the Indian's conception of the spiritual world and the sorcerer's influence therein. The sorcerer's lodge can be seen, wherein he is calling upon his familiar spirits, and they are coming and entering the lodge. As each spirit arrives, the lodge shakes. When they are all assembled, the sorcerer can use them as he pleases. The picture represents a prophet's lodge. It must be borne in mind that the sorcerer is also doctor and prophet. In prophecy he is supposed to be able to send these agents to the uttermost parts of his earth in a few seconds, and get information upon any subject by these messengers.[2]

Primitive prophecy was considered under the subject of their dream-theories. Such revelations came to any who were under favorable conditions. The power of sorcerers to send their spirit messengers for information to other localities for tribal advantage, is an early step toward national prophecy.

Henry tells the following of the Ojibways in illustration of this subject: "Before setting forward on the voyage, preparations were made for invoking and consulting the great turtle. They built a large wigwam for the use of the priest and reception of the spirit. The ceremonies began at night. The priest then appeared, and crept under the skins of the tent on his hands and knees. His head was scarcely within side when the edifice, massy as it has been described, began to shake, and the sounds of numerous voices were heard beneath the tent, some yelling, some barking as dogs, some howling like wolves, and in this horrible concert were mingled screams and sobs as of despair, anguish, and the sharpest pain. After some time these confused and frightful noises were succeeded by a perfect silence, and now a voice not heard before seemed to manifest the arrival of a new character in the tent. This was a low and feeble voice, resembling the cry of a young puppy. The sound was no sooner distinguished than all the Indians clapped their

---

[1] 4 Schoolcraft's Indian Tribes, 491.   [2] 5 ib., 422.

hands for joy, exclaiming that this was the chief spirit, the turtle, the spirit that never lied. Other voices which they had discriminated from time to time they had previously hissed as evil and lying spirits which deceive mankind. New sounds came from the tent. During the space of half an hour a succession of songs were heard, in which a diversity of voices met the ear. From his first entrance till these songs were finished we heard nothing in the proper voice of the priest; but now he addressed the multitude, declaring the presence of the great turtle, and the spirit's readiness to answer such questions as should be proposed. The questions were to come from the chief of the village, who was silent, however, till after he had put a large quantity of tobacco into the tent, introducing it at the aperture. This was a sacrifice offered to the spirit, for spirits are supposed by the Indians to be as fond of tobacco as themselves. The chief then desired the priest to inquire whether the English were preparing to make war upon the Indians. This question having been put by the priest, the tent instantly shook, and for some seconds after it continued to rock so violently that I expected to see it levelled with the ground. Then a terrific cry announced the departure of the turtle. The spirit soon returned, having in its absence crossed Lake Huron and proceeded as far as Montreal. It announced that the St. Lawrence was covered with boats full of soldiers coming to fight the Indians. Inquiries about private affairs were afterward made."

Prophecy among the Potawatomies suffered a loss of the respect formerly paid it, on account of the failure of the predictions of the famous brother of Tecumseh, and of his attempt to deceive the Indians.[1] His influence was great for a time. This Shawnee prophet well knew how, by surrounding himself with awe-inspiring mysteries, to produce an effect on the susceptible imaginations of the Indians. Bearing in his right hand the string of sacred beans and the magic fire, and carry-

---

[1] Keating, 133-34.

ing with him also an image of a dead body, the size of life, made out of some light material, he passed from wigwam to wigwam and from tribe to tribe, and his solemn, mysterious manner procured for him everywhere admission and confidence even among the wild and hostile Indians of the Upper Missouri.[1]

What a weird spectacle this famous sorcerer presented as he stood upon the eminence overlooking the battle at Tippecanoe, working his spells and hurling the imprecations of his spirit-world, which he was supposed to command, against the Americans under General Harrison! Truly in that defeat prophecy received its death-blow among the Red men of the forest. The Natches, who appear to have been considerably in advance of all the tribes in the United States and British America in civilization, did not have a priestly order, although some progress had been made in that direction. The eight guardians of the sacred fire were dedicated to that duty, but, as there were no offerings, libations, or sacrifices, these persons cannot be considered priests. On the contrary, they had conjurers among them who undoubtedly practised as did those of the barbarous tribes.[2] The power of prophecy was ascribed to them.

The American sorcerers practised another imposture. They used witchcraft to control the elements. Those around Freshwater Bay kept the wind in leather bags, and disposed of it as they pleased.[3] A Cree sorcerer sold three days of fair wind for one pound of tobacco. "There were among the Delawares," says Heckewelder, "old men and women who got their living by pretending to supernatural knowledge to bring down rain when wanted. In the summer of 1799 a most uncommon drought happened in the Muskingum country. An old man was applied to by the women to bring down rain, and, after various ceremonies, declared that they should have rain enough. The sky had been clear for nearly five weeks, and was equally clear when the Indian made this declaration. But

---

[1] Mollhausen's Journey to the Pacific, 72.   [2] McCulloh, 162.
[3] Hardy's Travels, 357.

about four in the afternoon the horizon became overcast, and, without any thunder or wind, it began to rain, and continued to do so till the ground became thoroughly soaked. Experience had doubtless taught him to observe that certain signs in the sky or in the water were the forerunners of rain; yet the credulous multitude did not fail to ascribe it to his supernatural power." When the Natches wanted rain, or when they desired hot weather for ripening their corn, they addressed themselves to the old man who had the greatest character for living wisely, and they entreated him to invoke the aërial spirits in order to obtain what they demanded. The old man, who never refused his countrymen's request, prepared to fast for nine days together; he ordered his wife to withdraw, and during the whole time he ate nothing but a dish of gruel boiled in water without salt, which was brought him once a day by his wife after sunset. They never will accept of any reward for this service, that the spirits may not be angry with them.[1] The Virginia sorcerers pretended to lay storms by going to the water's side and making offerings to the spirits of the waters. In Guiana the sorcerers thought they could control the rain and the clouds by incantation.[2] Those of Paraguay were thought to have the same superhuman control over the rain, hail, and tempests.

Among the Brazilians, the sorcerers made them believe that the fruitfulness and barrenness of the earth were owing to their influence. Among many of the tribes they boasted that the growth of plants and fruits was owing to them, and that all the blessings of heaven flowed only on account of their zeal and prayers.[3]

These accounts of the sorcerers show them to have been a set of professional impostors, who, availing themselves of the superstitious prejudices of the people, acquired the name and reputation of men of superior knowledge and possessed of supernatural powers. Many of these sorcerers were believed to

---

[1] 2 Du Pratz, Louisiana, 241.　　[2] Brett, 208.　　[3] 3 Picart, 18.

be able to work miracles. A young Comanche medicine-man pretended to bring the dead to life. He also ascended to the clouds far beyond the sun. He had several times ascended in the presence of the Comanches, remaining in the sky overnight and coming back next day. He succeeded in deluding the minds of his people in the following manner. It is given out that at a certain time he will visit the sun. He withdraws himself a short distance from the crowd, charging them to look directly at the sun until he speaks to them, then let their eyes slowly fall to the place where he is standing. As they do this, they will see dark bodies descend to receive him, with which he will ascend. His directions being complied with, the dark objects descend to him, and, being blinded by their continual gazing upon the sun, he bids them slowly raise their eyes, and the dark objects arise, while he conveys himself away and conceals himself until the appointed time of his return.[1] The Medicine Bluffs received the name from the following legend. Many years since, a noted medicine-man of the Comanche tribe, in company with some friends, rode up the slope of the hill, when this frightful precipice of two hundred or two hundred and fifty feet appeared before them, stopping them in their course. But the medicine-man was not to be stopped, neither turned aside. Uttering some words of Indian magic, he rode his horse over the precipice; but, to the astonishment of his friends, instead of being dashed to pieces at the bottom, he was gently borne across the chasm to the opposite bank of the stream, where, finding himself alone, he turned his horse to look for his friends, whom he beheld at the top of the bluff, afraid to follow and too proud to go around. To relieve them from their unpleasant position, he rode back and to the bottom of the perpendicular wall of rock, which rent at his approach, dividing the bluff into two parts by forming a chasm through the cliff several feet in width, through and up which he rode, rejoining his companions at the top, who then followed

---

[1] Battey's Quaker among Indians, 302-3.

him down through the pass thus made, now known as the Medicine-Man's Pass.[1] Wood, in his "New England Prospect," says, "The Indians report of one Passaconnaw that hee can make the water burne, the rocks move, the trees dance, and metamorphose himself into a flaming man. Hee will do more; for in winter, when there are no green leaves to be got, he will burne an old one to ashes, and, putting those into the water, produce a new green leaf, which you shall not only see, but substantially handle and carrie away; and make of a dead snake's skin a living snake, both to be seen, felt, and heard. This I write but upon the report of the Indians, who confidently affirm stranger things." Thomas Morton, writing of the same man, says he was "a Powah of great estimation amongst all kinde of salvages; he has been scene by our English in the heat of summer to make ice appear in a bowle of faire water; first having the water set before him, he began his incantations according to their usual accustom, and before the same had bin ended, a thick clowde darkened the aire, and on a sodaine a thunder clap was heard that amazed the natives. In an instant he showed a firme piece of ice. It floted in the middle of the bowle in the presence of the vulgar people, which doubtless was done by the agency of Satan, his consort."

Those dwelling about St. Francis River could make their rods to bud and shoot forth green branches. They could metamorphose themselves at pleasure. They were thought in many tribes to have power to bring the dead to life.

They so imposed on the Roman Catholic priests, who were predisposed to accept superstitions, that many of them believed most implicitly in their supernatural powers. One of them who labored among the Kootenais says he saw one of their sorcerers command a mountain-sheep to fall dead, and the animal, then leaping among the rocks, fell lifeless. "This I saw with my own eyes," says he, "and ate of the animal afterward. It was unwounded, healthy, and perfectly wild."[2]

---

[1] Battey's Quaker among Indians, 62, 63.   [2] Beach, 76-78.

Ascription of supernatural power often occurs on account of the possession of some mysterious object which is supposed to have a powerful spirit within it. Mr. Adair mentions a case among the Southern tribes in which a sorcerer had gained much distinction and had imposed upon the people by the use of a carbuncle nearly as big as an egg, which reflected the light with such strong flashes as to inspire terror in the minds of the superstitious natives.[1] Mr. Du Pratz, while among the natives of Louisiana, attained great distinction as a sorcerer by drawing down fire from the sun, to use their language, with a burning-glass. Some of the sorcerers among the Western tribes imposed upon the Indians by pretending to eat fire which they placed in their mouth and then extinguished the flame.[2] A sorcerer among the Cherokees who had been removed to the Western country had a knife which was magnetized, and he influenced the tribe to do as he wished by imposing on them by this mystery. Whatever he wished them to do he would announce when he was attracting the mineral substance.

They often impose on the people by finding out ahead of the tribe that an enemy is coming, and announce it as though it was revelation. Whatever they conjecture or learn from secret intelligence they predict as about to happen, with infinite pomposity, and are listened to with as much attention as though they were really inspired. When they call their spiritual agents, they retire into a tent, mutter awhile, then command, and the shade comes, which they interrogate, and, changing the voice, give the answers, and every one present believes. Before a battle, they ride around the ranks with fierce countenance, imprecating evil on their enemies. On account of this ceremony, if victory comes, the best part of the spoils is adjudged to them as the fruit of their office. Whatever they wish they extort from these credulous people. If they imagine themselves injured by any, they will command the persons to come to them and then lacerate them till the blood streams from

---

[1] American Indians, 87. [2] Lee and Frost, 164.

their body. They keep the people in dread by threatening to turn into a wild beast and tear them to pieces. This they believe they are able to do, and if they begin to roar like some ferocious animal the people will fly in every direction.

The belief in shamanism is universal in Alaska. The words and actions of the shaman, or sorcerer, are considered infallible by the Thlinkeets, and believed implicitly by them. A shaman has the faculty not only of calling spirits from the vasty deep, but also the power to make them come when he calls for them. Their mode of initiation is to retire to some forest or mountain and fast. Here the river-otter is said to come and visit them, from whom they get the secret of their profession. If the novitiate fails in this way, he repairs to the grave of some shaman, and remains over-night with a tooth or finger of the corpse in his mouth. Some of these shamans control a large number of spirits, and these he can command at will.[1]

Among the Chukchees and Koriaks, the head of every family performs the office of shaman.[2] This is evidence of their having made little progress from their primitive condition.

Among the more barbarous tribes the priestly office had never been separated from that of doctor and conjurer. Among a few of the tribes occupying the territory of the United States a division of these offices had begun to take place. The Cherokees appointed every year one of their tribe to make the sacrifices for the people.[3] The office of priesthood appears to have just been instituted among them. One family of the tribe was set apart for this office. He, however, continued to perform the office of "medicine-man" and sorcerer. He also interpreted omens and baptized their infants soon after birth, which was a custom from time immemorial among them. A priesthood had been established among the Powhatans of Virginia, and many of the tricks of these priests were discovered by the Europeans. They made the idols move and talk as they

---

[1] Dall's Alaska, 424–26.   [2] Ib., 513.
[3] 1 Logan's South Carolina, 26.

pleased, by being concealed in them, whilst another priest kept back the people, who were filled with curiosity, from discovering and profaning by their presence the holy of holies. These priests were celibates. The natives of Florida had priests who communed with invisible spirits and who alone were allowed within the temple with their gods.[1] The Florida priests were trained to their business by severe fasting, which induces visions and a supposed intimate correspondence with the deities.

Among the Ojibways, the medicine-men appear to have formed a secret society with a ceremony of initiation. They held secret convocations, which were held in high veneration by their deluded brethren. The chiefs never undertook anything of importance without consulting such a convocation. Among the Dacotahs, a sacred language had sprung up among their sorcerers, who had not yet, however, attained to a priestly dignity.[2]

Among the Eskimos, the angekok was sorcerer, doctor, and priest. They had, however, formed a caste in this world and in the next. The ordinary sorcerers did not rank with these angekoks, but were an inferior order who worked injuries to the people. The angekoks, before assuming the office, retired to a secluded spot and fasted until they dreamed of beasts and monsters, which they supposed to be real spiritual existences and became familiar spirits.[3] It will be noticed that these angekoks went through the same ceremony for obtaining their spiritual agent which every Indian did among the other wild tribes of America; but among the Eskimos it seems to have been confined to the angekoks. It shows they had taken one step in advance of the neighboring tribes in the establishment of a priestly hierarchy. The surrender of this primitive custom to the angekoks is quite significant. They used the superiority which they had begun to acquire to fasten their impostures upon the people, for they admitted to Europeans, says Mr. Crantz, that their pretended intercourse with the spiritual world

---

[1] Bartram's Travels, 497.   [2] Eastman's Chicora, 16.   [3] 1 Crantz, 194.

was a pretence to deceive the simple, and they avowed the falsehood of apparitions.[1]

The Caribs had a priesthood, and put all candidates for it through a pretty severe discipline. They fasted, became intoxicated with tobacco-juice, and did all other acts which prepared their minds, as they thought, to consult the genii. They always practised their art in the night-time, where and when their imposture could not be discovered.

Persons whose constitutional unsoundness induces morbid manifestations are indeed marked out by nature to become seers and sorcerers. Among the Patagonians, patients seized with falling sickness or St. Vitus's dance were at once selected for magicians, as chosen by the spirits themselves, who possessed and convulsed them.[2]

Traces of a priestly language are found among a few of the tribes. In Peru, the priests conducted the temple services in a language not understood by the masses, and the incantations of the priests of Powhatan were not in ordinary Algonkin, but some obscure jargon. The same peculiarity has been observed, and heretofore noticed, among the Dacotahs and Eskimos; but linguistic scholars, on searching, have found them among the last two tribes to be the ordinary dialects of the country, "modified by an affected accentuation, and by the introduction of a few cabalistic terms, which have made a slang such as rascals and pedants are very apt to coin."[3]

Among the most civilized aboriginal peoples a priesthood was found exercising all the offices assumed by them in the Old World civilizations. The attendants on the Peruvian temples composed an army of themselves. The whole number of functionaries who officiated at the Coricancha alone was no less than four thousand.[4] Among the religious ceremonies which occupied the priestly caste were baptism, confirmation, holy orders, extreme unction.

---

[1] 1 Crantz, 195-97. [2] Falkner's Patagonia, 116.
[3] Brinton's Myths, 303-4. [4] 1 Prescott's Peru, 100.

Baptism was general among all the Peruvian nations west of the Andes, and in some provinces took place two or three weeks after birth. In the southern provinces two years elapsed. All the relatives were assembled at this ceremony. On the day of the birth, the water with which the infant was washed was poured into a hole in the earth in the presence of a priest, who pronounced cabalistic words over the newly-born, intended to conjure away and exorcise all future malign influence. When the child attained puberty, confirmation took place, which consisted in imposing a new name and cutting the hair and finger-nails of the confirmed and sacrificing them to the Huacas. It will be borne in mind that these and all other parts of the body were superstitiously preserved from the possession of any one, and the dedication of these parts of the body to a deity was a solemn act of worship undoubtedly with them, however ridiculous it may appear to us. Penance was practised before the principal feasts, when they confessed their sins to a priest after they had previously fasted several days. Confession began in this strain: "Hear me, highlands, plains, condors, owls, grubs, and all animals and herbs, know that I wish to confess my sins." This is nonsensical, unless we recollect that they worshipped the things addressed, and hence they were confessing to their gods. After the confession had been made, they went through ordeals to prove whether they had concealed anything. By one of these ordeals they were required to throw a handful of corn into a vessel, and if there was an even number of grains the confession had been well made, otherwise not. Penance consisted in abstinence from many pleasures for a season, and occasionally in corporal punishment. Sometimes they were forced to put on new garments, in order that the sins might be left in the old ones. A priest assisted the dying by muttering incantations against the power of evil spirits. Holy orders, or the ceremony of the consecration of priests, was a matter of the highest importance among the ancient Peruvians. The priesthood contained a number of orders. The greatest respect was commanded by those of the sun; but each Huaca had its priest, who was respected in proportion as the Huaca was venerated. His occupation was to take care of the deity, and watch in his temple on the spot where his image was erected, to speak with him, and repeat his answers to the people, present their offerings, make sacrifices, celebrate their feasts, and teach their worship. Such employments occupied the priests of the dead. The Conopas also had priests, who interpreted their will and offered sacrifices when brought to them. The soothsayers and wizards formed a particular subdivision of the priesthood. Those most esteemed were the Socyac, who predicted the future by means of small heaps of corn; the Pacchacuti, who divined by means of spiders' feet; the Hacaricue, who foretold by the blood and intestines of rabbits; the Pichiuricue, who observed the flight of birds; the Moscoc, who interpreted dreams, sleeping by the clothes of him who consulted them, and receiving in a dream the answer.[1]

The Peruvian priests also acted as prophets, and could give an account of that which was done in very remote parts before any news thereof was brought. The battles that were fought, rebellions that broke out, and other remarkable accidents that happened at three hundred leagues' distance, they pretended to know the same day. They could also find stolen goods.[2]

Great was the surprise of the first Spanish ecclesiastics, who found, on reaching Mexico, a priesthood as regularly organized as that of the most civilized countries of the Old World. Clothed with a powerful and effective authority, which extended its arms to man in every condition and in all the stages of his life, the Mexican priests were mediators between man and divinity. They brought the newly-born infants into the religious society; they directed their training and education; they determined the entrance of the young men into the service of the state; they consecrated marriage by their blessing; they comforted the sick and assisted the dying. This sacerdotal authority also manifested itself in a species of confession,

---

[1] Rivero and Tschudi, 182-84. [2] 4 Herrera, 353.

which prevailed in Mexico as well as elsewhere, and concerning which the dogma obtained that a wrong or sin confessed to the priest and expiated through the medium of a penance imposed by him was blotted out and placed beyond the reach of human justice or secular power.[1]

As many as five thousand priests were attached to the principal temple in Mexico. The various ranks and functions of this multitudinous body were discriminated with great exactness. Those best instructed in music took the management of the choirs. Others arranged the festivals conformably to the calendar. Some superintended the education of youth, and others had charge of the hieroglyphical paintings and oral traditions; while the dismal rites of sacrifice were reserved for the chief dignitaries of the order. At the head of the whole establishment were two high-priests, equal in dignity, and with whom the sovereign advised in weighty matters of public concern. While engaged in immediate attendance at the temples, they lived in conventual discipline; but they were allowed to marry. Thrice during the day and once at night, when in active duty, they were called to prayers. They practised flagellation, and pierced their flesh with the thorns of the aloe,—

"In hopes to merit heaven by making earth a hell."

The great cities were divided into districts, and placed under the charge of a parochial clergy, who regulated every act of religion within their precincts, and administered the rites of confession and absolution. Priestly absolution was received in place of the legal punishment of offences, and authorized an acquittal in case of arrest.[2] The sick deemed it an indispensable condition to their recovery that every secret crime should be confessed to the priest.[3]

In all the towns of the Mexican empire there were as many complete sets of priests as there were temples. Some took

---

[1] Rivero and Tschudi, 19, 20.   [2] 1 Prescott's Mexico, 66, 68.
[3] 1 Bancroft, 124.

charge of the sacrifices, others were skilled in the art of divination. Others applied themselves to the composition of hymns. Those learned in science superintended the schools and colleges. Those who possessed literary talent compiled the historical works and collected material for the libraries. There were monasteries for each sex. In those for females they were under surveillance of a number of staid matrons of good character. On entering the monastery, each girl had her hair cut short. They all slept in one dormitory, and did not undress at night, in order that they might be ready to rise at ten o'clock, midnight, and dawn, for religious ceremonies. On these occasions a matron led the procession: with eyes bent on the ground, the maidens filed up one side of the temple, while the priests did the same on the other, so that all met before the altar. In a pantheon of as many divinities as that of the Mexican, and where all the phenomena of nature are attributed to some one or more of these divinities, it can be easily understood why a religious machinery, intricate and ponderous, should be required to propitiate the anger, humor the whims, and beseech the favor of such a vast number of capricious and active deities. The priests often went to the king and told him to remember the idols, who were starving with hunger, whereupon the princes sent to one another to prepare for war, because their gods demanded something to eat. Then they marched out and fought, only endeavoring to take prisoners, that they might have men to feed the gods.[1]

We hear from the accounts we have received that there were some celebrated preachers among the priests, and silvery-tongued orators played as successfully upon the emotions of the Mexicans as do our modern revivalists. Herrera says, "They had priests who preached dreadfully in the temples, putting men into horrid frights, by which means they moved them to do whatever they directed."[2]

The vast number of the Mexican priests, their enormous

---

[1] 3 Herrera, 213.   [2] 3 ib., 255.

wealth, and the blind zeal of the people, all combined to render the sacerdotal power extremely formidable. The king himself performed the functions of high-priest on certain occasions, and frequently held some sacred office before succeeding to the throne. The heads of church and state seem to have worked amicably together, and to have united their power to keep the masses in subjection. The sovereign took no step of importance without first consulting the high-priests, to learn whether the gods were favorable to the project. In Tezcuco and Tlacopan the pontifical dignity was always conferred upon the second son of the king. In Mexico a supervisor over the worship of the gods stood next in rank to the two high-priests. Among other dignitaries of their religious system were the chief of the sacrificers, who inherited his office, the keeper of relics and ornaments, the composer of hymns, the musical director, the treasurer, master over temple-property, and numbers of masters of special ceremonies.

The ordinary Mexican priests dressed in a black cotton cloth, which hung from the back of the head like a veil. Their hair was left uncut and painted black. Reed sandals protected their feet. There were certain orders, however, which varied from this. They were engaged a great part of the time with hymn-chanting and incense-burning. They also took the auguries, among which the priest went through the ceremony of sprinkling snuff on the altar in order to discover whether the gods would favor any national enterprise. If shortly afterward any footprint of an animal, particularly that of an eagle, was found impressed in the snuff, it was regarded as a mark of divine favor, and great was the shouting when the priest announced the augury.[1] We here see how the priests utilized the superstitions of the people in reference to the agency of animal spirits.

Among the Mexicans, each temple had its own lands and possessions, and even its own peasants to cultivate them. Thence was drawn all that was necessary for the maintenance

---

[1] 3 Bancroft, 431-38.

of the priests, together with the wood which was consumed in great quantities in the temples. A tract of country which went under the name of Teotlalpan (land of the gods) was undoubtedly so named from being the possession of the temples. There were, besides these, daily offerings from the devout, of provisions. Near the temples there were granaries for the provisions of the priesthood. The annual overplus, if any, was distributed to the poor. The priesthood received nearly as much homage as the deities themselves.[1]

The office of anointing kings was assumed by the two high-priests. The new king, with no covering except the girdle, ascended the temple of Huitzilopochtli, where he was met by one of the high-priests, who dyed his body with a certain kind of ink and sprinkled him four times with water which had been blessed. The king was then clothed with a mantle on which were pictured skeletons of the dead, and a medicine-bag tied to his neck containing charms against disease; after which he took an oath to maintain their ancient religion. The priest then instructed him in his duties as sovereign. The king during all this ceremony was upon his knees before the priest. The Mexican schools and seminaries were annexed to the temples, and the instruction of the young of both sexes was a monopoly in the hands of the priests. Generally the boys were sent there between the ages of six and nine years, and were dressed in black.[2] The seminaries for girls were guarded day and night by old men, and the maidens could not even leave their apartments without a guard. They were taught the tenets of their religion, and swept the temples and attended to the sacred fire. They also learned how to make feather-work and spin and weave mantles.[3]

The priests did not fail to assume an important part in marriage ceremonies, the most important part in which was the address of the priest to the betrothed couple, in which he defined their duties to each other. He exhorted them to be

---

[1] 1 Clavigero, 269-70.   [2] 2 Bancroft, 243.   [3] 2 ib., 245.

faithful to one another and maintain peace and harmony between themselves. He then tied the end of the man's mantle to the dress of the woman. After congratulations, they proceeded to the temple, where the priest perfumed them, then led them to the altar and placed a finely-woven shawl on each of their shoulders, in the centre of which was painted a skeleton, as a symbol that death only could now separate them from each other. He then perfumed them again, and led them to the door of the temple. Four days were spent in penance and religious ceremonies, after which their couch was prepared by two priests and the marriage consummated.[1]

Among the Mexicans, every distinguished man had a priest or chaplain to perform the ceremonies within his house, and when he died the chaplain was killed, to serve him in the same manner in the other world.[2]

The Mexican priests had to consecrate the ground on which they played their national game of ball, somewhat similar to tennis. This they did by blessing it and then throwing the ball four times about the court, when it might be played, but not before.[3]

Cortes says the priests were very strict in the practice of honesty and chastity, and any deviation was punished with death, and he was very desirous that the vice and profanity of the Spanish clergy should be concealed from them as much as possible, that they might not be led to undervalue the Christian faith.

It must have been an imposing sight to behold in Campeachy the priests, arrayed in long white mantles, perfuming the Spaniards with burning gum and bidding them depart.[4]

A tradition of the Mexicans would appear to indicate a period when sorcery was supplanted by their elaborate system of priestcraft. On departing from Michoacan, they left behind a sorceress who was worshipped by the people at the instiga-

---

[1] 2 Bancroft, 257-59.
[3] 2 ib., 341.
[2] 3 Herrera, 220.
[4] Cortes, Despatches, 7.

tion of an idol which had four priests connected with it. This woman, seeing herself abandoned, founded a town called Malinalco, and ever after, the inhabitants of that place were looked upon as great sorcerers. That part of the nation which proceeded toward Mexico appears to have fallen completely under the dominion of the four priests, who gave laws, and without whose approbation nothing was done, and who spoke through their idol, which they carried on their shoulders.[1]

The Zapotecs were a priest-ridden people. Their priests possessed great power, secular as well as sacerdotal. Among the Zapotecs, the wedding-day had to be fixed by the priest.[2] Yopaa, one of their principal cities, was ruled absolutely by a pontiff, in whom the Zapotec monarchs had a powerful rival. It is impossible to overrate the reverence in which this spiritual king was held. He was looked upon as a god whom the earth was not worthy to hold or the sun to shine upon. He profaned his sanctity if he so much as touched the ground with his foot. The officers who bore his palanquin upon their shoulders were members of the first Zapotec families. He scarcely deigned to look upon anything about him. He never appeared in public except with the most extraordinary pomp, and all who met him fell with their faces to the ground, fearing death would overtake them were they to look upon holy Wiyatal, as he was called. The most powerful lords never entered his presence except with eyes lowered and feet bared. Continence was strictly imposed upon the Zapotec priests, but this high pontiff was an exception, because no one could furnish him with a worthy successor, who must be of his own generating. On certain days in each year this high-priest became drunk, and while in this state one of the most beautiful virgins consecrated to the service of the gods was brought to him, and if the result of this holy debauch proved to be a male infant, it inherited his position.[3]

Among the Zapotecs there was a class of priests who made

---

[1] 3 Herrera, 190-91.   [2] 3 ib., 262.   [3] 2 Bancroft, 142-43.

the interpreting of dreams their special province. Each form of divination was made a special study. Some professed to foretell the future by the aid of stars, earth, wind, fire, or water, others by the flight of birds, by the entrails of sacrificial victims, or by magic signs and circles. There were hermits who passed their entire lives in religious ecstasy and meditation, shut up in dark caves or rude huts with no human companions.[1]

Among the Mayas, the temporal power of the priesthood was even greater than among the Nahua nations. Votan, Zamna, Cuculcan, and all the other semi-mythical founders of the Maya civilization united in their persons the qualities of high-priest and king, and from their time to the coming of the Spaniards ecclesiastical and secular authority marched hand in hand. The Itzas, at Chichen, were ruled in the earlier times by a theocratic government, and later the high-priest of the empire of the royal family of the Cheles became king of Izamal, which became the sacred city and headquarters of ecclesiastical dignitaries. The gigantic mounds still seen at Izamal are traditionally the tombs of both kings and priests. The priests were allowed to marry, and the office of high-priest was hereditary. Mictlan was another great religious centre and a shrine much visited by pilgrims. Here a sacerdotal hierarchy, hereditary in one family, ruled. Thus we see that while the priesthood had great power over even the highest secular rulers in all the Maya nations, yet the system by which the high-priests were members of the royal families rendered their power a support to that royalty rather than a cause of fear.[2]

The Mayas intrusted the more advanced education of youth entirely to the priesthood. The youths assisted the priests in their religious duties. Girls were placed in convents under the superintendence of matrons, who were most strict in their guardianship. In all the educational institutions of Yucatan the mysteries of astrology, divination, prophecy, and medicine

---

[1] 2 Bancroft, 201-13. [2] 2 ib., 647-48.

formed a great part of the instruction, and the youth of both sexes were familiarized with religious rite and ceremony.[1] Among the Mayas, no one could marry who had not been baptized, and, as the ceremony was elaborate connected with baptism, and no one could officiate thereat but a priest, we can see that it would have required a large body of clergy to attend to these ceremonies. This was remedied to some extent, however, by selecting five of the most honored men of the town to assist the priests in these ceremonies.[2] The Maya priests appear to have retained a primitive fetichistic superstition, for they had medicine-bags in which they kept fetiches of different kinds. They also appear to have had a superstitious feeling in reference to their pictographic manuscripts.[3]

A division of labor appears to have separated to some extent the ecclesiastical forces of the Mayas. The doctors were evidently a class distinct from the priesthood proper, although the priests do not appear to have yielded entirely the practice of medicine. Especially did they retain control over confessionals, which were considered as a means for the cure of disease. The doctors practised phlebotomy, drawing blood from those parts of the patient's body where the pain or malady lay. They believed disease was caused by spirits, and the practice of blood-letting and this primitive superstition are closely connected with each other. By a strange coincidence, blood-letting is found to be a cure for certain diseases, and is retained in the medical practice of the present day; but with the primitive peoples it was nothing but a superstition, and, with emetics, was the only cure, exclusive of spiritual influence. The Mayas, like the Nahuas, believed implicitly in the power of witches and wizards. The priests of Yucatan exercised even a greater influence over the people than those of Mexico. In order to retain this power, they appealed to the religious side of the people's character by thundering sermons and solemn rites. The king himself, when he paid his annual visit to the high-

---

[1] 2 Bancroft, 663-64. [2] 2 ib., 682. [3] 2 ib., 697.

priest to inaugurate the offering of first-fruits, set an example of humility by kneeling before the pontiff and reverently kissing his hand.[1]

The priests decided what trade a child should learn.

The priesthood of Yucatan were divided into classes, who performed different offices. Some preached, some taught, some were sacrificers. Others construed the oracles of the gods, and accordingly exercised great influence and held the highest place in the estimation of the people, before whom they appeared in state, borne in litters. The sorcerers and medicine-men foretold fortunes and cured diseases. The first step had been taken to divide the confessors into a class, for none but married priests could take confessions.[2]

The priests of Yucatan were so much venerated that they were the lords who inflicted punishments and assigned rewards, and were exactly obeyed. They were presided over by a high-priest. These priests appointed the festivals and ceremonies, administered the sacraments, divined and prophesied, and exorcised spirits. They were so much respected, they were sometimes carried shoulder-high.[3]

Herrera says, however, that they forged answers from the oracles to impose upon the people and get their presents, and also practised sorcery.[4]

Each of the numerous tribes of Guatemala had a distinct and separate body of priests, who, by means of their oracles, exercised a decided influence on the state. The Quiches were spiritually governed by independent pontiffs. The high-priests of Tohil and Gucumatz belonged to the royal house, and held the fourth and fifth rank among the grandees of the empire. The two high-priests of the Kahba temple in Utatlan were of the royal stock, and each had a province allotted for his support at Istlavacan. Sixty priests, diviners, and medicine-men exercised their offices even in modern times, for the influence of the native priesthood prevails in many localities.

---

[1] 3 Bancroft, 446.   [2] 3 ib., 473.   [3] Landa, xxvii.   [4] 4 Herrera, 174.

At Copan, a priest was so revered that a person who presumed to touch him was expected to fall dead immediately.[1]

In Nicaragua, the office of high-priest was held by the caciques, who each in turn filled the position for a year, removing from home to the chief temple. At the expiration of the term he received the honorable distinction of having his nose perforated. The ordinary priests had no fixed revenues, and lived on the offerings to the idols. Their sorcerers could produce death by a look. They had oracles, the answers from which came through the mouths of the priests. The chief priests of the temples exercised great influence on account of their sanctity and superior knowledge, and none dared approach them except the principal men of the state.[2]

The natives of the Isthmus had a priesthood sworn to perpetual chastity. Fasting and prayer for the needs of the people formed the greater part of their offices.[3]

The high-priest and four assistants among the natives of San Salvador were accustomed to meet to ascertain, by sorcery and enchantment, whether they should make war, and their decision was implicitly obeyed.[4]

Among the Chibchas of Bogota the priests were much respected. They were not allowed to marry, and lived an austere life. No sacrifice could be made but by the hands of a priest.[5]

Evidences of a recognition of special calls to the office of the priesthood appear. The priestly office among the Peruvians appears to have been hereditary; some attained to it by election; a man struck by lightning was considered as chosen by heaven; also those who became suddenly insane.[6] Mr. Southey says that among the Moxos of Brazil, who worshipped the tiger, a man who was rescued from but marked by the claws of that animal was set apart for the priesthood, and none other.

---

[1] 3 Bancroft, 489-90.   [2] 3 ib., 495-96.   [3] 3 ib., 499.
[4] Palacio, 66.   [5] P. Simon, 249.   [6] Arriaga, 20.

CHAPTER XII.

CONCLUSION.

The belief in the existence and proximity of a world of spirits, and a fear of such spirits, is the only solution of all the curious religious customs, ceremonies, and superstitions of pagan life. A degeneracy from monotheism has not taken place, but rather a gradual development from the rudest superstition. This is shown conclusively by the numerous survivals of the lowest forms of superstition in a higher culture. The elimination of these superstitions is gradually taking place, as their error is discovered and their inutility to the higher culture is manifest. This elimination is, and will always be, a slow process, because each individual has attained a different stage of progress from every other, and the more advanced will be ready to discard much that those less enlightened still cling to as a heritage of the past.

It is questionable whether the highest man will be able to eradicate from his nature every vestige of a superstitious fear or dread of the supernatural. Great progress, however, is made toward this end when a multitude of superhuman beings, who are supposed to have power over the forces of nature, and are at times malevolent in their disposition, are supplanted by one ruling power who controls all things in justice and by unchanging law. Our increasing knowledge of nature's laws is, however, working to diminish the domain of the supernatural. The paramount influence which surrounding nature has on the development of the human being is unquestionable. It is the more powerful the nearer the people is to the uncultured state, and diminishes in proportion as human art and science gain power over the forces of nature. For this reason a primitive people ascribe spiritual agencies to those results of nature's laws not understood by them.

Primitive animism is marvellously self-consistent. Its philosophy is the conservation and correlation of spiritual force which dwells in and controls matter. All the phenomena of nature are explicable thereby. It is "so coherent as to create a perfect plexus of ideas that mutually support and interpret one another; so persistent that even the more extravagant developments can survive for ages in defiance of accurate knowledge." It is the only philosophy that renders it possible to bring about a unity in mythological science, and by it alone can a religious evolution be made out. It is in perfect accord with modern science and thought upon the subject of man's social development.

All the doctrines of the present day have their source in animism. In the animistic philosophy is embraced a belief in the immortality of the soul, and its entity could not be destroyed, but continued in a never-ending circle of transmigration or emigration, which was the genesis of all superstition. The doctrine of the resurrection of the body was believed in, and all its parts preserved with sacred care. A belief in rewards and punishments existed in the primitive animism. Says the Aztec proverb, "Remember that evil, like a poisonous herb, brings death to those who taste it."

Apotheosis and translation were the highest prizes awarded the meritorious. Such subtle doctrines as the incarnation and immaculate conception are found as forms of transmigration. Prophecy, revelation, and miracles are all logical results of animism and found everywhere. Among the aborigines of America the modern ordinances of religion, such as the eucharist, baptism, penance, confession, and sacrifice, are found among their pagan rites.

Savage animism is not a degeneracy of a higher culture. In it we find no survivals which show inconsistencies with it; whereas in higher cultures we find survivals of primitive superstition wholly inconsistent with the more advanced beliefs. Their presence in the higher culture can only be explained by a survival. The whole scope of man's doctrinal history shows a progressive movement. If monotheism had been an original doctrine, traces of such a belief would have remained among all peoples. If the cure of disease by medication had been the original method, such a useful art would never have been so utterly lost that sorcery should wholly usurp its place. These two special characteristics of a higher civilization are not found in primitive culture, but all the primitive superstitions, in modified form or in outline, are found in the higher cultures.

Before closing this work, it is appropriate to notice what historical tradition says about the primitive social condition of the civilized races of America. The first important result of a hunting life is the scattering of the population in small masses, which requires a large area, which of itself renders any advance in civilization impossible, a relatively dense population, with its multifarious reciprocal relations, being an indispensable condition of civilization.

M. Pauw says of the different grades of civilization, "Cultivators come first, because their subsistence is the least precarious, their life the least turbulent," thus affording them leisure to think and reflect. Hunters are always savage. They dread the multiplication of their species, because game will be less abundant. They are the farthest removed from social organization. Never at peace with men or animals, their instincts are savage. Among the American aborigines the hunter condition was the most prevalent. Agricultural pursuits were found, however, among the more civilized. American agriculture was indigenous. This is proved by the fact that grains of the Old World were absent, and its agriculture was founded on the maize, an American plant. Their agriculture and their architecture show an indigenous origin of their civilization, as does also their mythology. Since we have traced a development in their religious belief and ceremony, let us see what evidence, if any, mythology will contribute toward disclosing the primitive condition of the most civilized nations, and the development of their civilization.

The Peruvian civilization was the highest reached on the American continent, but their traditions show a primitive barbarism. Many of the Peruvians descended, according to tradition, from animals. Several tribes trace their descent from the condor, and the eagle and animal forms were used as heraldic designs. Manco Capac banished cannibalism and human sacrifices and introduced peaceable pursuits. He was a social organizer, and a builder of cities. In six years after the founding of Cuzco he had a well-drilled army, with which the barbarous peoples that surrounded his little state were subdued.[1] Caste-distinctions were found in Peru, and their growth is indicated in the traditional descent of the three classes from gold, silver, and copper. The princes descended from gold, the nobles from silver, and the common people from copper.[2] This myth has historical significance, and in it is preserved the fact that the class of the nobility originated after the other two classes, for, says the myth, "at first there were only the Incas and other people." The caste system of the Peruvians varies from the Oriental in the absence of the priest and warrior castes. In Peru, priests were officers of the son of the Sun, and there was no warrior caste, because all were called upon to bear arms periodically, showing no ethnological conquest as in the Orient.

In knowledge, little progress had been made by the Peruvians, except, perhaps, in mechanical and agricultural pursuits. Agriculture was especially encouraged and patronized by the Incas, who turned the earth, at their annual ceremonial, with a golden plough. They had little knowledge of science. They thought rain was produced by a rain goddess, who poured water upon the earth from a pitcher. Anger was the predominant emotion of their gods, and their outbursts of wrath were manifested in eclipses, storms, and comets.[3] Their fire-worship was, in pre-

---

[1] Müller, Geschichte Amer. Urrelig.   [2] Des Jardins, Le Pérou, 29.
[3] Müller, Ges. Amer. Urrelig., 395.

Incarial times, connected with stone-worship,[1] but in later times with sun-worship. The sun was anthropomorphosed, and removed from the control of natural law. Stars were named after earthly animal gods and human beings, which were thought to be heavenly prototypes. They had no medical knowledge; their writing was pictographic. Their geographical maps were made of clay, with small stones in bas-relief to denote the few localities known. The gods of the Incas set us no moral examples. There were many immoral elements in their worship. Prayer was offered to these divinities by priests, but personal prayer was little used. Such was their civilization in its moral aspects.

A development of the civilization of the Muyscas of Bogota from savagery is confirmed by their myths. The former nakedness of the people is set forth in their traditionary clothing by Bochica, who found them naked. He had the fabulous age of two thousand years ascribed to him, in accordance with the custom of all ancient nations. All of this period was employed, until about the time of his death, in elevating his subjects.

The most remote antiquity is always the age of giants, and great convulsions of nature are thought to terminate and begin an epoch. The Mexicans had five such epochs. The first was that of the giants; the second was that of fire, from which the birds and one human pair escaped; the third was that of wind, from which, however, one human pair was again saved; the fourth was the age of water, from which a snake woman escaped, and from her the present race sprang. The snake woman, or the woman of the snake gens, shows the existence of the totemic system. The Aztec military orders were divided into gentes named after animals, showing a former primitive condition.

The Aztec government gave the Mexican religion its dark and sanguinary nature. The system of natural religion depends on the idea that prevails of the character of the divinities, whose

---

[1] Müller, Ges. Amer. Urrelig., 368.

nature depends on the traditional character of the apotheosized ruler. If an inexorable tyrant, his worship will be bloody. At the time of the discovery a powerful religious hierarchy had grown up in the Mexican empire. Four million priests officiated in their religious ritual, who also had great political influence. Besides these there were monks, who were confined in cloisters and were celibates. Learning and education were in the hands of the priests and religious orders. All boys had to pass through the ordeal of baptism by fire, in which they were drawn four times through that purifying element. They were a priest-ridden people. The Mexican civilization at the time of the conquest presented an incongruous mixture of good and evil. It was made up of Aztec and Toltec elements. The Aztecs were a semi-barbarous people, whose association with the more civilized but subjugated Toltecs was producing the inconsistency of a social compact made up of peaceful and sanguinary ingredients. Human flesh would be sold in market-places adorned with flowers. The taste for flowers undoubtedly indicates a relish for the beautiful, and we are astonished at finding it in a nation in which a sanguinary worship appeared to have extinguished whatever related to the sensibility of the soul. In the great market-place of Mexico the native sells no peaches, or roots, or pulque, without having his shop ornamented with flowers. The Indian merchant appears seated in an intrenchment of verdure.

Although the arts were in their infancy, yet those appertaining to worship and personal adornment were pursued to an extent that denoted a generous patronage.

Among the Mexicans the laws against theft were severe, and punished with slavery or death. Drunkenness was allowed in men after sixty, and in women after they were grandmothers. Fornication was allowed among the unmarried, but it was punished with death among the married. Their laws were utilitarian rather than moral. Cannibalism was sanctioned by religion. Phallic worship existed, according to the monuments, and at an annual festival licentiousness prevailed to such an extent that the noblest women were willing victims. The Toltecs thought that their great goddess Centeotl would triumph at last over the ferocious gods of their warlike conquerors, and human sacrifices would be abolished.

Among the Maya nations in their higher civilization, a former condition of savagery and totemism may be strongly suspected when the names of the fox, jackal, paroquet, and crow are found attached to them in the annals. Their traditions corroborate this.

In the cosmogony of the Quiches, of the four men first created, three were named after the tiger,—namely, Balam Quitze, the tiger with the sweet smile; Balam Agab, tiger of the night; and Iqui Balam, tiger of the moon. The Popol Vuh appears to intimate a totemism, and to recognize a metamorphosis of the fierce animals into stone when they threatened the destruction of the human race.

The Miztecs seem to have worshipped the deer, as their first gods were called deer, male and female, and these deities had children, from whom they descended. Traditionary descent from animals implies an early condition of savagery.

The process of social development received little aid from sorcerers, or priests, who were the religious leaders of the people. With few exceptions they were impostors. Hence the religious condition was most deplorable of those who were the most advanced in their civil organization.

Fear is the prevailing religious sentiment among all the tribes of America. Religion did not have much moral influence toward ennobling hearts or humanizing manners, but merely excited emotions of fear and increased fanaticism. Prayers were offered for material things, but touched not morals. Prayer was in the form of conversation with spirits. Hence among the savage tribes we find very little evidence, if any, of a moral sentiment. Neither among savage nor civilized was morality a religious necessity. Where a moral dualism occurs, it can be reduced to the simple terms of the Totonecs, who had a dualism, but " their evil gods were those of the Aztecs, their enemies and conquerors." Their worst barbarities were committed at the instigation of superstition. Even the custom of abandoning the infirm or sick arose from a superstitious fear of the evil spirits which were supposed to have taken possession of them.

The religion of the aboriginal tribes of America was a system of superstitions, all of which are explicable by the doctrine of the agency of multitudes of spirits, and in no other way.

INDEX.

A.

Absolution, priestly, 375; acquittal of criminals, 375.

Abstention from animal food, superstitious origin of, 49, 169, 237.

Agency, spiritual, 26, 69, 92, 349, 352, 377, 392; in disease, 51-61; in production of winds and storms, 349-352; in prophecy, 363, 364.

Agriculture, indigenous character of American, 387, 388.

Altars, tombs the primitive, 218-220; altar-mounds, 188-190.

Amulets, 71; amuletic character of fetichism, 141. See *Fetichism*.

Ancestors, worship of, 72-74, 80, 86-88, 91, 104, 110, 115.

Anchorite, 100.

Angekok, 371.

Animals, worship of, 221, 256, 266; worship of animal spirits, 253; fear of animal spirits, 253; animal dress, 248-253; animal dances, 251-253; worship of every variety of animal life, 255, 256; transmigration of human souls into animals, 48-51, 221, 254, 255; superstitions about white animals, 260; animal forms in art, 222, 223, 266-268; fabulous animals, 268-286; animals in rôle of creators, 222, 223, 268, 269; deluges produced by animals, 269, 270; winds produced by animals, 270; convulsive changes in nature produced by animals, 270, 271; superstitions about strange animals, 281, 282; descent of human race from animals, 221-223, 231-237, 242; descent of animals from human race, 242-245; animal names given human beings, 230, 231, 237; sexual unions of animals and human beings, 234-237; disease produced by animal spirits, 51-61.

Animism, 52, 71, 116, 117, 133, 134, 317, 321, 325, 326, 386; animistic origin of idol-worship, 116, 117, 123-125; animistic origin of fetichism, 141, 156; animistic origin of nature-worship, 317, 321, 325, 326; animistic origin of Sabaism, 326; coherency of, 386; persistency of, 386.

Anointing kings, ceremony of, 378.

Anthropomorphism, 80, 83-85, 89, 91; anthropomorphic character of plant-spirits, 299; anthropomorphic character of tree-spirits, 289; anthropomorphic nature of the heavenly bodies, 62, 326, 336-338, 347, 348; anthropomorphic character of deities, 92, 96-99, 107, 110.

Apotheosis, 76-78, 96, 102, 105, 106, 112, 114, 386.

Araucanians, locality of their spirit-land, 36.

Architecture, indigenous character of aboriginal, 387.

Areskoui, Iroquois deity, 87.

Astrology, 348, 381.

Astronomical knowledge, 336; crude ideas of heavenly bodies, 342, 343.

Athaensic, Iroquois deity, 87.

Atlas, or earth-upholding deity, of the New World, 113.

Atotarho, Iroquois cult-hero, 86.

Augury, 223, 226, 377.

INDEX.

Aztec sovereigns, 96, 97; military orders, 289; sanguinary character of Aztec religion, 389.

B.

Bacab, immaculate conception of, 106.
Bachue, Muysca goddess, 112.
Baptism, 103, 370, 372, 373, 382, 386.
Blackbird, mythical light-producer, 268.
Bochica, Muysca god, 112.
Bogota, civilization of, 389.
Bone-houses, 118, 178, 179.
Bones of the dead, 144; preservation of, 177, 193–195; preservation of the bones of animals, 157, 158, 193, 199; the bones the dwelling-place of the spirit, 193.
Buffaloes, worship of, 258.
Burial in temples, 178; burial in huts, 175; burial-customs, 163–196.
Butterfly, mythical creator, 269.

C.

Canis Major, 329.
Cannibalism, origin of, 144–152, 388, 390.
Captives, sacrifice of, 214.
Caste, system of, in Peru, 388; priestly caste, 371, 372.
Catalepsy, 198.
Cataracts, worship of, 315, 319, 320.
Ceremonies, burial, 169, 170, 172. See chapter on *Priestcraft* for religious ceremonies.
Charms, 134, 157, 264.
Chiefs, worship of dead, 77.
Chulpas, burial-towers of Peru, 191.
Cities of refuge, 323, 324.
Cloisters, 335.
Coatlicue, goddess of flowers, 102.
Composite forms, human and animal, in art and myth, 235, 267, 268, 276–278, 283, 284.
Confessional, 57, 58, 373–375, 383, 386.
Confirmation, 372.

Conjurer, influence of, 356, 357. See *Sorcery*.
Conopas, 160.
Convents, 335.
Copper, superstition about, 135.
Cosmogony, tribal myths about, 268–270.
Couvade, origin of, 58, 59.
Creators, 74, 75, 84, 87, 88, 91, 110, 113, 268, 269.
Cremation, 166, 168, 171–174, 187–190, 194, 196; cremation-mounds, 187–190.
Cross-roads, superstition about, 71.
Cultivators of soil, 387.
Culture-heroes, 76, 78, 86, 96, 107, 113.
Cumulative burials, 165.
Cure of disease, 55, 354–361. See *Exorcism* and *Sorcery*.

D.

Deities, strength of, 108, 113, 114; deities of Eskimos, 79; Iroquois, 87; New England tribes, 87, 88; Western tribes, 88–91; of tribes of Brazil, 92, 93; of Mexico, 93–102; of Yucatan, 104–107; of Guatemala, 108, 109; of Peru, 113, 114.
Deluge, 132, 269, 270.
Demonology, 27–29.
Demons, 28, 30, 31, 40, 53, 321; Toltec, 29; Peruvian, 29; local, 30.
Descent of human race from stones, 133; from springs, 315; from trees, 289; from mountains, 307, 308; from sun, 333, 334; from moon, 333; from animals, 222, 223, 231–237, 242.
Deucalion, myth similar to that of, 132.
Disease, 223; produced by spirits, 51–61; by sorcerers, 361, 362; cure of, 354–361.
Divination, 223, 381.
Division of labor, 382.
Doctors, 354; their method of cure, 354–360; influence of, 356, 357.
Dreams, 53, 61–68, 163, 223.
Dress, animal, 248–253.

E.

Eagles, worship of, 261, 262.
Earth, supported by animals, 311, 312; by men, 113, 312; supported on pillars of holy wood, 292.
Earthquakes, production of, 312.
Echoes, the voices of spirits, 42, 177, 302.
Eclipses, causes of, 340, 344–346.
Education in hands of priests, 374, 376, 378, 381.
Elements, worship of, 349; control of, by sorcerers, 365, 366.
Elopement of the moon, myth of, 333.
Embalming the dead, 167, 173.
Epilepsy, 60.
Epunamun, Brazilian deity, 92.
Erratic boulders, worship of, 136.
Eucharist, rite similar to, 152, 153, 386; eating gods, 152, 153.
Evil eye, myth of, 284.
Evolution, 13–15, 385, 387–90.
Exorcism, 14, 353, 354, 356, 383.
Expulsion of evil spirits, 27–29, 40; expulsion of, 14, 29, 353, 354, 356, 383; transmigration of, into animals, 50, 51; return of, from spirit-land, 37, 43, 44.

F.

Fabulous animals, 268–286.
Fairies, 23–25.
Family gods, 110, 111.
Fear of spirits, 253, 385.
Festivals to the dead, 72, 73, 77.
Fetichism, 141–144; fetichistic superstitions, 141–161, 259; animistic origin of, 141, 156.
Fire, mythical origin of, 293.
Flagellation, practice of, 375.
Flags, fetichistic origin of, 241.
Flamingoes used as fetiches, 161.
Flood, traditions of, 269, 270, 323.
Flying heads, 281.
Food-offerings to the dead, 200–205.
Fountain of life, tradition of, 132, 269, 270, 314.
Future life, 31, 32; rewards and punishments of, 31, 33, 50, 51, 204, 205.

G.

Gateways, guardian spirits of, 122, 123.
Gentes, animal, 231–237; tree gens, 289. See *Totemism*.
Geysers, superstitions about, 314.
Ghosts, 42, 69.
Giants, 78, 85, 86.
Gods, 84–102; of air, 352; rain, 103, 388; sea, 322, 323; of love, 100, 101; of mirth, 101; of flowers, 102; of medicine, poetry, and music, 106; of dead, 97; thunder, 83, 93.
Grave-posts, 117, 118.
Great Spirit, 15, 16, 85.

H.

Haunted places, 21, 22, 302–305, 309–311.
Hayti, mythical animation of, 312.
Heads, preservation of human, as fetiches, 143.
Heavenly bodies, worship of, 325–348; anthropomorphic character of, 326; personality of, 320, 332; animation of, 326.
Heavenly ladders, 67.
Heraldry and heraldic devices, 237–239, 241, 250.
Hermits, 381.
Heyokah, a Dacotah god, 84.
Hiawatha, 86.
Hieroglyphic writing, 239.
High-priests, 381–384; office hereditary, 381.
Human spirits, worship of, 69–71, 77, 82, 87, 88, 91, 110. See *Apotheosis* and *Translation*.
Hun Ahpu, a Quiche god, 108.
Hunter tribes, condition of, 387.

I.

Idols, 115, 123–130; vitality of, 116, 117, 123–125; idol pipe, 128.
Images, use of, in sorcery, 361; worship of images of the dead, 125, 126.
Immaculate conception, 76, 101, 111, 113, 386.
Immortality of human spirits, 31–33,

50, 51, 204, 205 (see *Spirits* and *Apotheosis*); immortality of animal spirits, 223, 224.
Impostors, 366, 371, 372. See *Sorcery* and *Priestcraft*.
Incantation, 354, 356.
Incarnation, 45-47, 78, 90, 102, 108, 386. See *Transmigration*.
Incas, worship of, 72, 114.
Indian corn, origin of, 293.
Indian summer, origin of, 181.
Infanticide, 38.
Inherence of spiritual life, 142-144.
Intercessory character of human sacrifices, 214.
Interchange of souls, 60.
Interment, 166, 168, 171, 174, 177, 194, 195.
Intoxicating herbs, superstitions about, 295-297.
Islands, worship of, 309; haunted, 309; sacred, 311.
Ixtlilton, a god of medicine, 99.

J.

Jouskeha, an Iroquois deity, 87.

K.

Kabibonocca, a deity, 82.
Kareya, a deity, 88.
Khanuk, a deity, 89.

L.

Lakes, worship of, 315, 319-322.
Legend of Mount Shasta, 308.
Licentiousness of Aztec religion, 390, 391.
Living, worship of the, 75.
Locality of the spirit-land, 35-43.
Longevity of gods, 112.
Lycanthropy, 246.

M.

Manabozho, a deity, 80-82.
Manco Capac, 114, 334, 388.
Mandioca, traditional origin of, 293.
Manitology, 221, 237.

Manitous, 222, 223, 226-229; manner of selection, 227-230.
Maracas, fetichistic nature of, 159, 160.
Mastodon, bones of, 84, 279, 280.
Mayas, civilization of, 391.
Medicine-bag, 158, 159, 382.
Mermaids, 277, 278.
Metamorphosis, 101, 130-132, 223, 243-249, 305, 306, 326, 327; origin in animal dress, 248-253; from eating animal flesh, 253.
Meteorology, 349-352; winds produced by spirits, 349-352.
Meteors, 330.
Mexitli, a Mexican deity, 101.
Milky Way, 329, 346.
Miracles, 367, 368, 386; ascribed to sorcerers, 366-368; dead brought to life, 368; belief of Catholic priests in miracles of native sorcerers, 368; power of working ascribed to those in possession of a mysterious object, 369; mantle, embarking on, 114; sea parts for passage of Quiches, 109.
Monasteries, 376.
Monotheism, 385, 387.
Montezuma, 76.
Moon, worship of, 343; myths of, 329, 332, 333.
Moral character of the religion of aborigines, 391; of convents, 335.
Mounds, burial, 178-187; altar, 188, 190; animal mounds, 241, 242; recent erection of, 179-181; civilization required in erection of, 179-181.
Mountains, worship of, 301-305; haunted, 202-205; metamorphosed into men and animals, 305, 306; traditionary descent from, 307, 308.
Mythology, comparative, 17.
Myths, star, 327, 328, 330, 331.

N.

Names, superstitions about, 21, 153-156; of living, 153, 154; of dead, 154-156; change of, 154.
Naology, science of symbolism, 221.
Nature-myths, 325.

INDEX.

Niagara Falls, worship of, 300.
Nondescript animals, 278, 279.
Northern lights, 330.

O.

Obsession, 52.
Omaha, a god, 91; evil spirit, 40.
Omens, 56, 62, 223, 224; cries of birds, 225, 226.
Oracles, 137, 138, 225, 226, 383.
Origin of trees, 292, 293; of plants, 293; of the color of red clover, 293.
Orion, 329.
Ornamentation, fetichistic origin of, 141.
Ouiot, a god, 75, 91.
Owls, worship of, 262, 263.

P.

Pachacamac, 334, 335.
Penance, 373, 375.
Persecution, religious, 335.
Peru, civilization of, 388; deities of, 113, 114; priesthood of, 372-374.
Phallic worship, 390.
Phlebotomy, 382.
Photographs, superstitions about, 140.
Piasan, legend of, 274-276.
Pilgrimages, 105, 134, 303, 304.
Plants, worship of, 293, 295, 296, 299; personality of, 294; spirits of, 294; anthropomorphic character of, 299; supernatural character of intoxicating and healing herbs, 295-298; origin of maize, 293; of mandioca, 293; of red clover, 293.
Pottery, 122; worship of burial-urns, 120, 121.
Prayer, 70, 71, 73, 74, 389, 391.
Priestcraft, 123, 353, 370, 372-381; priestly caste, 355, 356, 371-374; in Mexico, 374-380; language, 372; honesty of, 379; calls to, 384; maintenance of, 377, 378; dress of, 377; confessions to priests, 374, 375; education in hands of, 374, 376, 378, 381; imposture of, 353-356; temporal power of, 381.

Primitive superstitions, 19-22.
Primitive temples, 118.
Promethean legend, 97.
Prophecy, 363-365, 386.
Prophet, 363-365, 374, 386.
Protecting genii of towns, 122, 123.

Q.

Quahootze, a god, 89.
Quetzalcoatl, a Mexican god, 93; human nature of, 93-99; reforms of, 94, 95.
Quiches, civilization of, 391; deities of, 108, 109.

R.

Rabbits, worship of, 256.
Rain, sorcerers control, 365; produced by sorcerers, 365, 366; rain goddess, 388.
Relics, 70-72, 144.
Resurrection of body, 162-164, 194, 195, 197-199, 386; cases of resuscitation, 197, 198; resurrection of animals, 199.
Revelation, 386. See *Prophecy*.
Rivers, worship of, 315-317; spirits of, 316; music of river-spirits, 317.
Road to spirit-land; 357; difficulties of, 35; length of, 37; of the dead, 329.
Rock-temples, 301, 302.

S.

Sabaism, 325-332.
Sacrifice, 70, 71, 73, 196; of food, 200, 205; periodical renewal of food-offerings, 203; utilitarian character of, 205, 220; sacrifice of property, 205-208; of flowers, 205, 206; substitution of the images of property, 208; becomes a ceremonial rite, 208; human sacrifice, 101-103, 107, 109, 111, 208-216; suicides in sacrifices, 209, 211; intercessory character of human sacrifice, 214; sacrifice of children, 214-216; tombs the altars of sacrifice, 218-220; bodily mutilations, 216-

220; myth of the substitution of a spiritual being, 208, 209.
Scalping, fetichistic origin of, 142, 143.
Scomalt, a deity, 90.
Serpents, worship of, 263-266.
Shamanism, 370.
Shingebiss, an Ojibway god, 82, 83.
Shooting stars, 329.
Sorcerer, 52, 54, 57, 95, 96.
Sorcery, 142-144, 361; practice of, in cure of disease, 354-360, 382, 387; use of idols in sorcery, 138-140.
Spirits, worship of human, 69-71, 82, 113, 115; fear of, 14, 19; worship of evil spirits, 30; land of, 35-43; river-spirits, 316, 317; water-spirits, 322, 323; contest with, 22; subterranean abode of, 35.
Springs, worship of, 312-315.
Statues, worship of those containing ashes of the dead, 119, 120.
Stones, worship of, 130-135; animation of, 133, 134; transmigration of spirits into, 133; oracle-stones, 137, 138.
Stygian flood, 37-39.
Sun, myths of, 325-327, 330.
Supreme Being, 15, 16, 88, 92, 93.
Survivals of superstitions, 385-387.
Suspensions of the dead, 166-168, 170, 171, 174, 176, 177, 194.
Symbolism, 221, 237; symbol of land, 312.

T.

Tattooing, fetichistic origin of, 156, 339-441.
Tchimose, Haidah mythological being, 278.
Temples, primitive, 118.
Tezcatlipoca, a Mexican god, 94-96.
Thunder-bird, 271-274.
Tlaloc, Mexican god of rain, 103.
Toads, worship of, 256, 257.
Toltecs, 95, 96.
Tortoise, worship of, 258; earth on the back of, 312; shells of, as fetiches, 160, 161.
Totemism, 222, 230-239; totemic poles, 238.

Translation, cases of, 77, 78, 86-88, 91, 92, 107, 111, 328, 329, 332, 333.
Transmigration, 386; of human souls into animals, 48-51, 221.
Transmission of spiritual essence, 353.
Trees, worship of, 287-292; spirits of, 289, 290; anthropomorphic character of, 289; origin of, 292, 293.
Trimurti, 77, 93.
Tupa, a Brazilian god, 92.
Tupinamba thunder-god, 193.

U.

Underground origin of tribes, 200.
Unktayhee, a Dacotah god, 84.
Urns, burial in, 176, 189; worship of, 120, 121.

V.

Valor rewarded in future life, 32.
Viracocha, a Peruvian deity, 113.
Volcanoes, worship of, 308, 309; hell located in, 308.
Votan, a Maya deity, 104.

W.

Water-lily, origin of, 332.
Water-spirits, 322, 323; worship of, 312-326.
Winds produced by spirits, 349-352; by animals, 270.
Witchcraft, 361.
Woods, sacred, 177.

X.

Xbalanque, a Quiche god, 108.
Xipe, Mexican god of goldsmiths, 101.

Y.

Yehl, a deity, 89.

Z.

Zamna, a Maya god, 105.
Zipacna, a Quiche god, 108.
Zome, a Brazilian god, 93.

www.ingramcontent.com/pod-product-compliance
Lightning Source LLC
Chambersburg PA
CBHW051245300426
44114CB00011B/898